THE HOLY LAND UNDER MANDATE

IN TWO VOLUMES

VOLUME I

THE SURRENDER OF JERUSALEM, DECEMBER 9, 1917

In front, left to right: Hadj Abd-El Kadir El-Alami, Chief of the Jerusalem Police; Burhan Ed-Din Tahir El-Husseini; Amin Abd El-Latif El-Husseini; Sergeant James Sedgewick of the 2d 19th London Regiment; Dahoud Saleh El-Husseini; Sergeant Frederick Hurcomb of the 2d 19th London Regiment; Hussein El-Asali, Jerusalem Police; Hussein Hashim El-Husseini, Mayor of Jerusalem; Rushdi El-Muhtadi; Tewfik Salen El-Husseini; Akmed Sharraf, Jerusalem Police; Shukri Ghazzawi, Jerusalem Police. Behind: Selim Beiruti and Hannah Laham (holding the white flag of surrender).

THE HOLY LAND
UNDER MANDATE

BY
FANNIE FERN ANDREWS

With Illustrations

VOLUME I

BOSTON AND NEW YORK
HOUGHTON MIFFLIN COMPANY
The Riverside Press Cambridge
1931

The Riverside Press
CAMBRIDGE · MASSACHUSETTS
PRINTED IN THE U.S.A.

PREFACE

PALESTINE has witnessed many changes during her four thousand years of recorded history. But not since the Crusades has there been such a far-reaching transition as the ending of the Turkish administration by the World War, and the resulting circumstance of placing the country under a British Mandate. Before 1914, most of the literature on Palestine featured its religious associations, while to-day the focus of discussion is the Mandate with its puzzling complications. This book looks at Palestine in its new aspect.

The author's interest in the Mandates began with the Peace Conference at Paris in 1919. The breaking away from the historical method of annexing conquered territories, and the substitution of a plan providing for the well-being and development of peoples 'not yet able to stand by themselves under the strenuous conditions of the modern world,' seemed to the author, at Paris, the most impressive bit of idealism in the whole war settlement.

Being a new principle of international law, the statesmen and jurists of the world immediately began discussions on the legal consequences of the Mandatory System, and the author joined in the search after new definitions covering this plan of trusteeship. The result was a Doctor's dissertation on the Mandatory System. The work was timely and important; and as problems developed in the mandated territories, the author kept in close touch with the authoritative pronouncements on the legal status of the Mandates. Already an important body of literature has grown up on this phase of the subject.

Upon the publication, however, of the annual reports of the Mandatory Powers and the Minutes of the Permanent Mandates Commission, revealing, as they did, controversies and movements among the peoples under mandate, the author saw the need of a work that would describe the concrete functioning of the Mandates, that, in other words, would show how these documents of trusteeship cut into the customs and the aspirations of the peoples. This human aspect seemed indeed a primary circumstance in the whole Mandatory System. But to get this phase of the story, a visit to the territories was an obvious necessity. The author selected for a first study on the spot the 'A' Mandates, in the Near East — Palestine, Syria and 'Iraq — former Turkish provinces. The present volume embodies the results of a face-to-face acquaintance with the Palestine Mandate, which is offered as the first in the series.

This close-range investigation was dramatic and inspiring. In the attempt to understand the actual working of the Mandate, the author aimed to study everything that could in any way reveal the character and the motives of the peoples in Palestine. The process involved a study of the background of these circumstances, and the continually developing movements; it became, in fact, the unfolding of a drama that led into circuitous and unfamiliar ways. Each experience illumined the road and pointed to the next step.

The author hopes that this book may reveal to the reader a picture of the essential phases of the Mandate; and above all that it may impart a real sense of the imponderable elements — a factor of the utmost importance in wielding the scales of justice in this land of dual responsibility and of partisan reaction.

The largeness of the scope of the work and the delicate and intricate nature of the subject led the author to seek consultation with a number of persons whose knowledge and experience give them authority to speak. These persons may be divided into four classes: first, those whose experiences have led them into intimate associations with Palestine and the Near East — those, in fact, who have breathed the Eastern atmosphere; secondly, scholarly partisans, with high devotion to their cause; thirdly, those who witnessed the birth of the Mandatory System at the Peace Conference; and fourthly, scholars especially consulted as authorities in the Christian religion.

In addition, the author has received valuable information from officials of the Palestine Government, from the Mandate Section of the Secretariat of the League of Nations, from the Zionist offices in New York, London, and Palestine, and

from the Palestine Arab Executive. The Attorney-General of
Palestine has been especially helpful in giving accurate data.

To all who have rendered assistance the author is deeply
appreciative. This method of direct suggestion has continually given fresh impulse — an extremely significant process
for a study of this nature. The life of Palestine cannot be
reduced to simple terms; and the facts cannot be too thor-
oughly verified.

The author is especially grateful to Albert Howe Lybyer,
Professor of History in the University of Illinois, general
technical adviser of the King-Crane Commission, and Current History Associate on the Near and Middle East — for
his invaluable aid in the documentation of the Arab chapters,
and in the clarification of delicate situations; to Moses Bailey,
Professor of Biblical History in Wellesley College — for his
advice in the selection of subject-matter, based on his former
residence in Palestine, whose handiwork is reflected in several
chapters of the book; to Jacob Spafford, resident and devoted citizen of Palestine — for his untiring zeal in searching
out facts, and providing the author with documents and intimate touches of reality; to Elizabeth P. MacCallum, author
of 'The Nationalist Crusade in Syria,' valued member of the
Research Department of the Foreign Policy Association —
for her aid in elucidating obscure situations in Arab life.

The author expresses appreciation for the scholarly inspiration of Harry A. Wolfson — profound Hebrew scholar —
Professor of Jewish Literature and Philosophy in Harvard
University, who read line by line the chapters on the Jews,
and whose sympathy for the study continually urged the
work along; for the fine and delicate criticism of Philip Khûri
Hitti — leading Syrian scholar — Professor of Semitic Literature in Princeton University, whose reading of the Arab
chapters contributed to an accurate and inclusive text.

And also for the discriminating counsel of Manley O. Hudson, unique in the field of international law, Bemis Professor
of International Law in the Harvard Law School, whose personal library was an unfailing source for the unusual document and the obscure fact; for the authoritative survey of
Ray Stannard Baker, Director of the Press Bureau at the
Peace Conference, in daily consultation with President Wil-

son, who read Chapter XIII; and for the legal scrutiny of Felix Frankfurter, Byrne Professor of International Law in the Harvard Law School, who read the two chapters on 'British Personalities' and the chapter on 'Zionism and the World War.'

So, too, for the courtesy of David G. Lyon, Hancock Professor of Hebrew and other Oriental Languages, Emeritus, of Harvard University — who read the chapter on Christianity.

Finally, the author is deeply grateful to Dr. James T. Shotwell — historian and keen interpreter of world affairs — for his kindness in reading the book as a whole and writing the Introduction, and also for his continuous sympathy with the original plan to keep the work to the scholarly standard.

F. F. A.

Boston, Massachusetts
April, 1931

CONTENTS

PART II

THE PROBLEM OF ZIONISM IN PALESTINE

ILLUSTRATIONS

ILLUSTRATIONS

INTRODUCTION

THE pages which follow deal with one of the oldest and most recent, and one of the strangest, of the great problems of history. In an intimate personal narrative the author carries one's interest along that track of conquest which was followed in turn by the Pharaohs of Egypt, the kings of Assyria, and the army of Allenby. But conquest does not settle problems, it merely states their terms. The last of the Crusades was fought with the aid of the Jew and 'the Unbeliever,' both of whom shared with the Christian the sense that this little stretch of hill and plain was a holy land. The recovery of Palestine from the Turk was, therefore, but the opening of a new era, fraught with difficulties, if, for a time at least, illuminated by a new hope. These problems, stated in their local setting as well as in their relation to international policies, form the body of the book. And they have been approached in such a spirit of impartial, scholarly interest, so studied in detail and in their actual, practical setting, that the text, which has been read by specialists whose opinions differ most widely, is held by all to be a fair and helpful statement of the situation.

But what a situation it is! Zionism, on the one hand, mobilizing public opinion in Europe and America for the realization of hopes maintained with an ardor fed by two full streams of religion and nationality; the Arab world troubled and angered by what it regards as an unwarranted intrusion in its ancestral home; British interests involved, not only by the strategic location of this outpost along the road to India and Australia, but also by the fact that the Empire, which is a great Mohammedan power abroad, has in recent years cherished the most intimate and friendly relations with the Jews; and over and beyond these varied elements of the problem, the League of Nations, as the embodiment of a new sense of international responsibility, looking on, investigating, criticizing, and offering a world centre for the discussion of grievances. It would be hard to imagine a stranger page of the history of the Holy Land than this which Dr. Andrews here describes.

While readers will turn to this volume for many different reasons, the central interest of the whole story seems to lie, not in passing incidents, however dramatic or difficult of solution, but in the test which these incidents supply of a new device in government, that of the Mandate. It was President Wilson who inserted this into the state system of the world. It is doubtful if the full significance of this revolutionary act has been appreciated as yet. Planned as a bulwark against the exploitation of defenceless peoples, it was a frontier of democracy in unfamiliar places. It was therefore connected with two other Wilsonian principles, the 'self-determination of peoples' and the reform of colonial administration.

The Palestine Mandate belongs with the first of these rather than with the second. It connects more with the application of Wilsonian democracy to the submerged peoples of Eastern and Southeastern Europe than to African and Pacific colonies. It is not a substitute for pre-war colonial government, but an extension of the principle of self-determination which has not yet been given sufficient attention.

This is not the place to discuss how far the Treaty of Versailles, in providing for the freedom of the nations of Eastern and Southeastern Europe, violated the rights of those formerly in control. The point of interest is that the break-up of the great empires was justified by a theory of national liberty which was to become the starting-point for political responsibility. The initial efforts of the liberated nations in the great art of government, which have at times been so reactionary and unenlightened compared with the experienced administration of the past, should not blind us to the outstanding fact that constructive forces are at work in the new state structure, as yet largely undefined, but nevertheless vital and growing. And in proportion as the new nationalism adjusts itself to realities, the outlines of a new, democratic Europe become more and more evident.

It is against this background that the historian will probably place the history of the Palestine Mandate. It has less in common with the other Mandates than with those nations which form that fringe of Eastern Europe which extends from the Baltic to the Ægean.

That this is the setting for the study of the Mandates which were formerly in the Turkish Empire, the Treaty of Versailles itself indicated quite definitely. The other Mandates are, to all intents and purposes, left permanently under the trusteeship of the Mandatory State. There is no provision for their ultimate freedom, no suggestion that their tutelage is for the purpose of establishing independence. Quite different are the terms of the Mandates for Palestine and Syria. These, says the treaty, 'have reached a stage of development where their existence as independent nations can be provisionally recognised subject to the rendering of administrative advice and assistance by a Mandatory until such time as they are able to stand alone.' In these words the Covenant envisages the ultimate independence of Syria and Palestine, and the aim so clearly expressed must be a major consideration in judging the policy and administration of the Mandatory.

With reference to Palestine, this volume supplies, with great wealth of detail, the story of this last chapter of its unique history. Based as it is upon first-hand knowledge of the land and its administrators, documented with scrupulous, scholarly care, Dr. Andrews' narrative of the complex problems of race, religion, and politics should furnish the material for an objective judgment upon the part of all those interested in Palestine and its people and in the upbuilding of the safeguards of international justice for those 'peoples not yet able to stand by themselves under the strenuous conditions of the modern world.'

JAMES T. SHOTWELL

THE HOLY LAND UNDER MANDATE

∴

PART I
AN INTRODUCTORY SURVEY

THE HOLY LAND
UNDER MANDATE

..

CHAPTER I

ENTERING THE HOLY LAND

I was eager to leave Egypt. Not that I had failed to respond to the charm of the land of the Pharaohs, with its pyramids, the Sphinx, and the mysteries of ancient temples and tombs, vying with the fascination of the history-speaking Nile; nor had I been indifferent to the sullen currents of discontent constantly breaking forth in open resentment of England: all had made their impression — fervent, indelible. I had descried in the ancient monuments the symbols of old Egypt, and had looked upon the anti-British manifestations as serious forebodings. I shall not soon forget an event which happened on the day of my departure from Cairo. Standing under the rays of a blazing sun, watching a column of British troops parading through the streets, I remarked to a bystander, a tall, serious-faced Egyptian, 'What are they parading for?' With a quick satirical glance and a defiant toss of his head, he jerked out, 'Just to remind us they are here.' And so it really seemed.[1]

But my face was turned toward Palestine, Syria, and 'Iraq — the countries of the Mandate. In Cairo I stood at the gateway of this new adventure. The six o'clock train to

[1] Lord Lloyd, who had been trained in the Indian Civil Service, became High Commissioner for Egypt in October, 1925. Ahmed Pasha Ziwar was Prime Minister, but did not represent the wishes of the people of Egypt. Parliament had been dissolved, but no new election was ordered; the King's right-hand man, Nashat Pasha, was endeavoring to control the politics of the country. Lord Lloyd took hold firmly: Nashat Pasha was sent abroad in the diplomatic service; and Ziwar Pasha was supported in a conservative policy pleasing to the High Commissioner. Such was the political situation of Egypt at the time of my visit.

Kantara, a ferry ride across the Suez Canal connecting with the night train to Haifa, a change at Ludd to the Jaffa–Jerusalem Road at seven in the morning — and I would find myself in Jerusalem a few minutes after nine o'clock.

The train left on time, crowded with passengers and luggage — disgracefully crowded with luggage, for steamer trunks were actually obstructing passage in the corridors of the cars. As I look back on the scene, it seems to me that the passengers must have represented every nationality under the sun. The faces, the costumes, and the languages presented a diversity of race and custom such as I have never seen anywhere else in the world.

My husband and I talked with the passengers in our compartment. We were especially interested in two young men, Cypriotes, who had been studying engineering in New York for four years and were now on their way home to use their knowledge in their own little island, which, they said, needed engineers. Proud they were to have been born in Cyprus! They became confidential. One was leaving a sweetheart in New York, and the other was going home to a girl whom he had not seen for four years. We looked at the pictures of these bright-faced girls, which the boys proudly displayed. With the assurance of youth, they opened their bags and showed us gifts and souvenirs intended for the home folks. I exclaimed in admiration at the face of a beautiful doll which one of the boys affectionately explained was to go to a little sister, with curly golden hair, he said, and I wondered how this young Miss would have changed in four years! We were sorry when these earnest-minded, sentimental youths left the train to make connections with the steamer for Cyprus. They said they were sorry too, they were glad to have met us, they wished we could visit them in Cyprus, etc., etc., but they fairly jumped out of the car as if to hasten the moment when they would step again on their native soil.

After passing through the customs at Kantara,[1] we crossed

---

[1] Kantara may be considered the Gate of Palestine, although it is many miles from the frontier which is reached just beyond the village of Rafa. There are two Kantara stations. Kantara West is a solitary place with hardly a habitation. The custom house is here. Kantara East is on the other side of the Suez Canal and is the starting-point of the railway for Palestine. During the War, Kantara East was a great military camp for the operations against Palestine.

the Suez Canal on one of the ferries waiting to convey the passengers to the other side. It was about ten o'clock when we boarded this slow-moving, open boat. Standing in the bow, during the few minutes of the crossing, on this very warm night, we saw the lights on passing boats in the canal; while across we could see the stationary group of lights which marked our destination on the other side. It was a dark night; the atmosphere was mild, placid, still. I found it difficult to realize that we were crossing the Suez Canal. The dark and languid water gave no clew to the political and strategical importance of this connecting link between the Mediterranean and the Red Sea; nor did it in any way convey the picture of the twenty-six and a half million tonnage, commercial vessels representing nearly a score of nationalities, which annually pass through this stretch of one hundred and three miles of water. To me, on this romantic night, the Suez Canal was merely a passage leading to the mysterious land of the East.

After going through the passport formalities, we walked to the train where we found our luggage securely established in our sleeping-car compartment. But we did not go to bed until some time after the train had started. We were viewing the sandy panorama and noting the passengers who, though not so diversified in appearance as the Egyptian trainload, seemed a very interesting group.

The sun was just peeping over the edge of the desert as I looked out of the car window in the early morning. Camels and donkeys, goats and sheep dotted the curious landscape. Arabs beside their tethered camels passively viewed the speeding train, while others sedately riding their camels over the arid desert appeared at the stations as the train stopped. Still others could be seen in the distance quietly pursuing their course, apparently oblivious to everything foreign to their own particular quest. But what this might be no one could tell from any outward signs. Their immobile faces were enveloped in the Arab head-dress of the closely bound turban, a picturesque contrast to the long flowing robe worn by these Eastern desert folk. The garb quite satisfied my preconceived notion of these Arabs of the southern desert who call themselves Egyptians, and who, swarthy from their life in the open, gaunt from meagre fare, having nothing but the barest existence, undoubtedly are the replica of the ancient Hebrew tribes before their settlement in Canaan. My mind quickly reverted to the past: What a contrast, I thought, between the ancient caravan route through the desert, and this ride of a few hours on an express train carrying twentieth-century tourists into Palestine!

Intently gazing through the car window, lest any part of the picture should escape me, certain facts of Biblical story rushed to my mind. I visioned the journey of the patriarchs and the Holy Family travelling from Canaan into Egypt. It was along this line that Thothmes III led seventeen invading forces and expeditions. As the train entered Palestine, visible reminders of the past loomed along the route. There were the Crusader masonry walls, castles and churches; so recent are the Crusades — eight hundred years is but a little time in so old a land — that the stones have but slightly disintegrated, and not even yet have the Arabs exhausted these mines of ready-quarried blocks. The plain of Philistia has scores of these reminders of Crusading days. Older ruins there are, too: Byzantine, and Roman foundations, and walls. One sees modern Arab buildings curiously constructed with a medley of antiquities — perhaps a block from an ancient Jewish synagogue for a door lintel, Roman milestones, Greek inscriptions from early churches, old Arab tombstones built into the walls — all surmounted, maybe, by the Turkish crescent so often seen over a Moslem holy place.

But older than any of these superficial reminders of age are the 'tells,' those mounds of débris which have beneath them thousands of years of village life. On one of these 'tells,' Tell el Hesy, Mr. F. J. Bliss excavated eight superimposed cities.[1] Several of the 'tells' are conspicuous along the railway route. Indeed, so common are they a part of the landscape, the Semitic languages contain the particular word 'tell' to refer to these peculiar signs of remote antiquity.

We were only a few miles from the Mediterranean as the train continued through Philistia running parallel to this inhospitable shore — a line of almost unbroken surf. The villages were unattractive; for lack of building stone, most of

[1] F. J. Bliss, *A Mound of Eight Cities.*

the peasants' houses were of crude, sun-dried brick. A conspicuous exception was Gaza, the southernmost of the five allied cities of the Philistines, situated three miles from the sea. Built on a lofty mound, the place presented a more prosperous exterior than its crude surroundings. The town has flourished for some three thousand years and is now buoyantly reviving from the ruins of the recent War, having been occupied by General Allenby on the seventh of November, 1917. It has a population of some thirty-five thousand people, a typical Eastern city with its bazaars hidden in narrow, tortuous lanes.

For centuries Gaza was a centre of struggle between the Philistines and the Israelites. The story of Samson, as given in Judges XIII, *seq.*, is a particularly graphic picture of the perpetual struggle for the hegemony of Palestine. Gaza, whose Hebrew word perhaps means 'The Strong,' possessed such strength that even Alexander the Great, who conquered the whole of the East in a few years, had to lay regular siege to it before it fell; while a thousand years later, Omar, the Arab conqueror, had more difficulty in suppressing the town than even Jerusalem itself. Saladin in his turn put forth his greatest efforts in wresting it from the Crusaders; and to-day, though the Tartar hordes razed its walls and citadel, it is still a place of great strength and strategic importance.[1]

The Philistine plain, sometimes called one of the most lazily attractive parts of Palestine, has contributed very little to history, although in mythology Philistia has been fertile. Apparently the warm climate of the plain proved better for the growth of curious legends than the evolution of ideals. The Philistines settled here about the twelfth or eleventh century B.C., and gave their name to the entire country; yet, though they represented a higher culture than the contemporary Israelites, they died, almost forgotten; while their competitors on the rugged mountain ranges produced the idealism of the prophets.[2]

The train followed the route of the retreating Turks in 1917

[1] For a description of Gaza, written in May, 1917, see *Palestine of the Jews, Past, Present and Future*, p. 222 *seq.*, by Norman Bentwich, of the Egyptian Expeditionary Force. Mr. Bentwich is now the Attorney-General of Palestine.

[2] For a discussion on the origin of the Philistines, see George Adam Smith, *The Historical Geography of the Holy Land*, p. 169 *seq.*

past the one-time great and powerful cities of Ashdoud and
Ascalon, two of the most important cities of the Philistines.
Ashdoud, like Gaza, takes her name from her military strength.[1]
Her citadel was probably the low hill, beside the present village. Like Gaza, Ashdoud had experienced varying fortunes in
the war with Israel, and in common with the other Philistine
cities, had also suffered because of her position in the route
between Assyria and Egypt.

I resolved to return to Ascalon, the birthplace of Herod the
Great, which is best reached from the town of Mejdel directly
on the railway line. Ascalon, which is a rocky amphitheatre
in the low bank of the coast, having no natural strength, has
a long and varied history from the time of Joshua until its
final destruction by Bibars in 1270. In her period of greatest
fame, during the Crusades, Ascalon, as described by George
Adam Smith, 'combined within herself the significance of all
the fortresses of Philistia, and proved the key to south-west
Palestine.' [2] 'Askalôn is called A'lâ ar Râs, the Summit of the
Head, that is, the Summit of Syria. The city is also named
'Arus ash Shâm, the Bride of Syria.' [3]

In David's lamentation over Saul, Ascalon and Gath are
taken as two typical Philistine cities. *Publish it not in the
streets of Ashkelon.*[4] George Adam Smith remarks that the
'streets' were probably bazaars; and he says, 'There is a
sound of trade, a clinking of shekels, about the city's very
name.' [5]

Excavations were undertaken at Ascalon by the Palestine
Exploration Fund in 1920–21,[6] under the direction of Professor Garstang. A large public building in classical style, identified with the cloisters that Herod the Great is said to have set

[1] I Samuel v: 1, Joshua xv: 47.

[2] George Adam Smith, *The Historical Geography of the Holy Land,* p. 190.

[3] Guy Le Strange, *Palestine Under the Moslems,* p. 402.

[4] II Samuel i: 20.

[5] George Adam Smith, *The Historical Geography of the Holy Land,* pp. 191, 192.
Ascalon is very well watered. It is worthy of mention that onions were always extensively cultivated there. Through its Latin name Ascalonia and the Norman form
Escallion, Ascalon has given the word *shallot* to the English language. (*The Handbook of Palestine,* edited by Harry Charles Luke and Edward Keith-Roach, 1922, p.
83.)

[6] In 1862, the Prince of Wales, afterwards King Edward VII, visited Jerusalem and
did much to bring about the constitution of the Palestine Exploration Fund.

up, has been uncovered near the crossing of the central routes in the area, and a museum of the antiquities is to be found on the spot.

The fascinating journey past the cities of the Philistines came to an end at Ludd, the Arabic name of the ancient Lydda. Like all other inland towns of Sharon, it appears never to have been fortified. Throughout Roman times, and after the destruction of Jerusalem, Lydda became a refuge for the religious leaders of Judaism. Through the early centuries, the town was a far-famed centre of Rabbinical learning, and its schools were visited by students from the whole of the Jewish Diaspora. Later on, Lydda was emptied of everything Jewish and was made Pagan. Judaism disappeared, although Christianity finally got the upper hand.

The chief Christian interest of Lydda centres round her Saint George, whose fame has spread wherever English is spoken. Among all the saints, there has been none whose history is so significant. From obscure origins, Saint George became not only the virtual patron of Syrian Christendom, and an object of Mohammedan reverence, but patron as well of the most western of all Christian peoples. Saint George of Lydda is Saint George of England; he is also a venerated personage in Moslem legend. The original George was a soldier of good birth, and served as a military tribune under Diocletian. He was martyred in 303; and according to some authorities, Lydda was the scene of his martyrdom. At any rate, Lydda received his relics; and during the Crusading times, the town was called Saint George. The Arabs have perpetuated the Hebrew name Lod in their Ludd.[1]

The Mohammedans usually identify Saint George with the prophet Elijah — El Khudr, the forerunner of Messiah. Their name for Antichrist is Dajjâl, and they have a tradition that Jesus will slay Antichrist by the gate of Lydda. This notion sprang from an ancient bas-relief of Saint George and the Dragon on the Lydda Church. 'Could there be,' says George Adam Smith, 'a fitter scene for such a legend than the town where Hebrew touched Philistine, Jew struggled with Greek, and Christendom contested with Islam?' [2]

[1] George Adam Smith, *The Historical Geography of the Holy Land*, p. 163.
[2] *Ibid.*, p. 164.

To-day the town is the junction of the Kantara–Haifa and Jaffa–Jerusalem lines, and has a population of about five thousand Moslems and two thousand Orthodox Christians. The earthquake of 1927 seriously injured the modern half of Saint George's Church, while the half that goes back to the early centuries was left intact.

Two miles northeast of Ludd there is a small Jewish Colony, built on one of the lower spurs of the hills of Judea. The Colony is the creation of the Jewish National Fund which was founded by the Zionist Organization for the purpose of securing land in Palestine for national purposes, as a kind of public domain. The place is known by the Jews as Ben Shemen, meaning literally the Son of Oil, the original settlement having consisted of a factory for making olive oil and soap. The training farm was established in 1911, and the Colony sprang up around the farm.[1]

After a half-hour wait at Ludd, we changed to the Jaffa–Jerusalem Road. Instead of the regular Baldwin locomotive which had brought us across the desert from Kantara, a re-modelled Baldwin was used to take the train to Jerusalem. In order to make the sharp mountain curves, the engine was supplied with heavy water tanks jacketing the wheels, so as to add as much weight as possible.

For some miles the route was almost due south, steadily climbing among the rounded little foothills known as the Shephelah.[2] The Hebrew word Shephelah means 'lowland,' for the Judeans looked down upon these hills from their cities as if they were really a part of the Philistine plain. Had the Philistines named them, however, they would have been differently described. This was the debated border-land of the two peoples and the geographical setting of most of the Samson legend. It was here that David gained his early following in the days before we can be quite sure whether his greater loyalty was to the mountaineer Hebrews or to the five lords of Philistia.

---

[1] For a description of this Jewish Colony, which provided a billeting place for the British troops in 1918, see Norman Bentwich, *Palestine of the Jews, Past, Present and Future*, pp. 254–57.

[2] The word Shephelah, carried to Spain by the Phœnicians, is supposed to be the origin of the name Seville.

The train passed through the dense olive groves which surround the little Arab town of Ramleh, founded in the eighth century by Suleiman, son of the Khalif 'Abd-el-Melek. After overthrowing Lydda, Suleiman saw the necessity of building another town in the neighborhood which would command the junction of the roads from the coast to the interior with the great caravan route from Egypt to Damascus. He chose a site nearly three miles from Lydda, and called the town Ramleh, 'the sandy,' which, as George Adam Smith says, has 'no other feature to characterise it.' [1]

At Ramleh are to be found the most notable of the Crusader ruins, conspicuous from many miles away. The town contains the celebrated 'Tower of the Forty Martyrs,' which dates from the fourteenth century. The Tower was the minaret of a great mosque originally built by Suleiman, and is the only part of the mosque left standing. Ramleh also suffered much from the earthquake in 1927. To-day, it is known principally as a city in the Imperial Air Route to the East — Cairo–Ramleh–Amman–Bagdad. We could see the aerodrome between the station and the town.

Continuing in a southerly direction, the train followed the route across the southern border of the plain of Sharon, with hills and valleys and sites of ancient cities on either side. Our guide-book constantly piqued imagination; by consulting this detailed and accurate description of the route, we were able to identify the places on this ancient roadway. About a mile and a half away on the right was 'Akir, site of the Philistine city of Ekron, the city to which the Ark of the Covenant was brought from Gath, and from which it was taken to Bethshemesh, which in turn 'made haste to deposit it upon Jehovah's own territory of the hills.' [2] Like Lydda, after the destruction of Jerusalem, the Jews came to Ekron; for, like Lydda, it was situated in a valley leading down from Jerusalem. Some four miles south of Ekron was the hilltop village of Al Mughar, where legend says the five Amorite kings hid in the cave after the battle of Ajalon.

Soon the train passed round the base of Tell Jezer, the mound of débris from ancient Gezer. This is the most prom-

---

[1] George Adam Smith, *The Historical Geography of the Holy Land*, p. 165.
[2] *Ibid.*, p. 225.

inent object which the traveller sees on the Jaffa–Jerusalem Road. As early as 1400 B.C., Gezer was an important city. King Solomon acquired the place as a wedding gift from his royal Egyptian father-in-law. Gezer figured many times in the wars between David and the Philistines, and on account of its location, forming as it does an easy passage to Jerusalem, it has witnessed every invasion of the country. 'If all could rise who have fallen around its base — Ethiopians, Hebrews, Assyrians, Arabs, Turcomans, Greeks, Romans, Celts, Saxons, Mongols — what a rehearsal of the Judgment Day it would be!'[1] M. Clermont Ganneau discovered the site some forty years ago, and later identified it with the Mont Gisart of the Crusades. Gezer figures in the Tel al-'Amarna letters, and was excavated by Professor Macalister, who traced there the remains of Arab, Christian, Roman, Maccabean, Jewish, and Canaanite civilizations.[2]

From the Vale of Sorek Station, the route ran parallel with the ancient highway from Ekron along which the Ark was taken to Beth-shemesh.[3] It was in the neighborhood of the famous valley of Sorek that many events took place connected with Samson and Delilah. Our guide-book called attention to Zorah, the birthplace of Samson, which could be seen at the left on the summit of a high hill. And we also got a glimpse of another hilltop just opposite Zorah, which, as we were informed, was the ruined village of Ain-es-Shems, the modern site of Beth-shemesh. Ain-es-Shems was old when the Hebrews came into Canaan.

As we followed the Wady es Surar toward the east, the hills were more sharply defined; the markers at the side of the track showed steeper gradients, and the engine labored noisily up the crooked defile. This narrow pass seemed to me like the entrance to a distant world — a bit lonely to Western thought — a timeless land that belongs to all the centuries and yet belongs to none.

The next station was Artuf, situated in the centre of a low

---

[1] George Adam Smith, *The Historical Geography of the Holy Land*, p. 217.

[2] See R. A. S. Macalister, *Bible Sidelights from the Mound of Gezer*. London, 1906. Gezer is the only town in Palestine where, engraven in the rock in bi-lingual inscriptions, three of the city limits facing the cardinal points were discovered.

[3] At Beth-shemesh, Dr. Grant is conducting excavations for Haverford College.

hill, the supposed site of Ebenezer, the 'Stone of Help,' where the Philistines defeated the Israelites and captured the ark in the time of Eli. Then, beyond the Wadi Ismain, the rocky gorge which forms the pass to the Highlands near Jerusalem, could be seen the famous cave overhanging the valley in which Samson sought refuge from the Philistines, and where the men of Judah bound him with cords and delivered him to the enemy. As I looked at this, my childish admiration kindled anew for Samson, who broke his bonds and slew the thousand Philistines.

Finally, after zigzagging through this wild ravine, we reached Bittir, an ancient Canaanite city conquered by Joshua, and famous as the last stand of the Jewish Zealots under Jesus bar Cochba some eighteen hundred years ago. Never again since that time have the Jews been the principal inhabitants of their 'Promised Land.' At the little station there was a scramble among the passengers to buy fruit and refreshing drinks of sour milk, ladled forth in a single unwashed tin cup. Our dragoman, a Christian Arab, boarded the train at Bittir.

For a short distance, the train followed the Wady in a more northerly curve, and Jerusalem appeared in the distance. The railway emerges from the upper gateway of the Wady and continues its course on to the plain southwest of Jerusalem, which probably represents the ancient Vale of Rephaim. In a few moments we were at the Jerusalem Railway Station, twenty-five hundred feet above the Mediterranean.[1]

Around the railway station, cluster the houses of the German, or Temple Colony, established here between the years 1860 and 1870 by Hoffmann, brother of the German Court Chaplain. These Württemberg burghers formed a religious movement, actuated by their leader, whereby they hoped through agriculture, trade, and commerce, to build up the spiritual Temple. Their business efforts were certainly crowned with success, for when the War broke out in 1914, they had the best part of the trade in their hands. Shortly after the British occupation, however, they were all interned in Egypt, and were obliged to sell out their business to the

[1] By the Wady es Surar, Jerusalem is some twenty-eight miles from Ekron, thirty-eight from Ashdod, forty-five from Ascalon.

Jews, who were the only purchasers. Nearly all of them returned after the War, but they have not yet succeeded in regaining the footing they formerly had.

Though these Germans are Protestant, they do not belong to any current sect. When they built their meeting-house, they deliberately opened the building for a concert, in order to convince the Turks that it was not a 'church' in the technical sense.

The German Church [1] on the skyline is the building occupying the site acquired for the Catholics by the German Emperor on his visit to Palestine in 1898. They built the 'Dormition de la Sainte Vierge,' on the supposed site of the home of John the Evangelist, to which he took the Virgin, after Christ had said to him from the Cross 'Behold thy mother,' and to her 'Behold thy son.' The Catholics had long sought to acquire this site, but on account of its nearness to the Tomb of David, they had never been allowed to have it, on the ground that if a tower were built there, its shadow might obscure the Sacred Tomb. Through the bestowal of this favor, Emperor William had sought to placate the Catholics and adjust the delicate balance in the Reichstag.

There is a striking contrast between this action of Emperor William and that of his father, the Crown Prince Frederick, who, in 1869, while visiting Jerusalem after the opening of the Suez Canal, had been presented by the Sultan with the site of the Crusader Church, because of his membership in the order of the Knights of Saint John, turned the site over to his Protestant subjects.

Having stepped from the train, we looked about as if to get a view of Jerusalem, but the city wall, we were told, was a mile from the station. Presently an Arab porter offered to take our luggage, but before we had time to reply or to survey the interesting mass of Arab porters, Arab hotel agents, and the tourists, or to say a courteous good-bye to some of our fellow passengers, who were, as ourselves, coming to Palestine for the first time, we found ourselves in our dragoman's car, speeding rapidly along a white and very dusty road. The date was October 13.

Our destination was the American Colony, on the other

---

[1] There is no other German Cathedral, since there is no Episcopacy.

JERUSALEM FROM THE MOUNT OF OLIVES

side of the city. This is a unique community of about one hundred persons, founded in Jerusalem in 1881 by Horatio Spafford and his wife, of Chicago. The aim of the Colony is to render Christian service for the needy people of Jerusalem and of Palestine, without distinction as to race or religion. One of its principal activities centres around the help it gives to the native people in the care of children and young girls. From the beginning, the Colony was engaged in education, having had at one time as many as one thousand pupils under its care, who were in institutions belonging to different nationalities and religions. As, however, advanced methods and better equipped enterprises developed, the simple efforts of the Colony were rendered unnecessary. So, too, before there were nurses or hospitals for contagious diseases, the Colony served its fellowmen, as best it could, until such service was superseded by trained nurses and specially equipped hospitals. The Colony maintains a hostel for the accommodation of visitors to Palestine.[1]

The poor have been helped and fed by the Colony. During the War, soup was distributed to two thousand people a day, until the arrival of the British troops, on December 9, 1917. At that time, the Colony handed over to the British eleven hundred sick and wounded, for whom it was caring, and for whom only twenty-four hours' provision remained. The Colony had volunteered its services to the Turkish authorities in the hour of their direst need; wounded soldiers lay sometimes for hours on the sidewalks for want of care. Although there was not a trained nurse among the members of the Colony, this service was extended in token of the debt they felt they owed the Turks for their hospitality of thirty-five years.

The road over which we motored joins the route from Bethlehem to Jerusalem, and passes through a Jewish Colony along the west bank of the Wady er-Rabâbi, 'Valley of the Fiddle.' This, in antiquity, was known as the Valley of the Sons of Hinnom. Into this valley in 621 B.C., King Josiah cast the evil images which his father and grandfather had

---

[1] In 1929, the American Colony Aid Association gave a Playground to the Municipality of Jerusalem. For the full program of the Association, see Annual Report of the American Colony Aid Association for the year 1928–29.

established in the Temple. Here, the prophets said, was a burying-ground; and, for some reason, Jesus or his disciples took one of their words for Hell from the Wady's name — Ge (Valley) henna (Hinnom). Queer associations this little valley has had![1]

The Jewish Settlement in this valley has an interesting history. In 1868, Sir Moses Montefiore, who had paid more than one visit to Jerusalem where he had evinced great interest in the condition of his people, bought a considerable tract of land and built three rows of almshouses, which were occupied by the poor, free of rent, for two years. Upon his death, it was found that this was recorded as a 'Pious Foundation'; in other words, it was inalienable property. So numbers of poor Jews, appropriating the land, squatted there, and built for themselves the remaining rows of houses. More recently poorer Jews and Arabs have settled in the valley bed.

Like a landmark, above the lines of houses built by Sir Moses Montefiore, stands one of the three windmills of which Jerusalem boasts. And on this side of the valley, looms the British Ophthalmic Hospital of the Knights of Saint John, which has rendered inestimable service in improving the condition of the eyes of the people throughout the country for the last half-century. When this was established, there was no other institution of the sort in the whole region, and people came from the desert, from Syria, Trans-Jordan, and elsewhere to have their eyes treated and corrected. King George is the Grand Master of the English Order of the Knights of Saint John.[2]

Just above a large open reservoir, the carriage road crosses

---

[1] The Jewish Encyclopædia gives the following explanation: Ge-Hinnom, or Ge Ben- (Bene-) Hinnom: Name of the valley to the south and southwest of Jerusalem (Joshua xv: 8, xviii: 16; Nehemiah xi: 30; II Kings xxiii: 10; II Chronicles xxxiii: 6; Jeremiah vii: 31 et seq., xix: 2, xxxii: 35). Its modern name is 'Wadi al-Rababah.' The southwestern gate of the city, overlooking the valley, came to be known as 'the gate of the valley.' The valley was notorious for the worship of Moloch carried on there (comp. Jeremiah ii: 23). According to Jeremiah vii: 31 et seq., xix: 6 et seq., it was to be turned into a place of burial; hence 'the accursed valley Ge-hinnom' ('Gehenna' in the N.T.) came to be synonymous with a place of punishment, and thus with hell (comp. Isaiah lxvi: 24; Enoch xxvi, et seq.; and the rabbinical Hebrew equivalent).

[2] This is not as old as the Continental Order. A couple of years ago, an unveiling of the King's and Queen's portraits took place at the Hospital.

the valley by a low bridge. The reservoir, called the Birket es Sultan, or Sultan's Pool, was in Turkish days an important water supply for the city; there the winter rains were collected, held stagnant, and slowly used during the spring and summer; and in the late summer and fall, when the water was quite gone, cattle are said to have been butchered there. When the British came, in December, 1917, Jerusalem was dependent for its water supply on about fifty-three hundred cisterns, and a four-inch pipe bringing water to the Mosque of Omar from the spring at Solomon's Pools. Naturally, the first necessity was to provide water for the army. By February, the British had exhausted every possibility of drawing enough water from any supply in sight; and they finally decided that the Arroub water, thirteen miles south of Jerusalem on the Hebron Road, must be brought in.

The only water near Jerusalem is the spring in the Kedron Valley called 'The Virgin's Fount.' The British tried to make use of this spring. For eight days and nights, they had engineers pumping up the water for the purpose of ascertaining how much there was, and also what were the periods of irruption. It was found that the flow varied considerably in quantity, and, moreover, that the number of its irruptions varied in the twenty-four hours. The experiment showed that there was not sufficient water to supply the need, and also that the water itself was not perfectly pure. So the project was dropped.

Water was brought to Jerusalem from Solomon's Pools by a skilful bit of engineering work. This spring lies thirty-two feet higher than Jerusalem, and the conduit, by following the contours of the hills, stretches seventy thousand feet before reaching the city. Between the spring and Bethlehem, a drop of one foot in eight hundred was allowed; while between Bethlehem and Jerusalem, not more than one foot in fifty-two hundred could be spared.

The Arroub enterprise, according to Josephus, was the creation of Pontius Pilate, who hoped through its establishment to ingratiate himself with the Jews. He committed the unpardonable blunder, however, of taking money from the Sanctuary Fund to pay for the work, which so angered the Jews that they sent a delegation to Rome and had him removed.

This accounts for the fact, which Josephus mentions, that the Arroub water was never brought to Jerusalem.

The conduit was forty miles long.[1] In one part, opposite Rachel's Tomb, where the course crosses a dip, there is a syphon, the principle of which was evidently understood at that time. This was composed of thousands of stone pipe sections, about three and one half feet cube, some of which show the Jewish bevel, while others bear the name of the contractor.

Thus this great work had lain idle and useless for about nineteen hundred years; although during the four hundred years of Turkish occupation, the prospect of reviving the project was frequently discussed. Forty-five years ago, fifteen hundred pounds were expended on a survey. But it was reserved to the British during four months of the War to bring the plan to completion!

This supply was found, however, to be insufficient for the needs of Jerusalem. There has been a real shortage of water for the past seven years; and five years ago it became so acute that plans were made to supplement the supply. This time the water was taken from Ain Farah, a spring lying fourteen hundred feet below Jerusalem, which necessitated three relays of pumps. The addition of this spring, lying far below the surrounding country, and drawing its supply from the foot of abrupt, imposing rocky mountains through clefts in the rock, therefore not as liable as springs near the upper surface to be influenced by the shortage of rain, greatly enhanced the supply and proved a real boon when the flow from the other springs was diminished. Thus Jerusalem has enjoyed, through British effort, a healthier and infinitely larger water supply than it ever had in its most halcyon days under Solomon or Herod.

Ain Farah has an interesting background. To reach it, one has to pass through Anathoth, Jeremiah's birthplace. Here is the only flowing brook to be seen in this part of the country. Hither the flocks from all the surrounding region come down at noon 'to lie down in green pastures:... beside the still

---

[1] Although the Arroub supply lies only thirteen miles from Jerusalem, the conduit had to take a circuitous route of forty miles in order that the water might flow by its own gravitation.

waters.' This is popularly accepted as the place where David, as shepherd boy, gained the experience which afterwards, as the Sweet Psalmist of Israel, enabled him to write the superb composition of the Twenty-Third Psalm.

The road continues north, up the Jerusalem side of the Wady to the Jaffa Gate, more properly called Bab el-Khalil, the Hebron Gate. On December 11, 1917, two days after the Turkish parlementaire conveyed the surrender of Jerusalem to General Allenby, the British General made his official entry, walking into the city by the Jaffa Gate, followed by his staff and by representatives of the French and Italian contingents. It was at the entrance to the Citadel,[1] David's Tower, as the Citadel of Jerusalem is still called, a massive fortress of five mighty towers, probably occupying the site of Herod's Palace, where General Allenby caused to be read to the people in English, French, Italian, Arabic and Hebrew, the following notable Proclamation:

To the inhabitants of Jerusalem the Blessed, and the people dwelling in its vicinity.

The defeat inflicted upon the Turks by the Troops under my command has resulted in the occupation of your city by my force. I therefore here and now proclaim it to be under Martial Law, under which form of Administration it will remain so long as military considerations make it necessary.

However, lest any of you should be alarmed by reason of your experiences at the hands of the enemy who has retired, I hereby inform you that it is my desire that every person should pursue his lawful business without fear of interruption. Furthermore, since your city is regarded with affection by the adherents of three of the great religions of mankind, and its soil has been consecrated by the prayers and pilgrimages of devout people of those three religions for many centuries, therefore do I make known to you that every sacred building, monument, holy spot, shrine, traditional site, endowment, pious bequest, or customary place of prayer of whatsoever form of the religions, will be maintained and protected according to the existing customs and beliefs of those to whose faiths they are sacred.

EDMUND HENRY HYNMAN ALLENBY
General Commanding-in-Chief,
Egyptian Expeditionary Force[2]

9th December, 1917

[1] The picture of the Citadel appears on the new Palestinian currency.

[2] Proclamation of Martial Law in Jerusalem. (Repealed by Section 73 of the Palestine Order-in-Council, 1922.) Legislation of Palestine, 1918–1925. Compiled

Around the Jaffa Gate, there have been many changes during the last half-century, such as the building of the Jaffa Road in 1866 — the first driveway since Roman times — and the construction of the first buildings outside the walls. At the Jaffa Gate, also, there began the first paving of the streets of the city since the Roman occupation, which involved the enlargement and improvement of the sewerage system.

The Russian buildings to the northwest were the first habitations outside the walls. Before there were houses beyond the city limits, it was all a man's life was worth to reach the gates after nightfall. Robbers prowled about the walls after dark, in the hope of overtaking some belated stranger who got there after the gates were closed. With the increase of dwellings outside, however, and the growth of the Consular power, security became more stable; and in time the 'Gates were not closed by night' or at the hour of Friday prayers. Now the area of the city outside the walls greatly exceeds that enclosed by Suleiman's walls of 1542.

Our automobile must go around the walls, for carriages and motor vehicles may not go through the narrow streets within the city. Some of the modern city's most enterprising busi-

by Norman Bentwich, Attorney-General of Palestine. Orders-in-Council and Ordinances, vol. 1, p. 599.

The scene of Allenby's entry into Jerusalem is recorded in a large colored photograph, which I saw on the wall of Sir Ronald Storrs' room, in the Governorate, outside the Damascus Gate.

The picture is a striking contrast to the spectacular entry of Kaiser Wilhelm II on October 29, 1898, who, riding with pomp and ceremony, was the central figure of an imposing procession. The preparation for the Kaiser's entrance is an interesting bit of history: There was a moat around the Citadel, faced with scarp and counterscarp. One of the sides was outside the wall, running southward from the Jaffa Gate to the angle of the east Citadel wall, which connects at this place with the city wall enclosure. Except for a wall which was built as a screen between the Jaffa Gate Tower and the Citadel, a person might glide down the counterscarp into the moat, and walk into the city at the bottom of the depression. The moat was filled up to the level of the street and afforded a much larger and more commodious entrance into the city than that offered by the limited and sinuous Jaffa Gate entrance.

As the Greeks were feverishly excavating their portion of the Muristan to put up their row of buildings, before the arrival of the Emperor, it suited both the authorities and the Greek Convent people to dump the earth into this moat for a causeway. The Greeks feared that the Emperor, seeing unoccupied building land, might ask it of the Sultan, who perhaps would give it to him regardless of their rights.

Through this opening the German Emperor, clothed in the garb of a Crusader, rode in on a white charger, furnished by the Sultan; whilst the conqueror, Allenby, had a screen of soldiers close that opening and walked reverently into a city sacred alike to Christians, Moslems, and Jews.

ness is carried on along the Jaffa Road, through which we passed, parallel to the northwest wall.

The Greek Convent owns the strip of land lying northeast of the road. Here, there is a row of stores and offices two stories high, where the banks are situated, and where the most important part of the trade is carried on. Most of the business is in the hands of the Jews; and it is very marked that on a Saturday only a few of the stores can be found open. Although liberal, the Jews are scrupulously careful about the matter of observing the Sabbath in closing their places of business.

The Municipal Offices occupy the apex between the Jaffa Road and the new road leading to the railroad station; while farther west another apex is formed by the Allenby Hotel.

We soon came to the hotel, at one end of which is the road which passes in front of the post-office building. This contains the Department of Posts, Telegraphs and Telephones. Financially, this Department has proved the most satisfactory of the State services in Palestine. Prior to the British Occupation, Posts and Telegraphs were administered by two separate Departments. There was no public telephone service during the Turkish régime; while the postal service was so unreliable that certain of the European Powers maintained their own services between Europe and various towns in Palestine. All foreign mails were landed at and dispatched from Jaffa; but the Turkish post-office, which was housed near the Jaffa Gate in the upper story of the Greek row of buildings lining the wall toward the gate, was the only service allowed to use the railway to Jerusalem. The mails of other nationalities had to be conveyed by road.[1] The telegraph service was also poor and very limited. During the Military Administration, however, a beginning was made in the reorganization of the posts and telegraphs, but no public telephones were installed. At the present time, cables are dispatched satisfactorily to all parts of the world, and it is possible to telephone from Jerusalem to Cairo.

The new telephone service started with eighty subscribers in July, 1920, and by January 1, 1929, there were three

[1] *The Handbook of Palestine*, p. 210. Edited by Harry Charles Luke and Edward Keith-Roach. 1922.

thousand two hundred and thirty-two.[1] The Post-Office Building, which belongs to the Municipality, used to be run as the Jerusalem Hotel. During the War, a part of it was used for censoring, and other War services.

The road continues in an easterly direction, skirting the north wall. A hundred yards from the corner we came to the New Gate. This was obtained from the Turks by the Catholics, who had for many years occupied the northwest corner of the city within the walls. There, the Parochial Church of San Salvador and the Franciscan Convent are situated; and during the last half-century the Frères Chrétiens established near by their large day and boarding school. On the outside, opposite the northwest corner of the wall, the French hospital, served by the Sœurs de Saint Joseph, was established; and later the huge Notre Dame de France five-story hospice was built. After that, the great structure of the Sœurs Réparatrices was erected close to the wall, opposite the hospital; so that it was quite natural that the Catholics should desire an easy communication between their establishments within and those without the walls. They spent much time and money in their efforts to secure this opening from the Turks.

A little farther on to the left, we saw the fine new Nies Building of the American School of Oriental Research. The structure, which was built about three years ago with the money left by Mrs. Nies in her will, occupies the main building facing Saladin Road, while the Director's home is built at right angles to it, facing north. In the main building, there is an imposing lecture hall which contains Jerusalem's most up-to-date archæological library; and around the entire property is a substantial wall, surmounted with an iron railing.

Since the British Occupation, excavations have been carried on to a greater extent than ever before. The Government invites the coöperation of any nation or society willing to lend

---

[1] The British Report on Palestine for 1928 states that the number of subscribers' lines increased eleven per cent during the year 1928, and that additional trunk lines were erected between Jerusalem and Hebron, Jerusalem and Bethlehem, and Jaffa and Haifa. It is also stated that the Egypt–Palestine trunk service was extended to Trans-Jordan and worked satisfactorily. (Colonial No. 40. Report by His Majesty's Government in the United Kingdom of Great Britain and Northern Ireland to the Council of the League of Nations on the Administration of Palestine and Trans-Jordan for the year 1928, p. 64.)

a helping hand. Excavation works have been carried on by Danes, Germans, Americans, and Englishmen. From the 1928 Report on Palestine, we find the following interesting information: 'A Records Office and Library is being organized by the Department of Antiquities with the object of collecting and arranging all archæological information available about Palestine monuments and archæological sites, whether published or unpublished, in order that it may be made available for study.' [1]

Foremost among the excavators are the Universities of Pennsylvania and Chicago, which have undertaken respectively the sites of Bethshan and Megiddo. This involves long years of work. Harvard has brought much to light at ancient Samaria. Haverford is busy at Beth-shemesh, and Xenia Theological Seminary, of St. Louis, Missouri, laid bare the hidden secrets of the supposed Kirjath Sepher, under the leadership of Dr. Kyle; while Dr. Badè, of the Pacific School of Religion, has worked on the identification of Mizpah at Tell el Nusbeh. Dr. Sellin (a German) has been engaged on the Tell at ancient Sechem, the modern Balata, near Nablus. [2]

After Egypt had finally and clumsily rejected Mr. Rockefeller's munificent gift of ten million dollars for an archæological museum, Palestine was made the beneficiary to the extent of one fifth of that sum for a building, on condition that within three years it would be completed. The site, stipulated in the gift, was Kerm esh Sheikh, where King

[1] Colonial No. 40. Report by His Majesty's Government in the United Kingdom of Great Britain and Northern Ireland to the Council of the League of Nations on the Administration of Palestine and Trans-Jordan for the year 1928, p. 98.

[2] Excavations have been conducted during the year at Ain Shems (Beth-shemesh), by Dr. Elihu Grant, for Haverford College (Haverford, Pennsylvania); at Tell Beith Mirsin, by Professor W. F. Albright, for the American School of Oriental Research, Jerusalem, and the Xenia Theological Seminary, St. Louis, U.S.A.; at Shukbeh, by Miss D. Garrod, for the British School of Archæology in Jerusalem; at Balata, by Professor E. Sellin, assisted by Dr. Welter, for the Vorderasiatisch-Ægyptische Gesellschaft; at Tell el Mutasellim (Megiddo), by Mr. P. L. O. Guy, for the Oriental Institute of the University of Chicago; at Wady Khureitun, by Monsieur René Neuville; at Wady Gerizim, by Dr. A. M. Schneider; at the Monastery of Saint Euthymius, by the Reverend D. J. Chitty, for the British School of Archæology in Jerusalem; at Jerusalem of a portion of the Tyropæon Valley, by Mr. J. W. Crowfoot, for the Palestine Exploration Fund; at Tell el Qadar and Jericho, by Professor J. Garstang, for the Liverpool Institute of Archæology; at Tell Fara, by Professor Sir Flinders Petrie, assisted by Mr. Starkey, for the British School of Archæology in Egypt. (Colonial No. 40. Report on Palestine, 1928, p. 98.)

Edward, as Prince of Wales, had his camp, opposite the northeast corner of the city wall. Part of the money is to be devoted to equipment, and a sum is to be retained for upkeep. Lord Plumer's letter of acceptance follows:

Dear Mr. Rockefeller:

I beg to acknowledge the receipt of your letter of Oct. 13th.

On behalf of the Government of Palestine I beg to thank you most sincerely for your generous contribution toward the cost of building, equipping and endowing an archæological museum in Jerusalem. The museum will be built and maintained in accordance with the plans specified in your letter.

I can assure you that your gift will be widely appreciated. It cannot fail to be of far reaching and permanent benefit to Palestine.

Believe me

Yours sincerely

(Signed)   PLUMER [1]

At the foot of the hill from the Nies Building, we came to the Damascus Gate, 'Gate of the Pillar,' according to the Arabic name. The present city walls are the work of Suleiman the Magnificent in 1542; and of the four principal gates, which face the cardinal points, the Damascus Gate is the gate of honor, having been used for the entry of all the Governors and certain other functionaries. It is finished off with turrets and battlements, is higher, larger, and the most ornamented of all the entrances to the Holy City.[2]

[1] *Palestine Weekly*, November 18, 1927.

[2] On either side of the gate the old guard-houses are plainly to be seen, and under the street leading down to the Tyropæon Valley which forks from the Damascus Gate Street, there is to be seen, through a grill in the sidewalk, a grist-mill in use today, on the old level of the now partly buried ancient gate! These remains are regarded by the partisans of the Church of the Holy Sepulchre as the Third, or Agrippa Wall; while those who do not consider the site of the church as authentic, regard them as the Second Wall, outside of which, according to the Epistle to the Hebrews, the site of the Crucifixion is to be sought. The date of the Third Wall, which was constructed because of the existence of an unprotected suburb, was A.D. 42, therefore, after the date of the Crucifixion.

The city is very neatly and definitely bounded on the west, south, and east sides by the valleys of Hinnom and the Kedron. The north side had no definite boundary, but a steadily rising plateau running northward. This was the only side from which the city was ever taken. It was here that the forty attacks were made. According to Josephus, Solomon's North Wall corresponded roughly with the Jaffa Gate. The historian records that a suburb grew up later on this side, and because it was unprotected, a second wall was built, starting from the northwest corner and circling round to the northeast corner of the Temple Enclosure. In the year 42, when a second suburb had grown up and needed defence, another wall was built by Agrippa; hence there were three walls — but only on the north side.

But when the carriage road to Jaffa was built, and the railroad line from Jaffa to Jerusalem was constructed, in 1892, the Jaffa Gate became first in importance; thus leaving the Damascus Gate in the shade of its past glory.

Opposite the Damascus Gate, on the right side of the Nablus Road, the Catholics built Saint Paul's Hospice for the reception of Catholic pilgrims. It was very substantially and heavily built, although not more than a third of the contemplated building was constructed. The workmen were obliged to go through more than thirty feet of rubbish to reach the rock on which they were to rest their establishment. The building contains a large basement in which is to be seen the finest collection of the birds of the country — the work of expert German taxidermists, collected by the former Superior, the late Pater Schmitz. On the main floor, there is a handsome church, and there are also spacious dining-rooms; while the bedrooms are found in the upper stories. Various German States of the Union, as well as private individuals, by paying a certain sum, were privileged to have their name and arms attached to different rooms or halls, which still bear their names. Here the Lazarists conducted schools for the native children. To-day, the Palestine Government pays rent for the building, which houses the Governorate.[1]

The knoll behind Saint Paul's Hospice is called 'Gordon's Calvary.' Because of certain rock appearances on the south face of this elevated precipice, and in view of a tradition among the Jews that this was the Place of Stoning, wherefore there might be skulls lying around, General Gordon, who came to Jerusalem in 1882, concluded that this was the place of Crucifixion; and since that time, the place has been called 'Gordon's Calvary.'

This faces Solomon's Quarries which extend under the city for fifteen hundred feet in a direct line. It is estimated that enough stone has been taken out of the cavern to build the temple erected by Solomon and the whole of Jerusalem thrice over. More than three thousand years have passed since the workmen removed the stone for Solomon's structures, in the

[1] The part of the building devoted to a church is kept closed; and is not used by the Government officials.

building of which 'there was neither hammer nor axe nor any tool of iron heard in the house.' [1]

We saw the restored Eudoxia's Church of the fifth century, which marks the spot of the stoning of Stephen. Here, parts of the mosaic floor, the outline of apse, chancel, and pier were found, and were crowned with a noble structure, showing in a depression in the chancel the spot of the stoning. Beneath the atrium were found Christian tombs of that period, closed by a 'rolling stone,' and 'stone door' turning on its tenons[2]— besides many other Jewish tombs. In the monastery adjoining the church, the Dominicans conduct the scholarly École Biblique et archéologique française, with its remarkable library.

We soon reached the apex formed by the English 'Men's College'; and then Saint George's Cathedral. This was the necropolis which the Jews prepared for Helena, Queen of Adiabene, to show their gratitude for her kindness in bringing shiploads of wheat to help the poor Jews during the famine which had been foretold by Agabus. Helena became a convert to Judaism and expended her substance in relieving the poor Jews. Josephus, in describing the Third Wall, speaks of its reaching almost to the Monument of Helena of Adiabene.

A little farther on, spanning the course of the lateral feeder of the Kedron watercourse, stood, until Emperor William's visit, the old Roman bridge; and a hundred yards away, where the first hairpin bend occurs in the road, we found ourselves on the old Roman road over which Paul was sent away hurriedly at night to Cæsarea, when the centurion discovered that there was a plot on foot to kill him.

About nine-thirty, our motor entered the American Colony compound through a large gateway, and stopped at the door which leads into a courtyard. We were warmly welcomed to the hostel. The main building of the American Colony was originally the home of a private Mohammedan aristocrat — one of the earliest and one of the most pretentious buildings outside the walls. In Damascus fashion, the rooms are built around a central court, where a fountain plays, encircled by

---

[1] I Kings vi: 7.

[2] Instead of hinges, in ancient days, there were tenons above and below the doors, which thus swung in sockets.

garden beds. On three sides of the court, the rooms are two and three stories high. Being thus above the ground, the Moslem women could go around négligée, doing their scrubbing and washing without fear of the intrusion of masculine eyes. The perforations in stones projecting from the walls on either side indicate the position of the clotheslines.

The proprietor of the house, Rabah Effendi, who was known to be a man of wealth, brought marble from abroad for the flooring of the parlor and the bedrooms. He also embellished the ceilings with gilt stars — in the blue vault of heaven — and from this, the mansion was popularly referred to as 'the house whose owner had dissolved gold to whitewash it!'

In the gardens are the Halazone or snail flower (caracalla) with its rich sweet odor, the lovely heliotrope and the ivy geraniums which in May produce the effect of a wall of pink flame. Flowering cactus grows at each end of the court, while in the centre the light sky-blue plumbago blossoms all summer. In the early spring, violets and cyclamen bloom very freely; and at Easter time the lily, amaryllis, and lilacs join in a profusion of fragrance and color. Fan palms and acanthus plants add variety and beauty.

Across one end of the court lies the large cistern that conserves the water of the winter rains — now pumped up automatically by electricity. This is most gracefully screened by a mass of dark pink ivy geraniums on the verandah of the upper porch. The Colony introduced the city water for drinking purposes, because of its purity; but on account of the chlorinating of this supply every twenty-four hours, which caked and choked the range pipes, they returned to the cistern water.

After our hot and dusty ride, the varied hues of the flowers and the green of the vines were delightfully refreshing. We were given a room on the ground floor, a spacious large-windowed room looking on the Damascus Road. I drew the draperies aside as if to get a clearer view. The white road and the intermittent passing of a camel, or a donkey mounted by a turbaned, long-robed Arab, fitted appropriately into this Eastern picture. But to be living on the Damascus Road — that to me was the inexpressible charm!

We responded to the call for breakfast. The food might well have been served in our own dining-room at home, the breakfast of bacon and eggs, the coffee, the cereal, and the muffins having been prepared by an American cook. The milk from the Colony dairy and the home-made jam completed the picture of an American breakfast. And after the thrilling entry into this unfamiliar land, this touch of America was most welcome and indeed a bit stabilizing. Before the meal was finished, however, I was brought back to this country of Palestine and plunged into another series of reactions. It was known that I had come to study the Mandate, and this I soon found was interpreted to mean first and foremost a study of Jewish-Arab relations — a study of conflict. I heard both sides in the hour's conversation, and as I recall my later interviews on the subject, I think this first exposition was perhaps the most impartial of them all. It was well that it was, for I was ill-prepared at the beginning to weigh or to estimate the testimony of partisan pleaders.

Unpacking that morning was no ordinary matter. Anxious and puzzling thoughts accompanied the process. I took out the various Mandatory documents and reports I had brought for reference, and glanced at my notes describing interviews on the Near-East Mandates. In London, I had talked with Sir Frederick Lugard, member of the Mandates Commission, with officials of the British League of Nations Union, and with certain members of the British Parliament; in Paris and Geneva, I had spent several weeks discussing with numerous experts the many phases of the Near East situation. This morning, however, I laid aside the documents and notes on Syria and 'Iraq, and centred my thoughts on Palestine. Dozens of letters of introduction to important people in all three mandated territories lay on the table; but as I ran through those for my immediate study, I could easily classify them as British, Moslem, Jew, and Christian. What a cleavage of interests, I thought, in this, the Holy Land!

We accepted Mrs. Vester's invitation to dinner, where in her delightful home we met the Director of Education for Palestine, some distinguished archæologists who were starting the next day on an exploring expedition, and also some prominent women of Jerusalem who, like our hostess, were devoting their lives to human welfare among the native people of Palestine. Mr. Vester was in Damascus, from which disquieting rumors had just been received — rumors which proved to be facts, for in less than a week Damascus was bombarded.

Never, it seemed to me, was a dinner party so electric, so interesting, and yet so delightfully social. This was life in Palestine, and it was life I had come to see! Truly I had made a beginning during this, my first day's sojourn in the Holy Land!

CHAPTER II

STUDYING THE LIFE OF THE COUNTRY

EVERY experience, every circumstance revealed the value of personal contact in approaching the problems of this complicated Mandate. A first-hand study of data is always the strongest asset for a student of politics, whatever institution he may be attempting to describe; but for Palestine, actual association with the people and the life of the country is the foremost requisite for accurate and penetrating judgment.

On the spot, as I re-read the Balfour Declaration, it became strikingly clear to me that my previous study of Palestine had ignored — what I now perceived to be the centre and core of the situation — the human aspect of the problem. I had dwelt on the legal nature of the Mandate, as outlined in the Covenant of the League of Nations, and in the terms of the Mandate approved by the Council of the League. I had speculated on the principle of trusteeship under which the Mandatory Government administers its trust; but now, for the first time indeed, I began to see living people in these documents of the Mandate. How these instruments cut into the motives, the customs, and the aspirations of the people — this was to be my new study.

The task was extensive and various. My scheme of investigation included formal interviews: with British Mandatory officials, with Arab notables, with Jews and Christians, and with prominent British and American residents. To mingle with people, regardless of race, creed, or station; to see them living their normal lives; to read what they read; and to know what others were writing about them — all became part of my study. And finally, to get the setting for the story, I planned to study the country itself, including its historical sites. On these lines I started on my quest.

Fundamental to all this was the reading of the daily newspapers. I subscribed for the 'Palestine Bulletin,' the daily four-page sheet, and also the 'Palestine Weekly' — the only papers printed in English. Both these publications are conducted by Jews and naturally emphasize Jewish aspirations and plans, although in fact one finds a surprisingly interesting digest of current happenings throughout the world. There are also in Palestine more than a score of periodic publications in Arabic and about a dozen in Hebrew. In addition to the 'Palestine Bulletin' and the 'Palestine Weekly,'[1] the principal Jewish papers are: 'Doar-ha-Yom,' a morning daily, published in Jerusalem; 'Ha-Aretz,' an evening daily, published in Tel-Aviv; and 'Davar,' an evening daily, also published in Tel-Aviv. 'Davar' has a weekly English edition.[2]

The principal Arabic papers are 'El-Karmel,' published in Haifa; 'Falastin,'[3] published in Jaffa; and 'Mirat-esh-Sharq,' published in Jerusalem — all being edited by Christians. There are also 'Jamia-el-Arabiyya,' published in Jerusalem; and 'Sirat-el-Mustaqim,' published in Jaffa or Tul-Kerem.

[1] The *Palestine Weekly* has a Hebrew supplement in Latin characters.

[2] Other Jewish papers are:

Mischar w' Taasia, Economic Magazine (Hebrew), Tel-Aviv.

Palestine and Near East (fortnightly) (English), Tel-Aviv, published by the same organization.

Moznayim, literary weekly, Jerusalem and Tel-Aviv.

Ketubim, literary weekly, Tel-Aviv.

Boust'nai, agricultural weekly, Tel-Aviv.

Ha-Poel ha-tzair, Labor weekly, Tel-Aviv.

Kirjath Sepher, quarterly bibliographical review (Hebrew), published by the Hebrew University, Jerusalem.

[3] *Falastin* has a weekly English edition.

On the occasion of Lord Balfour's visit to Palestine, in 1925, *Falastin* printed a Special Edition in English, dated March 25, 1925. The following appeared on the front page:

LA PALESTINE

Jaffa, March 25th, 1925.   Wednesday

A Special Edition in English issued on the occasion
of the visit to Palestine of LORD BALFOUR,
the statesman with whose name is associated the Declaration
which to the Arabs signifies the death knell of
all the hopes they cherished when the victorious
British Armies entered their country in 1918

'For we wrestle not against flesh and blood, but against principalities and powers, against the rulers of the darkness of this world, against spiritual wickedness in high places.'

Ephesians VI: 12.

J'ACCUSE!

The former is the organ of the Mejlissites, who have in the main Husseini family connections.[1]

Knowing little of Arabic or Hebrew, I was limited to the reading of translations, through which I learned to some extent what the different communities were thinking and talking about. In my endeavor to get a complete view of the situation so far as it concerned the publications of the country, I also read the 'Official Gazette' of the Government of Palestine and the 'Commercial Bulletin' of the Department of Commerce and Industry. Although these are for sale, probably not more than ten per cent of the population read them. The 'Official Gazette,' which is printed in English, Arabic, and Hebrew, appears semi-monthly and contains the laws and enactments; [2] while the 'Commercial Bulletin,' printed in English only, is a monthly periodical of trade and business. The Health Department publishes annual reports, besides the monthly short bulletins; and there is also an annual volume containing statistics of shipping, trade, oranges, olives, etc., etc.

The language problem of Palestine looms on every side. With the occupation of the British, Arabic was substituted for Turkish as an official language; while the Mandate pro-

[1] In *Annuaire du Monde Musulman* (L. Massignon, Paris, Leroux, 1929) the following Arabic publications are listed:

Bethlehem	*Jerusalem*
Beît Lahm (monthly)	*Aqsa*
Sawt al Sha'b	*Beît al Maqdis*
Haifa	*Dâr al mo'allimîn* (monthly)
Karmel (daily)	*Jamia al Arabia* (organ of the Supreme Moslem
Nafîr	Council)
Salâm	*Jazîrat al 'Arab*
Ordonn	*Lisân al 'Arab* (daily) (discontinued?)
Zohrat al Jamîl (monthly)	*Mir'ât al Sharq*
Jaffa	*Raqîb Sahiyoûn*
Akhbar (daily)	*Rawdat al ma 'ârif* (monthly)
Falastin (daily)	*Sabah*
Hoqoûq (monthly)	
Istiqlal	
Nafas 'asriya	
Jazîra (daily)	

Recent references have been made in the Press to *Al-Yarmuk* and *Al-Zamer* — Arabic publications. There is also the publication *Al-Salam* which was recently established by groups hoping to foster friendship between Jews and Arabs.

[2] Reports of cases involving decisions on points of law are published from time to time in English special supplements to the *Official Gazette*.

vides that 'English, Arabic, and Hebrew shall be the official languages of Palestine,' and that 'any statement or inscription in Arabic on stamps or money in Palestine shall be repeated in Hebrew, and any statement or inscription in Hebrew shall be repeated in Arabic.' [1]

Exceptional facilities are given in Palestine for an informed public opinion — a striking contrast to the mandated territory of Syria, where I found the newspapers very carefully censored. The use of the Press by the Palestine Administration, as a means of conveying information to the people, is a good illustration of British justice and good sense. A conspicuous example is found in the method of enacting Ordinances. The Palestine Order-in-Council of 1922 [2] requires the text of every draft Ordinance to be published in the Press — Arabic, Hebrew, and English—at least one month before it comes before the Executive Council. The aim of this publicity is to give opportunity for suggestions and criticisms, as a result of which several desirable alterations have been made before the promulgation of certain Ordinances.

The framing of an Ordinance is first considered by the Executive Council, which consists of the High Commissioner, the Chief Secretary, the Attorney-General, and the Treasurer. All important draft Ordinances are submitted for the scrutiny of the Secretary of State in London, after which they go to the Advisory Council, which consists of the members of the Executive Council, the five heads of Departments and one of the District Commissioners. With the final approval of the Secretary of State, they are published in the 'Official Gazette' and communicated to the Press as draft Ordinances. It is during the month following that public opinion has the opportunity of expressing itself before the final enactment. It should also be mentioned that where some legislative measure introducing a new principle is proposed, the matter is often considered by a special Committee or Commission on which there may be non-official representation.

[1] Article 22 of the Mandate. See also 'Use of Official Languages.' Legislation of Palestine, 1918–25. Compiled by Norman Bentwich, Attorney-General of Palestine. Printed for the Government of Palestine by Whitehead Morris Limited, Alexandria, 1926. Regulations, Public Notices, Proclamations, vol. 2, pp. 390, 391.

[2] Palestine Order-in-Council, as amended by the Palestine (Amendment) Order-in-Council, 1923. Legislation of Palestine, 1918–25. Ordinances and Orders-in-Council, vol. 1, p. 6, Part III.

The British Administration has in more than one way shown its desire for the free expression of public opinion. In 1921, on June 3, the King's birthday, Sir Herbert Samuel, the British High Commissioner, announced that it was the desire of the British Government to ensure in Palestine 'a free and authoritative expression of popular opinion.' [1]

From the very beginning, the proceedings of the Advisory Council, constituted in October, 1920, were made public through the Press. The setting-up of this Advisory Council, meeting once a month, was in itself an appeal to public opinion. As originally constituted, it consisted of ten official members, and also of ten unofficial members nominated by the High Commissioner — four Moslems, three Christians, and three Jews.

The High Commissioner declared in his Report on the Administration of Palestine, 1920–1925, that: 'No attempt was made to control the expression of opinion. Except for a few weeks after the disturbances of 1921, there has been no censorship of the press; nor has any subsidy been paid to any newspaper.' [2] The Government has even defended itself through the Press. When the American Zionist Medical Unit publicly accused the Department of Public Health of having allowed the water supply of Jerusalem to become contaminated by typhoid germs, the Department communicated a refutation of the statement to the local Press.[3]

The use of the Press by the Administration as a means of acquainting the people with the financial position of the country at the beginning of 1924 is a fair illustration of this method of conveying information to the public. The following statement was communicated to the Arabic and Hebrew Press:

On the whole, the budgetary situation is not unsatisfactory. The total revenue collected by the Civil Administration since its establishment on 1 July, 1920, including the estimate for the present year up to 31 March, 1924, is 6,972,000 pounds, and the total expenditure for the same period is 6,729,000 Egyptian pounds, showing a

[1] Cmd. 1499. An Interim Report on the Civil Administration of Palestine, during the period 1st July, 1920–30th June, 1921, p. 10.

[2] Colonial No. 15. 1925. Report of the High Commissioner on the Administration of Palestine, 1920–25, p. 44.

[3] Philip Graves, *Palestine, the Land of Three Faiths*, p. 200.

favourable balance of 243,000 Egyptian pounds. But the prospects of the future indicate that the most careful economy on the part of the Government is still necessary.

The people learn through the Press of the changes in the personnel of the Administration. A good example of this is the proclamation by the Chief Secretary, on assuming the office of High Commissioner during the absence of Lord Plumer. The following appeared in the 'Palestine Weekly' for January 27, 1928:

By his Excellency George Stewart Symes.
Administering the Government of Palestine.
WHEREAS by an Order-in-Council of His Majesty King George V dated the tenth day of August, 1922, it is ordered inter alia that if the High Commissioner be absent from Palestine the person appointed to be Chief Secretary to the Government of Palestine shall, during His Majesty's pleasure, administer the Government of Palestine, first having taken the oaths in the said Order directed to be taken by the High Commissioner and in the manner therein prescribed, which having been done the Chief Secretary is by the said Order authorised, empowered, and commanded to do and execute during His Majesty's pleasure all things that belong to the Office of the High Commissioner according to the tenour of the said Order and according to His Majesty's instructions and the laws of Palestine;

AND WHEREAS His Excellency the High Commissioner is absent from Palestine and I have this day taken the said oaths;

NOW, THEREFORE, I, George Stewart Symes, Chief Secretary to the Government of Palestine, do hereby proclaim that I have this day assumed and taken over the administration of the Government of Palestine, and I do hereby enjoin all officers of the Government, civil and military, and all inhabitants of Palestine to take notice thereof and to give their ready obedience accordingly.

Given at Jerusalem, this twenty-first day of January, one thousand nine hundred and twenty-eight.

G. S. SYMES
Officer Administering the Government [1]

All publications, with the exception of those issued by the Government, come under the provisions of the Ottoman Press Law of 1327.[2] My later experiences brought me in contact

---

[1] Proclamation. The *Palestine Weekly*, January 27, 1928, p. 62.

[2]   THE PRESS LAW
Dated 11 Rejab 1327 (29 July, 1910).
    16 Tamuz 1325
(Amended by the Law of 26 Rabi Awwal 1330 (3rd March 1328).

with some of the violations of the Press Law. The editor of
one of the Arabic papers boasted to me of having broken the
law several times, and laughed at the penalty. In the early

(Amended by the Law of 23 Rabi Awwal 1331 (16th Shebat 1328).
(Amended by the Law of 13 Rabi Akhar 1331 (9th March 1329).
(Amended by the Law of 22 Dhil Hijjah 1331 (9th Tashrin Thani 1329).
(Amended by the Law of 16 Shawal 1322 (25th August 1330).

It is prescribed in Section 1 of the Press Law that 'Every paper or daily or periodical pamphlet must have a responsible editor (Mudir)'; while Section 3 declares
that 'The owner of a newspaper if possessing the requisite qualifications may also assume the duties of a responsible Mudir.' According to this same Section, the following particulars must be registered when application is made to publish 'a newspaper
or daily or periodical pamphlet': 1. The title of the newspaper or pamphlet. 2.
Where it will be published. 3. The subject of which it will treat. 4. The periods of
its publication. 5. The name, description, age, domicile, and nationality of the ap-
plicant. 6. The name, description, age, domicile, and nationality of the responsible
Mudir. 7. The language in which it will be published. Section 4 states the penalties
for failure to conform to these regulations; they include a fine; and in case of a second
offense or unlawful content, a fine and imprisonment may constitute the penalty.
Section 9 prescribes the penalty of a fine 'if a newspaper or periodical pamphlet is
published without the name of the responsible Mudir being written at the beginning
or at the end of it.' Section 10 lays down rules for those who desire 'to sell newspapers, books, pamphlets, pictures or other printed matters in the streets and bazaars.' The person desiring to engage in this occupation 'must apply to the Police
Department'; and the certificate given him for such purpose limits him merely to a
displayal of the title, the name of the author and the price of the publication. 'It is
forbidden to use titles or headings contrary to public morals or to cry out with the
purpose of attracting buyers, utterances against the honour or reputation of a person
or body or which generally are likely to excite the public.' Any one who contravenes
these provisions is liable to a fine or imprisonment. Section 11 extends the responsibility for the penalty concerning the contents of newspapers, and daily and periodical
pamphlets, not only to the responsible Mudir, but also to the writer, the printer, the
seller, and distributor; and where damages are awarded the owner also is responsible.
Provision is made in Section 12, for any person to secure redress who 'deems himself
materially or morally, prejudiced by any publication made in a newspaper or daily or
periodical pamphlet.' Such a person may file a claim for damage against the persons
responsible under Section 11. Sections 13 and 14 contain restrictions with regard to
the publication of court proceedings; and Section 15 states the penalty for the publication of 'Laws or regulations before they are officially promulgated.' Restrictions
are laid down in Section 16 concerning 'insulting or defamatory publication' against
a community or religion, or spreading animosity, or approving acts which are by law
regarded as criminal offences. A fine or imprisonment is the penalty for such offences. It is stated, however, that 'Scientific and philosophic discussions based on
sound arguments on the subject of religions shall not be deemed to be insulting publications.' The remaining Sections of Part II of the Press Law mention such matters
as 'threats to reveal through the press anything likely to compromise the honour or
good reputation of a person'; the publication or transmission of 'news without foundation or documents falsified or fabricated or falsely attributed to any person'; the
publication of 'books, pamphlets, articles or pictures contrary to public morality or
offensive to decency'; the right to reply, in the same paper, by a person against whom
a publication has appeared. Part III of the Press Law is devoted entirely to the subject of Defamation; and Part IV deals with Miscellaneous Provisions.

days, certain papers were suspended, and some rather amusing law-suits are recorded. At one time, the Police prosecuted 'Haaretz' for dubbing their band as 'Jazz,' but they lost the case. Another paper was prosecuted by Colonel Symes for printing an imaginary political 'dream,' but the paper won the suit.

The following interesting statement on Press censorship and Press prosecutions appeared in the Report on Palestine for 1924:

1. There is no Press Censorship in Palestine.

2. Only two Press prosecutions were instituted in 1924: one for contempt of Court, and the other for blasphemy, under Article 15 of the Press Law.

3. Under the Ottoman Law a newspaper is required to publish the correction of any false statement it has made, with equal prominence to the original false statement. This provision has been exercised on some occasions by Government.

4. 'Al Tabl,' an Arabic newspaper of Damascus, was temporarily excluded from Palestine on account of defamatory and scurrilous articles against Arab Officers of the Palestine Government.[1]

The Press was an important factor in the unfortunate disturbances of August, 1929. In naming the immediate causes of the events, the British Commission of Inquiry states: 'A further... cause... is the liberty of expression in which some sections of the Press in Palestine were allowed to indulge.' [2]

The Report of this Commission recommends that:

(a) Steps should be taken to ensure that the attention of senior officers of the Palestine Government is in future called to any articles appearing in the Press in Palestine which are of an inflammatory character and likely to excite the feelings of the people of that country. (b) The Palestine Government should examine the Press Law now in force in that country with a view to making provision, if such provision does not now exist, which would enable them to obtain from the Courts a conviction in any case in which it is proved that articles tending to a breach of the peace have been published in a newspaper in Palestine.[3]

With reference to Press control, the Report on Palestine and Trans-Jordan for the year 1929 states that:

[1] Colonial No. 17. Appendices to the Report by His Britannic Majesty's Government on the Administration under Mandate of Palestine and Trans-Jordan for the year 1924. Appendix V, Press Prosecutions.

[2] Cmd. 3530. Report of the Commission on the Palestine Disturbances of August, 1929, p. 156.

[3] Ibid., p. 167.

A stricter surveillance has been instituted over the Press, and the Government are prompt to take action against any newspaper which contravenes the provisions of the Ottoman Press Law by publishing articles calculated to provoke enmity between communities or endanger the peace.[1]

The following case may be cited to illustrate the nature of later court action against the Press. The editor of the 'Palestine Bulletin' was prosecuted under the Contempt of Court Ordinance No. 12, 1929,[2] for having published in the 'Palestine Bulletin' of February 9, 1930, an article with reference to judicial proceedings pending in the Courts of Justice calculated to prejudice such proceedings and to bring into contempt the Court before which such proceedings were pending.

The following is the decision of the Court:

We order the respondent to publish within eight days in the Palestine Bulletin the apology which he has offered through advocate, and in the same issue to publish a complete copy of this judgment and of that in the proceedings in Attorney-General v. Zalman Rubashoff (without which this judgment cannot be understood), and we further order that Schwartz pay a fine of L.P. lo and be detained, and if necessary, lodged in the Jerusalem Central Prison until this sum be paid.

Delivered this 27th day of February, 1930.

(Signed)   MICHAEL F. J. McDONNELL
Chief Justice

The 'Palestine Bulletin' published the apology and the judgment. The following is the apology:

The Palestine Bulletin apologize humbly, abjectly and absolutely for the Contempt of Court which they have committed in the article headed 'Injustice to the Jews' published by them in the issue of the 9th February, 1930, and express their regret for such publication.

In its Report to the Council of its Seventeenth (Extraordinary) Session, the Permanent Mandates Commission commented as follows on the influence of the Press in the Palestine disturbances:

[1] Colonial No. 47. Report by His Majesty's Government in the United Kingdom of Great Britain and Northern Ireland to the Council of the League of Nations on the Administration of Palestine and Trans-Jordan for the year 1929, p. 8.

[2] High Court No. 10/30. Attorney-General v. Responsible Editor Palestine Bulletin, Sch. Schwartz.

The mandatory Government agrees with the Commission of Enquiry that this state of mind was maintained by the continual incitements of the Jewish — and, more especially — of the Arab local Press. It has however been established that the Administration did not always use at the right moment its powers under the Press Law to suspend seditious prints.[1]

The newspaper proved a valuable approach to the study of Palestine; but I soon realized the need of wider reading, of which I was forcibly reminded in my interview with Sir Ronald Storrs, then Governor of Jerusalem.[2] While I was telling him the object of my visit, he interrupted with the genial inquiry, 'What have you read?' He knew I had written a Doctor's thesis on the Mandatory System, but he suspected, for all that, I might know very little about actual life in Palestine. He suggested my reading certain books, and we both concurred in the agreement that I should come to him again after I had finished them. It was strenuous work, this reading, after my daily round of interviewing and sightseeing. I found myself far into the night poring over books and newspapers, writing out interviews, recording observations, and noting significant facts about the day's experiences.

Most useful and indeed fascinating was the 'Handbook of Palestine,'[3] mentioned by Sir Ronald Storrs, which was issued under the authority of the Government of Palestine. British foresight in stimulating public interest and intelligence is strikingly illustrated in the issue of this comprehensive little book. It describes the mandated territory of Palestine in clear and accurate outline: the history and geography, the peoples and religions, the archæology and art, the geology and natural history, the government and government activities, the communications and general information for tourists, the outstanding customs and organized activi-

[1] C. 355. M. 147. 1930. VI. Permanent Mandates Commission. Minutes of the Seventeenth (Extraordinary) Session Held at Geneva from June 3 to 21, 1930, including the Report of the Commission to the Council and Comments by the Mandatory Power.

[2] Sir Ronald Storrs was appointed Governor and Commander-in-Chief in Cyprus, August, 1926.

[3] *The Handbook of Palestine*, edited by Harry Charles Luke and Edward Keith-Roach. 1922. Issued under the authority of the Government of Palestine, and published by Macmillan and Company. This and other timely books were for sale at the book-shops in Jerusalem.

ties in the life of the country — a truly illuminating story for
one who wants to know Palestine. The editors of the book,
Harry Charles Luke, Assistant Governor of Jerusalem when
the book was written, and Edward Keith-Roach, then Assistant Chief Secretary to the Government of Palestine,[1] were
peculiarly qualified to do this unique piece of work. The
'Handbook' gave me just the information I was seeking. It
was the framework to which I could attach face-to-face
observations.

The Introduction to the book, written by Sir Herbert
Samuel, the High Commissioner, who from July, 1920, to
July, 1925, held this office, gives an amazingly graphic de-
scription of the country. He writes:

If I were called upon to express in a single word the distinguishing characteristic of Palestine I should say Diversity — diversity of
religions, diversity of civilizations, diversity of climate, diversity of
physical characteristics. If the traveller wishes for coolness in the
summer, he may live 3000 feet above the level of the sea; if he
wishes for warmth in the winter, he may live 1000 feet below. He
may find among the Beduin of Beersheba precisely the conditions
that prevailed in the time of Abraham; at Bethlehem he may see
the women's costumes, and, in some respects, the mode of living of
the period of the Crusaders; the Arab villages are, for the most
part, still under mediæval conditions; the towns present many of
the problems of the early nineteenth century; while the new arrivals from Eastern and Central Europe, and from America, bring
with them the activities of the twentieth century, and sometimes,
perhaps, the ideas of the twenty-first. Indeed, it is true to say that
in Palestine you can choose the climate, or the century, that you
prefer. And these conditions are found in a country so small that it
is easy to motor in a single day from the northernmost town to the
southernmost, and in a morning from the eastern boundary to the
sea.

These diversities would be enough to lend to Palestine an unusual
interest; but her position as the birthplace of religions renders that
interest unique. Still farther is it enhanced by the conditions of the
present time.

Palestine has witnessed many and great changes in the four thou-

[1] Mr. Keith-Roach now occupies the position of Deputy District Commissioner,
Jerusalem Division.

Mr. Luke held the office of Chief Secretary under Lord Plumer and Sir John
Chancellor. He was Acting High Commissioner, in the absence of Sir John Chancellor, during the August disturbances of 1929. On June 13, 1930, the King approved
the appointment of Mr. Luke as Lieutenant-Governor of Malta to succeed Sir
Thomas Best.

sand years of her recorded history. But it is necessary to go back to the time of the Crusades for a change as fundamental as that which is involved in the ending of the Turkish administration and the substitution of a British Mandate. An era of new development opens widely before her. A multitude of new problems arise. To the importance of the country as a centre of religious associations, new political and economic considerations are added.

In these circumstances a 'Handbook of Palestine' — accurate and readable as this Handbook is — will be of service; both to those whose interest is distant, and to those who, more fortunate, are able to visit the country, to experience the charm of its scenery and climate, to come into contact with its history, to study at first hand the many complexities of its present-day problems, and, above all, to hear the voice of its spiritual appeal.

What a challenge to investigation and study! How these words of Sir Herbert Samuel draw one to seek an intimate contact with this land of diversity, and to experience its charm and complexity of life! To study at first hand, listening to 'the voice of its spiritual appeal' — what a precious opportunity!

Further reading of 'The Land of Three Faiths,' by Philip Graves, and 'The Truth About Mesopotamia, Palestine and Syria,' by J. de V. Loder — other books mentioned by Sir Ronald Storrs — widened and illumined the background, which gave me eyes to see and ears to hear as I daily pursued the fascinating search. Sir Ronald Storrs might well have been satisfied with his enthusiastic student!

My interviews went on apace. They brought me early in contact with the Zionist Executive and the leaders of Jewish thought, on whom I relied for accurate information concerning the Jewish situation in Palestine. My itinerary for visiting the Jewish Colonies was planned in Jerusalem; in fact, I had hardly been in the city a day when this began to take shape. The Colonies are the backbone of Zionism. The outstanding expression of the Zionist idea, they form the centre of the Arab-Jewish controversy, apparent on every side, and are continually breaking out in unexpected channels. To understand this subtle atmosphere, one should visit the Colonies and study their structure; and likewise their history, if one would hope to get at the root of the problem.

It was like going to the fountain-head to talk with Colonel Kisch, Chairman of the Palestine Zionist Executive. His appointment, as head of the Zionist activities in Palestine, followed the Churchill Statement of British policy,[1] which clearly repudiated 'political Zionism,' for which the Zionist Executive had previously stood.[2] The Statement made it plain that the British Government 'had no such aim in view as that Palestine should become as Jewish as England is English,' and that the special position of the Zionist Executive in Palestine did not entitle it to share in any degree in the government of that country.

Coming to the office after this declaration, Colonel Kisch, a British officer of a distinguished Anglo-Jewish family, who had served his country in France and Mesopotamia, became especially noted for his tact in allaying the irritation which, because of the extreme claims made by certain members of the Zionist Executive, had grown up between that body and the Government.

Colonel Kisch explained the case of the Jewish National Home, its present situation and the possibilities for the future. He had invited us to his home for tea; and as I remember him, there was a man, overworked in a task more important to him than anything else in the world! His spirit seemed to be one of accommodation, and I admired his comprehensive grasp of the Palestinian problem as a whole.[3]

[1] Cmd. 1700. Correspondence with the Palestine Arab Delegation and the Zionist Organisation. Presented to Parliament by Command of His Majesty, June, 1922. No. 5. The Colonial Office to the Zionist Organisation, 3d June, 1922, pp. 17–21.

[2] Dr. Eder, Acting Chairman of the Zionist Commission in 1921, stated before the Commission of Inquiry on Jewish-Arab disturbances in Jaffa as his view of the Zionist ideal, that there can be only 'one National Home in Palestine, and that a Jewish one, and no equality in the partnership between Jews and Arabs, but a Jewish predominance as soon as the numbers of that race are sufficiently increased.' These claims, the report of the Commission asserts, 'are at the root of the present unrest, and differ materially from the declared policy of the Secretary of State and the High Commissioner for Palestine.' (Cmd. 1540. Palestine. Disturbances in May, 1921. Reports of the Commission of Inquiry with Correspondence Relating Thereto. Presented to Parliament by Command of His Majesty, October, 1921, p. 57.)

[3] Colonel Kisch has become a Palestinian citizen, as well as a number of other English Jews resident in Palestine. It is a curious anomaly that Colonel Kisch and other Englishmen, by becoming Palestinian Citizens, are privileged by their passports to travel, under the ægis of Great Britain, in 'France, Italy, Austria, Germany, Spain, Switzerland, Egypt, 'Iraq, Persia, Syria, and U.S.A.' Then there follows this note: 'Unless specially endorsed this passport does not entitle the holder to enter the United Kingdom, or any British Dominion, Territory, Protectorate, or Mandated Territory.'

Other important interviews were arranged. It was a delightful group of Jewish ladies and gentlemen whom I met at tea one Sunday afternoon at the home of Miss Millstein, now employed in the Department of Immigration and Travel. Professor Patrick Geddes, of Edinburgh, had given me an introduction to her, and had told me, when I visited him in his interesting Tower at Edinburgh, of the pleasant year he had spent at her house while working on the architectural plans for the Hebrew University, and also the town-planning scheme for Tel-Aviv.[1]

I received Miss Millstein's invitation from the Government House Kavass who came to deliver it by hand. An imposing picture was this tall Arab, with his scarlet suit adorned with medals, wearing a silken striped turban around his 'tarboush.' He formerly belonged to the British Consulate.[2]

It was ingeniously arranged by my hostess, on this Sunday afternoon, that I should have a personal conversation with each of her guests. After I had talked with one after another, each occupying for a while the chair at my right, I found I had been discussing the whole series of problems which were at the time agitating Jews and Arabs. Two of these, the Urtas Springs and the 'Stamps' cases, namely, were at the time under consideration by the Department of Justice and the Supreme Court. Three of the lawyers present explained the

---

[1] In the 1928 Report on Palestine, we read: 'A comprehensive town-planning scheme for Tel-Aviv, originally drawn by Professor Patrick Geddes, was passed after substantial amendment.' (Colonial No. 40. Report by His Majesty's Government in the United Kingdom of Great Britain and Northern Ireland to the Council of the League of Nations on the Administration of Palestine and Trans-Jordan for the year 1928, p. 39.)

[2] Kavass means 'Archer.' He is a 'footman' such as the Turkish Government granted to a Foreign Consul or Prelate to guard his house and archives, and, when walking abroad, to precede him with a heavy silver-headed mace, with whose iron ferrule the pavement was rhythmically struck, so that people would make way for the coming dignitary of Church or State. Most of the Consuls or Prelates had two Kavasses, sometimes four. They were clothed in broadcloth, usually dark blue. They wore the 'sirwal,' or baggy trousers, and a short zouave jacket, much ornamented with gold thread, generally bearing on the back — or breast — or fez the Kavass coat of arms of the country, or the Church he was representing. The baggy trousers had also a proportionate embellishment of gold thread. A curved sword, frequently heavily sheathed with silver, was slung with cords and many tassels from his shoulder and hung by his side. Besides, he almost always carried in his hand (if not going in state with his mace) a rawhide whip, chased with silver. Accompanying the 'sirwal' was a pair of the same colored cloth gaiters, heavily trimmed.

Jewish arguments as a lawyer would present his case in court
— an incomparably valuable procedure for my investigation.

I became exceedingly interested in the cases. We were all
conscious of the alarming water shortage in Jerusalem in the
autumn of 1925, evidences of which were apparent on every
side. The water supply, as we have seen, has always been a
problem for Jerusalem, situated as it is on two hills, and having but a single spring in the valley of the Kedron, from which
water flows only intermittently.

It was a specially interesting sight to watch men and women filling goat-skins from the reservoir in the sacred Haram
area, between the Dome of the Rock and the Mosque al-Aksa.
These water-carriers were engaged in distributing water in
these primitive containers to many parts of Jerusalem. The
water in the Haram was drawn from a vast hidden reservoir
fed from the Pools of Solomon, two miles south of Bethlehem.

Wherever we went, we saw the urgent need of supplying
Jerusalem with more water. For the poor, the situation was
most embarrassing and critical. They were obliged to stand in
queues and wait long hours for their turns to come, though, as
a matter of fact, the amount they had to pay was nominal
compared to pre-war days, when a skinful cost twenty-five
cents. Naturally, there could be little or no street-sprinkling,
and the shortage obviously militated against the erection of
new buildings. At the American Colony, as the springs began to diminish, the water was turned on on alternate days,
instead of daily as was customary. Later, the supply was
available only every third day, and indeed, three days would
sometimes elapse without getting a drop of city water. At
such times, the Colony fell back on its old water supply in
cisterns.

During the previous May, an attempt was made to relieve
the effects of the drought. On May 25, 1925, an Ordinance
was passed,[1] authorizing the taking of water from the spring

[1] 'Urtas Springs Ordinance, 1925.' An Ordinance to enable the authority undertaking the public supply of water to Jerusalem to acquire temporarily water available from the spring at Urtas village for the purpose of relieving the water shortage
of Jerusalem. (Legislation of Palestine, 1918–25. Compiled by Norman Bentwich,
Attorney-General of Palestine. Printed for the Government of Palestine by Whitehead Morris, Limited, Alexandria, 1926. Vol. 1, p. 513, No. 13 of 1925.)

in the Arab village of Urtas [1] for the purpose of supplying Jerusalem with necessary water. According to the Ordinance, the water from Urtas was to be used for augmenting the supply contained in the Reservoirs situated at Solomon's Pools. The water was to be taken for a period not exceeding twelve months.

It was provided that enough water should be left in the spring to supply the daily needs of the inhabitants of the village of Urtas and also such other persons as had habitually used the waters of the spring, for drinking and other domestic purposes and for their animals, as well as for the irrigation of lands belonging to such inhabitants, which, at the date of the Order authorizing the use of the spring, were irrigated and planted with trees or other permanent plantations.

Authorization was given to enter upon land privately owned, for the purpose of erecting at or near the spring a pumping engine, to lay pipe-lines from the spring to the Reservoirs at Solomon's Pools, and to do such other work as might be necessary to carry out the project: provided that the owner of such land should receive compensation for any direct loss or damage suffered by him as a result of the aforesaid works. In order to ensure the purity of the water, authorization was given to prevent access to the spring by the public, either by enclosing it with a fence or by other means necessary for the purpose. It was stipulated that any person unlawfully entering such enclosure would be guilty of the offence prescribed by Article 258 of the Ottoman Penal Code. [2]

Provision was also made for giving compensation to any inhabitants in the village of Urtas who should suffer loss by

---

[1] Of Urtas, Solomon says in Ecclesiastes: '… I planted me vineyards: I made me gardens and orchards, and I planted trees in them of all kind of fruits: I made me pools of water, to water therewith the wood that bringeth forth trees.' (Ecclesiastes II: 4–6.)

Josephus relates how Solomon the King used to ride out in the early morning surrounded by his bodyguard, with his hair powdered with gold, as far as Ethan, with which Urtas has been identified, to inspect his gardens.

[2] Ottoman Penal Code, Article 258: 'Those who wilfully throw stones or other hard substances or dirt upon a man or into his house, or other building, or courtyard, or garden, and those who enter a place where they have no right of entry, or pass through a place through which they have no right of passage, are, in addition to taking from them a fine, of likewise from six bishlicks to ten bishlicks, also imprisoned for from 24 hours to five days.' (A *bishlick* is equal to fifteen cents.)

the destruction or damage to vegetables or other annual plants or crops, planted on land which at the date of the Order was irrigated by water from the spring, because of the cessation or diminution of water ordinarily used for such purposes. Compensation was also provided for any inhabitant who should suffer loss by reason of being prevented from planting vegetables or other annual plants or crops on land, which at the date of the Order was cultivated and irrigated by water from the spring, owing to the cessation or diminution of the supply of water to an extent sufficient to prevent such cultivation.

The Ordinance further stipulated that if any dispute should arise regarding the amount of water available for any inhabitant, or as to the amount of compensation to be given him in case of loss, the matter was to be referred to a single arbitrator, appointed by the High Commissioner, and that the award of the arbitrator should be final.

The Urtas Springs Ordinance was a striking blow to that little Arab village; and all the Arabs of Palestine joined in a vociferous protest against the Government. The water was taken, they said, for Jewish building purposes in Jerusalem; and to substantiate the accusation, they pointed to the exceptional amount of building in process at the time. Every provision of the Ordinance stirred the very fibre of the Arab nature. That anybody should say how much water should be left in this village spring, or that privately owned land should be taken and the inhabitants restricted, under penalty, in going to their age-old rendezvous, were preposterous notions, the Arabs said, the like of which they had never heard before. There was little comfort in the offer of compensation for those who should suffer loss, and bitter contempt for any plan for the settlement of disputes. The spring was theirs, and nobody had a right to usurp their property. This was the gossip in the sûks and bazaars throughout Palestine.

The Executive Committee of the Palestine Arab Congress sent a long communication, under the caption, 'Spoliation in Palestine,' to the Secretary of State for the Colonies in London. The letter reiterated the contention that the Urtas Spring water was needed only for the building activity of the Jews in Jerusalem, and that this 'should not by any means be taken as a legitimate excuse for the Government to legalize the illegal and trample down the uncontested and legally verified rights of the Arab owners.' The statement was made that the water of the Urtas Spring was 'barely sufficient to meet the needs of the village and its orchards and cattle.'

Commenting on the enactment of the Ordinance, the letter observed that:

> It is an unprecedented attitude that a Government should, when committing an illegal or a high-handed action, enact a new law to legalize it.... It cannot be contended that the said Ordinance is of public interest because the water is to be sold by the Municipality and not distributed gratis, which makes it in this respect a commercial enterprise, although the rightful proprietor of the water is not paid for it.

In conclusion, the following appeal was made:

> In view of the above, the Executive Committee of the Palestine Arab Congress appeal to your Excellency for the revocation of the outraging Ordinance of Artas Spring and redemption to the owners thereof all losses thereby incurred.

The inhabitants of Urtas brought suit to restrain the Government from using the Urtas Spring. They said that the Ordinance was void because it failed to respect Arab rights guaranteed by the Mandate; and in support of their contention, they cited Article 2, which makes the Mandatory responsible 'for safeguarding the civil and religious rights of all the inhabitants of Palestine, irrespective of race and religion.'

The case came before the Supreme Court of Palestine which acted under the authority of the Palestine Order-in-Council of 1922 and the Amendment of May 4, 1923.[1] According to the Order-in-Council, 'no ordinance shall be promulgated which shall be in any way repugnant to or inconsistent with the provisions of the mandate.' And to the great elation of the Arabs, the Court held that this Ordinance was repugnant to and inconsistent with the Order-in-Council of 1922, and with Article 2 of the Mandate, because it failed to safeguard the civil rights of all the inhabitants.

---

[1] Legislation of Palestine, 1918–25. Compiled by Norman Bentwich, Attorney-General of Palestine. Printed for the Government of Palestine by Whitehead Morris, Limited, Alexandria, 1926. Vol. 1, pp. 1–22. The Palestine Order-in-Council, 1922, as amended by the Palestine (Amendment) Order-in-Council, 1923.

The arguments of the Chief Justice allayed Arab fears and quieted fanatical conjecture.

In this case [the Chief Justice said] the High Commissioner has passed an Ordinance enabling a Water Board to control the springs of Urtas and take water from the inhabitants of that place for the benefit of the Municipality and inhabitants of another place, namely Jerusalem. There is a provision [he continued] for compensation for damages to vegetables and crops limited to such amount as may be awarded by a person to be appointed by the High Commissioner from whose award there is to be no appeal. For damages owing to a decreased supply of water for drinking and domestic use, for watering animals and irrigating trees no compensation is to be given, but the person mentioned above and called an arbitrator is to be empowered to decide how much water the villagers should have.

Further, he explained:

If the Ordinance does not pretend to provide full compensation for water rights infringed, that can hardly be called a 'safeguarding the civil rights of all the inhabitants,' because it is a recognized principle of sound legislation that when private property is taken for public purposes, the persons damaged by such taking should be adequately compensated.

The Court did not deny the right of the Government to take the water for the public interest, as the Chief Justice explained to me afterwards, but it did say that there should be full compensation and that the Court must decide what the compensation shall be. This, the Chief Justice said, could not be settled by arbitration. In his Judgment, the Chief Justice queried:

whether the reference of all disputes to a person called an arbitrator whose award shall be final is not of itself sufficient to invalidate the Ordinance as being repugnant to the Order-in-Council 1922, and repugnant to the Mandate.

As to the functioning of this arbitrator, the Chief Justice said:

The person who is called an arbitrator in this Ordinance is a Judge of some sort, appointed by the High Commissioner as in the case of other Judges and Magistrates with judicial powers to award damages. What again [he asked] is the meaning of the words 'whose award shall be final'? Every award is in a sense final if it disposes of all the matters referred, and final in the sense that there is no appeal, but it is not final in the sense of being executable without further procedure or that it settles the question for good and all and cannot be set aside and corrected.

If the last suggested meaning is the meaning of 'final' in the Ordinance and it appears to be so, then this person called an arbitrator is just a new sort of Judge, and what is called an 'award' is just a judgment from which there is to be no appeal. To substitute this judicial arrangement for the ordinary courts established by the Order-in-Council, 1922, is repugnant to that Order, and is not a 'safeguarding of the civil rights of all the inhabitants' as required by the Mandate.

The Judgment of the Senior British Judge upheld the arguments of the Chief Justice; and the Court decided that the Ordinance was not valid.

The Arabs were jubilant, and lost no opportunity in airing their views on the decision of the Supreme Court.[1] In the report of the Executive Committee of the Palestine Arab Congress, submitted to the High Commissioner, there appeared the following arraignment of the Government:

In its headlong law-making rush, the Palestine Administration tumbled into many pits of legal errors and entangled itself with such effective and far reaching consequences that its own law courts began to throw such laws to the wall, as the High Court of Justice did in the Artas spring case.[2]

But the Government did not accept the decision of the Supreme Court. An appeal was made to the Judicial Committee of the Privy Council,[3] which reversed the decision of the Court with regard to the specific situation, although it sustained the contention that Ordinances, repugnant to or inconsistent with the provisions of the Mandate, must be considered invalid by the courts.

Their Lordships were in agreement with the Supreme Court that Article 2 of the Mandate 'does not mean that all the civil rights of every inhabitant of Palestine which existed at the date of the Mandate are to remain unaltered throughout its duration; for if that were to be a condition of the Mandatory's jurisdiction no effective legislation would be pos-

[1] Murra v. The District Governor of Jerusalem, June 25, 1925.

[2] Report on the State of Palestine submitted to His Excellency the High Commissioner for Palestine by the Executive Committee, Palestine Arab Congress, on the 13th of October, 1925, p. 21.

[3] Jerusalem–Jaffa District Governor v. Murra, Law Reports, 1926. Appeal Cases, p. 231.

sible.' This view, they observed, was taken by both the Chief Justice and the Senior British Judge.

But their Lordships differed from the judgment of the Supreme Court on the matter of compensation. Article 2 does not

in their Lordships' opinion, mean that in every case of expropriation for public purposes full compensation shall be paid. Their Lordships agree that in such a case, and in the absence of exceptional circumstances, justice requires that fair provision shall be made for compensation.... In their Lordships' opinion the key to the true purpose and meaning of the sentence quoted from Article 2 of the Mandate is to be found in the concluding words of the Article, 'irrespective of race and religion,' and the purpose of the Article is to secure that in fulfilling the duty which is incumbent upon every Government to safeguard the rights from time to time belonging to the inhabitants of the territory the Mandatory shall not discriminate in favour of persons of any one religion or race. There is no suggestion that any such discrimination is to be found in the Ordinance now under consideration.

But, their Lordships asserted, even if 'legislation providing for the appropriation of property to public uses without proper compensation would be an infringement of the Mandate, and therefore of the Order in Council (which is contrary to their Lordships' opinion), it does not appear to their Lordships that the Urtas Springs Ordinance would be invalid on that ground.'

This decision, as one would imagine, caused great consternation among the Arabs; and they expressed their feelings without restraint. The Jews, on the other hand, began to discuss the legal implications of the decision, not only as it affected the Arabs, but as it might be applied to the interests of the Jews themselves. They emphasized especially the approval in principle of the 'right to appeal to the Law Courts against a violation of rights' given them in the Mandate. A long and detailed statement appeared in the 'Palestine Weekly': instances were enumerated in which the decision of the Privy Council might be used as a precedent in ameliorating the condition of the Jews. 'Although this time,' the author of the statement declared, 'the case was one of alleged infringement of the rights of the Arabs, nevertheless in the future we may use this precedent in order to protect our own interests, e.g., it would be worth while to complain about some of the extremely peculiar restrictions in the Immigration Regulations and of the way they are executed.'

Hearty assent was given to the decision of the Privy Council with reference to the concluding words of Article 2 of the Mandate, namely, 'irrespective of race and religion.' The conclusion that 'no such discrimination can be found in the Urtas Spring Ordinance,' so the writer stated, 'can also be applied to the Kabbarah case and many similar cases, in which the Arabs complain of alleged violations of their rights.... From now on,' the writer concluded, 'no small group of inhabitants will be able to protest and to hold up undertakings of public benefit and of necessity for the country, merely because their minute interests have suffered.'

The other case, under consideration while I was in Palestine, in which the Arabs claimed that their rights were violated, involved the use of 'E. I.,' signifying *Eretz Israel* or the Land of Israel, on the Palestine postage stamps. The word 'Palestine' was printed on the stamps in the three official languages, but after the Hebrew text were these letters, 'E. I.' This aroused great bitterness among the Arabs. They interpreted it to mean the recognition by the Government of the extreme Jewish claim to Palestine. The case was taken to the Supreme Court.[1]

The Petitioner charged that the Hebrew lettering, 'Palestine E. I.,' was contrary to Article 82 of the Palestine Order-in-Council;[2] and also to Article 22 of the Mandate for Palestine,[3] because the letters 'E. I.' did not appear in the English or Arabic surcharges.

---

[1] Husseini *v.* Postmaster-General of Palestine. The application was by way of a Mandamus addressed to the Postmaster-General concerning the inscription on the stamps. The decision of the High Court was not reported in the Palestine Law Reports or elsewhere.

[2] Article 82 of the Order-in-Council, 1922: 'All Ordinances, official notices and official forms of the Government and all official notices of local authorities and municipalities in areas to be prescribed by order of the High Commissioner, shall be published in English, Arabic and Hebrew. The three languages may be used in debates and discussions in the Legislative Council, and, subject to any regulations to be made from time to time, in the Government offices and the Law Courts.' Legislation of Palestine, 1918–25. Compiled by Norman Bentwich, Attorney-General of Palestine. Orders-in-Council and Ordinances, vol. 1, pp. 20, 21.

[3] Article 22 of the Mandate: 'English, Arabic and Hebrew shall be the official languages of Palestine. Any statement or inscription in Arabic on stamps or money

The Senior British Judge said that the provisions of the Palestine Order-in-Council are enforceable in the Courts; but he asserted that it was doubtful 'whether a postage stamp comes within the terms of Article 82, and even if it does,' the Judge continued, 'the Article only requires that the three official languages shall be used in official documents, and does not prescribe that the wording of either of the other official languages shall be a literal translation of the English.'

On the other hand, the Senior British Judge declared: 'The position as regards Article 22 of the Mandate is different.... The terms of the Mandate,' he said, 'are enforceable in the Courts only in so far as they are incorporated by the Palestine Order-in-Council, 1922, or any amendment thereof.' But he proceeded to point out that: 'Although as regards legislation the Palestine Order-in-Council, 1922, and the Amending Order-in-Council of 1923, both contain a provision prohibiting the passing of an Ordinance inconsistent with the Mandate, there is no similar provision with regard to executive acts, either in general or with special reference to the terms of Article 22.'

And the important statement was made that: 'In so far as the Mandate is not incorporated into the law of Palestine by Order-in-Council, its provisions have only the force of treaty obligations and cannot be enforced by the Courts.' The Senior British Judge therefore concluded: 'It is unnecessary to consider whether the lettering on the postage stamps is in accordance with Article 22 or not. The Petition must be dismissed.'

The Chief Justice concurred in the opinion of the Senior British Judge. 'But,' he said, 'there is another point raised by the Petitioner which requires to be dealt with. It is said,' he continued, 'that the High Court has power to, and should interfere wherever the action of an official person or Government department infringes or denies the rights of a citizen.'

in Palestine shall be repeated in Hebrew, and any statement or inscription in Hebrew shall be repeated in Arabic.'

C. 529. M. 314. 1922, VI. League of Nations. Mandate for Palestine.

(Cmd. 1785.) League of Nations. Mandate for Palestine, together with a Note by the Secretary-General Relating to its Application to the Territory known as Trans-Jordan, under the provisions of Article 25. Presented to Parliament by Command of His Majesty, December, 1922.

Then there followed a fine bit of legal reasoning on what constitutes the rights of a citizen and the competence of the Court to make redress for the violation of such rights. Let us see how carefully the Chief Justice unfolds his thesis:

It is the duty of the Postmaster-General [he said] to convey letters on payment of certain postal rates. These rates are paid into the Post-Office in return for documents which are attached to the letters deposited for transport, and these documents are called postage stamps. All the people of Palestine, not excluding the Arab majority, have a right to send letters in this way and to buy stamps, but without stamps letters cannot be sent. All stamps are surcharged with a statement of the Country of Issue in the official languages. The surcharge appears as Palestine or its equivalent in each language, but following the Hebrew word for 'Palestine' are two initial letters which signify 'Land of Israel.' It is said that Palestine is not an Arabic word, but that the Arabs call this country Southern Syria. Nevertheless the Arabs are content to let the word 'Palestine' stand.

But the Petitioner says he is an Arab and that he together with persons of his race complain that they cannot exercise the legal right of sending letters by post without purchasing and using a document in which their country is described as the Land of Israel, that this is an offence to all Arabs including the Petitioner and a moral injury for which the High Court ought to find a remedy. The further contention that this is an infringement of Article 22 of the Mandate and that the use of initials meaning 'Land of Israel' is a mere imposition on the Government and the people and not a repetition in Hebrew of the official name 'Palestine' in English and Arabic — this has been dealt with by my learned brother in his judgment, and I agree that this Court has no general authority to superintend the carrying out of the Mandate.

But the point of real interest is the former one, the claim that this Court ought to find a remedy for a moral injury which is said in this case to be an offence to the national pride of the Arab Nation, who are compelled to use a document in which their country is described as the Land of the Jews.

I do not think that matters of sentiment or politics come within the scope of our authority unless expressly so included by some instrument of Law. Had the Postmaster-General refused without reasonable ground to convey a letter or issue a stamp demanded in accordance with the Laws or rules governing his department, that could have been an infringement of right for which a legal remedy would lie, but we cannot go so far as we are asked in this case, and interfere with a public department in a matter which has to do with sentiment and politics.

The decisions in the Urtas Springs and the 'E. I.' cases

were momentous pronouncements for the Arab population.
The law of Palestine, and the highest courts in interpreting
the law, had proved, they felt, unquestionably inimical to
their interests.[1] So, too, were these decisions profoundly important for the Jewish National Home. All my interviews
with Jewish leaders touched upon the essentials of the cases
and the concomitant reactions of the Arabs. The atmosphere was full of excitement, but so subtle were the manifestations, one had to be a part of it to appreciate its full
import.

My Jewish interviews were by no means confined to the
intellectual class. I talked with Jews wherever I met them.
Our Jewish chauffeur, on our motor trip to the Jewish Colonies, was of a wholly different type from the Jews I had met in
Jerusalem. He was a young university student from Austria,
and was just recovering from an attack of malarial fever con-
tracted while engaged in draining the swamps of the Nahalal
lands, in the Plain of Esdraelon. He was a wholesome youth,
an idealist, a friendly fellow, always ready with a kind word.
His genial nature was especially evident when we visited the
American Hadassah Hospital, where three weeks before he
was a patient under the same roof. He was acquainted with
some of the sufferers whose faces brightened as he gave them
a cheering word.

[1] In connection with the Urtas Springs and the 'E. I.' cases, one should read the
judgment given by the Supreme Court in the Hebrew Telegrams Case, on May 2,
1929. This was an adverse decision against a Jewish Petitioner, who applied for an
order to issue to the Postmaster-General directing him to accept telegrams in Hebrew characters. In this case, the refusal of the Postmaster-General to accept telegrams in the Hebrew characters is supported by the Attorney-General, who cited as
authority a Public Notice appearing in the *Official Gazette* of the Government of
Palestine, issued on October 1, 1926. Section 3 of the Notice reads: 'Telegrams may
be sent in any of the three languages, but if in Hebrew, they must be written in Latin
characters, it not being practicable at present for the Post-Office to transmit telegrams in Hebrew characters.' The Petitioner alleges that the rule is invalid because
it is contrary to the terms of the Mandate and the Order-in-Council of 1922. In reply
to this, the Attorney-General says that this regulation was in force at the time of the
issue of the Palestine Order-in-Council; and that Article 74 (1) of that Order declares
that: 'The Proclamations, Ordinances, Orders, Rules of Court, and other legislative
acts which have been issued or done by the High Commissioner or by any Department of the Government of Palestine on or after the 1/17/20 shall be deemed to be
and always to have been valid and of full effect and all acts done thereunder and all
prohibitions contained therein shall be deemed to be valid.' 'Hence it is clear,' the
Court decided, 'that this regulation has the force of law by virtue of the Order of
1922 and the provisions of Art. 17 of that Order.'

When we visited the Children's Orphanage,[1] pleasantly situated on the slope of Little Hermon overlooking the Plain of Esdraelon, the children flocked about our chauffeur like any other group of youngsters who saw some new people arriving, and who detected, as children will, a sympathetic face. They besieged him with questions, both boys and girls; and, although we could not understand their Hebrew, our chauffeur, if one could judge from the ringing laughter, enjoyed to the brim the questions and sallies of these Jewish war orphans from the Ukraine. This was during the noon lunch hour.

The children go to school four hours, and work on the land four hours. Besides this, each child, as the Director explained, has his own garden which he tends during recreation hours, and in which he takes a personal pride. It was interesting to study these individual efforts of the children, for the garden almost invariably, we were told, reflects the characteristics of the owner. There were at the orphanage, which was supported by Jewish funds from South Africa, about eighty boys and half as many girls. There were children from the best and from the poorest families.[2] Many a tragic experience lay in the background of these orphans. I think I shall never forget the face of a little girl of eight who remembers seeing her father and mother murdered by the Turks; or of the little boy of twelve who witnessed the murder of his father, and who, as the Director told us, almost faints at the sight or smell of blood. Children stay at the orphanage until they are sixteen, when they can work for some one else; and at twenty-one they are free. One can only rejoice at the opportunity given these children to live in these pleasant circumstances, gradually forgetting the past and living for the new life.

We felt the sympathetic interest of our young chauffeur throughout the whole trip. His one desire seemed to be to show us the Colonies in a way to win our approval. When we arrived at Haifa, the end of his journey with us, my husband paid the bill for the automobile and passed him an extra

[1] The Children's Orphanage was founded in 1923. It escaped attack during the disturbances in August, 1929, but in September of that year, there was a raid on the cattle of the farm by Bedouin Arabs, and one of the guards was wounded.

[2] They were Jewish children, made orphans in the post-war massacres in the Ukraine.

amount for his services. Looking up with his mild blue eyes, he returned the money, saying that he got his pay from the Company, and therefore could not accept this. 'But,' he added almost wistfully, 'if you would give me a letter telling that I have been satisfactory, I should like it.'

One should visit the Jewish Colonies with an open mind and with practical imagination. There are various systems of settlement in Palestine.[1] In the first place, there are the Jews who come to the country with private means with which they buy land and farm independently. Then, there are the Colonies, which may be divided into three classes. In the first, we find the large agricultural settlements of Rishon-le-Zion, Petach-Tikweh, and Rosh-Pinah, founded during the last forty or fifty years by Edmond de Rothschild. Rishon-le-Zion, meaning 'The first in Zion,' a large village eight miles south of Jaffa, is the earliest of the Rothschild settlements. It was founded in 1882 by seventeen immigrants upon what was then desert land. To-day, it is the chief exporting centre of wine production in Palestine. The wine-cellars here are said to be among the largest in the world. In 1907, the wine-growing Colonies were formed into an association called 'La Société Co-opérative Vigneronne des Grandes Caves de Rishon-le-Zion et Zichron-Jacob.'[2] The association has developed to an average yearly output of about a million and a half gallons, the greater part of which is exported.

The second class of Colonies are the coöperative or profit-sharing — farms worked by a group of settlers and their families. In this class are: (1) the Colonies in which the settlers are individual proprietors, who pay for their land by annual instalments to the Zionist organization which was the original purchaser; (2) the Colonies which are run on the same lines as the above, and in which there is a system of coöperation in the buying of tools and farm implements and in the sale of produce; (3) other Colonies where all the land, or a considerable part of it, is worked in common, the workers receiving their pay out of the proceeds; and (4) the few settle-

[1] See *The Jewish Colonies in Palestine.* Admiralty Naval Staff, Intelligence Department (I. D. 1203, London, 1919).

[2] The Zichron-Jacob cellars near Haifa, founded by Baron Edmond de Rothschild, were constructed in 1884.

THE WINE CELLAR AT RISHON-LE-ZION

ments worked on a communal basis, where the people appor-
tion the work in the interest of economy in time and labor,
and draw food, clothing, and other necessaries of life from a
common store.[1]

The third class of Colonies is organized on the system of
small-holding settlements, composed of families working in-
dividually. It is true, however, that the coöperative system
is applied in these Colonies wherever it is found to be useful.

There are now 115 Jewish settlements in Palestine, grouped
in four districts, namely: in Judea, 43; in Samaria, 18; in
Lower Galilee, 43; in Upper Galilee, 11. The total population
of these settlements is now about 32,000. More than 30 of
them are built on land belonging to the Jewish National Fund,
which was established by the Zionist Organization for the
purpose of acquiring land to remain the property of the Jewish people. The settlements were founded with the assistance
of the Keren Hayesod (Foundation Fund), and also of the
Zionist Organization. The total area of the Jewish Settlements exceeds 1,200,000 dunums (four and one half dunums
equal one acre).[2]

Our trip to the Jewish Colonies began at Nahalal, situated
five kilometres from the Tel-Shemam station on the Haifa–
Nazareth Road. The Biblical name for Nahalal is 'a well-
watered pasture.' The group of Jewish pioneers who founded
the Colony in 1921 chose the name Nahalal, in preference to
Mahalul, used by the Arabs for centuries, and called such
even in the Talmud. It might be said that 'a well-watered
pasture' represented the hope of the colonists with regard to
the land on which they settled; it certainly did not indicate
the condition of the soil. This was one of the swampiest sections in Palestine, when the twenty men, led by Eliezer Joffe,
set up a tent one August evening in 1921. Nahalal is the gateway to the fertile Emek Valley.

Seventy-five families settled there. The population according to the census taken in April, 1927, numbered 548 — of

---

[1] Major Newman, to whom I am indebted for this clear analysis of the co-
operative colony, warns us that the word 'communal' must not be mistaken for
'communist,' an error, he says, which has caused a distinctly false impression regarding these settlements where Bolshevism finds practically no adherents at all.

[2] *The Statesman's Year-Book*, 1928, pp. 186, 187.

which 188 were men, 162 women, 101 boys, and 97 girls. The settlers obtained from the Keren Hayesod (Palestine Foundation Fund) all the sums required for settlement, in the form of a loan. They established a small-holding workers' settlement. Each of the families cultivates 100 dunums of land (25 acres); they carry on mixed farming, and sell their produce in Haifa through a coöperative system. The Girls' Agricultural School of the Women's International Zionist Organization, accommodating 40 pupils, is also situated in the Colony.

The founding of Nahalal is an interesting story. Its founders were men and women who came to Palestine in the early 1900's from Russia and Poland, inspired by the ideal of returning to the soil of Palestine for their existence. At first, they served as farm laborers in the older Jewish villages which then employed only Arab labor. But always they looked forward to the day when they would own their own parcels of Palestinian land. Recruited from labor settlements and farms, these pioneers conceived the idea, in 1919, of forming a small-holding settlement of their own. They were divided as to whether they should organize a *moshav ovdim* or a *kevuzah*,[1] but they decided in favor of the former, believing that in the latter form of settlement the individual is not stimulated to exert himself to the utmost.

Four principles govern the conduct of the Colony: the land is nationalized; the principle of self-labor is maintained; every member of the community must buy all his commodities and sell his produce through the coöperative village store which conducts a coöperative dairy and runs a village auto-bus to carry milk and other farm products to the market in Haifa. All members of the community pledge themselves to administer mutual aid, either in nursing the sick, or ploughing, building, etc.

When the seventy-five families first settled in Nahalal, the

[1] The difference between *kevuzah* and *moshav ovdim* is as follows: the *kevuzah* is a sort of 'communistic' colony where the workers receive no monetary compensation; all their needs in nature are covered from a joint treasury of the colony. The income of the treasury consists mainly of the proceeds from the sale of the products. *Moshav ovdim*, on the other hand, is a colony conducted on individualistic and coöperative basis, namely, each farmer lives in his own house, is alone responsible for his land and its income, although the products are sold on a coöperative basis. All work on a *moshav ovdim* (translation: 'settlement of workers') must be done by the farmer himself or by members of his family, no outside labor being permitted.

place was, as we have said, a tremendous swamp. The Palestine Foundation Fund granted the Colony $15,000 for building a road, and then $50,000 for drainage. About $75,000 was obtained for colonization credits, which, however, did not come in a lump sum. The money was provided by the Zionist Organization as it was received in contributions from Jews throughout the world. This naturally caused delay, which hampered the progress of Nahalal; but as I was told, the persistence and the courage of the pioneers won out.

The centre of the Colony contains the most important communal buildings — the school, public offices, coöperative stores, etc. Thus, the communal life is concentrated in the heart of the whole settlement. In view of the round shape of the hillock on which Nahalal is situated, a circular road has been built, on the outer side of which are to be found the farmyards of the colonists. Between this ring and the central buildings are the plots belonging to the professional men and artisans.

On our motor ride to Haifa, we passed a number of new Jewish settlements, some of which were founded by Hasidic Jews. It was interesting to see the beginning of these new settlements — the rough wooden barracks, and the people who had never done work of this sort trying and apparently succeeding in becoming farmers.

We arrived at Ain Harod in the morning, and the Secretary of the Colony explained to us the plan of organization. This is the largest experiment in coöperative agricultural and industrial colonization in Palestine; it comes under the fourth group of the second type of Colonies. Ain Harod was made possible by a grant of 10,000 dunums of land from the Jewish National Fund. Of these, 8600 dunums are under cultivation, being probably the largest percentage in any Jewish Colony.

In order to understand the system which governs Ain Harod, one would do best to contrast it with Nahalal. Whereas Nahalal is a pure *moshav ovdim*, Ain Harod is a pure *kevuzah* — in fact, one of the most successful of its kind. This Colony, lying at the foot of the mountains of Gilboa in the Valley of Jezreel, founded in 1923, is settled by members of the Gdud Avodah, the so-called Labor Battalion; its popula-

tion comes from eastern Europe. Those who have studied the
development of the Colony believe that much of its success is
due to the fact that residence in the Colony is carefully restricted; we were told that only those who can pass the most
rigid moral and physical tests are admitted.

The population in April, 1927, numbered 435; men 166,
women 147, boys 73, girls 49. The colonists in Ain Harod have
aimed to make their Colony self-supporting. The village
boasts a tailor-shop, a smithy, a carpenter's shop, a shoemak-
er's shop, a hospital, as well as a large dining-hall [1] with a stage
for concerts and theatrical performances. The Colony is
chiefly engaged in grain and forage cultivation, plantation of
forests, fruit trees, the vine, olives, figs, apples, and pears.

Although communistic in government, Ain Harod, as the
Secretary pointed out to us, is communistic in the primitive
sense of the word. He described it as an idealistic communism, without the political implications usually attached to the
term. The Colony is governed by an elected committee which
meets at frequent intervals and determines the nature of the
work to be done; it assigns specific duties to each member of
the community.

What is considered, even by the Jews themselves, as a dar-
ing experiment in education, is being conducted at Ain Harod.
Here, the children, graded into four different groups, are
placed apart from their respective parents, and see the latter
only for brief periods during meal-times. The rest of the time
the children are under the guidance of a school-teacher who
alone is responsible for their cultural and mental development.

I shall never forget a scene in the kindergarten which
seemed to me at the time quite touching. As we were watching the work of the children, who were sitting around a low
table, the Secretary of the Colony, who had ushered us in,
suddenly bent over a little girl, who was sitting back to him,
and kissed her. 'That's my little girl,' said he. I have always
been puzzled at the incident. The Secretary was beaming
with pleasure, while the little girl, on the other hand, maintained an unusually serious countenance. So far as I could
see, she made no response to the kiss, unless it was (and this
is what I could not make out at the time, nor have I come to a

[1] A portrait of Herzl hangs upon the wall.

conclusion since) that she showed just the slightest bit of resentment for having been kissed. At any rate, I still remember the serious little face. Curious, naturally, to know where her mother was, I asked the Secretary, who responded frankly, 'She is sick in Haifa.' There are many human touches in these pioneer settlements!

The Secretary told us that the Colony has not only been able to take care of its own need; but that it was sending some of its surplus to neighboring Colonies. It is a fact, that up to the present time this settlement has not obtained its full equipment from the Keren Hayesod. Inasmuch as the duties of the settlement are placed equally upon the shoulders of each member, the profits are equally divided. The first-class doctor receives the same remuneration as the last-joined laborer.

Ain Harod is still housed in temporary barracks; emphasis is placed on establishing the community on a sound financial basis. But, as the Secretary told us, the residents hope that in the near future they will be able to erect permanent houses of a beautiful type. One could only wish to see their desires realized.

From Ain Harod, we saw on the other side of the road the small-holders' settlement of Kfar Ezekiel; and as we motored along, we passed Afuleh, the Jewish town rising with remarkable rapidity in the heart of the Plain. We stopped at Balfouria, named in honor of Lord Balfour, which is a small-holders' settlement containing a number of American families. We inspected the hotel there, which is owned by a man from Chester, Pennsylvania.

Jewish authorities wish to make it clear that the communal type of settlement in Palestine is not a post-war development, a product of the wave of immigration that came from Russia and Poland after 1921. They point out that during the last years before the World War, the Zionist Organization entered the field of agricultural settlements, which took the form of coöperative farms, and that the present villages of Ben Shemen and Hulda in Judea and Kinnereth and Dagania in Lower Galilee have grown directly out of them.

That the *kevuzah* is a product of Palestine itself seems especially true of Dagania, which is the oldest coöperative Colony in the Holy Land. This is divided into two sections, Dagania A and Dagania B. The former settlement was founded in 1908, with aid from the Jewish National Fund. The second Dagania was established in 1921, with the assistance of loans from the Palestine Foundation Fund.

Both settlements, because of their identical nature and their proximity to each other, are generally referred to as Dagania. This is one of the most beautiful Colonies in Palestine to-day. With its famous farm-stock, two well-built residences of several stories, and groves of flourishing trees, Dagania is beautifully situated at the south end of the Sea of Galilee. A considerable amount of corn is grown for fodder, and the land is cultivated for the growing of bananas, sugarcane, oranges, olive trees, vegetables, etc. Income is also derived from cattle, poultry, and bees, while nurseries have been started for the growing of flowers and vegetables. One of the cherished places at Dagania is the grave of A. D. Gordon, famous labor philosopher and a worker in Dagania A, as well as one of its founders.

The communal type of settlement is to be found here in its purest form. Both land and stock are owned in common by all the members. The homes, too, which are unusually comfortable, for Colonies, set off by tropical gardens, are the property of the entire community.

Dagania B, which is immediately north of Dagania A, was founded when the members of the latter Colony felt convinced that their settlement was an economic and social success. The second Colony, so we were told, has repeated the achievement of the parent settlement, having adopted the same principles as to government and the selection of personnel. The members of the Colony point to the fact that not only has Dagania maintained its own obligations, but has even been able to reap sufficient of a surplus to be invested in a number of enterprises in various parts of Palestine. One of the principal sources of revenue comes from dairying, and a special milk train transports milk to the Tiberias and Haifa markets.

The amount expended by the Zionist Organization in Dagania A for land and its improvement was $21,105, and $118,610 for improvements and equipment. According to the survey made by the Joint Palestine Survey Commission, the excess of communal expenses over communal income was $13,755. The colonists point out, however, that this does not include the value of grain and fodder sold, or $4000 increase in storehouse inventory.[1]

If I were to express in a single word the distinguishing characteristic of the Jew in the Colonies, I should say Idealism; and this is especially true of the young people. In fact, the idealism of the young Jew manifests itself everywhere. At Tel-Aviv one afternoon, where I had gone to visit some of the industrial plants, I was accompanied to various places by a young Polish Jew who was sent by the Manager of the Immigration Office to take me to the places I wished to see. The Manager himself had planned to receive me, but at the last moment found himself obliged to look after the disembarking of a fresh load of immigrants from Russia. As we drove through the residential streets, the young Jew called attention to certain houses, saying, 'Don't you think they are beautiful?' And when we came to what was probably considered one of the finest houses in the town, he looked directly into my face and exclaimed, 'Don't you think it is very beautiful? A gentleman from Europe was here last week, and he said that this house was the most beautiful building he had seen anywhere in the world!' The young man said this with absolute sincerity.

Unquestionably, Tel-Aviv, or the Hill of Spring, is a unique illustration of Jewish activity in Palestine. Two decades ago, its site was nothing more than endless stretches of sand-dunes, running in a mile or so from the coast, to the north of Jaffa. To-day, the population is estimated at 45,000; it is entirely Jewish. Tel-Aviv is the only wholly Jewish city in the world.

It was founded in 1909, as a garden-city and a resort for Jewish merchants and clerks whose economic interests bound them to the harbor city of Jaffa, but who desired to

---

[1] Nahalal, Ain Harod, Dagania, and Kiryath Anavim (Dilb), which are described in this chapter, have not yet begun to repay the sums advanced to them by the Keren Hayesod. According to the agreement, repayment will fall due only after the elapse of a certain number of years following their organization.

All the facts about the Jewish Colonies which I have cited in this chapter have been obtained from Jewish authorities, or as a result of my personal observation.

live outside the city. The site of Tel-Aviv was purchased in 1909 for two thousand pounds sterling, while to-day it is worth approximately ten million pounds.[1] Upon the outbreak of the World War, there were in Tel-Aviv 182 villas, with small adjacent gardens and a population that did not exceed 980. An index to the city's growth is found in the building statistics, which show that there are at present some 3000 houses, the number in 1924 being 1936. Most of these dwellings comprise 3 rooms each. There are, however, about 600 houses which contain 8 or more rooms and 150 whose room capacity is 21 or more, while the average number of rooms per house is 6.

The rapid growth of Tel-Aviv was due to the building activities and the expansion of industry. According to the census of 1925, there were 2185 independent industrial and commercial undertakings in Tel-Aviv. Among the most important of these is the Palestine Electric Corporation, which is founded on the plan of Pinhas Rutenberg, the Jewish engineer, whose plan means the harnessing of the Jordan for the electrification of the whole of Palestine. The industries include the making of cement, bricks, and other building materials. There is also the furniture-making plant of Gouralsky and Krinizi. The textile industry has established a number of factories in Tel-Aviv, the most important being the 'Lodzia,' and the Delfiner Silk Factory. The Levkovitz Hide Tannery gives employment to a substantial number of Jewish workers; while other factories of importance are the Lieber Chocolate Factory, and the Dror Furniture Company.

Tel-Aviv has a municipal council, magistrates, a police force, theatre, exhibition grounds, factories, banks, hotels, libraries, schools, hospitals, post-office, railway station, cinemas, electricity, omnibuses, cabs, and daily, weekly, and monthly periodicals.

A large factor in the systematic development of Tel-Aviv is the importance attached to town-planning and the development of the street and traffic system. The streets have been laid out to facilitate the continuing expansion of the city. Allenby Road is the central artery, on which most of the places of business are located. Allenby Road and Herzl Street

[1] Figures received from Jewish authorities.

are parallel and are cut by the Rothschild Boulevard which leads straight to the sea.

Typical of the spirit which animates the Jewish pioneers throughout Palestine is the emphasis placed on the educational development of the youth of Tel-Aviv. At the very beginning, schoolhouse planning found a prominent place in the scheme for the city's growth. Among the first of the buildings was a high school, which was intended, not only for the children of the neighborhood, but also for those in any part of the world who might wish to come there for a Hebrew education.[1] The funds for this were provided by a wealthy English Jew, Mr. Moser, of Bradford. The Jewish High School, or Lycée, is an exclusively Jewish institution, with a staff of some thirty or more teachers and three or four hundred boys, ranging from six to eighteen years of age. In the school there is a chemical laboratory, carpenters' shops, and other modern equipment. The Lycée prepares for the university, and is for that reason in touch with Continental, British, and American universities.

The educational system of Tel-Aviv begins with the kindergarten and the public elementary schools, and ends with the technical schools. There are now somewhat more than fifty schools in the city, the majority of which are co-educational. The city maintains a Gymnasium, a Teachers' Seminary, trade schools, and technical schools. Instruction in the elementary schools is provided free of charge. There is also the Tachkemoni School in Tel-Aviv, the educational institution supported by the Mizrachi, the orthodox wing of the Zionists.

The religious life of the community has developed simultaneously with education and industry. Originally, there was only one synagogue, a small building to which the inhabitants came for worship, but during the years since 1909, a number of synagogue buildings were erected. Recently there has

[1] A considerable number of American boys have been sent to the High School at Tel-Aviv. Some have studied there after high-school graduation, before entering college; and in a few instances, which have come to my attention, young men have gone to Tel-Aviv after college, before entering the Law School; while others have taken summer courses without interrupting their studies at home. Some American families have taken up residence in Palestine for a year or two years at a time for the chief purpose of putting their children into Palestinian schools.

been built what is known as 'The Great Synagogue,' the most imposing Jewish religious structure in Palestine.

We see in all this Jewish life an unquestionable record of intelligent achievement. There are here the elements of a stirring drama — idealism and pertinacity within, opposition and suspicion without. I sought to evaluate the basic circumstances of the latter: why the opposition; why the suspicion? And what of the Mandate, which is designed to promote the well-being and development of peoples 'not yet able to stand by themselves under the strenuous conditions of the modern world'?

CHAPTER III

STUDYING THE LIFE OF THE COUNTRY — *continued*

On the part of the Arabs, there was practically universal resentment toward the Jews — those who had come in with the Balfour Declaration. But there were numerous degrees of resentment; my Arab interviews revealed various shades of opinion. I had conversations with Arab editors, with members of the Executive Committee of the Palestine Arab Congress, with the Secretary and the President of the Moslem-Christian Society, and also with pro-Arab residents in Jerusalem. In these interviews, I discovered one point on which all were agreed: that as a race the Arabs deserve the right to be independent in their own country; that Palestine is their country; and that the Jews are intruders. Yet, as to the form and extent of Arab independence, there was no unanimity of opinion. Some expressed their ideas more feelingly than others; though in no instance, and this is important to note, did the Arab case receive a consecutive, logical, or appealing presentation. That I found to be the great weakness of the Arabs. As a high official in the Government said to me, 'The Arabs have grievances, but they have the worst lawyer in the world to present them.'

It was an Arab who surrendered Jerusalem to the British. The enemy, the Turk, had gone away in the night, leaving the Letter of Surrender with the Mayor of Jerusalem.

The surrender of the Holy City is one of the most dramatic incidents of the World War. Early in the morning of December 8, 1917, the inhabitants of Jerusalem were startled by the snapping sounds of machine guns. For six months they had been accustomed to the thud of the cannon bombarding Gaza, and for the preceding seventeen days, they had heard the near cannon hammering at Neby Samuel; one day they witnessed the collapse of the minaret attached to the mosque. But now the fighting was at their very doors!

The suspense continued throughout the day. In the afternoon, the Turkish Commander issued an order that no women

or children should occupy the upper stories of the houses, as
there was to be street fighting. The Commander was to hold
out until the last man fell! This was the darkest moment for
the inhabitants of the Holy City. They were not afraid of the
bombardment of the encircling army, for they knew that
their undertaking would be fraught with mercy. But they
were fearful of being crushed between the upper and nether
millstones; for with the Turkish army shut up in Jerusalem,
they would be eaten out of house and home in twenty-four
hours!

About eight o'clock on the morning of the 9th, Hussein
Hashim El-Husseini, the Mayor, next-door neighbor of the
American Colony, rapped at the door saying, 'Tell Mother,
for she will be glad to hear it, I am on my way out to the military outposts on the Jaffa Road with the Letter of Surrender,
left by the Governor last night.' The Mayor explained that
the Governor, acting on orders received from headquarters at
midnight, had drafted a Letter of Surrender, with the aid of
the Mufti, and had withdrawn the army, leaving the act of
surrender in charge of the Mayor.

Hussein Hashim El-Husseini asked for a horse or buggy to
use on this errand, but neither was available, for all had been
requisitioned long before. He thereupon went to the Italian
Hospital, which had been requisitioned by the Military, and
tearing a sheet in halves, attached it to a broomstick. Armed
with this flag of truce and the Letter, the parlementaire and
his party set out on the important mission to the northwest
outskirts of the city, along the Jaffa Road.[1]

At the toll-house, on the left side edge of the road, they met
two British sergeants stationed as sentinels, but, as they were
not qualified to accept the Letter, the parlementaire and his

---

[1] 'A person is regarded as a parlementaire who has been authorized by one of the
belligerents to enter into communication with the other, and who advances bearing
a white flag. He has a right to inviolability, as well as the trumpeter, bugler or
drummer, the flag-bearer and interpreter who may accompany him.' (Article 32 of
the Hague Convention Respecting the Laws and Customs of War on Land. Convention IV of 1907. The Hague Conventions and Declarations of 1899 and 1907. Edited
by James Brown Scott.)

In this party, there was no trumpeter, bugler, drummer, or interpreter; for there
were no trumpeters, buglers, or drummers left in Jerusalem. The parlementaire and
two flag-bearers were accompanied by three members of the Jerusalem police and
other members of the Husseini family. (See frontispiece.)

party waited under their protection. On the arrival of a major, the Letter was presented to him, but he had no authority to receive the important document. Later, an artillery colonel reached the spot, and he too declined it. Soon Brigadier-General Watson came riding up; and again the Letter was refused. At last, a message was sent to the Corps Commander, General Sir John Shea, who met the party at the post-office about 1 P.M. It was to him that the Letter of Surrender was officially delivered. Thus ended the fortieth — but bloodless — siege of Jerusalem!

The Mayor was a member of the ancient Husseini family, the leading Arab family in Jerusalem. His father, Selim Effendi, had had a long and successful career as Mayor of Jerusalem. During his fourteen years of service, the city underwent more civic changes than at any previous time. The streets were paved, which entailed the enlarging of the old city sewers, and led to the uncovering of the old Roman pavement, so that for the first time macadamizing was used in road-building.

The most outstanding member of this important family is Musa Kazim Pasha, the older brother. He is President of the Moslem-Christian Society, and Chairman of the Arab Executive. He served under the Turks as Governor in Yemen. The British appointed him Mayor of Jerusalem, but afterwards superseded him by Raghib Bey. He is now the leader of the Arab group, which persistently refuses to coöperate with the Government of Palestine, so long as the Mandate recognizes the Balfour Declaration. It is this group also which is most violently opposed to the Jews.[1]

With vivid recollection, though in many respects a repetition of previous discussions, I recall my interview with Musa Kazim Pasha El-Husseini. The unique setting at his home, together with the personality of the Head of this ancient House, gave a touch of Arab life more eloquent perhaps than words. After climbing a long outside flight of stairs under the intense glare of an October sun, we (my interpreter and myself) were ushered into a large room with faded carpet, cov-

[1] Musa Kazim Pasha was Chairman of the Palestine Arab Delegation which went to London in 1922 after the disturbances in May, 1921, and also Chairman of the Commission which went to London in the spring of 1930, after the August riots in 1929.

ered furniture, and closed windows. The servant shut the door as she went to announce our arrival. The atmosphere was close, humid. We had been seated a few minutes when the door opened, and Musa Kazim Pasha, a tall, slender figure, in a gray suit of clothes, set off by the red fez, entered the room and greeted me in Arabic. He seated himself languidly on a sofa, one arm resting on the back. As I watched the far-away look in his red-brown eyes and perceived the occasional cough which appeared to rack the frail physique of the old man, I thought of the glories and downfalls of his interesting race. He seemed to be worn out with hopes and disappointments, yet, with a tenacious resentment, he rallied to the Arab cause.

I was about to begin conversation with him when the door opened and there entered a tall, energetic-looking, pleasant-faced young man, the nephew of Musa Kazim Pasha, who had evidently been invited by his uncle to be present at the interview. He was ready and alert, and he spoke in English. All the arguments of the Arabs were on the tip of his tongue: he rehearsed grievance after grievance against the Jews; and just as fluently arraigned the British, dwelling particularly on the burning questions of the day — the Urtas Springs and the 'Stamps' controversies. There was little coherence in what he said, but there was, none the less, tremendous seriousness and frank appeal.

When the Pasha talked, he seemed to be thinking more on the past, though his chief thesis touched the immediate past. He stressed the 'British Promises' for Arab independence, and invoked the McMahon letters of 1915 to prove that Palestine was included in the Arab independent zone. He rehearsed the whole story down to the granting of the Mandate, placing the burden of his argument on broken treaties and brutal betrayals.

The Arabs, he said, went into the War on the side of the Allies in return for the promise of Arab independence. He had seen, he asserted, a copy of the correspondence between Sir Henry McMahon and Hussein, the Sherif of Mecca, which, he reiterated, contains in unmistakable terms the pledge to liberate the Arabs and set up an independent government. With cold disdain he described the British-French intrigues for the

MUSA KAZIM PASHA, PRESIDENT OF THE MOSLEM SUPREME
COUNCIL *(left)*, AND EMIR EFFENDI EL HUSSEINI, GRAND
MUFTI OF PALESTINE
On their departure for London with the Arab delegation

control of the Near Eastern Arab countries, which culminated in the Sykes-Picot Treaty of 1916; and with supreme indignation denounced the Balfour Declaration of 1917 which gave the Jews a National Home in Palestine. Each of these agreements, he observed, was in direct conflict with all of the others. This miserable story of Arab betrayal, Musa Kazim Pasha reflected, lies at the root of all the troubles in Palestine; and justice to the Arabs, he exclaimed, can never be given so long as the Balfour Declaration is recognized. There he paused and languidly listened to my expressions of thanks and appreciation for his illuminating interview.

Jaffa was the scene of my next Arab interview. We set out from Jerusalem about eight in the morning, having accepted an invitation to attend the Annual Police Sports which were held in a field to the right of the road leading into Jaffa, just back of the German Colony.[1] We were also to lunch at the Cliff Hotel in Jaffa, where I was to meet Isa Elisa, the Editor of 'Falastin.'

Leaving Jerusalem by the Jaffa Road, the first sight, as we got to the outskirts, on the right hand side, was the water tank that supplies the city with water; and a few hundred yards farther on, we saw the monument [2] erected in the open field, just opposite the toll-house, to commemorate the surrender of the Holy City to General Allenby — now, forsooth, nearly lost sight of in the midst of a Jewish settlement which has since grown up here.

On the right side of the road which zigzags down to the Kalonieh Valley, we passed Lifta, which is probably the ancient Nephtoah. Mozah is probably represented by the modern village of Kalonieh. The road wound back and forth until we reached Kastel, an old Roman fort. There was quite

---

[1] The field that skirts the road is called 'Solomon's Harbor.' In winter, sometimes, the sea water comes up into the field, and in digging up the earth, old rusty anchors have been found, hence the appellation, 'Solomon's Harbor.'

[2] The monument was erected in the field, off the road, on higher ground than that where the toll-house stood, in order to command attention.

The following is the inscription which runs around the base of the monument:

'Near this spot the Holy City was surrendered to the 60th
London Division, 9th December 1917.
Erected by their comrades to those officers Co's & men who
Fell in fighting for Jerusalem.'

a descent to Dilb, and later a rise to Enab, the Bible Kirjath-jearim,[1] where the Ark was brought from Beth-shemesh, and where it rested for twenty years. It was here from the house of Obed Edom that David carried the Ark to Jerusalem 'with shouting, and with the sound of the trumpet.'[2] In Crusader days, there was a large nunnery in this vicinity, which is still called by the natives 'Deir el Banat' — 'Convent of the Girls.' The Crusader Church exists intact at Enab.

We stopped at Dilb — 'Kiryath Anavim,' the Biblical name meaning Grapetown — to visit the Jewish Colony. Nowhere in Palestine did one find greater devotion to the cause of Zion, nor firmer determination to overcome each and every difficulty in achieving the great aim. Every visitor to Palestine who studies the Jewish Colonies becomes absorbed in the story of these pioneers. In 1917, the Zionists in the Ukraine founded an agricultural school for the training of those who intended to go out to Palestine. As we learned from our friends in Jerusalem, the group consisted of ten university graduates, a printer, a druggist, a book-store keeper, a carpenter, and small merchants. For two years this interesting group studied agriculture, at the end of which time part of them went to Palestine to clear the land and make the beginnings of a settlement.

The terraced hillsides, the waterworks, the barns, houses, and the school reflected the indomitable courage and intelligence of this group of young men and young women — seventy-five of them.[3] Everybody is impressed with the youthful appearance of these people; we were told that no member of the Colony was more than forty years old.

I was greatly interested in the school, and especially the kindergarten, which is carried on in accordance with the communal system. This, to the visitor, is perhaps the most strik-

---

[1] The Town of the Woods. (Jeremiah XXVI: 20; Joshua IX: 17.)

[2] II Samuel VI: 15.

'The course of the Ark's return,' says George Adam Smith, 'is certain.... The plague which the Ark had brought upon Philistia clung about it still. As stricken Ashdod had passed it on to Gath, Gath to Ekron, and Ekron to Beth-shemesh, so Beth-shemesh now made haste to deposit it upon Jehovah's own territory of the hills: *To whom shall he go up from us?* The nearest hill-town was Kiriath Jearim, *the Town of the Woods.*' (George Adam Smith, *The Historical Geography of the Holy Land*, pp. 224, 225.)

[3] The population in April, 1927, was 79; 33 men, 29 women, 10 boys, 7 girls.

ing aspect of the Colony. The property is held in common, the work is allotted on lines of economy, and the children are cared for on the same basis. This plan releases the mothers for field and household duties.

The colonists have planted many pines and fruit trees. There are sixty different kinds of eucalyptus trees in the forest nursery. They have also cows for dairying purposes and they sell their milk in Jerusalem and other places. When we visited the Colony, we saw a newly arrived herd of Holstein cows in the barnyard. Tormented by flies, and desperate with the heat, they appeared to us scarcely likely to measure up to the hardiness of their courageous and persistent owners.

The cost of establishing this Colony was £22,500. This covered the price of the land and the outlay for clearing it, the building of houses and waterworks, and the purchase of farming implements and animals. The money was supplied from Zionist funds; the land was provided by the Jewish National Fund, or Keren Kayemeth, and the grants and loans by the Palestine Foundation Fund, or Keren Hayesod. The Colony was established nine years ago, and already the colonists are paying all of their running expenses, although as yet they have paid no interest on the borrowed capital.[1]

Two miles beyond Enab, at Saria, we found ourselves on the edge of the western ramparts of Judea, where we got a view of the Mediterranean, which marked the end of our journey. From this elevation, the road dropped through a mountain gorge to one thousand feet above sea-level at Bab el Wad, the Gate of the Valley, and thence more slowly to the foothills of the Shephelah at Latroon (Turon), a Crusading stronghold of Richard I in the Third Crusade, and supposed to be the home of the penitent thief. Half a mile northwards, on the other side of the road, we passed Amwas — the Emmaus of the Plain, another of Richard's strongholds, and the Nicopolis of later Roman days. In front of us here was the Plain of Sharon and to the right the Valley of Ajalon, which has always been the easiest passage from the coast to Jerusalem. Joshua came this way when he drove the Canaanites down to Makkedah in the Shephelah, and, because of the

[1] Facts obtained from Zionist authorities.

length of time necessary for its accomplishment, bade the sun and the moon to stand still: 'Sun, stand thou still upon Gibeon; and thou, Moon, in the Valley of Ajalon'; [1] down Ajalon the early men of Ephraim and Benjamin raided the Philistines; [2] in 166 B.C., Jonathan Maccabeus drove the Hellenizing Syrians from Judea; [3] and in A.D. 66, Cestius Gallus, heading a Roman army, came up to Jerusalem by way of Ajalon, set it on fire, but harried by the sudden attacks of the insurgent Jews, who smote the Romans by the thousands, retreated the same way he had come up; and here, too, Allenby, supported by the Fleet, broke the Turkish lines and pushed up to Jerusalem.

For some three miles after leaving Latroon, there was a rise in the road, which after leaving Kubab, dropped again for two miles to the Plain of Sharon, and ran level for another four to Ramleh, identified with Joseph of Arimathea's home. Joseph, who 'begged the body of Jesus' from Pilate, and 'laid it in a sepulchre ... wherein never man before was laid,' [4] is commemorated in a fine twelfth-century church, which was transformed a century later into a mosque. This has a lofty tower, from which all the convergent roads may be surveyed for miles.[5]

Leaving Ramleh, two hundred and fifty feet above sea-level, the road dropped gently for ten miles until Bethdagon and the famous orange groves of Jaffa came into view. Finally, we came in sight of the sea — and then on to Jaffa, a town of 45,000 inhabitants.

A long and interesting story weaves itself about this Arab town, whose name was first recorded in history in the sixteenth century B.C. According to mythology, Jaffa was the place where Perseus rescued Andromeda from the sea-monster; and it was from this port that Jonah essayed to flee from Tarshish.

In the fifteenth century B.C., Jaffa was a Phœnician city under Egyptian suzerainty. It later became Philistine, and remained so for about a thousand years, during which period the cedar logs were landed here for King Solomon's Temple

---

[1] Joshua x: 12.   [2] I Chronicles vii: 21; viii: 13.
[3] I Maccabees xi.   [4] Luke xxiii: 52, 53.
[5] See description of Ramleh in Chapter I, p. 11.

after being floated down from the Lebanese ports by Hiram, King of Tyre. Under the Maccabees, Jaffa was a typically Jewish town, but became a Roman Free City after its conquest by Pompey. At one time in the next century, it was given by Mark Antony as a love-token to Cleopatra.

Christianity was introduced into Jaffa at an early period. In the house of Simon the Tanner,[1] Peter had the vision of the sheet sent down from Heaven preparing him to go to Cornelius in Cæsarea;[2] and one can now see at the southern end of the old city the site of the house of Simon the Tanner, which is shown in a little mosque. It was also at Jaffa that Peter brought Tabitha to life.[3]

The next outstanding fact in the history of the city is the Treaty of Jaffa which King Baldwin I made with the Genoese, under which Jaffa was constituted a country, the investiture of which was always given to the heir to the throne of Jerusalem. Captured from the Crusaders and destroyed by the brother of Saladin in 1187; subsequently retaken by Richard Cœur-de-Lion; sacked by Bibars in 1267; and stormed by Napoleon in 1799 — Jaffa certainly has had a stormy history. I had expected to see marks of depredation from the World War, but neither at Jaffa nor at Jerusalem was there any fighting. On account of the lack of labor, however, and also because of the scarcity of money, Jaffa suffered material damage during the evacuation. An orange-garden proprietor, for example, was allowed to stay behind to attend to his property, but was given only four men to help him. At least ten per cent of the gardens were destroyed because of the conditions under which the order of evacuation was carried out.

As we motored from the modern Jewish town of Tel-Aviv into Jaffa, I shall never forget the perceptible and almost sudden change when we passed from one municipality into the other. The street was continuous, yet the boundary between the two places could not have been more distinctly marked than by the vivid contrast in the shop windows of the Western Tel-Aviv and the gay bazaars lining the streets of Jaffa. I wondered what had taken place, and curiously looked around as if to study the scene; but before I could come to any conclusion, I found myself riding peacefully along a

[1] Acts ix: 43 and x: 6.   [2] *Ibid.*, x: 10–48.   [3] *Ibid.*, ix: 38–42.

street of Oriental picturesqueness and charm — typical of Eastern Arab life. We motored through narrow and winding streets to the oldest part of the town up to the Cliff Hotel, situated on a rocky hill overlooking the Mediterranean Sea. The Cliff Hotel was built by a former Austrian Consul, Count Caboga, a Knight of Saint John. This explains the Malta crosses carved on the capitals, and also the Moorish windows. The property was inherited by a native whom the Consul adopted, but who afterward sold it to the Sisters of Charity, the present proprietors.

Luncheon was served on the piazza, from which we looked down upon strings of camels laden with building materials, plodding along the hot beach on their way to Tel-Aviv. As we sat and talked with the Editor of 'Falastin' — the history of Jaffa in the background and the blue Mediterranean before us — it almost seemed as if another page of Jaffa history were being written. There was the Arab denouncing the Jew, and standing defiant of the Government which allowed the intruder to enter. With stinging sarcasm, he pointed to the Russian ship in the roadstead, flying the red flag — bringing in more of the hateful race; and there was Tel-Aviv, risen like black magic from a plain of bare sand to a completely Jewish town, the only wholly Jewish town in the world — and that, indeed, in the Holy Land! To the Arabs, the power house, the factories, the schools, shops, and electric tramcars of this Jewish centre meant the blasting of their precious hopes.

Back again in Jerusalem. Through the courtesy of Sir Ronald Storrs, an appointment was arranged with an Arab official of the Government for three o'clock one afternoon at the Governorate. At the appointed hour, my husband and I walked into the reception-room, which, one might casually observe, was rather poorly furnished for a public waiting-room in a British Government building. The sofa on which we sat, although it may have had a meritorious history, was much the worse for wear, and indeed the room as a whole could make little boast of its appointments. Certainly neither the Jews nor the Arabs could accuse the Administration of extravagance in this direction.

We had been waiting several minutes when a tall, slender man, perhaps in the forties, dressed in Western clothes except for the fez, came bounding up the stairs. Making apologies for being late (he said he had been showing the Mosque of Omar to Lady Plumer and her guest), he asked us to his office, and there with true Arab politeness answered the questions which I had carefully prepared beforehand. He talked freely of Jewish and Arab grievances, but always from the Government's standpoint. Obviously, he was of a different political party from Musa Kazim Pasha! When we rose to go, he asked if he might take us to the Mosque of Omar, or if he could render any other service; but since we had already visited the Mosque and our stay in Jerusalem was nearing its end, we reluctantly declined his invitation. It was a pleasure to have sat with this Arab gentleman for the half-hour; and I regret even now that we could not have taken advantage of his escort to the sacred shrine.

At a dinner party given by the American Consul and Mrs. Heiser, I met Mahmoud Ch. El-Husseini, an official in the Land Registry.[1] A cultured and scholarly gentleman, he approached the Arab question from the historical viewpoint. He urged me to read certain books, and the next day, just as we were leaving for our trip to the Jewish Colonies, a messenger brought me a book which Mahmoud Ch. El-Husseini had especially mentioned the evening before. On the card accompanying the book he had written the following: 'You are going to meet Miss Newton soon.[2] She will tell you all about it.' I had told him of my intended visit on Mount Carmel; and he was comfortably assured that I would get from Miss Newton the important facts about the Arab cause.

The next morning at eight o'clock, by appointment, Jamal-el-Husseini, Secretary of the Palestine Arab Congress, came to see me. Mrs. Vester had very kindly arranged for the interview in her library; and as we drank our Turkish coffee, we talked of the Jewish Colonies. Here, I listened to an arraignment such as I had not heard before. This young man of open countenance, tall and well-groomed, centred his exposition on

---

[1] He was later moved to the Administration quarters, and, still later, retired.

[2] An Englishwoman living on Mount Carmel, who gives time and money to the Arab cause. She was one of the witnesses for the Arabs before the Commission on the Palestine Disturbances of August, 1929.

the social side of Jewish immigration, describing especially the domestic life in the 'communist' Colonies. He pointed out in detail what he considered to be the moral depravities of the system. The influence, he said, of such centres of immorality on the surrounding life was a matter of very serious concern; a situation, he affirmed, which should certainly be known by those who were trying to make an impartial study of Zionism.

Everybody would agree, of course, that all the essential phases of Jewish life in Palestine should be included in a study such as I am making; but this conversation shows very plainly that my appraisement of the Jewish Colonies is bound to differ from the Eastern view, even when that view is sincerely detached from prejudice. Nevertheless, in my study, I must see the picture, not only from the point of view of Western standards, but of the Orient as well; for it is the transplanting of twentieth-century Western modes into a country of Eastern mediæval customs that jars the old and stirs up disharmony and strife.

In the midst of all the confusion and dissension, however, there are evidences of a common civic life, and a responsible feeling for the public welfare. Civic agencies began to be built up in Palestine almost as soon as the country was occupied. Secondary only to the immediately necessary work of giving the people of Jerusalem a water supply which would be free from the evils of the private rain-fed cisterns, and of combating the unspeakable conditions resulting from the lack of any kind of sanitary arrangements either in the old city or in the new, or of solving the grave and harassing problem of averting starvation, the military authorities planned and carried out a remarkable program of civic improvement. Large sums of money were spent on the roads of Palestine,[1]

[1] Before the War no motor-car — or, to be exact, only one — had ever been seen in Palestine, for there was no road there on which an owner would trust either his car or his life. The exigencies of war necessitated the building of several roads, but these were war roads, intended only to serve military purposes. During the seven years of civil government all of these war roads have been reconstructed and made permanent and new ones made, so that one can travel in a car in comfort now from Dan to Beersheba and from the Mediterranean to the Arabian Desert. All the towns of Palestine are connected by first-class roads, and the mileage of the secondary roads is increasing so rapidly that before long every village in the country will be accessible in all weathers to its neighbors. (Albert M. Hyamson, *Palestine Old and New*, p. 46.)

and on rebuilding or strengthening the bridges destroyed during the military operations.[1]

Still uncertain of their tenure, the military authorities endowed the country with public gardens, Chambers of Commerce, and the Jerusalem School of Music.[2] Under the auspices of the Pro-Jerusalem Society,[3] indigenous industries that had been allowed to die out were revived. But aside from these obviously useful projects, attention was given to certain phases of junior citizenship. Branches of the Boy Scouts and Girl Guides were organized, which proved their usefulness in many ways. These organizations have developed continuously and have become recognized institutions in the life of Palestine. On all public occasions such as the arrival of a new High Commissioner, a public funeral, or public function of any kind, the Boy Scouts are in evidence. They are responsible for the direction and smooth-working of the ingress and egress of the crowds, and other allied duties.

There are the Baden-Powell Boy Scouts, founded in April, 1913, and the Jewish Boy Scouts, organized after the War. The Baden-Powell Boy Scouts are members of the 'Boy Scouts Association,' founded by Sir Robert Baden-Powell, and are in direct connection with the Imperial Headquarters in London. The Jewish Boy Scouts, although similar to the Baden-Powell, are not directly dependent on London. They are grouped in Jerusalem, Jaffa, and Haifa, and in the larger Jewish Colonies in connection with the Jewish schools. The Association contains about five hundred Girl Scout troops, and it has also a Sea Scout troop. A complete Hebrew translation of 'Scouting for Boys' has been published. The Jewish Labor Federation has established a scout association for working boys and girls, and there are also a number of independent Jewish and Arab troops.

The Baden-Powell Boy Scouts Association has now in the vicinity of sixty scouters and sixteen hundred scouts, all Moslem or Christian. The majority of the troops are in Gov-

[1] A steel bridge was thrown across the Ghoraniyeh passage of the Jordan River.

[2] This was subsequently presented to the Jewish community.

[3] See Chapter VIII.

ernment schools. In 1923, the Director of Education was appointed Camp Chief for Palestine.[1]

The Girl Guide Association was started in Palestine in the year 1919, in connection with the Girl Guide Association in England. The 1927 Report on the Administration of Palestine gives the following information concerning the Girl Guide Association in Palestine: 'There are 260 guides, 10 rangers, and 85 brownies, most of them Arabs, and 48 guiders. Guiders and guides are drawn from all classes, and the movement is already widely popular.'[2]

The educational department has also enlisted the schoolchildren of Palestine in planting trees. In 1922, an 'Arbor Day' was inaugurated for Government schools, with the cooperation of the Department of Agriculture; more than 10,000 trees were planted in or near the school grounds by the children themselves. The responsibility for tending the trees rests on the schools, each generation of children handing them on in good condition to its successor. A day similar to 'Arbor Day' is celebrated in all Jewish schools.[3] On Arbor Day, 1924, 18,348 trees were planted in Government school gardens; in 1925, 13,300 trees were planted; and the day continues to be observed. The interest in preserving trees and protecting forests dates back to October, 1920, when the Woods and Forests Ordinance was passed.[4]

Almost at the inception of the Civil Administration, the Government exerted its authority over the general appearance of the country. 'With a view to preserving the charm

[1] See Colonial No. 5, p. 25; see also Colonial No. 26, p. 30, and Colonial No. 31, p. 33. (Reports on the Administration of Palestine.)

[2] Colonial No. 31, Report by His Britannic Majesty's Government to the Council of the League of Nations on the Administration of Palestine and Trans-Jordan for the year 1927, p. 33.

During the visit of Princess Mary, the Girl Guides formed the guard of honor.

[3] Report on Palestine Administration, 1922, p. 30.

[4] Cmd. 1499. An Interim Report on the Civil Administration of Palestine, during the period 1st July, 1920–30th June, 1921, p. 23.

An Ordinance to provide for the regulation of Forest Lands and the protection of Trees. (This Ordinance has since been repealed by 5 of 1926.) Legislation of Palestine, 1918–25. Compiled by Norman Bentwich, Attorney-General of Palestine. Orders-in-Council and Ordinances, vol. 1, p. 93.

In 1926, there were fourteen government forest nurseries, with over a million trees in stock. In 1927, the entire forest area of Palestine, excluding artificially created forest, was assessed at 300,000 acres.

and preventing the vulgarization of the country,' the High Commissioner wrote in his Interim Report, 1921, 'the placarding of advertisements has been prohibited throughout Palestine, except, in towns, in places allotted for the purpose by municipalities, in the railway stations and on business premises for the purposes of the business conducted there.' [1] The Advertisement Ordinance, restricting the display of advertisements, was passed in July, 1920.[2]

The Government's early interest in the appearance of the towns is shown in the enactment of the Town-Planning Ordinance, in November, 1920, for the purpose of preventing, as the High Commissioner said in his Interim Report, the chaotic methods of building new streets and quarters which had hitherto prevailed in Palestine.[3]

A Central Town-Planning Commission was established by Ordinance in January, 1921,[4] to control and guide the lines of development and expansion of the old, and the design of the new towns of Palestine. In 1923, Jerusalem, Jaffa, Haifa, Nablus, Tiberias, Ramleh-Ludd, Beersheba, and Gaza were declared Town-Planning Areas, within which no construction was possible without permit from a Building Commission. In 1924, Beisan was declared a Town-Planning Area, and the boundaries of the Jerusalem and Haifa Town-Planning Areas were withdrawn.

The 1928 Report on Palestine contains the following interesting statement on the activities of the Central Town Planning Commission:

The Central Town-Planning Commission held seven meetings during the year, and its Adviser, Mr. Holliday, gave constant

[1] Cmd. 1499. An Interim Report on the Civil Administration of Palestine, during the period 1st July, 1920–30th June, 1921, p. 20.

[2] An Ordinance to provide for the Regulation of Advertisements. Legislation of Palestine, 1918–25. Compiled by Norman Bentwich, Attorney-General of Palestine. Orders-in-Council and Ordinances, vol. 1, p. 60.

[3] Cmd. 1499. An Interim Report on the Civil Administration of Palestine, during the period 1st July, 1920–30th June, 1921, pp. 19, 20.

[4] An Ordinance to secure the orderly planning of Towns and to control the erection of Buildings and the laying out of Streets. (This Ordinance has been amended by the Town-Planning (Amendment) Ordinance, No. 16 of 1922. Section 26 (c) of the original Ordinance has been repealed by Section 3 of the Town-Planning (Amendment) Ordinance. 1922.) Legislation of Palestine, 1918–25. Compiled by Norman Bentwich, Attorney-General of Palestine. Orders-in-Council and Ordinances, vol. 1, p. 120.

counsel to local authorities. In consequence of the earthquake in 1927, schemes of reconstruction were prepared for the towns of Nablus, Ramleh, and Lydda, and are being put into execution.

The general town-planning scheme for the area of Jerusalem is still under preparation; but schemes for four suburbs, including the areas around the new archæological museum and the General Post-Office, were approved. A scheme has been prepared for preserving the area around the ancient walls free from new building.

A comprehensive town-planning scheme for Tel-Aviv, originally drawn by Professor Patrick Geddes, was passed after substantial amendment.

Detailed schemes for areas on Mount Carmel above the present town of Haifa were approved; and a joint committee of the Harbour Board and technical members of the Central Town-Planning Commission was constituted to frame a plan for the laying out of the area affected by the harbour.

Tulkarem and Afuleh were declared town-planning areas.

The model building bylaws were applied, with certain modifications, in Tiberias and Jaffa.

The fees for building permits which are imposed by the municipal authorities were revised. In place of the basis taken in the Ottoman law of the area of the ground, the cubic content of the proposed building is adopted in the new scale.[1]

As far back as 1908, a group of humanitarian people organized a Society for the Prevention of Cruelty to Animals,[2] but during the War, the work ceased to be carried on. During the British occupation, however, anti-cruelty work was carried on under Army auspices; and in 1921, the Society, called the S.P.C.A.,[3] was re-started under the Presidency of the High Commissioner, Sir Herbert Samuel. The Veterinary Hospital in Jerusalem was taken over by the Society on lease from the municipality and conducted entirely under the Society's management. The efforts of the Society were, and are now, limited by the amount of voluntary support forthcoming from the public.

In January, 1921, a great step was taken toward forward-

[1] Colonial No. 40. Report by His Majesty's Government in the United Kingdom of Great Britain and Northern Ireland to the Council of the League of Nations on the Administration of Palestine and Trans-Jordan for the year 1928, p. 39.

[2] The Charter was granted in 1908, the year that the Turkish Constitution was adopted.

[3] The Society was first called R.S.P.C.A., but after much correspondence with the Royal Society, the R. was dropped, inasmuch as, owing to restricted funds, the Palestine Society was unable to keep to the standard of the Royal Society.

ing the welfare of women and children in Palestine. On that date, a meeting was held, composed of representatives of the various women's organizations interested in social welfare. The object of the meeting, which was presided over by Lady Samuel, wife of the High Commissioner, was the formation of a Women's Council, which had for its aim the coördination of the work of organizations whose purpose was to better the conditions of women and children. From the earliest conception of the idea, it was understood that the Palestine Administration would welcome such an effort. At an informal gathering preceding the January meeting, the Civil Secretary of Palestine was present, and the women were assured that the officials of the Administration were willing to recognize the Council as a consultative body on all matters relating to the welfare of women and children.

At the meeting in January, thirty-three persons were present, representing organizations of all nationalities and denominations from all parts of Palestine. Lady Samuel presided, and the proceedings took place in the three official languages. A Provisional Council was elected which drew up a Constitution for the formation of a 'Union of Women for Social Work in Palestine'; and at a later meeting the Constitution was adopted, and plans made for active work.

Conspicuous among the organizations represented on the Council was the Social Service Association, a voluntary body representing women of all nationalities and denominations interested in social work. This was formed in the autumn of 1918 for the purpose of dealing with some of the many social problems which arose at the end of the War. The Association had done most effective work in raising the moral tone of Jerusalem which had suffered immeasurably during the war years. The founding of a Girls' Home was one of its successful activities. For two years, under the skilful directorship of a woman who came from England for the purpose, the Home received girls and helped them over a difficult time, and trained them to earn their own living. Although at the end of that time, the Home was closed because of lack of funds, the need for such an institution became more and more apparent. Many young girls with their children were being put into prison for lack of better accommodation.

The Social Service Association brought the matter before the Chief Secretary, Sir Wyndham Deedes, who issued an appeal for funds to re-start the Home. This being successful, it was decided to enlarge the scope of the work, and with the consent of the Chief Justice, the Home took in young female offenders who would otherwise have gone to prison. A Government grant was made which covered the cost of food and clothing, while the rent and repairs and the cost of the Social Service cases was borne by the Association. Thus, the Home was run jointly for Reformatory, Rescue, and Preventive cases.

The policy of the Palestine Administration, in recognizing and working with forces in the country potentially able to improve civic life, is notably reflected in the attitude of the Government toward the Social Service Association and the Women's Council. Soon after the Council was organized, the Civil Secretary made the following statement: 'The Administration will be willing at all times to refer to the Council questions affecting women and children in Palestine, and that while the Administration cannot in the meantime bind itself to give effect to any resolutions which the Council may subsequently pass in respect of these matters as referred, it will, nevertheless, give serious attention and attach full weight to the resolutions emanating from such a body.' [1]

Later on, however, the Council found that the effectiveness of its work depended on a still closer connection with the Administration. Moreover, it was felt that to bring the country into line with enlightened principles regarding the treatment of women and children commensurate with the standards of an English Administration, there should be a trained woman working as a Government official, and coöperating with the Council.

On representing this view to the Administration, Miss Nixon, a woman of great experience in all forms of social work, was appointed to care for women and children for whom the Government was in any way responsible. Although the money for this appointment was privately provided for the first year, so satisfactory and necessary had the work proved that from April 1, 1921, Miss Nixon was appointed on the

[1] Palestine Women's Council. Report 1921–22, page 3.

staff of the Palestine Government as Inspector of Female Prisoners, under the Department of Public Security, with the rank of a Senior Service Official.[1]

The Women's Council became an invaluable adjunct to the Palestine Administration. It was constantly making inquiries concerning conditions affecting women and children, and sending in suggestions for improvements. The Young Offenders Ordinance [2] was passed by the Government after submission to the Council for their consideration. This Ordinance introduced a system of voluntary Probation Officers into whose care offenders of either sex below the age of twenty might be committed by the courts. The officers were appointed on the recommendation of the Council. The Ordinance also enables the Court to commit to a Reformatory or Industrial Home any female offender up to the age of eighteen.

The Industrial Employment of Women and Children Ordinance, enacted in 1927,[3] was the direct result of inquiries made by Miss Nixon and the Women's Council. This Ordinance prohibits female and child labor in dangerous trades, and child labor under twelve years of age entirely; and limits the employment of persons from twelve to sixteen years of age to eight hours (not more than five to be continuous) in twenty-four, and on not more than six days a week. Such persons may not be employed from 7 P.M. to 6 A.M. nor women from 10 P.M. to 5 A.M. Women must have a rest period of eleven consecutive hours in twenty-four. Agriculture and

---

[1] The Criminal Law Amendment Ordinance of 1927 brought the law with regard to disorderly houses, indecent assault and graver offences of the kind against women and children into accord with modern standards. (Colonial No. 31. Report by His Britannic Majesty's Government to the Council of the League of Nations on the Administration of Palestine and Trans-Jordan for the year 1927, p. 21.)

Criminal Law Amendment Ordinance (No. 2), 1927. An Ordinance to Amend the Criminal Law regarding parties to offences, attempts to commit offences and other matters connected therewith. (*Official Gazette* of the Government of Palestine, No. 199. 16th November, 1927.)

Miss Nixon is still on the staff of the Palestine Government.

[2] An Ordinance to amend the law relating to the punishment of young offenders. Legislation of Palestine, 1918–25. Compiled by Norman Bentwich, Attorney-General of Palestine. Orders-in-Council and Ordinances, vol. 1, p. 258.

[3] An Ordinance relating to the employment of women and children in Industrial Undertakings. *Official Gazette* of the Government of Palestine. Gazette Extraordinary. 29th November, 1927.

undertakings in which members of the proprietor's family alone are employed are excluded from the scope of the Ordinance.[1]

The Director of Public Health has asked the coöperation of the Council on more than one occasion. A conspicuous instance was that which concerned the supervising and training of midwives. The Council's method of dealing with this situation is a good illustration of the wise and thorough methods of that body. The Council appointed a sub-committee to collect information, and the Director of Public Health supplied the committee with a full report of existing conditions. After careful consideration, however, the committee reported that it 'has felt itself so far unable to send in any recommendations for the amelioration of conditions. It was found that the present mentality of the women of the country was such that they do not seek professional skill on the part of the midwives. And any attempt to enforce ideal conditions would at present be unworkable. It was felt, therefore, that education must precede reform; and that the establishment of Infant Welfare Centres and the dissemination of simple pamphlets on the subject of health and hygiene to the people of Palestine in Arabic and Hebrew were as much as could be accomplished immediately.' [2]

In the Report of the Palestine Administration for 1923, we read that in the Midwives' Training School of the Government Hospital, Jerusalem, eleven women (three in 1922) passed the qualifying examination.[3] And in the Report for 1927, there is the following statement: 'Twenty-six pupil midwives and eleven midwives with foreign qualifications were licensed, bringing the number of trained and licensed midwives up to 221. Yet midwives are reluctant to settle in the villages to practise among the peasantry, where their attendance is a crying need.' [4]

[1] Colonial No. 31. Report by His Britannic Majesty's Government to the Council of the League of Nations on the Administration of Palestine and Trans-Jordan for the year 1927, p. 69.

[2] Palestine Women's Council. Report, 1921–22, p. 5.

[3] Colonial No. 5. Report on Palestine Administration, 1923, p. 29.

[4] Colonial No. 31. Report by His Britannic Majesty's Government to the Council of the League of Nations on the Administration of Palestine and Trans-Jordan for the year 1927, p. 42.

In 1928, there were 291 midwives licensed to practice; and 44 of the midwives licensed in 1928 underwent their training in Palestine.[1]

In the 1926 Report, the statement is made that: 'The last years have seen a remarkable growth of Infant Welfare work in Palestine. The Hadassah Organization now maintains or supervises some fifteen centres in Jerusalem, Tel-Aviv, Haifa, Tiberias, and in Jewish settlements. Local Committees have started the same activities in Nablus, Haifa, Ramleh, Acre and Bethlehem and are securing the interest of the local populations. The British Superintendents of Midwifery at Jerusalem and Nablus will train nurses in the work.'[2]

The 1928 Report states that infant and child welfare work was extended considerably, and that nine new Infant Welfare Centres were set up. 'Most of the centres serve the urban population, but there are a few in the Jewish settlements and one in the Arab village of Jifna.'[3]

The Council also brought about a reform in the manner of giving women justice in the land courts of Palestine. In view of the difficulties experienced by women in this direction, the Council requested the Administration to allow a competent woman to look into cases where women's claims were concerned. The request was granted: the statement was made that, where any woman qualified to speak on behalf of others, presented herself to the Court, the Judges would certainly allow her to appear and argue their rights.

When the change in the Penal Code was under consideration, the draft sections which relate to women and children were sent to the Council for their comments. A few emendations and suggestions were made. Later, the Civil Secretary suggested to the Council the formation of Women's Visiting Committees for hospitals and similar institutions. This mat-

[1] Colonial No. 40. Report by His Britannic Majesty's Government to the Council of the League of Nations on the Administration of Palestine and Trans-Jordan for the year 1928, p. 56.

[2] Colonial No. 26. Report by His Britannic Majesty's Government to the Council of the League of Nations on the Administration of Palestine and Trans-Jordan for the year 1926, p. 36.

[3] Colonial No. 40. Report by His Majesty's Government in the United Kingdom of Great Britain and Northern Ireland to the Council of the League of Nations on the Administration of Palestine and Trans-Jordan for the year 1928, p. 56.

ter was placed in the hands of the Social Service Association, and as a result of their efforts, hospital visiting was established in the Government and Jewish hospitals in Jerusalem. Volunteers were found who were willing to undertake visiting and to teach women prisoners. In the 1925 Report, the following statement is made: 'Women prisoners at Jerusalem are employed in the repair of prison clothing and instructed in needlework by English ladies.' [1]

The Council was asked by the Administration to form a Society for helping discharged prisoners. As the majority of the prisoners were men, it was decided that Miss Nixon and three members of the Council should sit on a joint committee with a representative selection of competent men, and should work as a related committee to a Prisoners' Visiting Board, which had also been proposed. The committee was formed, and established regular relations with the Administration.

At the end of Sir Herbert Samuel's term as High Commissioner for Palestine, he gave public recognition of the Women's Council and the valuable service it had rendered Palestine:

A number of women, British, Palestinian and others have formed a Palestine Women's Council, representing over fifty organisations in the country, and affiliated to the International Council of Women. This body keeps a watch upon many questions of social welfare, helps to mould public opinion with regard to them, and offers valuable suggestions to the central and district administrations. It has also established a small home for wayward girls, which is utilised as a State reformatory. The Government has in its service as a full-time officer an Englishwoman, charged with the duty of inspecting the prisons and other government establishments, and of proposing measures relating to the welfare of women and children and the prevention or suppression of social evils. [2]

Another institution which focusses its efforts on improving the conditions of girls and women in Palestine is the Y.W.C.A.,

---

[1] Colonial No. 20. Report by His Britannic Majesty's Government to the Council of the League of Nations on the Administration of Palestine and Trans-Jordan for the year 1925, p. 32.

Another matter in which the Council is interested is raising the age of consent.

The Council has also undertaken an inquiry into the condition of street beggars and lepers.

[2] Colonial No. 15. Report of the High Commissioner on the Administration of Palestine, 1920–25, p. 15.

which maintains a Hostel[1] in Jerusalem and an Employment Bureau. The Hostel endeavors to combine two aims: that of welcoming tourists, and of providing a home for girls and women who are earning their living. During the year 1927, three hundred and ninety-one persons, representing ten nationalities, with occupations varying from domestic servants to journalists, hospital sisters, missionaries and students, stayed at the Hostel. The motto of the Employment Bureau is, 'By love serve one another.' Four hundred and forty-six girls of twelve nationalities applied to the Bureau for work during the year 1927. Of this number, one hundred and eighty-three were placed.

A very important activity of the Association is its club work. There are the regular club members, consisting of young women over sixteen years of age, and the junior members — girls between the ages of eleven and sixteen, all of whom are admitted irrespective of race or religion. The club work of the Association has gradually developed, until now, 1929, there are five centres in Palestine, with a total membership of about five hundred. In Jerusalem, the membership is very cosmopolitan, including Arabs, Greeks, Armenians, Russians, English, Americans, and Germans, with a number of Jewish and Moslem members; while in the smaller centres it consists almost wholly of Palestinian Christians. The program of the club provides for an informal after-school education — by means of classes, lectures, discussion circles, and libraries.

Quoting from the 1929 Report:

There are three outstanding needs of the Palestinian girls at the present time: a higher standard of physical education, with adequate opportunities for outdoor and indoor recreation; professional and technical training for careers, other than those of teaching and nursing, including the important branch of domestic service; and a wider and deeper spiritual outlook, especially as regards her social responsibilities, which will lead her to feel she has a vital part to play in working out the Divine purpose in the Holy Land.

Among all the institutions for bettering life in the Holy Land, none is more potent nor more far-reaching than the

---

[1] It was as 'The House of World Friendship' that Wyndham House was first conceived, when the plan was set on foot to acquire it in 1921, and it has kept this ideal before it, whether friends come from near or from far.

Y.M.C.A. The spirit which animates this humanizing effort makes for fraternity and brotherliness. The mixing of all creeds and classes tends to obliterate cleavage and suspicion, the principal source of disunity and strife.

Besides the Y.M.C.A. centre in Jerusalem, there is a live branch at Jaffa and another at Nablus. The property of the Y.M.C.A. in Jerusalem consists of about nine acres. The site dominates the old city, and its building is situated on the principal street, leading to the railway station. It is to have as its opposite neighbor the new Government Offices which are yet to be built.

The new building, which is to be erected at a cost of $1,000,000, will contain the first auditorium in Jerusalem suitable for lectures, concerts, etc. A fine organ has been presented for the purpose. The building will also contain a gymnasium, swimming-baths, a cafeteria, and about one hundred rooms for a hostel. It will be furnished with elevators and will have the first central heating plant in Jerusalem. On the grounds, there will be half a dozen tennis courts, a soccer field, and a grandstand.

The foundation stone bears the inscription: 'To the Glory of God and in remembrance of His Only Begotten Son.' The 'Jesus Tower' will give an extensive view of much of the Promised Land, east and west, and here will be inscribed: 'Where the feet of Jesus have trod is the Holy Land.' Here also there will be a reproduction in mosaics of the oldest geographic representation in the world, found expressed in Medeba, Trans-Jordan, thus harking back to A.D. 499. On the floor, bronze tablets will immortalize the memory of Y.M.C.A. men who in great crises have given their lives. An 'Upper Room,' as referred to in the Gospel, will be displayed. The doorway leading into the tower will be low, thus enforcing humility; on the wall will be a representation of Christ's parable 'The Pharisee and the Publican praying in the Temple.' Only such trees and vines as the Bible mentions will adorn these gardens. A great carillon of bells has been donated, and the tower is to be reflected in a narrow lake in front.

There is to be a public library of over 100,000 books, and special attention will be given to such as deal with Palestine.

It is expected that the most complete collection of books on Christology in existence will be assembled here. There is also to be a Biblical Museum in the cruciform vestibule. An education section will be established which will enable young men to qualify as engineers, mechanics, etc. There will also be a 'School of the Prophets,' where ministers, Bible teachers and missionaries can pursue special courses. Provision will also be made for women Christian workers.

One can hardly estimate the extent of the influence which this institution will exert in the Holy Land.[1]

The nature of civic and social improvement in the life of Palestine is interestingly set forth by Sir Herbert Samuel in his last Report as High Commissioner:

Throughout the country [he said] efforts have been made in various ways to maintain the standard that should mark the Holy Land. Public gaming and lotteries are prohibited. Cinema films are subject to censorship. Branches of the Royal Society for the Prevention of Cruelty to Animals are active in some of the towns. The liquor traffic is controlled. Houses of ill-fame have been almost entirely suppressed, and — a point seldom observed by the visitor, for a negative fact is not often noted — the country is free from disfigurement by advertisements. An Ordinance, enacted in July, 1920, before any vested interests had appeared, restricts the posting of placards to notice boards, provided in suitable places by the municipalities, and to railway stations. In this one country at least, the beauties of the landscape and the amenities of the towns are free from the intrusion of the hoarding.[2]

To the tourist who gets merely a bird's-eye view of Palestine, this normally developing civic and social life is entirely unobserved, and yet it colors the whole problem of the Mandate. Quite lost from view, as well, unless one looks beneath the surface, are some of the official plans, inaugurated by the Administration, to encourage common thought and action among the different elements of the population. A keen observer might see, for example, the significance of British

---

[1] It was reported from Palestine in March, 1929, that Mohammedans, with headquarters at Haifa, had organized a Young Men's Moslem Association to correspond, in a general way, to the Young Men's Christian Association. The purpose is to foster adherence to the Moslem faith, perpetuate its traditions and practices, and combat European influences that are considered hurtful to the religion.

[2] Colonial No. 15. Report of the High Commissioner on the Administration of Palestine, 1920–25, p. 15.

policy in establishing official holidays, and inviting the different communities to take part in the celebration.

On December 22, 1923, the Chief Secretary issued a circular, declaring that: 'June the 3rd, the Anniversary of the birthday of His Majesty the King, will be a general Government holiday.' [1] At first, the day was celebrated in the 'Pub-

[1] Colonial No. 9. Report by His Britannic Majesty's Government on the Palestine Administration, 1923. No. Adm. 2026. Chief Secretary's Circular No. 287, p. 25.

The circular also declared that: In addition, the following days will be observed as official holidays in 1924 by the members of the respective communities:

1. *Christians* —

	Western Churches	Orthodox Church
New Year's Day	1st January	14th January
Epiphany	6th January	19th January
Good Friday	18th April	25th April
Easter Monday	21st April	28th April
Ascension Day	29th May	5th June
Whit-Monday	9th June	16th June
Christmas Day	25th December	7th January, 1925
Boxing Day	26th December	8th January, 1925

Note. — These dates are according to the Gregorian Calendar (New Style).

2. *Moslems* —

Return from Nebi Musa of Sanjaq al-Sherif	15th May
Sheker Bairam (Fitr, 3 days)	5th–7th May
Qurban Bairam (Adha, 3 days)	13th–15th July
Maulud al-Nabi	10th October

Note. — The President of the Moslem Supreme Council states that, as the Moslem Festivals depend upon the appearance of the New Moon, it is possible that they may be changed by a day or so shortly before the Feast concerned.

3. *Jews* —

1st Day of Passover	19th April
7th Day of Passover	25th April
Pentecost	8th June
1st Day of New Year	29th September
2nd Day of New Year	30th September
Day of Atonement	8th October
1st Day of Tabernacles	13th October
8th Day of Tabernacles (Rejoicing of the Law)	20th October

Note. — The Secretary of the Chief Rabbinate states that all Jewish Feasts begin half-an-hour before sunset on the previous evening, and terminate half-an-hour after sunset on the date shown, with the exception of the Day of Atonement, when, for the convenience of persons fasting, work should cease two hours before sunset on the previous day.

The following days are holidays of obligation binding on all Catholics of the Latin Rite, and every facility should be given to Roman Catholic Officers of the Government to attend Mass on these days:

The Circumcision	1st January
The Epiphany	6th January
St. Joseph's Day	19th March
The Ascension	40 days after Easter
Corpus Christi	Thursday after Trinity Sunday
SS. Peter and Paul	29th June
Assumption of Our Lady	15th August
All Saints	1st November
Immaculate Conception	8th December
Christmas Day	25th December

G. F. CLAYTON,
Chief Secretary.

The legal holidays under the Bills of Exchange (Protest) Ordinance, 1924, enumer-

lic Garden' at the invitation of the then Governor Sir Ronald Storrs. Later, when Lord Plumer arrived, and took charge of the function, invitations were issued to the leading members of each community to come to his garden for tea. At the reception in 1927, Colonel Symes, the Chief Secretary, read the list of honors conferred by H.M. the King upon Palestine officials and notables. This ceremony took place in the presence of Government officials, foreign consuls, heads of the various religious communities and other notables. The British anthem is always played on the King's Birthday.

All the people are asked to suspend business at 11 A.M. and to maintain silence for two minutes on Armistice Day. The proclamation of the High Commissioner in 1925 [1] was a forceful appeal to the people to unite in commemorating those who fell during the War, and to recall the ideals which prompted the great sacrifice. In 1926, Memorial Services were held in Saint George's Cathedral, attended by Lord and Lady Plumer, Government officials, Consuls, and notables. The

ates the holidays of the different religious communities which are recognized by the Government for members of those communities. They are treated as legal holidays for the purpose of protesting bills-of-exchange.

Birthday of His Majesty the King (June 3rd)
Shakar Bairam (3 days)
Qurban Bairam (4 days)
Mauled Al Nabi (1 day)
New Year's Day } (according to both
Christmas Day   the Gregorian
Easter Monday } and Julian
Ascension Day   calendars)
Passover (first and last days)
Pentecost
New Year (2 days)
Day of Atonement
Feast of Tabernacles (first and last days)

23rd January, 1925. (Legislation of Palestine, 1918–25. Regulations, Public Notices, Proclamations, etc., vol. 2, p. 452.)

[1] 'The 9th of December, the day on which, in 1917, Jerusalem was taken by the Allied Troops, is rightly celebrated throughout this country as a day of Victory.

'I ask that the 11th of November, the day on which the fierce struggle which had been carried on for more than four years ceased, may be kept as a day of Remembrance for those who fell during that struggle.

'I trust that all in this country will endeavour to attend a place of worship on that day.

'I appeal to all citizens to suspend business at 11 A.M. on that day and to maintain silence as far as possible for a period of two minutes.

'All Government Offices will be closed until 12 noon.

'1.10.25.   (Sgd.)   PLUMER, F. M.

'*High Commissioner*'

principal synagogues were crowded, where prayers were offered for the protection and well-being of His Britannic Majesty and for the health of Lord Plumer and his officials.

There was also the usual parade of the Jewish ex-service
men. About three hundred marched in the parade, which was
led by Colonel Kisch. Lord Plumer addressed these ex-
soldiers, after which they marched to the War Cemetery on
the Mount of Olives, where a short Memorial Service was
read by Rabbi Grayewski, former Chaplain to the Jewish
force.

Let us read the description of this Armistice Day Observance which appeared in the 'Palestine Weekly': [1]

The anniversary of the Day on which the great powers ceased
hostilities in the Great War seven years ago, was celebrated with
impressive ceremony at Jerusalem on Wednesday morning. His
Excellency the High Commissioner and Lady Plumer, the members
of his Advisory and Executive Councils, prominent officials in the
Government service, members of all clergy in the Holy City, the
Consuls and notabilities among the residents attended a solemn
service and thanksgiving, with a memorial for the Glorious Dead at
St. George's Anglican Cathedral. Lord and Lady Plumer later laid
a wreath at the foot of the Memorial Cross in the War cemetery on
Mount of Scopus. Services of thanksgiving and memorial were also
held at the Catholic Cathedral, and at the Synagogues of the Hur-
vah and Rabbi Yochanan Ben Zakkai, where Chief Rabbis Kook
and Meir delivered orations. The services were largely attended.

At the eleventh hour of the morning three guns fired to signify
the commencement of the Great Silence. Hundreds stood with
bared heads in the Russian Compound to commemorate the sacred
Two Minutes. All over Jerusalem the solemnity of those two minutes were observed.

Thousands had flocked to the Russian Compound to witness the
Parade of Jewish ex-servicemen, mostly ex-legionnaires of the Jewish Battalions. A large crowd of Jewish ex-soldiers had come the
same morning from Jaffa, carrying wreaths for the graves of Jewish
soldiers in the War cemetery. About three hundred ex-servicemen
had gathered in the Compound, with an imposing array of medals
gained in service in Gallipoli and other fronts. Colonel F. H. Kisch,
C.B.E., D.S.O., accompanied by Colonel N. de M. Bentwich,
O.B.E., M.C., arrived at about 11.20 A.M., and Colonel Kisch took
command of the parade. He was assisted by Captains Coussins,
Harris, Levi, Jacobs, Lieutenants E. H. Samuel and M. Nurok, and
the regimental sergeant-majors and company sergeant-majors,
formerly of the Jewish battalions. Lord Plumer arrived, in com-

[1] *The Palestine Weekly*, November 13, 1925.

pany of Lady Plumer, and attended by Captain Drummond, at noon precisely. He was greeted by Colonel Kisch, and then inspected the ranks.

Following the inspection, His Excellency delivered a short address. He was happy to meet them he said. It was above all the duty of ex-soldiers to maintain the bond of union created during the Great War. He urged them to observe the ideals of those who fell in the interest of their motherland and nation. The supreme sacrifice had been paid by the Glorious Dead, who had given their all for these ideals. It would be his pleasure to meet them at every Armistice Day ceremony during the time he was in Palestine.

After passing and saluting H.E. the High Commissioner, at the saluting base, the parade proceeded under the command of Colonel Kisch to the War Cemetery, where the service was held by Rabbi Grayewski, former Chaplain to the Force. Wreaths of the Jewish Community and ex-Legionnaire's Club 'Menorah' were laid in the Cemetery.

This breathes real patriotic fervor, such as one finds in Armistice Day programs in any part of the world. But it is significant that the Jews were the only part of the population which entered whole-heartedly into the observance of the day.

The Armistice Day celebration in 1928 is described as follows by a friend of mine in Jerusalem who attended the service:

For Armistice Day celebration in 1928, Lord Plumer having gone on leave, and Sir John Chancellor, the new High Commissioner, not having arrived, it devolved on Mr. H. C. Luke, Chief Secretary, Acting for the High Commissioner, to play the part. By announcement through the press and from the pulpit, people were asked to be in their (unreserved) seats by 10.25 A.M. Punctually at 10.30 the Chief Secretary and party came in and marched up to the front seats on the right hand side of the church. This side was filled exclusively with British Tommies and uniformed policemen and officers; whilst on the opposite side were officials and civilians, among whom were a few Jews, some Mohammedans and some Arab Christians. The Clergy of the Greek Orthodox, Armenian, Coptic, Syrian, Abyssinian and Russian Churches, in their gorgeous vestments, had already been conducted into the chancel. Then to the singing of the Recessional, the Bishop, preceded by a clergyman bearing aloft a golden cross, and followed by the canons and clergy, a banner and the choir, marched in.

An abbreviated form of the Church of England morning service was conducted, during which two hymns were sung. In the reading of the Scripture, both the Greek Patriarch, and the Syrian Bishop took part, each reading an extract in his own tongue.... The sermon was preached by Bishop McInnes from the text in Revelations: 'And there was silence in heaven for the space of half an hour.' This fitted in with the two minutes of silent prayer. Then came the firing of the gun, the congregation standing; then the trumpets sounded the Last Post, followed by the 'King's Silence.' Again the gun sounded — followed by trumpets, Reveille, the National Hymn, and the Blessing.

A Memorial Service for the fallen is conducted each year, on the 15th of April, at the War Cemetery on the Mount of Olives by the Bishop of Jerusalem.[1] At this time, flowers are laid upon the graves of those twentieth-century Crusaders who fought for Palestine against the Turk. On the cross, which rises from the centre of the monument, erected to commemorate the fallen, is a double-handed sword, such as Richard and Baldwin wielded. This is emblematic of the continuity between the early wars against the infidel and the twentieth-century struggle for human justice. On the wall of the monument are the regimental crests of those who took part in the capture of the Holy City. In the centre above the gateway, one reads, in English, the inscription:

The Land on which this Cemetery stands is the Free Gift of the People of Palestine for the perpetual Resting Place of those of the Allied Armies who fell in the War of 1914–1918 and are honoured here.

The same appears in Arabic on the right, and in Hebrew on the left.[2] British, Arabs, and Jews are thus honored in the same burial-place for their share in liberating Palestine.

December 9, Liberation Day, has hitherto been observed

[1] In this cemetery, there lie 24 Jews, 3 Christian Turks, 16 Germans, and 2615 British. Among these, there are 100 unknown graves. In the cemetery are also buried two chaplains, and one British Sister who succumbed to malaria. The Moslems who were among the war prisoners, or of the Indian troops, were not buried here, but at the end of Talpioth on the Plain of Rephaim. The War Cemeteries in Palestine are situated at Beersheba, Gaza, Ramleh, Deir al-Belah, Jerusalem (Mount of Olives), Sarona, Wilhelma, and Haifa. Some 10,000 dead are buried in these cemeteries which are cared for by the Anglo-Palestine War Graves Committee.

The sites of all the cemeteries were presented to the Imperial War Graves Commission by the People of Palestine, in pursuance of a resolution spontaneously proposed by the non-official members of the Advisory Council in December, 1920. The War Cemeteries at Ramleh and Jerusalem were formally dedicated in May, 1927, by Field-Marshal Viscount Allenby: a Memorial to the 54th Division was unveiled at Gaza on the 27th of April the same year.

[2] This inscription is set up at the entrance to each cemetery.

as a Government holiday in Jerusalem. On the first Liberation Day, the Mayor and representatives of each community called on the Governor, where they met the High Commissioner, who received their congratulations. The thanks of the populace were formally tendered and transmitted by telegram to the King, Lord Allenby, etc. The officials were invited to tea by the Municipality. The school-children paraded, and there was also a military review.

Later, the celebration of Liberation Day became a religious function. Until the year 1929, the year of the unfortunate disturbances, the High Commissioner issued a Liberation Day Proclamation, that of 1925 [1] being fairly representative of these public announcements. In this year, in compliance with Lord Plumer's wishes, there were two services — a special service on December 9 at Saint George's Cathedral, primarily for soldiers and ex-service men; and a general service on December 8.

The Liberation Day service in Jerusalem was an impressive and unique ceremony, conducted under the direction of the Anglican Bishop, and attended by the High Commissioner and the heads of the Administration, as well as the Mayor and the principal notables of the city. The Patriarchs of the Greek Orthodox and Armenian churches attended and took part in the service. The leading ecclesiastical dignitaries of the Syrian, Coptic, and Abyssinian churches had seats by the High Altar, and representatives of the Jewish community formed part of the congregation. The Consuls of the Foreign Powers attended, irrespective of the Church to which they belonged. Parts of the services were conducted in English, others in Arabic, Hebrew, Greek, and Armenian.

In his last Report on Palestine, Sir Herbert Samuel expressed what he considered to be the real significance of the observation of Liberation Day. 'This annual service,' he

---

[1] 'I am grateful for the response to my appeal that the 11th of November — Armistice Day — should be kept as a day of "Remembrance."

'I hope that the 9th of December, the day of the deliverance of Jerusalem, will be observed in a similar spirit as a day of Thanksgiving, and that every citizen will endeavour to attend his own place of worship on that day.

'It will be observed as a Public Holiday.

'(Sgd.) PLUMER, F. M.
'*High Commissioner*'

said, 'simple as it is, and sincere, appears to me profoundly significant; for it is of good augury for the growth of the spirit of religious harmony, for which mankind is eager, and for which Jerusalem may yet be again a centre.' [1]

That the purpose of these observances has fallen far short of realization; that, indeed, the achievement of an harmonious Palestine seems perhaps more remote than ever — these considerations, I believe, should not alter the circumstances nor condemn the motive.

It is a conspicuous fact that the Catholics have always abstained from the observances of the public holidays. The Mohammedans, on their part, have protested against them. Immediately after the occupation, before the Arab cause became articulate, the great majority of the population joined in celebrating whatever festivities were in vogue; for the people had just emerged from systematic and enforced tyranny, when no man dared to say his soul was his own. When, however, the new Jewish immigration began, and the Advisory Council was established in which questions were aired and debated, there grew up among the Arabs a sullen opposition and a retirement from active participation in the celebrations; they came to look upon these manifestations of British loyalty with distrust, and brushed them aside as of little concern to their interests. There was always, of course, the exception in the case of Arabs in Government employ.

Let us read the Arab Proclamation of 1928 on the observance of Liberation Day: [2]

Some people have received invitations to attend a Thanksgiving service to be held at the Saint George's Cathedral on December 9th, 1928, in commemoration of the liberation of Jerusalem and its conquest by Field Marshal Lord Allenby.

The Arab nation protests strongly against the organisers of this odious ceremony through which they wished to give this day a religious character. The Arab nation have not assisted British troops to occupy their country on such an improper basis.

If Arabs fought in the ranks of the Entente and helped British troops occupy this country, it was on the basis of the well-known pledges given to King Hussein by His Majesty's Government and of the promises made to Arabs themselves by the French and the

[1] Colonial No. 15. Report of the High Commissioner on the Administration of Palestine, 1920–25, p. 51.

[2] Liberation Day was not observed in 1929.

English Governments in the Proclamations issued on October 5, 1918, which guaranteed that the Arabs would be granted the hopes for independence.

The two powers having broken their pledges and promises to Arabs and placed the latter under an arbitrary régime, drawing its might from the sword and the gun, it is an ugly action on the part of the senders of the invitation to the Deliverance Day Ceremony to alter truth and to be unjust to Arabs themselves in such a vile manner.

On this occasion we would like to remind certain foreigners dwelling in this country and living on its resources that Arabs have still dignity and self-respect and they could no longer bear the insults inflicted on them wilfully.

The Secretaries of the Arab Executive trust that every Arab in this country will refrain from attending such ceremonies designed to humiliate him as well as his noble fathers and ancestors.

One must recognize the logic and the usefulness of these official efforts to unite the different elements of the population through concentration on British institutions and wider world relationships, yet, on the other hand, the conviction must be clear that the basis of a common civic life in Palestine, if one is ever to develop, rests more on the structure of the government than upon conciliatory civic devices. The complexity of the problem increases with the growth and organization of the different communities which, to a greater and greater degree, base their claims on their origins in the past — powerful and penetrating factors in the present life of Palestine. He who would understand the Mandate of the Holy Land must seek acquaintance with the forces which make its complex background. One must, in other words, get a vision of the land as a whole; no part can be omitted in the process.

CHAPTER IV

THE GEOGRAPHY OF PALESTINE

NOTHING has contributed more to the determination of the history and the life of Palestine than the physical nature of the country; and no force so definitely and arbitrarily circumscribes its present and future. To know the real Palestine one must get, so to speak, 'the lie of the land.'

'Within the limits of a province,' says Sir Herbert Samuel, 'Palestine offers the varieties of soil and climate of a continent. It is a country of mountain and plain, of desert and pleasant valleys, of lake and sea-board, of barren hills, desolate to the last degree of desolation, and of broad stretches of deep, fruitful soil.' [1] What other country of the size of Palestine can offer such an extraordinary picture of diversity!

Palestine has always been the meeting-place of East and West, the pathway of conquerors, and the trade-route between North and South. This little country, so small, indeed, that one may motor in a single day from its eastern boundary to the sea, is limited on the north by Syria, the French mandated area; bounded on the west by the Mediterranean Sea, on the south by Egyptian and Hedjaz territory; and on the east by Trans-Jordan and the Desert. At the most, the area of Palestine is very little more than nine thousand square miles, excluding Trans-Jordan.

The smallness of the country is a startling discovery to many a visitor to Palestine. Its history has been so extensive and varied, and of such importance to the world, that one instinctively expects to find an area with physical dimensions in consonance with the great drama enacted on its soil. But after one has taken the motor ride over that long journey 'from Dan to Beersheba' [2] — a distance of one hundred and

[1] Cmd. 1499. An Interim Report on the Civil Administration of Palestine, during the period 1st July, 1920–30th June, 1921. Presented to Parliament by Command of His Majesty, August, 1921, p. 3.

[2] An area in the extreme north of Palestine, previously included in the territory of Syria, was transferred to Palestine, as from the 1st of April, 1924, in accordance with

RECORD OF RAINFALL IN JERUSALEM — Since the Year 1861.

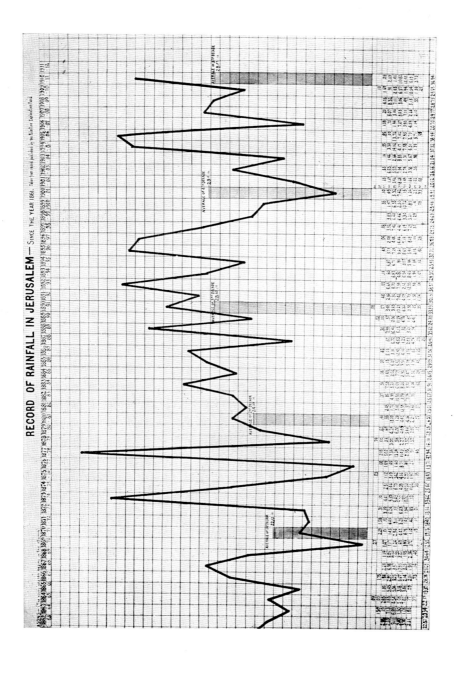

fifty miles! — his idea of the size of the Holy Land begins to undergo a process of readjustment, which at every turn pursues the visitor through this perplexing little country.

On arriving in Palestine, one is immediately conscious of the outstanding characteristic of its climate, namely, the division of the year into a rainy and a dry season. Palestine has a dry hot summer and a rainy winter. The spring lasts from the beginning of March to about the end of May, when the hot season begins. From the middle of May to about the end of October, the sky is almost cloudless.[1]

After the long period of constant sunshine, when the ground is parched and white with dust, the first rains seem like a blessing from heaven. As I came out of the offices of the Zionist Executive in Jerusalem, soon after my arrival, about the third week of October, I stepped into a heavy downpour of rain, the first of the season and quite unexpected. Although I should have been drenched had I not sought immediate shelter, and even as it was my shoes were buried in white mud, there was a real feeling of relief from the dazzling sun and the hot and dusty road. I was curious to know the cause of this arbitrary climate.[2]

Looking at the physical map of Palestine, one sees three vertical sections: the Maritime Plain, with varying widths, a few hundred feet above the sea, reaching from Acre, its northern extremity, to Gaza, its southern limit; the Central Range, an extension of the Lebanon chain; and the Jordan Valley, varying in width from two to sixteen miles, and separating Palestine proper from Trans-Jordan. The map also shows the rectangular-shaped desert in the south,[3] whose four corners

the terms of the Palestine–Syria Boundary Convention of 1920. This area contains twenty villages with a population of nearly 9000. It includes Tel-el-Kadi, the ancient Dan, and its inclusion has restored to Palestine her Biblical boundaries 'from Dan even unto Beersheba.' (Colonial No. 12. Report on Palestine and Trans-Jordan for the year 1924, p. 5.)

[1] The average yearly rainfall is twenty-six inches. See chart, giving Record of rainfall in Jerusalem since the year 1861, facing p. 100.

On the climate of Palestine, see Robinson, *Physical Geography of the Holy Land*, chap. iii, and George Adam Smith, *Historical Geography of the Holy Land*, chap. iii.

[2] Not being a geographer, I have to a great extent invoked outstanding writers on the geography of Palestine. George Adam Smith still ranks as the leading authority.

[3] The Negeb. (George Adam Smith, *The Historical Geography of the Holy Land*, pp. 50–52.)

are Rafa and Gaza on the west and Beersheba and al-Auja on the east.

These four geographical sections are the key to the climate of Palestine, and in turn to its history. They are the same to-day as they have been for four thousand years. The Maritime Plain [1] is one of the most famous warpaths of the world; it is the level and open part of the Bridge between Asia and Africa. At Acre, the width of the Plain is about four miles, having a wide margin of sand on the coast. It continues to widen out toward Haifa, where it expands into the Plain of Esdraelon, which extends eastward to the Jordan Valley. South of Haifa, at Mount Carmel, the Plain is barely two hundred yards wide; while southward from Athlit to Ascalon it expands to a width of twenty miles. Along this highway Thothmes, Ramses, Sennacherib, Cambyses, Alexander, Pompey, Titus, Saladin, Napoleon, and Allenby led their armies.

All the invaders found their way into Palestine by land. With the exception of the headland of Mount Carmel, the shore along the whole coastline is conspicuously uniform and low, consisting mainly of long shallow curves of low sandy beach. The currents are parallel to the coast, which is almost always a lee-shore, the prevailing winds being from the south-west. This inhospitable coast has always served as a natural barrier of defence, and in consequence has never produced a maritime people. In the Bible, the straight coast is always a limit which 'the Almighty has set between sea and land.' [2] In Numbers, it is said: 'And as for the western border, ye shall even have the great sea for a border: this shall be your west border.' [3] The Hebrew name for the West is the Sea.

---

[1] The Maritime Plain between Carmel and Joppa was called in Hebrew 'Sharon,' probably meaning 'The Level,' but in Greek, 'The Forest,' from a great oak forest which once covered it. To the south the name for it was Pelesheth, Philistia, or, poetically, 'The Shoulder of the Philistines,' from its shape as it rises from the sea. The Hebrew word *darom* or *daroma*, meaning south, was applied by the Jews shortly before our era to the whole of the Maritime Plain southwards from Lydda; in Christian times Daroma extended inland to the Dead Sea, and absorbed both the Shephelah and Negeb. The Arabs confined the name to a fortress south of Gaza — the Darom of the Crusaders. (George Adam Smith, *The Historical Geography of the Holy Land*, p. 52.)

[2] George Adam Smith, *The Historical Geography of the Holy Land*, p. 132.

[3] Numbers xxxiv: 6.

Eastward from Philistia, the southern part of the Maritime Plain, is the so-called Shephelah, or low hills, which extend as far north as the Vale of Ajalon. The name Shephelah is also probably used for the low hills that separate Carmel from Samaria. The Shephelah is separated from the Central Range by broad valleys running north and south.[1] The formation of these low hills, which range from 500 to 1500 feet, is of limestone or chalk, very soft and irregular. This was the debatable ground between the plain and the hill country, and was always the battlefield between the two. A land of glens and moors, of caves and broken rocks, it was just the home for strong border-men like Samson. To-day it is inhabited by Bedouin tribes and offers the same physical characteristics which make it still a border-land, wild and difficult to control.

From the Shephelah, eastward, we come to the Central Range, which is divided by the Plain of Esdraelon into two sections, the hill country of Galilee [2] to the north and the hills of Samaria and Judea to the south. To the north of Galilee is the great gorge of the Litâny or Kasimiyeh, cutting off Lebanon; to the east are the valley of the Jordan and the Lake of Galilee; and to the west, the narrow Phœnician coast.

The province of Galilee is divided into four parts: there is, first, the Jordan Valley with its two lakes, running along the eastern edge of Galilee; second, the Plain of Esdraelon; third, Lower Galilee, consisting of a series of long parallel ranges, all below 1850 feet, which, with broad valleys between them, cross the plateau above Tiberias to the maritime plains of Haifa and Acre; and fourth, Upper Galilee, a series of plateaus, with a double water-parting, and surrounded by hills from 2000 to 4000 feet. At the southern end of the hills of Galilee rises Mount Tabor, 1845 feet above the sea. Then the range becomes continuous and increases in height near Safed, which is 2750 feet high. The highest points of the range are Jebel Jermak, 3934 feet high, northwest of Safed, and Jebel Heider, 3440 feet.

'The controlling feature of Galilee is her relation to these

[1] Vale of Ajalon, Vale of Sorek, Vale of Elah.

[2] Galilee means 'The Ring.'

great mountains,' says George Adam Smith. It was on **Tabor** that Deborah and Barek assembled their forces,[1] and dashed down the precipitous mountain to meet Sisera and his 'nine hundred chariots of iron, and all the people that were with him.' [2] The old tradition identifies the mountain as the scene of the Transfiguration, and was accepted by Raphael for his great picture.[3] During the Greek period, there was a town of some size on the Top of Tabor, and during the war with Rome, Josephus fortified it, although it was afterwards taken by the Romans. Here, after many centuries, Saladin fought the Crusaders and captured the hill; and near its base, Napoleon drew up his army against the Turks. Tabor was always a favorite place of pilgrimage; and to-day an excellent road leads to its top from which can be distinguished almost the whole of Northern Palestine.

Both Upper and Lower Galilee are generally fertile, owing to the moisture brought by the westerly winds to the Lebanons and thence dispensed to Galilee all the year round. Both Upper and Lower Galilee are well wooded, and where the land has not been stripped by war, trees grow to the tops of the hills, and grass and flowers grow in great profusion. The road over which we motored from Nazareth to the Bay of Carmel is lined with open woods of oak,[4] although frequently we saw, as at Nazareth, outcrops of white limestone quite as bare and dusty as in Judea. Fosdick speaks of 'Galilee, with its oaks and sycamores.' [5] Besides the orange, almond, date, and other trees native to this region, there is a very interesting tree — the carob, which, perhaps, was the famous 'Oak of

---

[1] '... and he went up with ten thousand men at his feet: and Deborah went up with him.' (Judges IV: 10.)

[2] Judges IV: 13.

[3] Fosdick says that the Transfiguration probably took place on a shoulder of Mount Hermon. (Harry Emerson Fosdick, *A Pilgrimage to Palestine*, p. 21.)

[4] The recognition of the importance of the oak tree is indicated in the following Regulation: 'All persons are prohibited from felling, cutting, lopping, burning, uprooting, barking, marking, or otherwise injuring any oak trees, whether growing in State Forests, or in the forests that are the property of an individual or of a community, except in accordance with the provisions of a forest license, issued by the Chief Forest Officer or his representative duly authorised.' (*Official Gazette*, March 1, 1921.) Legislation of Palestine, 1918–25. Regulations, Public Notices, Proclamations, etc., vol. 2, p. 37.

[5] Harry Emerson Fosdick, *A Pilgrimage to Palestine*, p. 14.

Basan.' It has the hard wood of the oak, and long, twisted, flat pods which make excellent fodder. The carob, although it throws a very dense shadow, allows cereals to grow right up to its trunk, whereas, according to one observer, eucalyptus prevents anything from growing in a radius of nine times its own shade.[1]

The wild flowers of Galilee are the loveliest in all Palestine.[2] On these hills, in the springtime, wherever one looks, there are scores of varieties of brilliant blossoms. The anemone, poppy, cyclamen, phlox, ranunculus, lupine, oleander, charlock, asphodel, squill, daisy, birthwort, and a host of others — all are growing in glorious profusion. Even in the arid places, on the rocks, as it seems, these little blossoms conspire to beautify the landscape. Well might this spectacle impel the Master's words: 'Consider the lilies of the field, how they grow; they toil not, neither do they spin: And yet I say unto you, that even Solomon in all his glory was not arrayed like one of these.' [3]

The Plain of Esdraelon lies only about two hundred feet above the level of the Mediterranean. It is usually regarded as one plain, connecting the sea with the Jordan Valley. In reality, however, it is not one, but several plains, as described by John Kitto, writing in 1841:

This great plain possesses the elements of great fertility, having a rich alluvial soil, about three feet deep, resting on a substratum of gravel and whitish limestone. As seen from above, it is not a perfect level, but a tract of gentle undulations, in the midst of the hills which inclose it on every side. It is destitute of trees; but so rich and spontaneously fertile is the soil, that Morison thinks that, if it were cultivated as it ought to be, it would alone suffice to supply the whole of Galilee with corn, even were that province as populous now as it was in ancient times. But, he says, it was in his time almost entirely uncultivated, although so covered with green herbage, as to evince what Nature could do if seconded by man.[4]

And in our own day, let us see what man has done with the

---

[1] Myriam Harry, *A Springtide in Palestine*, p. 80.

[2] See Ludwig Preiss and Paul Rohrbach, *Palestine and Transjordania* (1925), p. iv, for a description of the flowers of Palestine.

[3] Matthew VI: 28, 29.

[4] John Kitto, *Palestine: The Physical Geography and Natural History of the Holy Land*, pp. cxv, cxvi.

Plain of Esdraelon, which Sir Herbert Samuel portrays so graphically:

This is a belt of rich, deep soil, which stretches for forty miles from the sea at the Bay of Acre eastwards down into the Jordan Valley; it is some nine miles broad, between the range of Mount Carmel and the hills of Samaria in the south, and the hills of Galilee about Nazareth and Mount Tabor in the north. When I first saw it in 1920 it was a desolation. Four or five small and squalid Arab villages, long distances apart from one another, could be seen on the summits of low hills here and there. For the rest the country was uninhabited. There was not a house, not a tree. Along a branch of the Hijaz Railway an occasional train stopped at deserted stations. A great part of the soil was in the ownership of absentee Syrian landlords. The River Kishon, which flows through the valley and the many springs which feed it from the hillsides, had been allowed to form a series of swamps and marshes, and, as a consequence, the country was infested with malaria. Besides, public security had been so bad under the former régime that any settled agriculture was in any case almost impossible.

By an expenditure of nearly nine hundred thousand Egyptian pounds about 51 square miles of the valley have been purchased by the Jewish National Fund and other organisations; twenty villages have been founded, with a population numbering at present about 2,600; nearly 3,000 donums (about 700 acres) have been afforested. Twenty schools have been opened. There is an Agricultural Training College for Women in one village and a hospital in another. All the swamps and marshes within the area that has been colonised have been drained, and cases of malaria are proportionately rare. An active trade in dairy produce has sprung up, mostly finding a market, by means of the railway, in Haifa. The whole aspect of the valley has been changed. The wooden huts of the villages, gradually giving place to red-roofed cottages, are dotted along the slopes; the plantations of rapidly growing eucalyptus trees already begin to give a new character to the landscape; in the spring the fields of vegetables or of cereals cover many miles of the land, and what five years ago was little better than a wilderness is being transformed before our eyes into a smiling country-side.[1]

Of the historical significance of the Plain of Esdraelon, Kitto gives the following dramatic account:

The historical celebrity of this plain is very great. It is that 'mighty plain' — μέγα πεδίον as it is called by many ancient writers — which has in all ages been the famous battle-ground of nations. In the first ages of the Jewish history, as well as during the

[1] Colonial No. 15. Report of the High Commissioner on the Administration of Palestine, 1920–25, pp. 34–35.

Roman Empire, the Crusades, and even in later times, it has been the scene of many a memorable contest. In this great plain, Barak, descending with ten thousand men from Mount Tabor, fought with the kings of Canaan, 'by the waters of Megiddo.' Here King Josiah was slain in battle with the Egyptians. And 'it has been the chosen place for encampment in every contest carried on in this country,' to use the words of Dr. Clarke, 'from the days of Nabuchodonosar, King of the Assyrians, until the disastrous march of Napoleon Buonaparte from Egypt into Syria. Jews, Gentiles, Saracens, Crusaders, Egyptians, Persians, Druses, Turks, Arabs, and French, warriors out of every nation which is under heaven, have pitched their tents upon the plain of Esdraelon, and have beheld their banners wet with the dews of Tabor and of Hermon.' [1]

What has been called a national feature of Galilee is the volcanic nature of her range. Here and there, through open fissures of the limestone, there are lava deposits. One sees an extinct crater near Gischala, and dykes of basalt, while upon the plateau above the lake are scatterings of lava. Hot sulphur springs, which remind one of volcanoes, flow by Tiberias.[2] In fact, the whole province has been shaken by terrible earthquakes. The earthquake in 1837 overthrew the walls of Tiberias: hardly a house remained intact; and almost a third of the population perished. Strangely enough, however, the 1927 earthquake caused only slight material damage to the place. Though some of the houses were cracked, there were

[1] John Kitto, *Palestine: The Physical Geography and Natural History of the Holy Land*, pp. cxv, cxvi.

[2] The medical hot springs of Tiberias were famous before the city came into existence. The cemetery on which the city was built is believed to have been that of Hamath, later Emmaus, a village to the south that clustered round the springs. To these springs tradition attributes the virtue of cleaning Tiberias and making it habitable by Jews. (Albert M. Hyamson, *Palestine Old and New*, p. 211.)

On April 17, 1929, the High Commissioner of Palestine signed an agreement, awarding the concession for the exploitation of the Tiberias Baths to the group of pre-war concessionnaires and their associates. The agreement, called the Tiberias Baths Agreement, was signed by Sir John Robert Chancellor, by virtue of his office as High Commissioner, on the one part, and Suleiman Bey Nassif of Haifa, Amin Rizk of Brumana, Lebanon, Joshua Suprasski of Tel-Aviv, Jacob Gesundheit of Tel-Aviv, and Bernard A. Rosenblatt of New York of the other part. The concessionnaires have eighteen months from the date of signing in which to form a new company for working the enterprise and to raise the prescribed capital. The concession was granted for a period of forty years, and the capital of the Company must be at least 40,000 Palestinian pounds. As soon as the thermal bath establishment is completely erected, the Company must pay to the High Commissioner an annual rent of 3,000 Palestinian pounds. (Colonial No. 47. Report on the Administration of Palestine and Trans-Jordan, for the year 1929. Appendix III, pp. 194–200.)

few casualties. Many towns in Palestine, however, suffered loss of life and property, notably Nablus, Ramleh, and Lydda. In Trans-Jordan, especially at Es-Salt and Amman, the damage was great; and several villages were almost completely destroyed.[1]

Josephus, who was Governor of Galilee thirty-four years after Jesus' ministry there, said that the nature of the people was also volcanic. He describes them as 'ever fond of innovations, and by nature disposed to changes, and delighting in seditions.' [2] Yet Josephus proudly said of them, 'The country hath never been destitute of men of courage.' [3] 'The Galileans,' according to the Talmud, 'were more anxious for honour than for money; the contrary was true of Judæa.' [4] Says George Adam Smith: 'Their fidelity, often unreasoning and ill-tempered, was always sincere'; and he adds: 'For this cause also our Lord chose His friends from the people; and it was *not* a Galilean who betrayed Him.' [5]

As to the political geography of Galilee: we are again indebted to George Adam Smith for his lucid analysis. He points out three chief factors which have influenced its interesting life: (1) the proximity to classic scenes of Hebrew history; (2) the great world-roads which crossed Galilee; and (3) the surrounding heathen civilizations. Here, indeed, we see a combination fruitful of dramatic possibilities!

It is not true, as some writers have implied, that Galilee

---

[1] The Government made loans for reconstruction purposes after the earthquake. The following appears in the Report for 1928:

EARTHQUAKE RECONSTRUCTION LOANS

The advances on account of earthquake reconstruction loans may be summarized as follows:

Advances in 1927–28....................£P. 26,454
Repayments in 1928......................   212
Total outstanding.................£P. 26,242

These loans were made principally to persons residing in Nablus, Ramleh, Lydda, and Nazareth. (Colonial No. 40. Report by His Majesty's Government in the United Kingdom of Great Britain and Northern Ireland to the Council of the League of Nations on the Administration of Palestine and Trans-Jordan for the year 1928, p. 14.)

[2] *Life*, xvii; *Antiquities*, xx, vi, 1; *War*, i, xvi, 5; *ibid.*, ii, xvii, 8; Tacitus, *Annals*, xii, 54.

[3] *War*, iii, iii, 2.   [4] Quoted by Neubauer, *Geog. du Talm.*, p. 181.

[5] George Adam Smith, *The Historical Geography of the Holy Land*, pp. 423, 424.

was remote and provincial at the time of Christ. She had traditions and a history. Carmel, Kishon, Megiddo, Jezreel, Gilboa, Shunem, Tabor, Gilead, Bashan, the waters of Merom, Hazor and Kadesh — all were within touch or sight. Galilee shared with Judea the exploits of the Maccabees.

That the Messianic tempers were stronger in Galilean than in other Jewish hearts is most certain. While Judæa's religion had for its characteristic zeal for the law, Galilee's was distinguished by the nobler, the more potential passion of hope. Therefore it was to Galilee that Jesus came preaching that *the Kingdom of Heaven is at hand;* and it was the Galilean patriotism which He chose to refine to diviner issues.... Galilee was vindicated also in the affections of the Jews themselves. It is one of the most singular revolutions, even in Jewish history, that the province, which through so many centuries Judæa had contemned as profane and heretical, should succeed Judæa as the sanctuary of the race and the home of their theological schools — that to-day Galilee should have as many holy places as Judæa, and Safed and Tiberias be reverenced along with Hebron and Jerusalem. The transference can be traced geographically, by the movements of the Sanhedrim. After the defeat of the last Jewish revolt at Bettir (A.D. 134), the Sanhedrim migrated north from Jabneh in the Philistine plain to Oshah just north of Carmel, and thence gradually eastward across Lower Galilee to Shaphram, to Beth She'arim, to Sepphoris — nay, to the unclean and cursed Tiberias itself. Here the last Sanhedrim sat, and the Mishna was edited. You see the tomb of Maimonides in Tiberias, and most of the towns of Lower and some of those of Upper Galilee have a name as the scenes of the residence or of the martyrdom of famous Rabbis.[1]

We are, as Mr. Fosdick points out, forever indebted to George Adam Smith for explaining the significance of the world highways in Jesus' homeland.

Galilee [he says] is covered with roads to everywhere — roads from the harbours of the Phœnician coast to Samaria, Gilead, Hauran and Damascus; roads from Sharon to the valley of the Jordan; roads from the sea to the desert; roads from Egypt to Assyria.... They ran over Lower Galilee by its long parallel valleys, and even crossed the high plateau of Upper Galilee on the shortest direction from Tyre and Sidon to Damascus.[2]

These highways gave content to much of the teaching of Jesus: they were the setting of many of the parables. As Mr. Fosdick says:

[1] George Adam Smith, *The Historical Geography of the Holy Land*, pp. 424, 425.
[2] *Ibid.*, pp. 425, 426.

Some one is always going somewhere. The prodigal son goes to a far country (Luke xv: 13); the traveller falls among thieves (Luke x: 30); the merchantman is off with his caravan in search of fine pearls (Matthew xiii: 45); friends on a journey arrive unexpectedly, requiring hospitality (Luke xi: 6); the householder leaves his servants and the nobleman his subjects to travel widely and return again (Matthew xxv: 14, 19; Luke xix: 12–13).[1]

In his discussion of the third great factor which influenced the lives of the Galileans, namely, their environment, George Adam Smith contrasts Galilee with Judea.

In the neighbourhood of Judæa [he says] we have seen great deserts, some of which come up almost to the gates of the cities, and have impressed their austerity and foreboding of judgment upon the feelings and the literature of the people. The very different temperament of the Galilean was explained in part by his very different environment. The desert is nowhere even visible from Galilee. Instead of it, the Galilee of our Lord's time had for neighbours the half Greek land of Phœnicia, with its mines and manufactures, its open ports, its traffic from the West; the fertile Hauran, with its frequent cities, where the Greek language was spoken, and the pagan people worshipped their old divinities under the names of the Greek Gods; and Gilead, with the Decapolis, ten cities (more or less) of stately forums, amphitheatres, and temples.[2]

Such was the environment in which Jesus grew to manhood and conducted his Galilean ministry. The Lake of Galilee, the focus of the whole province, became the centre of his work. In Jesus' time, there were woods and gardens around the lake and fleets of fishing boats. Josephus says that there were two hundred and four cities and villages in Galilee, the smallest of which numbered about fifteen thousand inhabitants.

The chief industries at the Lake of Galilee were fishing, boat-building, and fish-curing. These occupations, which were famous throughout the Roman world, provided a livelihood for thousands of families. The fisheries were free to all and were very profitable. Jesus selected his Disciples from the ranks of these hardy workers, whose speech and the appurtenances of their simple craft became largely the language and symbolism of the Christian religion.

[1] Harry Emerson Fosdick, *A Pilgrimage to Palestine*, p. 189.

[2] George Adam Smith, *The Historical Geography of the Holy Land*, p. 431.

South of Esdraelon, the Central Range rises again in the hills and high valleys of Samaria. The earliest name given to this section of the Central Range, excluding Carmel, was Mount Ephraim. The imposing headland of Carmel is the most striking object on the western side of central Palestine. Geographically it is a branch of the Central Range, though it is cut off from it by the Shephelah. Carmel has never had a history of its own; it has either been merged in that of the coast or of Samaria. It holds much the same place on the west as Bashan or Gilead fills to the east. Rising about 1800 feet above the plains of Acre and Esdraelon, Carmel extends fifteen miles from end to end; and as its name Carmel, the Garden, suggests, it is perennially green, which it owes to a heavy dew fall. It is the first of the mountains of Palestine to receive the western rains.[1]

Throughout the Old Testament, Carmel stands for fertility. It was the symbol for beauty, and sanctity, and reflected the goodness and the righteousness of God.[2] 'From the beginning of time its woodland valleys, its pure springs, and the caves in its rocky recesses, had given solitude and protection to the faithful worshippers of the God that made it.' [3]

It was on Carmel that Elijah's great conflict with the priests of Baal took place.[4] Here it was that the debate, whether Jehovah or Baal was the supreme lord of the elements, was fought out. Somewhere on the southeastern point of the mountain, at a height of 1685 feet, there is the traditional 'Place of Burning,' which commemorates the miracle of Elijah: the three years' drought was broken; rain came at last; and the famine was ended. Carmel was from early times a holy mountain, venerated both by Jew and Gentile. To the Jews Elijah is Eliayahu Hanavi, Elijah the Prophet; to the Christians, Mar Jirgis, or Saint George; to the Moslems, El Khudr, or the Evergreen One.

The hills of Samaria fall naturally into two great divisions.[5]

[1] The Government of Palestine has endeavored by re-afforestation to repair the ravages to its thick forests; there were once oaks and carobs, olive groves and vineyards.

[2] Solomon's Song vii: 5; Isaiah xxxv: 2.

[3] W. Basil Worsfold, *Palestine of the Mandate* (London, 1925), p. 206.

[4] I Kings xviii: 19–40.

[5] The description of the geography of Samaria is summarized from Charles Foster Kent, *Biblical Geography and History*, pp. 34–38.

The first extends from the plains of Esdraelon and Jezreel to the one great valley which, following the Wady el-Ifzim, cuts through Samaria from the northwest to the southeast, running between Mount Ebal and Mount Gerizim. This valley is from a quarter to half a mile across, though the summits of the mountains are two miles apart. The territory north of this line resembles Lower Galilee in many ways; and to the east, the valleys have plenty of water, and a rich soil. The northernmost of the hills, separating the valleys, is Mount Gilboa which rises to a height of from 1200 to 1650 feet. Although the bare limestone crops out at many points, villages and cultivated fields are found on its broad top. The next great valley south of the Plain of Jezreel is that through which the Wady Farah flows into the Jordan.

In the northwest, the hills of Samaria descend gradually and are intersected by wide valleys which open into the Plain of Sharon on the west and Esdraelon on the north. In these valleys are rich fields of grain or olive orchards. Southern Samaria lies to the south and west of Mount Ebal, and in many ways resembles northern Galilee. It is an elevated plateau, the descent in the east to the Jordan being exceedingly steep and rocky. On the high central plateau north of Baal-Hazor are open plains, well-watered and covered with grain fields. The western part of Southern Samaria contains deep but open valleys, with trees and grass and many well-tilled hills. Prosperous villages, some capping the summits of rounded hills, and others far down in sheltered spots in the deep valleys, are scattered throughout this entire region.

Of Ebal and Gerizim, Kitto has written:

The two mountains are separated only by a narrow valley, and they exhibit a remarkable analogy of size, figure, and height. It was perhaps for this reason, as well as from their convenient proximity, with a valley intervening, that, on taking possession of the Promised Land, it was ordered that assembled Israel should hear and respond to the curses of the law, declared from Mount Ebal, and to its blessings from Mount Gerizim. The blessings and the curses may seem to have remained upon these mountains; for, while Gerizim is fertile and of pleasant aspect, Ebal is utterly barren.[1] This

[1] This is similar to the observations of Benjamin of Tudela in the latter part of the twelfth century. (*Early Travels in Palestine. The Travels of Rabbi Benjamin of Tudela.*)

superiority of Gerizim may be owing, not only to its having a northern aspect on the side towards the valley, so that it is less than Ebal scorched by the hot suns of summer, but to its slope of ascent being less abrupt, so that the soil is more liable to accumulate on its surface, and less subject to be washed down by the autumnal rains. Gerizim was deemed by the Samaritans the holiest of mountains; and upon it they had their temple, in which, rather than in that at Jerusalem, they held that men ought to worship. The temple exists no longer; but a remnant of the people and of their worship still lingers in the valley below, where is still the city called Shechem in the Old Testament, and Sychar in the New, and whose classical name of Neapolis is now exhibited in the modern one of Nablous.[1]

Samaria's position in religious history is admirably summed up by George Adam Smith:

It is therefore in full harmony with the geographical data that the story of the patriarchs brings both Abraham and Jacob, on their entrance into the Promised Land, at once to Shechem, and that the Book of Deuteronomy selects Ebal and Gerizim as the scene of a great inaugural service by all Israel on taking possession of the country — a service the performance of which the Book of Joshua duly records. Both of these passages, in Deuteronomy and in Joshua, are from the hands of a writer, the Deuteronomist, whose ruling principle is the centralisation of Israel's worship in one sanctuary, and that ostensibly Jerusalem. His mention of Ebal, therefore — and it is the only sacred site which he names — stands out in all the greater relief, as a proof of the natural attractiveness and central position of the district of Shechem. After the disruption of Israel, these qualities of Shechem were not found to atone for her weakness as a fortress, and she soon ceased to be the capital of the Northern Kingdom. It was to the Samaritans that the district owed the revival of its claims to be considered the religious centre of the land. But this was in the interest of as narrow and exclusive a sectarianism as ever sought to monopolise the liberal intentions of nature. The abuse was gloriously atoned for. It was by this natural capital of the Holy Land, from which the outgoings to the world are so many and so open, that the religion of Israel rose once for all above every geographical limit, and the charter of a universal worship was given. *Neither in this mountain, nor yet at Jerusalem, shall ye worship the Father; but the hour cometh, and now is, when the true worshippers shall worship the Father in spirit and in truth.*[2]

The narrow tableland of Judea meets the valleys and mountains of Samaria ten miles to the north of Jerusalem.

---

[1] John Kitto, *Palestine: The Physical Geography and Natural History of the Holy Land*, pp. xxxviii, xxxix.

[2] George Adam Smith, *The Historical Geography of the Holy Land*, pp. 333, 334.

This plateau has been very accurately described as 'a long zigzag central spine which throws out a series of deep spurs to east and west.' [1] The plateau averages about fifteen miles wide and forty miles long. South of Hebron the range becomes lower and finally loses itself in the desert. On the western side of the watershed the plateau of Judea extends about halfway to the sea, broken by deep valleys. On the east side it descends abruptly within twenty miles, from a maximum of over 3000 feet above sea-level to 1300 feet below, to the Lower Jordan and the Dead Sea. The slopes descend in a series of terraces sometimes terminating in walls of cliff, such as the Mount of Temptation above Jericho; they are deeply seamed by profound cañons such as Mar Saba and the Wady Qelt.

The landscape has the appearance of yellow limestone, although Judea is not wholly barren. There are some breaks in the tableland which are rich in vegetation: at Bethany, and the Valley of Hinnom, near Jerusalem; the Gardens of Solomon and other spots around Bethlehem; and in the neighborhood of Hebron, the famous Vale of Eshcol. Between Hebron and the Wilderness there is a considerable area where the soil is almost free from stones, and abounds in red and green fields.

In some places, where the soil is held upon the hillsides by terraces or piles of stone, it is very productive; it supports patches of grain, olive trees and luxurious vines. These stand out in striking contrast to the rocky background. Indeed, the prevailing impression of Judea is of stone. As it has facetiously been remarked, the uplands look as if they had been stoned to death.[2]

[1] *The Handbook of Palestine*, p. 3. Edited by Harry Charles Luke and Edward Keith-Roach.

[2] Commenting on the stones of Palestine, Fosdick says: 'I never understood the many passages in Scripture about stones until I went to Palestine. Readers of the Bible will recall many passages in Scripture where stones are sacred, but not every one will have noticed how frequently in Old and New Testament alike their commonness, cheapness, and troublesomeness are implied. "The king made silver to be in Jerusalem as stones" (I Kings x: 27) is a meaningful picture of Solomon's wealth when one has lived even a little while on the Judean ridge. Dashing one's foot against a stone (Psalm XCI: 12) is a symbol of trouble; having a stony heart (Ezekiel XXXVI: 26) is a picture of impenitence; gathering stones out of the highway (Isaiah LXXII: 10) or out of a vineyard (Isaiah v: 1-2) — as needful now as ever — is a metaphor of

But Judea lacks water perhaps more than soil. On the whole plateau, the only gleams of water are the pools at Gibeon, Jerusalem, Bethlehem, and Hebron. There is not a single perennial spring. We have already described the Pools of Solomon, from which Jerusalem gets part of its water; but, in contrast to Galilee, Judea lacks the streams and the moisture which come from the snow-clad Lebanons. In winter, the rains rush down the rocky hills and valleys, where there is little soil to absorb the moisture; so that instead of enriching the soil the rains continually wash it away. The inhabitants of Judea have always had to struggle for soil and water.

The eastern slope of the Judean plateau is called the Wilderness of Judea. The cultivated land extends only about four or five miles east of the central watershed, and the barren wilderness comes up to the fertile fields about Bethany. The only village of any importance in this desolate region is at Engedi, where, as Kent describes it, a beautiful spring bursts out of the cliffs overhanging the Dead Sea and transforms the barren desert into what seems by contrast a little paradise of trees and gardens.[1]

It was, as Fosdick says: 'Somewhere into this arid waste, this weird desolation, slashed by barren wadies and baked in merciless heat, the Master went when he was tempted (Matthew iv: 1–11), and down through this wilderness from Jerusalem to Jericho the victim in the Master's parable was travelling when he fell among thieves (Luke x: 29–35).'[2]

Only those who have travelled through the Wilderness of Judea can fully appreciate this scene of desolation. Indeed, as one motors over the winding road from Jerusalem to Jericho, and experiences the weird sensation of dropping from 2500

spiritual preparedness. The Master pictured an unreliable life as stony ground (Matthew xiii: 5–6, 20–21) and described a disdained request as asking for bread and receiving a stone (Matthew vii: 9). One does not notice until he goes to Palestine how common such figures are in Scripture, but, having been there, one can supply in imagination the very gesture and tone of voice with which John the Baptist must have said that God was able of these stones to raise up children unto Abraham (Matthew iii: 9), and Jesus said of the multitude that welcomed him to Zion on the first Palm Sunday, "If these shall hold their peace, the stones will cry out" (Luke xix: 40).' (Harry Emerson Fosdick, *A Pilgrimage to Palestine*, pp. 6, 7.)

[1] Charles Foster Kent, *Biblical Geography and History*, p. 39. See p. 121, note 3, *infra*.

[2] Harry Emerson Fosdick, *A Pilgrimage to Palestine*, p. 16.

feet above sea-level to 820 feet below, he feels the full force of this bare and dismal waste. As I came to the end of this amazing ride, and gazed upon the verdant oasis of Jericho, I was completely bewildered — startled, almost, at the contrast between this fascinating panorama and the rugged wilderness of the mountains and the terrifying precipices I had passed on the route.

The modern Jericho, the lowest town on the face of the earth, has about a thousand inhabitants; and most of them are Moslems. It is one of the hottest places in Palestine, and has, since the occupation of the British, become a popular winter resort.[1] The town is filled with orchards and gardens and is often called the 'City of Palms.' The stream which runs through the place, dividing into numerous rivulets, has its source in Elisha's Fountain which was restored in 1906. It was near this spring that the earliest Jericho, the Canaanite stronghold which fell to Joshua, was situated. The four separate sites which have been discovered testify to the existence of four different cities of Jericho. The present town marks the site of the Crusaders' Jericho, and an old tower supposed to date from that period is still to be seen.

The Wilderness of Judea has always exercised a powerful influence upon the life and thought of the people in this part of Palestine.

When you realise [says George Adam Smith] that this howling waste came within reach of nearly every Jewish child; when you climb the Mount of Olives, or any hill about Bethlehem, or the hill of Tekoa, and, looking east, see those fifteen miles of chaos, sinking to a stretch of the Dead Sea, you begin to understand the influence of the desert on Jewish imagination and literature. It gave the ancient natives of Judæa, as it gives the mere visitor of to-day, the sense of living next door to doom; the sense of how narrow is the border between life and death; the awe of the power of God, who can make contiguous regions so opposite in character. *He turneth rivers into a wilderness, and watersprings into a thirsty ground.* The desert is always in face of the prophets, and its howling of beasts and its dry sand blow mournfully across their pages the foreboding of judgment.[2]

---

[1] The newly constructed Winter Palace at Jericho was almost completely wrecked by the earthquake of 1927. Three Indian tourists were killed and buried in the building.

[2] George Adam Smith, *The Historical Geography of the Holy Land*, p. 314.

I shall never forget the 'howling waste' of the Wilderness of Judea. It is a grewsome reminder of the past, and a constant generator of gloom.

From Jericho to the Jordan River, a distance of five miles, the road falls another 470 feet. We find ourselves now in the deepest trench on the earth's surface.[1] The Jordan Valley, or Ghôr, is a perpendicular stretch of valley more than one hundred and sixty miles long and varying in width from two to fifteen miles broad. It falls 1292 feet below the sea-level at the coast of the Dead Sea.

In this long trench reaching from the Lebanons to the Red Sea, there are six distinct sections: the Beka'a, or valley between the Lebanons; the Upper Jordan, from its sources at the foot of Hermon through Lake Huleh to the Lake of Galilee; this Lake itself; the Lower Jordan to its mouth at Jericho; the Dead Sea; and, thence to the Gulf of 'Akaba, the Wady 'Arabah.

Geologists tell us that the Ghôr was once an ocean-bed from which the granite peaks of Sinai alone protruded. Deposits of limestone were laid upon the ocean-bed and rose upon the water in long folds, two of which are now the ranges on either side of the Jordan Valley. Major R. W. Brock describes the geological condition of the Ghôr as follows:

The Ghôr is still in a youthful condition. Its walls are still precipitous; tributaries have succeeded in excavating only narrow cañons, down which they plunge in waterfalls. Faulting of the Dead Sea deposits and the earthquakes which still occasionally disturb the district give warning that the fissuring and faulting and deepening of the Ghôr may still be proceeding, and that its dark sides may once more glow with streams of molten lava and the green plateau of Damascus again be lighted up by a wide crescent of volcanic fire.[2]

---

[1] No other part of the earth, uncovered by water, sinks to three hundred feet below the level of the ocean. The other depressions of the surface of the continents below ocean-level are: Asia: the level of the Caspian Sea is more than 80 feet below that of the Black Sea; and part of the Caspian coasts, a depression between Lake Elton and the Ural, in which a lake used to lie, but it is now dry, is 151 feet below the Black Sea. In Africa there is the Fayum, part of which is a few feet — 5 to 20 feet — under sea-level; and the Shott Melr'ir marshes and salt fields in the Sahara, which are from 95 to 279 feet below the Mediterranean. (George Adam Smith, *The Historical Geography of the Holy Land*, note 2, p. 468.)

[2] Major R. W. Brock, R.E., *The Palestine Pocket Guide Books*, vol. III.

The Jordan rises 3000 feet above sea-level near Banias. It first enters Lake Huleh,[1] whose surface is seven feet above the sea, and then within a distance of ten miles drops 690 feet, narrowing into a turbulent stream, dropping nearly forty feet a mile as it enters the Lake of Galilee. This rapidity of current has given the river its name. Jordan means the 'Downcomer.'

The surface of the Lake of Galilee is 682 feet below sea-level.[2] The Lake is thirteen and a half miles long and seven and a half miles wide, its greatest depth being one hundred and sixty feet. The turbulent Jordan makes the northern part of the Lake muddy, but the rest, except in the vicinity of the town of Tiberias, is good drinking-water.

Below the Lake of Galilee, the river becomes a turbid stream from 90 to 100 feet broad and from three to twelve feet deep, extending a distance of sixty-five miles until it enters the Dead Sea. On the western side are the mountains of Galilee and Samaria, rising from 800 to 1500 feet above the valley floor, with the Vale of Jezreel between them. On the east are the hills of Gilead, some 2000 feet above Jordan and broken by the valley of the Yarmuk and Jabbok. In general, between the Lake of Galilee and the Dead Sea, the Jordan passes through a long narrow vale twice expanding — at Bethshan and at Jericho — to the dimensions of a plain.

Down this broad valley there curves and twists a deeper, narrower bed — perhaps 150 feet deeper, and from 200 yards to a mile broad. Its banks are mostly of white marl, and within these it is packed with tamarisks and other semi-tropical trees and tangled bush. This jungle marks the Jordan's wider bed, the breadth to which the river rises when

[1] Lake Huleh is probably the waters of Merom of the Book of Joshua. (Joshua XI: 5–7.)

The British Report for 1929 states that: 'As regards the Concession for the drainage and reclamation of the swamps of Lake Huleh, the concessionaires, having failed to implement the agreement for a revised concession, fell back on their rights under the Ottoman instrument and entered into possession of the Heuleh Area in January, 1929.' (Colonial No. 47. Report on the Administration of Palestine, 1929, p. 14.)

[2] The Lake, as in Biblical days, is liable to sudden storms, and the local boatmen avoid, so far as possible, crossing its centre after midday. There are three motor boats and thirty-seven sailing craft on the Lake. The motor boats operate between Tiberias, Semakh, and Tabgha.

in flood.[1] In the Old Testament, it appears as the Pride of Jordan and always as a symbol of trouble and danger.[2]

In this hollow is the Jordan itself, 'a groove,' as George Adam Smith aptly describes it, 'in the bottom of an old sea-bed, a ditch as deep below the level of the ocean as some of our coal-mines are.'

There is [he continues] no yellow marl by the river itself. Those heaps and ridges, which in higher parts of the valley look like nothing but the refuse of a chemical manufactory, have here all been washed away. But there are hardly less ugly mudbanks, from two to twenty-five feet high, with an occasional bed of shingle, that is not clean and sparkling as in our own rivers, but foul with ooze and slime. Dead driftwood is everywhere in sight. Large trees lie about, overthrown: and the exposed roots and lower trunks of the trees still standing are smeared with mud, except where they have been recently torn by passing wreckage. There are, however, some open spaces, where the river flashes to the hills above and an easy path is possible to its edge. But in the lower reaches this is mostly where the earth is too salt to sustain vegetation, and so it may be said that the Jordan sweeps to the Dead Sea through unhealthy jungle relieved only by poisonous soil.[3]

As we motored on the Trans-Jordan side of the river, we could feel only disappointment and gloom at the ugly desolation. The only touch of cheer in the whole place was the pink oleanders, growing and actually blossoming amid the tangled mass. A pathetic scene it was — so in contrast to the Jordan of our imagination.

In the sixty-five miles from the Lake of Galilee to the Dead Sea, the descent is 610 feet, or an average of nine feet a mile. The valley of the Jordan never seems to have been a populous place, although some towns were built in it. On the Palestine side of the river, throughout the ancient world, the valley was famed for its corn, dates, balsam, flax, and other products.[4] There are three principal reasons why the valley has had so few towns. In the first place, the heat is intolerable and dries up all vegetation which is not constantly watered. At Jericho, the temperature in July is over a hundred, and it rises as high

---

[1] George Adam Smith, *The Historical Geography of the Holy Land*, p. 484.

[2] Jeremiah XII: 5; XLIX: 19.

[3] George Adam Smith, *The Historical Geography of the Holy Land*, pp. 485, 486.

[4] See George Adam Smith, p. 487, and also Le Strange, p. 17 f.

as 118° in August. Secondly, the valley was infested with wild beasts. The Old Testament speaks often of lions; and although the lion has not been seen for eight hundred years, other wild beasts still roam in the jungle of the Jordan. Thirdly, the valley was frequently overrun by Bedouin, which proved perhaps the most serious hindrance to the settlement of any considerable population. There was no strong site capable of resisting the desert swarms; neither Jericho nor Bethshan ever successfully sustained a siege.

Jordan has been associated not only with two of Israel's greatest prophets — Elijah and John the Baptist, but with their successors on whom the Spirit was bestowed. Elisha, who took up the mantle of Elijah, as he went up 'into heaven by a whirlwind,' [1] was the first in Israel to employ the river for sacramental purposes. He said unto Naaman the leper, 'Go and wash in Jordan seven times, and thy flesh shall come again to thee, and thou shalt be clean.' [2]

John the Baptist called on Israel to wash and be clean; and it was at Jordan that John, toward the close of his ministry, proclaimed the Christ. 'There cometh one mightier than I after me, the latchet of whose shoes I am not worthy to stoop down and unloose. I indeed have baptized you with water: but he shall baptize you with the Holy Ghost. And it came to pass in those days, that Jesus came from Nazareth of Galilee, and was baptized of John in Jordan. And straightway coming up out of the water, he saw the heavens opened, and the Spirit like a dove descending upon him: And there came a voice from heaven, saying, Thou art my beloved Son, in whom I am well pleased.' [3]

Between the Lake of Galilee and the Dead Sea, the Jordan falls nearly six hundred feet. The Dead Sea, called by the Arabs Bahr Lut (the Lake of Lot), [4] is fifty-three miles long and ten miles wide at its greatest breadth. The wondrous blue green surface of the Sea is 1290 feet below the level of the Mediterranean, while the bottom, near the entrance of the Jordan, is 1300 feet lower. The Dead Sea receives, besides the

[1] II Kings II: 1.   [2] *Ibid.*, v: 10.

[3] Mark I: 7–11.

[4] Geologists believe that it is physically possible that tradition is correct when it fixes the sites of Sodom and Gomorrah beneath the oily waters of the Dead Sea.

Jordan, four or five smaller streams, but has no outlet for its waters except through evaporation.

It has been estimated that six and a half million tons of water fall into the Dead Sea daily; and because of the extraordinary evaporation, the water remaining is impregnated to an unusual extent with mineral substances. The salt of the Dead Sea comprises one of the greatest mineral assets of Palestine. The average percentage of salts in the strong brine is at least twenty-five per cent, of which thirty-four per cent is sodium chloride, four to seven per cent potassium chloride, and up to one per cent or more magnesium bromide.[1]

The volume of the Dead Sea is somewhere in the region of 120,000,000,000 cubic metres; hence the area contains roughly 30,000,000,000 tons of mixed salts, of which possibly 1,500,000,000 tons are potassium chloride. This makes Palestine the richest country in the world for potash resources; and they occur under the most favorable conditions. The salts appear as a strong brine, immediately ready for evaporation and crystallization for the production of pure salts by the natural heat of the sun.[2]

Intensely saline springs exist along the banks of the Dead Sea, and in the region is to be found the finest and purest bitumen, as well as quantities of excellent sulphur. It is reported also that marble, porphyry, and other fine classes of stone are to be found, and there is also evidence of the existence of coal and oil. According to the report of Professor Blackenhorn, copper mines were worked near the south end of the Dead Sea in Byzantine times.[3]

In 1921, Moses Novomeysky, a Jewish engineer, and a citizen of Palestine, in association with Major Tulloch, began negotiations to secure the concession for the exploitation of the mineral salts of the Dead Sea. On May 22, 1929, a

[1] *The Handbook of Palestine*, pp. 240, 241. Edited by Harry Charles Luke and Edward Keith-Roach. 1922.

[2] *Ibid.*

[3] Halfway down the western bank of the Dead Sea lies Engedi — the spring of the wild goat — the only place on this side of the Sea where good fresh water can be found. There is also a plain about a mile square, skirting the shore, with hot and cold water springs and luxurious vegetation. The first cucumbers for the Jerusalem market are grown here.

Preliminary Agreement was concluded; [1] and on January 1, 1930, the final Agreement for the Concession was signed in London by the Crown Agents for the Colonies on behalf of the High Commissioner for Palestine and Trans-Jordan,[2] and by Messrs. M. Novomeysky, T. G. Tulloch, and E. W. D. Tennant on behalf of the Palestine Potash Company, Limited.[3] This is an English Company with a registered capital of 400,000 Palestinian pounds and a paid-up capital of 125,000 Palestinian pounds. The Company is incorporated in England and has its office in London.[4]

[1] See Cmd. 3326. Documents relating to the Dead Sea Salts Concession, presented by the Secretary of State for the Colonies to Parliament by Command of His Majesty, May, 1929.

[2] The High Commissioner is empowered to bind the Governments of the two countries.

[3] The concession relates only to the salts of the Dead Sea. The Government reserves the right to the 'gold silver or other precious metals and their ores precious stones antiquities and mineral oil (hereinafter referred to as 'the excepted substances') whether under the waters of the Dead Sea or under or upon the Concession Lands or any other lands in the occupation of the Company. (Report on the Administration of Palestine and Trans-Jordan, 1929. Appendix II, p. 184.)

[4] Ibid., p. 182.
See also the following statement in Cmd. 3317, 1929. Dead Sea Salts Concession:
'In accordance with an undertaking given in the House of Lords on the 23rd of May, 1928, the names of the financial supporters of Major Tulloch and Mr. Novomeysky are given below:
  Messrs. Basil Montgomery and Company, London;
  Messrs. C. Tennant, Sons and Company, Limited, London;
  Messrs. Pauling and Company, Limited, London;
  Mr. Leslie Urquhart (Chairman of the Russo-Asiatic Consolidated
   Company, Limited, London);
  The Jewish Colonial Trust, Limited, London;
  The Palestine Economic Corporation, New York.
'It is understood that the Earl of Lytton, G.C.S.I., G.C.I.E., will be the Chairman of the Company that will be formed to operate the Concession, and that Directors of some of the firms mentioned above will be on the Board of Directors of that Company. It is also understood that it is the intention of Major Tulloch and Mr. Novomeysky, in agreement with their financial supporters, that the Articles of Association of the Company should contain a provision to the effect that the Chairman of the Company should be a British subject, and that British subjects, or British subjects and Palestinian citizens together, should form the majority of the Board of Directors of the Company.'
See discussion on Dead Sea Concession in Minutes of the Fifteenth Session Permanent Mandates Commission. Sir John Chancellor said that: 'The concession had been granted to Major Tulloch and Mr. Novomeysky. A company had now been floated by them to work the concession. The Chairman of the company was Lord Lytton. Several financial houses, British and American, were interested in the company. All of them were firms of good standing, so far as the accredited representative was aware.' (Minutes of the Fifteenth Session Held at Geneva from July 1st to 19th, 1929, pp. 89, 90.)

The Company began operations toward the end of 1929. The first steps w^re to mark the Concession area, to construct facilities for evaporation purposes and to carry on experimental tests. The Report on the Administration of Palestine for 1929 states: 'By the spring of 1930, the number of workers had increased to seventy. Lorries and tractors had arrived, internal roads were being built, the pipe-lines laid, and a small consignment of asphalt was exported.' [1]

And the travellers who have ridden around the hairpin bends on the Jerusalem–Jericho Road will be glad to know that the Government has improved the road 'for the purposes of the concessionnaires, particularly by elimination of dangerous curves.' [2]

The names and nationalities of the holders of the Dead Sea Concession are interesting factors in the enterprise: The Right Honorable The Earl of Lytton, British; Ernest William Dalrymple Tennant, British; Lieutenant-Colonel Harold Josiah Solomon, British; Lieutenant-Colonel David Lyell, British; Mr. Bernard Flexner, U.S.A.; Mr. Felix Warburg, U.S.A.; Mr. Israel Benjamin Brodie, U.S.A.; Mr. Edward Friedman, U.S.A.; Major Thomas Gregorie Tulloch, British; Mr. Moses Novomeysky, Palestinian.[3]

Among these names there is but one Palestinian, and he is a Jew. The Arabs have protested against the Concession. The Commission on the Disturbances of August, 1929, stated that this and the Concession to Mr. Rutenberg for the generation of electricity [4] is one of the secondary Arab grievances. The Arab argument is given as follows:

The Arabs argue that by the grant of these concessions valuable natural resources of Palestine have been handed over to individual Jews and that the profits that may be expected to result from these enterprises will benefit foreign capitalists and not the people of the country. They contend that the Government of Palestine should either themselves have developed these resources for the benefit of all the people of that country, or should have entrusted their development to the Zionist Organisation in accordance with the latter part of Article II of the Mandate which limits the profits to be

---

[1] Colonial No. 47. Report by His Majesty's Government in the United Kingdom of Great Britain and Northern Ireland to the Council of the League of Nations on the Administration of Palestine and Trans-Jordan for the year 1929, p. 223.

[2] *Ibid.*   [3] *Ibid.*, p. 173.   [4] See p. 231, n. 1, *infra.*

drawn by the Organisation from any undertaking of this character and prescribes that any additional profits shall be utilised for the benefit of the country in a manner approved by the Palestine Government.[1]

The development of these natural resources is an important element in the functioning of the Mandate; and, especially in view of the enormous possibilities of the Palestine Potash Company, they may prove to be one of the decisive factors in determining the future of the country.

But the geography of this part of Palestine presents another interesting phenomenon. Along the east coast of the Dead Sea is a uniform sandstone, whose variegated hues cause the wonderful color effects of the 'Mountains of Moab,' which rise to the height of 2500 to 3000 feet above the shore.

One afternoon, soon after our arrival in Palestine, we were invited for a ride which would find us on the Mount of Olives for sunset. As I looked across the Wilderness to the Dead Sea, and beyond to the plateau of Moab with its slopes reflecting the shining amber of the sandy shore, the blue of the sea seemed to have changed to red, giving a radiating brilliancy like the sun in the fulness of its glory. This is one of the most startling color scenes to be found anywhere in the world; and, significantly enough, it is a part of the everyday experience in this region. These atmospheric effects constitute one of the permanent elements which influence, without doubt, the thoughts of those people whose imagination is daily quickened at the sight of the gorgeous and mystical spectacle. Color, it is held, has a distinct influence on the Eastern mind. The costumes, we know, are less colorful in the desert than in the fertile land. We observed this interesting phenomenon in our journey across the desert into Palestine — a matter of small moment, it seemed to us then — though, in reality, an obvious index to the costumes of the people in this part of the world.

Who can know Palestine, lacking acquaintance with its charm or geographical lie? What of the history which links the contact of the ages with the mountains, the valleys, and the lakes of this little country? It is a stimulating process to

[1] Cmd. 3530. Report of the Commission on the Palestine Disturbances of August, 1929, p. 132.

SUNRISE OVER THE DEAD SEA

learn the story of those who conquered the rugged ways, and of others who have succumbed to their pressure. Such a study invokes imagination and leads to fanciful conjecture — a profitable experience it is and enlightening to our main thesis.

But in Palestine there are still other circumstances more subtle even than these physical phenomena. There are the ruins of the dead past, which in spite of all the vigorous life and perplexing contacts, are an ever-present element. Hoary antiquity is part of everyday experience; so that life has not only a contemporary but an historic dimension. The human race is very old; by the measure of the human mind, it has always, in Palestine, been inconceivably ancient. The oldest document in Genesis refers to the 'mighty men which were of old'; and Job speaks of the ancient kings 'who built up ruins for themselves.' So throughout history, the people of Palestine have been reminded of man's brevity, God's eternity; and in view of the ruins of ages long gone by, man's clearest thinking has developed about the God 'who is the same yesterday, to-day, and forever.'

CHAPTER V

THE RELIGIOUS SETTING — (1) JUDAISM

PROBABLY the most amazing aspect of the Palestine of to-day is the lack of religious harmony — and this in a land where religion plays the leading rôle! As I went about the country, I became curiously conscious of the dominating force of religion in the daily life of the people. There are, for example, three 'Sundays' in Palestine: Friday for the Moslem, Saturday for the Jew, and Sunday for the Christian. And there are, as we have seen, the numerous Holy Days which are rigorously observed by the three communities.

These observances not only sustain and stimulate religious fervor, but, as one can readily see, emphasize and perpetuate the distinctions between the different faiths. The religion to which a person adheres is known to all — a condition hardly paralleled in any other country in the world. Those familiar with Palestinian costumes are able to distinguish by a person's clothing to which religion, often to which sect of his particular faith, he adheres.[1]

This religious disunity makes for social disharmony; and

[1] While most of the Jews, and many of the Christians and Moslems, wear ordinary European clothing, the red tarbûsh or fez, with the broad white turban wound about it, is usually worn by the Moslem men of the cities, while Christians wear the tarbûsh with no turban or one considerably narrower. Moslem women of the city are completely veiled, women of the poorer classes wearing black, those of higher station often wearing white. Druse women, mostly of the north, conceal the entire person except for one eye. Christians and Moslem peasants do not veil the face at all. The Christian women of Bethlehem wear a costume, by some supposed to be of Crusader origin: there is a much-embroidered red jacket, cut somewhat like a European man's waistcoat, full skirts, and a red cap similar to the man's tarbûsh, though narrower at the top, with coins sewed about it; when this cap is tall, seven or eight inches, it designates not only that the wearer is a Christian from Bethlehem, but that she is married. Most of the women of the country wear coins upon their head-dress: the coins are usually sewed to the cloth cap or kerchief making a sort of fillet over the forehead; when they lie flat against the head, the woman is from one of the villages not more than ten or twelve miles north of Jerusalem; but when they stand on edge, they indicate that the woman comes from farther north. The yoke of the dress, when embroidered predominantly in red, shows her to be of the tribe of Kais; the blue needlework is from the rival tribe of Yemen. This tribal division, however, does not follow the religious distinctions.

the Mandatory must have been cognizant of the situation before undertaking the Mandate, for religious friction in Palestine was notorious. The terms of the Mandate [1] hold Great Britain responsible for the protection and regulation of the religious interests in Palestine; but at the same time confine her authority within very definite limits. Nine of the twenty-eight articles of the Mandate define the responsibility and also the limitations.

Specifically: the Mandatory is responsible for safeguarding the religious rights of all the inhabitants, irrespective of religion; [2] respect must be fully guaranteed 'for the personal status of the various peoples and communities and for their religious interests,' and 'in particular,' the Waqf must be administered and controlled 'in accordance with religious law and the dispositions of the founders'; [3] the Mandatory must ensure to all 'complete freedom of conscience and the free exercise of all forms of worship, subject only to the maintenance of public order and morals,' and there shall be no discrimination of any kind between the inhabitants of Palestine on the ground of religion, neither shall any person be excluded from Palestine on the sole ground of his religious belief; [4] the Mandatory is responsible for 'exercising such supervision over religious or eleemosynary bodies of all faiths in Palestine as may be required for the maintenance of public order and good government,' and 'subject to such supervision, no measures shall be taken in Palestine to obstruct or interfere with the enterprise of such bodies or to discriminate against any representative or member of them on the ground of his religion'; [5] Article 20 declares that 'the Mandatory shall coöperate on behalf of the Administration of Palestine, so far as religious, social and other conditions may permit, in the execution of any common policy adopted by the League of Nations for preventing and combating disease, including diseases of plants and animals'; the Administration of Palestine must 'recognize the holy days

---

[1] C. 529. M. 314. 1922. VI. League of Nations, Mandate for Palestine.

Cmd. 1785. League of Nations. Mandate for Palestine, together with a Note by the Secretary-General Relating to its Application to the Territory known as Trans-Jordan, under the provisions of Article 25. Presented to Parliament by Command of His Majesty, December, 1922.

[2] Mandate, Article 2.   [3] *Ibid.*, Article 9.

[4] *Ibid.*, Article 15.   [5] *Ibid.*, Article 16.

of the respective communities in Palestine as legal days of rest for the members of such communities.' [1]

In every case, however, the Mandatory is responsible to the League of Nations, and this is particularly emphasized with reference to the preservation of existing rights in the Holy Places. Article 13 expressly states that the Mandatory 'shall be responsible solely to the League of Nations in all matters connected herewith'; and that 'nothing in this Mandate shall be construed as conferring upon the Mandatory authority to interfere with the fabric or the management of purely Moslem sacred shrines, the immunities of which are guaranteed.' Article 14 enjoins upon the Mandatory the appointment of a special Commission 'to study, define and determine the rights and claims in connection with the Holy Places and the rights and claims relating to the different religious communities in Palestine'; but it circumscribes the action of the Mandatory in the selection of the members and the determination of the functions of the Commission. All this must be submitted to the Council of the League of Nations for its approval: 'the Commission shall not be appointed or enter upon its functions without the approval of the Council.' This Commission has not yet been appointed.

The last Article of the Mandate provides that 'in the event of the termination of the mandate hereby conferred upon the Mandatory, the Council of the League of Nations shall make such arrangements as may be deemed necessary for safeguarding in perpetuity, under guarantee of the League, the rights secured by Articles 13 and 14.' [2]

Obviously, then, the religious situation is an extremely important element in the Mandate. Indeed, viewed from the religious angle, Palestine is the most interesting as well as the most problematical of any country in the world; and it therefore follows, if one hopes to understand the real nature of the Mandate, and the full responsibility of the Mandatory Power, he must be acquainted with the religious setting.

The Jews base their claim to Palestine on the history of Judaism, from Abraham down the centuries. When the Abrahamites 'left the land of Chaldea' and went into Ca-

[1] Mandate, Article 23.
[2] *Ibid.*, Article 28.

naan,[1] there was enacted the first act of the drama which was to make Palestine the central pivot of the Jewish faith.

The migration of the patriarchal Israelites from Canaan to Egypt; the fostering of the germ of Israel's national consciousness through the teachings of Moses, who led his people out of Egypt to the banks of the Jordan; and the conquest of Canaan which resulted in acquiring national territory: — all are decisive landmarks in this early Jewish history.

Then began the long struggle to retain the territory of Palestine. Under the government of Samuel, the Philistines became masters of the Israelites, and held their country in entire subjection. But when the situation became too acute for the Israelites, they united their interests and elected Saul King over Israel. After Saul's death, the tribes of Levi and Judah made David King. He consolidated the interests of the tribes and delivered the country from the Philistines.

David seized Jerusalem, made it his capital, and selected the place which for more than ten centuries, with the exception of a brief interruption during the Babylonian Exile, was the site of a central shrine of the Jewish nation.

Solomon built the first Temple. He also erected a magnificent palace and built the Walls of Jerusalem larger and stronger than they had ever been.[2] He developed the resources of the country, and his reign marked the period of the greatest temporal prosperity for Israel. But at the same time it also marked the commencement of its decline. Damascus threw off the yoke of the Israelites, and dissensions sprang up in the interior. The last years of Solomon's reign disclosed an absolute departure from the idea of the one God, and upon his death, the kingdom fell into two parts: Judah to the south and Israel to the north.

With the division of the kingdom, the social structure and religious convictions deteriorated under foreign influence. The northern kingdom of Israel, composed of the Ten Tribes, fell an easy prey to the encroachments of their neighbors, and in 722 B.C., the northern kingdom was destroyed by the

[1] Josephus, *Antiquities of the Jews*, i, vii.

[2] The building of the Walls of Jerusalem fulfills David's prayer: '... Build thou the walls of Jerusalem.' (Psalm LI: 18.)

Assyrians. The inhabitants were sent to the east, and colonists substituted in their stead.

Judah was also sinking into decay, and when Josiah died, mortally wounded as he was, defending Judah against the Egyptians, the Kingdom of Judah was virtually destroyed. Nebuchadnezzar deported King Jehoiakin and his whole court, and about forty thousand of the principal inhabitants, among whom was the Prophet Ezekiel. He also took away the remaining treasures of the Temple; Ezekiel and the forty thousand captives were sent to Media, but the King, court, and treasure were taken to Babylon.

A revolt, however, in 587 B.C., by the last King, Zedekiah, a son of Josiah, so enraged Nebuchadnezzar that he demolished Jerusalem and burnt the Temple. Thereupon followed a second and much more numerous deportation of the inhabitants, so that only the poor of the land were left 'for vine-dressers and husbandmen.' All the rest were carried captive to Babylon in 586 B.C.[1]

In the year 538 B.C., Cyrus [2] conquered Babylon, and gave permission to the Jews to return to their native country. Only some of them, however, came back, and the new Jewish State was wholly comprised within the ancient limits of Judah.[3] The exiles of the northern kingdom did not return. They are usually referred to as the Lost Ten Tribes.

The first efforts of those who came back to Jerusalem were devoted to the erection of the new Temple. This was promoted by the Prophets Haggai and Zechariah, who saw the need of a visible religious centre which would be the rallying point for a united nation. This was in 520–515 B.C., Ezra and

[1] During this time, great messages were delivered by the Prophets Ezekiel and Jeremiah. It was in this period that the sublime, anonymous Prophet wrote chapters 40–66 of the Book of Isaiah. Although these messages were not fully understood by those who were living under the Babylonian yoke, they served as the guiding-star in the achievement of the ultimate goal. The greatest need at the time, however, was for definite and uniform religious laws which would bind the Jews together as a nation.

[2] This Cyrus is called God's shepherd by Xenophon as well as by Isaiah: 'That saith of Cyrus, He is my shepherd, and shall perform all my pleasure; even saying to Jerusalem, Thou shalt be built; and to the temple, Thy foundations shall be laid.' (Isaiah XLIV: 28.)

[3] Josephus relates that: 'Now the number of those that came out of captivity to Jerusalem, were forty-two thousand four hundred and sixty-two.' (Josephus, *Antiquities of the Jews*, XI: i, 3.)

Nehemiah established a set form of ritual, following Ezekiel and the priestly legislation in Leviticus and Numbers. The object aimed at was to elevate all the people to a high spiritual plane, in accordance with the Biblical injunction, into 'a kingdom of priests.'

During the two following centuries of the Persian supremacy, there developed the so-called school of the Soferim, the Scribes — those versed in the Scriptures. A large part of the Scriptures, received into the Bible after the Pentateuch, were collected, compiled, and put into writing. They were preserved on parchment rolls and in books. There were set down the traditions of the earliest times, the chronicles of the people's past, and the Psalms produced by the religious enthusiasm of a long series of poets. All were put into literary form. The importance of this work to the world can hardly be estimated; for it must be admitted that if this compilation had not been made at that time, the world to-day probably would never have had access to these great expressions of faith and spirituality. Certainly, the literature of the world would have been that much poorer.

At the downfall of the Persian monarchy in 332 B.C., the Jews were forced to compete with Hellenism under the Macedonian supremacy. For a century Judea was the scene of conflict between the Egyptian and Syrian dynasties; and in 203 B.C., she was declared a Syro-Macedonian province. Hellenistic culture made rapid progress; a party favorable to this new influence was formed among the Jews. Judaism was therefore divided between Hellenists and the traditionally faithful Jews, known as Assidæans.

During the reign of King Antiochus Epiphanes, the Assidæans revolted. At the head of the insurgents, was the hoary priest Mattathias, who with his distinguished son Judas Maccabæus, fought for the dearest traditions of the Jews. The Syrian-Greek yoke was thrown off. Thus, after living under alien rule for nearly four hundred years, Judea became an independent state, and remained such for a century.

By the conquests of John Hyrcanus I, the dominions of Judea were considerably extended.[1] During this period, the

[1] John Hyrcanus (135–104 B.C.) waged aggressive wars on all sides. He made a campaign east of the Jordan in the old territory of Moab; took Shechem and

form of government was a theocracy, presided over by a high priest, who at the same time enjoyed political power, and ruled the country with the title of 'High Priest and Uniter of the Jews.' When, however, the eldest son of Hyrcanus took the reins of government, he assumed the title of king; and from that time on the Asmonean princes (Maccabees) retained the title of king.

Under the reign of the Maccabees, three famous parties arose: the Sadducees, the Pharisees, and the Essenes. This, as Dubnow says, 'by no means testifies, as many would have us believe, to national disintegration, but rather to the intense spiritual activity of the people.'

> The unbending religious dogmatism of the Sadducees [he continues], the practical sense of the Pharisees in religious and national concerns, the contemplative mysticism of the Essenes, they are the most important offshoots from the Jewish system as held at that time. In consequence of the external conditions that brought about the destruction of the Maccabean state after a century's existence (165–63 B.C.E.), the Pharisee tendency, which had proved itself the best in practice, won the upper hand.[1]

In 63 B.C., the Romans, under Pompey, captured Jerusalem, and the Asmonean Hyrcanus II reigned thereafter under Roman suzerainty. In 58 B.C., the Maccabean Dynasty came to an end, and the Dynasty of Herod came into power. Under Herod, the Jewish territories were divided as follows: (1) Judea, including Idumæa; (2) Samaria; (3) Galilee; (4) Peræa ('the country beyond'); (5) the territory which later

destroyed the temple on Mount Gerizim which pretended to rival Jerusalem; conquered the Idumæans in the south and made Jews of them by compulsory circumcision; recovered Joppa and Gazara; and finally, toward the end of his reign, after a long siege conducted by his sons, captured the city of Samaria and totally destroyed it. (George Foot Moore, *Judaism*, vol. I, p. 56.)

[1] S. M. Dubnow, *Jewish History: An Essay in the Philosophy of History*, pp. 80–82.

In explaining the difference between the Sadducees and the Pharisees, Moore says: 'The primary cleavage between the Sadducees and the Pharisees was on the doctrine of revelation. Scripture is the only authority, said the Sadducees; Scripture and Tradition, said the Pharisees. Next to this the most important doctrinal difference between the two was in the field of eschatology. The Pharisees believed in the survival of the soul, the revival of the body, the great judgment, and the life of the world to come. The Sadducees found nothing in the Scriptures, as they read them in their plain sense, about the resurrection of the dead or retribution after death, and rejected these new imaginations along with the subtleties of exegesis by which they were discovered in the Law.' (George Foot Moore, *Judaism*, vol. I, p. 68.)

became the tetrarchy of Philip. The Hellenistic towns east of the Jordan — Philadelphia, Gerasa, and Pella — together with Scythopolis west of the Jordan, formed a more or less compact political unit under the name of the Decapolis.

Herod the Great died in the year of the birth of Christ, 4 B.C., reckoned according to the accepted chronology as determined by Dionysius Exiguus in A.D. 525. Before Herod died, he divided his kingdom among his three sons — Archelaus, to whom he gave Samaria, Judea, and Idumæa; Philip, who received the districts of the Hauran (S.E.); and Herod Antipas, who was awarded Galilee and Peræa. In A.D. 6, Samaria, Judea, and Idumæa were added to the Roman province of Syria, but they were governed by procurators of their own.

The power of the native princes became merely nominal as the power of the Roman Governors increased; and as time went on, the Jews were kept in perpetual ferment by the intolerance of the tribute collectors and the audacity of the soldiers accompanying them, and by bribery and corruption of the worst kind. At length, under the profligate administration of Gessius Florus, 'there being scarcely a crime of which historians do not accuse him,' [1] a national insurrection broke out with great violence.

During the Passover, A.D. 70, Titus besieged Jerusalem with an army of sixty thousand Romans,[2] and the Temple was reduced to a heap of ruins.[3] The human losses sustained by the Jewish people in the course of the war are computed to be more than a million, and about the same number were taken captive.[4] Titus in his march toward Rome wantonly exposed the Jews to be devoured by wild beasts in the amphi-

---

[1] C. S. Mitchell, *Records of Events Connected with the History of the Jews*, p. 471.

[2] When the Temple quarter was assaulted, Titus used his utmost endeavors to protect the Temple from injury; but because of the burning of the palace of the high priests, where twenty thousand Romans perished, those remaining, exasperated at the loss, determined to wreak their vengeance on the Jews by destroying their Temple. After the soldiers had effected an entrance, Titus forbade any one to deface the fabric; but the fury of the soldiers was such that Titus was helpless.

[3] In sacking the city, the Romans, to disengage the gold and silver that had melted and concreted round the stones of the Temple, fulfilled the prophecy of Micah, by ploughing up the foundations: 'Therefore, shall Zion for your sake be ploughed as a field...' (Micah III: 12.)

[4] The figures given by Josephus are much larger.

theatres of the various cities through which he passed. Large numbers of Jews were sent to labor on the public works in Egypt, and thousands were put into the slave markets, when, after the demand was satisfied, the Jews could not be sold at any price. The words of the great lawgiver were thus verified: 'And the Lord shall bring thee into Egypt again with ships, by the way whereof I spake unto thee, Thou shalt see it no more again: and there ye shall be sold unto your enemies for bondmen and bondwomen, and no man shall buy you.' [1] Sixteen thousand Jews were reserved for the victor and the rest were sent to Spain. Though many Jews were deported from Palestine, a large population remained in the land, living on the soil and enjoying a certain form of government under the Patriarch for many centuries after the destruction of the Temple.

Ever since the Babylonian Exile, there existed large Jewish communities outside of Palestine, in almost every known part of the world. These Jewish communities were known by the general term Diaspora which was spiritually dependent upon Palestine.

The terrible consequences of the unsuccessful revolt against the Romans rendered impossible any political action, for the time being, on the part of the few survivors, who for the most part located on the coast. Bereft of property and living in great distress, they had only one thought beyond the struggle for a bare existence, namely — to preserve their spiritual ideal. Even before Jerusalem had entirely succumbed to the Roman destruction, a new Jewish centre was founded at Jamnia, near the coast at Jaffa under the leadership of Jochanan ben Zakkai, who had been a member of the Sanhedrin in Jerusalem. At Jamnia, the Sanhedrin was reconstructed, and it functioned as the legislative body of the Jewish people. The *hakhamin* (the 'learned') in Jamnia endeavored to collect their spiritual possessions, and to tabulate and correlate the religious Law, both that which was written and that which was traditional.

Gradually, the attitude of the Romans toward the Jews became less harsh, and in consequence Jewish communities began to come again into existence in the depopulated

[1] Deuteronomy xxviii: 68.

centres; the seats of learning flourished more and more; and there is even evidence that there were individual Jews owning land and slaves.

In the year 116, in the reign of Trajan, there was a great Jewish revolt throughout the Roman world: in Egypt, Cyrene, Cyprus, Babylon, and possibly also in Palestine. When, however, the Emperor Hadrian came to Judea in 130, it looked as if the Jews had found favor with him. It is said that he even gave them permission to rebuild the Temple. The Emperor decided to rebuild Jerusalem — but as a heathen city. Moreover, his plan included proscriptions against some of the essential observances of Judaism, which if followed out, would have rendered the Jewish religion in danger of extinction. So again, the whole Jewish people rose to defend their principles; while some of the Jews still nursed the hope of political restoration.

The revolt was led by Bar Cochba, inspired by Rabbi Akiba, the greatest scholar of that time. The revolt at first had phenomenal success. Immediately on the outbreak of the rebellion, the provinces of Judea, Samaria, and Galilee were evacuated by the Romans. Julius Severus, the greatest soldier of his age, was sent to restore Roman prestige, but even he could not prevail against Bar Cochba. This Jewish leader attracted recruits from all countries, and those who could not serve in person sent of their treasure. Even non-Jews joined the rebel forces.

Bar Cochba succeeded in reorganizing the Jewish State, as attested by the coins bearing his name. But it was plainly impossible to withstand the Romans indefinitely; stronghold after stronghold fell. Bether alone remained: the Romans entered the fortress, and after a stubborn battle defeated the Jews and put them to death. Most of the Jews — men, women, and children — wherever they were caught, were massacred, and the rest were sold into slavery. In the fall of Bether, alone, half a million Jews, including fugitives from the other cities, are said to have lost their lives. This disastrous defeat cut off the last remnant of hope for the immediate restoration of 'an earthly kingdom.'

After this, Hadrian was determined to suppress non-conformity to the official Roman religion. On the site of

Jerusalem arose the new pagan city Ælia Capitolina; and where the Temple of the Jews once stood, a heathen temple was erected. Not only this, but the Holy Places of the Christians at Bethlehem, and of the Samaritans on Mount Gerizim, were similarly defiled. No Jews were allowed in the new city,[1] and for two centuries afterward they were not permitted to live on the soil on which Jerusalem had stood.

The Jews were treated more humanely under Hadrian's successor, Antoninus Pius; and in consequence, the religious leaders began to return. The Sanhedrin was reëstablished at Usha,[2] but was afterwards transferred to Sepphoris and finally to Tiberias, which continued to be a centre of Jewish life and learning until about the tenth century. The ruins of synagogues, which date from this period, show the importance of the Jewish population of Galilee during the second and later centuries of the Christian era. The labors of the Palestinian scholars are embodied in the Mishnah,[3] the Palestinian or 'Jerusalem' Talmud,[4] and kindred literary output.

Until the conversion of the Roman Emperor, about the year 312, there is little to record in Jewish Palestinian history. Constantine, previous to this, had placed Judaism on a level with other religions of the Empire, and had recognized its Patriarchs and other officers of equal rank with the officers of other faiths. The Patriarch of Judea was officially regarded as the spiritual head of all the Jews of the Empire.[5]

---

[1] See Sir G. A. Smith, *Atlas of the Historical Geography of the Holy Land*. London, 1915.

[2] About ten miles inland from Haifa.

[3] The Mishnah, which means 'repetition,' or that which is learned by heart, was the result of a compilation and discussion carried on for more than two centuries. It was completed about A.D. 200. This was a codification of law relating to all aspects of life and all branches of religious observance. The Mishnah was based on the Scriptures, and set forth merely the traditional law.

[4] The Mishnah was subjected to further discussion in the academies of Babylon and Palestine for three centuries, and the record of this work was Gemara, or 'completion.' The Mishnah and the Gemara, text and commentary, together constitute the Talmud. The compilers of the earlier period of the Talmud are known as the *Tannaim*; and those of the later, *Amoraim*.

Darmesteter says: 'The Talmud of Jerusalem was not widespread, and counted for little in the development of the Middle Ages.' (James Darmesteter, *Selected Essays*, p. 260.)

[5] The Patriarch maintained intercourse with the communities in dispersion by

But after the conversion of the Emperor, he promulgated laws restricting the religious, political, and civil rights of the Jews. In 326, when Helena, the mother of Constantine, visited Palestine for the purpose of discovering the place of the Crucifixion, intense interest was aroused in the Holy Land. This militated against the Jews; the Law of Hadrian, for example, which had forbidden Jews to live in Jerusalem, but which had been falling into desuetude, was reënacted. The Jews were allowed, however, to mourn there, on the payment of a certain sum, once a year, on the anniversary of the destruction of the Temple.

In 361, Julian expressed sympathy for the Jewish people, and among his many acts consistent with this spirit, was his letter to the Jewish communities of the Empire stating his intention of rebuilding the Temple. The Emperor really placed funds aside for the work, collected building material, and set to work a large number of workmen to clear away the débris which for centuries had covered the site of the Temple. The Jews, however, took little heart in the project, believing, as they did, that they could take no step toward freedom until the coming of the Messiah, whom they eagerly awaited. The lack of participation by the Jews and several mysterious fires, coupled with the fatal arrow which struck Julian in battle, defeated the attempt to rear the Jewish Temple.

Theodosius abolished the Sanhedrin in 425, and Palestine ceased to be the dominant centre of Jewish learning. Babylon, which hitherto had existed as a secondary centre, now took the leading place. Tiberias, however, still continued to be a centre of Hebrew learning for many centuries; [1] and for two hundred years, after the division of the Empire in 390, when Palestine fell to Byzantium, Tiberias was the religious capital of Palestine.

In his comprehensive analysis of the spiritual development of Judaism, Darmesteter describes the Talmud as follows:

Finally, there are the successors of the Messianists and of the

delegates whom he sent periodically to visit them. One object of these visits was to collect the tax imposed for the support of the Patriarch. Another was doubtless the publication of the calendar. (George Foot Moore, *Judaism*, vol. i, pp. 108–09.)

[1] It was here, in the ninth century, that the system of vocalization, now in use in Hebrew Bibles, received its final shape.

zealots, building around the sacred Book, in defiance of Roman torches, that triple impregnable wall — the Talmud. In the sixth century of our era is completed the immense encyclopædia which embraces with absolute impartiality all variety of opinions, in all the branches of science and of belief, that were formulated during a period of six centuries in the schools of Palestine and Babylonia. It is a work without apparent unity, since it reproduces the infinite contrast presented by the thousands of minds of which it is the sum total. In turn, according to the voice that speaks, it manifests a strange narrow-mindedness by the side of unequalled breadth, now dull and again brilliant; open to science and closed to it; presenting all the timidities of thought and all its audacities; but penetrated throughout by a spirit of faith and of hope that brings unity into this chaos — faith in the one God, and hope for justice to come. The superficial mind often saw nothing more in this book than the babble of refined casuistry, of a reasoning and subtle superstition. It failed to perceive the vital force in consequence of which Jewish thought was enabled to pass through the intellectual night of the Middle Ages without being extinguished.[1]

If we now turn our attention to Babylonia, which was one of the centres of the Diaspora, we may note the results of an intellectual activity covering about eight hundred years — from the third to the middle of the eleventh century. The 'Babylonian Talmud' was put into permanent form about the year 500.[2]

In 611, the fate of the persecuted Jews in Palestine seemed about to turn in a more favorable direction. The Persian King, Chosroes II, invaded Palestine, and as the Jews regarded the Persians as deliverers, all the Jews in Galilee who were capable of bearing arms joined the invading forces. The Christians of Galilee suffered severely. Jerusalem was taken by storm in 614; its Christian inhabitants were massacred, and its churches destroyed. Palestine remained in the hands of Persia fourteen years, and it looked as if Rome and Christianity had been driven out of the country forever.

In 628, when Palestine reverted to Byzantium, and the Emperor Heraclius visited Jerusalem, he was met by the monks who urged him to exterminate the Jews, saying that

---

[1] James Darmesteter, *Selected Essays*, p. 259.

[2] George Foot Moore says that the Palestinian Talmud reached substantially the shape in which it has come down to us in the schools of Galilee in the last quarter of the fourth century, and the Babylonian Talmud about a century later. (George Foot Moore, *Judaism*, vol. I, p. 4.)

it was his Christian duty to destroy them, young and old. The Emperor did as he was asked, and as a result the only survivors of the Jews of Judea were those who hid underground or fled into Egypt.[1]

The triumph of Heraclius was short-lived; in 635, he was defeated by Omar, the head of the new religion which had arisen in Arabia. Mohammed died in 632, and Omar was the second Caliph. He vigorously strove to gain adherents to Mohammedanism. In 640, the Greeks were driven out of Palestine; permanent disabilities were put on the Christians; and the ordinances concerning the Jews were more severe than either of the others. If the Jewish ordinances had been put into operation, the Jews would have been placed in exceedingly bad circumstances; but the benign Caliph generously allowed them privileges, so that their condition proved to be much better even than before the Moslems came. But the last vestige of hope of rebuilding their Temple was gone forever. In 688, the Caliph Abd al-Melek erected the beautiful mosque, now known as the Mosque of Omar, on the Temple site.

In the eighth century, the wars ceased; and there arose a peaceful era in Palestine which witnessed the growth of industry, the sciences, and the arts. In the second half of the eighth century, there sprang up in Babylon, as an active revolt against the Talmud, the sect known as the Karaites. They urged a return to the literal Biblical laws. There was a considerable immigration of Karaites into Palestine, and a large number of them settled in Jerusalem as *Abelim*, or Mourners for Jerusalem.

When Palestine became subject to Egypt in the latter part of the ninth century, persecution of the Jews had ceased; there were considerable numbers of Jews in Jerusalem, as well as other parts of Palestine, living normal lives. Jews were to be found in all occupations, but were especially prominent as dyers, tanners, and money-changers. At the end of the tenth century, however, they suffered from the persecution of Hakim, the insane Caliph; and in consequence, the Jewish population of Jerusalem diminished, although the city continued to be a place of pilgrimage.

[1] Albert M. Hyamson, *Palestine: The Rebirth of an Ancient People,* p. 14.

During the First Crusade, when Jerusalem was taken, in 1099, and every Moslem — man, woman, and child — was killed, so that the Crusaders had to wade knee-deep in blood to reach the Church of the Holy Sepulchre, the Jews were driven into their synagogue and burned to death.[1] But another respite for the Jews came in the peaceful period of the Frankish Kingdom. It was during this time that Jewish pilgrims, pious and learned men, visited Palestine to investigate the condition of the land for the benefit of their co-religionists in Europe, and also to pray at the Western Wall,[2] the only remnant of the Temple, and at the other Jewish Holy Places. These men, among whom was Jehuda Halevi, the Spanish poet and philosopher, who came to Palestine in 1140, visited the graves of illustrious Jews who lay buried in the sacred soil. Now that the crusading zeal had lost its energy, the Jew was better off in Palestine than in some of the states of Europe; though, as one might infer, the former Jewish population had been practically annihilated by the warfare through which they had passed.

The Jewish practice of journeying to the Holy Land continued; and some of the visitors wrote accounts of their travels, giving information regarding the number and condition of the Jews settled in the towns of Palestine.

The best known of all mediæval Jewish travellers was Benjamin of Tudela,[3] who traversed throughout the length and breadth of Palestine about the year 1165. He came into Palestine from Tyre, which, as he says, contained about four hundred Jews, mostly 'ship-owners and manufacturers of the celebrated Tyrian glass.' He describes Acre as 'the frontier town of Palestine'; and because of its large port on the Mediterranean, 'it is the principal place of disembarkation of all pilgrims who visit Jerusalem by the sea.' He records about

[1] H. Graetz, *History of the Jews*, vol. III, p. 308. English translation. Philadelphia, 1893.

[2] This is called the Wailing Wall, clearly recognized as Moslem property, but the Jews are strongly contending for the legal right to worship there.

[3] *Early Travels in Palestine. The Travels of Rabbi Benjamin of Tudela*, pp. 80–90. The Hebrew Preface to this work gives the following description of Benjamin of Tudela: 'The above-mentioned Rabbi Benjamin was a man of wisdom and understanding, and of much information; and after strict inquiry his words were found to be true and correct, for he was a true man.'

two hundred Jewish inhabitants here, and 'many Jewish sepulchres'; while Cæsarea, 'the Gath of the Philistines of Scripture,' was inhabited by about ten Jews and two hundred 'Samaritan Jews, commonly called Samaritans.' He describes Cæsarea as 'very elegant and beautiful, situated on the sea-shore'; and Sebaste as 'richly watered, and surrounded with gardens, orchards, vineyards, and olive trees.' There were no Jews here. Nablus, situated between Mount Gerizim and Mount Ebal, contained no Jewish inhabitants, but was 'the abode of about one hundred Cutheans, who observe the Mosaic law only, and are called Samaritans.' Mount Gerizim is described as 'rich in wells and orchards, whereby Ebal is dry like stone and rocks.' He gives a long description of Jerusalem: 'It is a small city strongly fortified with three walls. It contains a numerous population, composed of Jacobites, Armenians, Greeks, Georgians, Franks, and indeed people of all tongues. The dyeing-house is rented by the year, and the exclusive privilege of dyeing is purchased from the King by the Jews of Jerusalem, two hundred of whom dwell in one corner of the city, under the tower of David.... The city contains no building stronger than the tower of David.' He speaks of two hospitals, one of which 'harbours and furnishes four hundred knights, who are ever ready to wage war, over and above those knights who arrive from the country of the Franks and other parts of Christendom.' He refers to the 'large place of worship, called Sepulchre, and containing the sepulchre of that man,[1] is visited by all pilgrims.' 'Jerusalem,' he says, 'has four gates, called the gates of Abraham, David, Sion, and Jehoshaphat. The latter,' he continues, 'stands opposite the place of the holy temple, which is occupied at present by a building called Templo Domino. Omar Ben Al-Khataab erected a large and handsome cupola over it.... In front of it you see the western wall, one of the walls which formed the Holy of Holies of the ancient temple; it is called the Gate of Mercy, and all Jews resort thither to say their prayers near the wall of the court-yard.... Very little water is found at Jerusalem; the inhabitants generally drink rain water, which they collect in their houses.' 'From the valley of Jehoshaphat,' he proceeds, 'the

[1] The reference is to Jesus.

traveller immediately ascends the Mount of Olives.... From hence the Dead Sea is distinctly visible.... Mount Sion is also near Jerusalem, upon the acclivity of which stands no building except a place of worship of the Nazarenes' (Christians). The traveller further sees three Jewish cemeteries, where formerly the dead were buried. He then goes to Bethlehem. 'Twelve Jews,' he says, 'dyers by profession, live at Bethlehem. The country abounds in rivulets, wells, and springs of water.' Of Hebron he says: 'The ancient city of that name was situated on the hill... whereas the modern town stands in the valley, even in the field of Machpelah.... On the confines of the field of Machpelah stands the house of our father Abraham... and, out of respect to Abraham, nobody is allowed to construct any building on that site.' At Beit Jaberim, he records that there were three Jewish inhabitants; at Toron de los Caballeros, three hundred; and at Beith Nubi, 'the city of the priests,' two. The latter are dyers. Describing Ramleh, 'where you still find walls erected by our forefathers, as is evident from the inscriptions upon the stones,' he says that the 'city' contains about three Jews, but it was formerly very considerable, for a Jewish cemetery in its vicinity is two miles in extent. Hence to Jaffa, 'the Japho of Scripture on the coast; one Jew only, a dyer by profession, lives here.' Ibelin, he writes, 'the ancient Jabneh, where the site of the schools may still be traced... contains no Jews.' There were no Jews at Asdoud, 'formerly a city of the Philistines, at present in ruins.' Ascalon, 'which is in fact the new Ascalon,' he describes as 'very large and handsome; and merchants from all parts resort to it.... There are here about two hundred rabbinite Jews.... From hence back to Saint George, which is Lydda, and in a day and a half to Serrain, the Jezreel of Scripture.... It has one Jewish inhabitant, a dyer.' Tiberias contained about fifty Jews, and he writes that the waters, 'which spout forth from under ground, are called the warm baths of Tiberias.' At Gish, there were about twenty Jewish inhabitants, and at Alma, fifty. Here also there was 'a large cemetery of Israelites.' 'Half a day,' he writes, 'brings you to Kades... on the banks of the Jordan. ... This place contains no Jews. A day's journey brings us to Belinas, the ancient Dan, where the traveller may see a cave.... In front of the cave, you may still trace vestiges of the altar of the image of Micha, which was adored by the children of Dan in ancient times.' From Dan, Benjamin of Tudela went on to Damascus.

After the fall of Jerusalem in 1187, there was a considerable Jewish immigration into Palestine; for under Saladin's rule, there was freedom for the Jews. Nablus, Cæsarea, Jericho, and Jaffa opened their gates to Saladin; and Jerusalem became a Jewish centre. Under the reigns of Saladin and his brother, Moslem Palestine had become a haven of refuge for the persecuted Jews of Europe. In 1211, two years before the Dominican Inquisition, the Sultan gave a friendly welcome to three hundred Rabbis of England and France who visited Palestine to investigate the prospects of a Jewish immigration on a large scale.

During the later Crusades, however, the Jews suffered severely, and many a community which had flourished in the time of Saladin, including that of Jerusalem, was destroyed. There were only two Jews to be found in Jerusalem when Maimonides (Moses ben Maimon),[1] the famous Spanish Talmudist, philosopher, and physician, visited there in 1267, just after the overthrow of the Franks. The Moslem Government was favorably disposed to a Jewish settlement in Jerusalem, and so with the aid of the Jewish residents of the neighboring villages, Maimonides was able to form once again a Jewish community in Jerusalem. As a result of his efforts, one of the old synagogues was rebuilt. A Rabbinical College was established, and Jewish students from neighboring countries began to come to Jerusalem. Jewish centres developed in Safed, Acre, Ramleh, and Sarafend.[2] Maimonides himself landed at Acre, but soon afterward left for Egypt.[3] About twenty years after, there came a Jewish immigration into Palestine from the Rhine Provinces.

During the following century, the condition of the Jews in Palestine continued to improve, and again Palestine became a centre of Jewish pilgrimage. Many of those who came

[1] George Foot Moore, *Judaism*, vol. II, pp. 81, 393.

[2] Jewish Encyclopædia, vol. IX, p. 91. New York. 1905.

[3] Maimonides reduced the Talmud into a code known as the Mishmeh Torah ('Double of the Law'). This was divided into fourteen books.

engaged in agriculture, industry, and commerce; and a large number devoted the remainder of their lives to Jewish scholarship. It is a fact, that during this period Palestine became again a centre of Jewish learning, where distinguished European scholars studied and taught. It was principally in Jerusalem that the latter settled; although artisans, merchants, and physicians were also to be found there. The new Jewish population of Hebron devoted themselves more to weaving, dyeing, and the manufacture of glassware; while in the south, the newcomers adopted a pastoral life.

During the fourteenth century, a large number of Jewish settlers came from France, where, until their expulsion in 1394, they were the victims of confiscation and massacre. In the earlier half of this century, the rumor spread in Europe that the Jews had bought Mount Zion and the Holy Sepulchre, although it was known that the Christians had rebuilt the churches at Jerusalem, Bethlehem, and Nazareth. This brought new persecution. But it was a fact that the spiritual power of the Jews was so strong that the rule of the Chief Rabbi of Jerusalem was accepted by Jews throughout Egypt and Syria.

But again, the Jerusalem Jews were to suffer reverses. Following a change in political conditions, plague, famine, and economic depression made inroads on the community after the middle of the fifteenth century. Emigration began, and a traveller who visited the city in 1481 reported that there were only two hundred and fifty Jewish families there. It is said that within a few years the number had decreased to seventy families, and that they were all in a state of poverty.

Jerusalem Jewry was not to remain in this condition long, however. In 1492, the Jews were expelled from Spain, and a few years later, from Portugal. Most of these exiles, who called themselves Sephardim, from the Hebrew word for Spain, turned eastward — some to North Africa, but the greater numbers to Turkey and her province Palestine. The Moslem lands were the only ones in which the Jews felt secure.

Palestine profited greatly from the immigration of these

exiles, who were for the most part men of wealth and learning.[1] The number of Jews in Palestine increased so largely that the place of the one congregation was taken by four. The community was under the direction of Obadiah of Bertinoro, who had settled in Jerusalem some years earlier, and who again secured considerable influence over the Jews of the East. Safed, under the guidance of Joseph Saragossi, developed into a Jewish centre almost as important as Jerusalem; and its Jewish population was increased to ten thousand.

With this Sephardic immigration from Spain came the Jewish mysticism of the Kabbala.[2] Everywhere, this 'mist-shrouded symbolism' had aroused the Jews to new hope. Then, too, the spiritual current which seized these exiles, as they came in sight of their ancestral home, kindled a passionate 'longing for Zion.' The immigration of the Spanish Jews really marked the first significant 'Return' to Palestine. Many of them hoped for political resurrection.

These feelings found expression in the modern Kabbala, founded by Ari (Isaac Luria), at Safed. During the sixteenth century there were many Messianic movements among the Jews. The outstanding ones were the Kabbala of Isaac Luria, the Messianic claims of Solomon Molko and the more practical works of Joseph Nasi. Luria imparted to his circle of Kabbalists at Safed the doctrines by means of which he hoped to establish the moral system of the world on a new basis. Molko preached throughout Palestine and announced that the Messianic kingdom would come in 1540.

Nasi's influence began during the reign of Suleiman the Magnificent, when the Jews had full liberty. This freedom led to an increase in the number of Jews in Jerusalem; and many merchants of considerable wealth, particularly from

[1] H. Graetz, *History of the Jews*, vol. IV, pp. 396 *seq.* English translation. Philadelphia. 1893.

[2] The literal meaning is 'tradition.' Throughout the age of the Tannaim and Amoraim, down to the close of the Talmuds, Kabbalah is used *only* of the tradition in Scripture, not of the unwritten law, nor of the theosophic tradition to which the name was subsequently attached. Bacher, *Terminologie*, I, 165 f. (George Foot Moore, *Judaism*, vol. I, p. 239. Note.)

Darmesteter says: The Kabbala opens to the imagination its great and beautiful mystic avenues where the thought of Spinoza often wandered in his youth. (James Darmesteter, *Selected Essays*, p. 263.)

Italy, settled there. At this time, Joseph Karo, the re-nowned Jewish jurist, settled at Safed,[1] and made the city the intellectual centre of Jewry.

Suleiman the Magnificent stands out in Jewish history as the protector of the Jews of Europe. During his reign, Turkey became the land of refuge for the fugitives who escaped European cruelty. The same policy was continued by Suleiman's successor, Sultan Selim, at whose court Joseph Nasi, whom Selim had made a duke, rose to be a considerable dignitary. Suleiman had presented him with the town of Tiberias for the purpose of settling Jews there; and to make the grant doubly secure, Suleiman obtained the assent of his heir and of his heir's heir to the gift. Nasi had the walls of Tiberias built, and invited the persecuted Jews of Italy to settle there. Large numbers left Italy, and especially on the expulsion of the Jews from the Papal States. Nasi encouraged agriculturists and artisans to settle; he planted mulberry trees for the breeding of silkworms, and introduced the manufacture of wool and silk.[2] Nasi's energies, however, were after a time directed to other channels, and this pro-mising experiment of Tiberias was given up.

We may speak of the sixteenth century as marking a renaissance of Judaism in Palestine. This was a striking contrast, however, to the succeeding two centuries, when the local government sank gradually into a condition of neglect and corruption; and when not only the Jews, but the people of all races and religions suffered in consequence. The first decades of the seventeenth century found the Jews reduced by oppression and poverty to a low level. The principal means of existence was the alms which the pious Jews of Europe were accustomed to send to their co-religionists in the Holy Land, who were expected to devote themselves to prayer and study.[3]

---

[1] In 1588, the first printing-press in Palestine was set up at Safed by the brothers Abraham and Isaac Ashkenasi.

[2] Albert M. Hyamson, *Palestine: The Rebirth of an Ancient People*, p. 43.

[3] Writing in 1914, Cohen says: 'In Palestine, where in 1880 as many as 30,000 of the 35,000 Jews lived wholly or mainly upon the charity received from their brethren abroad (the *Chaluka*), the economic situation has since considerably improved, but there are now still 55,000 out of an increased population of 100,000 who are solely dependent upon this means of subsistence.' (Israel Cohen, *Jewish Life in Modern Times*, p. 212. Cohen cites Dr. E. Auerbach, *Palaestina als Judenland*, p. 13.)

It is an obvious fact, therefore, that the condition of the Jews in Palestine was affected by the Jewish situation in various parts of Europe. The Jews of Poland, for example, who at the beginning of the sixteenth century had assumed the hegemony over the Jewry of the world,[1] were in the seventeenth century subjected to such a period of massacre and spoliation that they were no longer able to send the customary revenues. This led directly to the starvation of the Jews in Jerusalem.

In the second half of the seventeenth century, mysticism reached its zenith in Turkey, the cradle of the 'practical Kabbala.' In Smyrna, the false Messiah, Sabbatai Zebi appeared, and for a quarter of a century (1650–76), attracted a tremendous number of adherents in the East and in the West.

Near the end of the eighteenth century, the population of Jerusalem had mounted to more than ten thousand inhabitants, one tenth being Jews. At that time, there were twelve Jewish colleges in Jerusalem, supported or endowed by pious Jews in Europe. Safed, in the mean time, had declined in importance. Its misfortunes, arising from the plague in 1742 and the earthquake in 1769, forced practically all the survivors to emigrate to Damascus. There were only seven families left in this one-time important Jewish centre.

Within a very few years, however, Safed revived, through a new immigration of Russian Jews, especially of the newly formed sect known as Chassidim,[2] who, inasmuch as they came from Russian Poland or Austrian Galicia, lived under the protection of the Russian and Austrian Governments.[3] In

[1] This marks the displacement of the Sephardic (Spanish, in a broader sense, Romanic) element, and the supremacy of the Ashkenazic (German-Polish) element. (S. M. Dubnow, *Jewish History: An Essay in the Philosophy of History*, p. 143.)

[2] As to the nature of Chassidim, Cohen says: 'The only sect of the eighteenth century that has remained within the fold of Israel is that of the Chassidim, founded by Israel ben Eliezer, of Miedzyboz, in Podolia, who was famed as a worker of miracles through the name of God, and known as the *Baal Shem Tob* ("Master of the Good Name"). But the Chassidim do not differ from the rest of orthodox Jewry on any point of dogma; they differ simply in their conception of the religious life. They regard fervour of faith as its highest essential and as superior to profundity of Talmudical learning, and although they have their own houses of prayer and their own ritual, they fully accept and acknowledge the authority of the Oral Law.' (Israel Cohen, *Jewish Life in Modern Times*, p. 278.)

[3] Turkey abolished the Capitulations prior to the outbreak of the war between Turkey and the Allied Powers in 1914.

the early nineteenth century, Austria sent a representative to Jerusalem to look after their interests. Both Austria and Russia repeatedly brought pressure in Jerusalem on behalf of their nationals.

A significant tendency in Judaism began to develop in the early part of the nineteenth century, when the Jews of Western Europe had begun to reap the benefits of the movement for their emancipation, which was initiated by the French law of 1791 giving Jews full rights of citizenship. Coming under the influence of modern life and culture, some of these emancipated Jews regarded much of the Rabbinic tradition as an anachronism; and in order to adapt the ancient religion to modern conditions, they began to adopt changes in the tenets and practices of Judaism. This action is generally known as Reform Judaism.

The movement began in Germany at the close of the eighteenth century. It rejected many traditional customs, and expunged from the Prayer Book all references to the coming of a Messiah and the restoration of Zion. Until this movement started, Jews had regarded their dispersion as a punishment for their sins, and fervently prayed for their restoration to the Holy Land. The Reformers declared that the dispersion was not a punishment, but a divinely appointed means of spreading the teachings of Judaism throughout the world. Although these doctrines found a limited number of adherents in Germany, they gained wide acceptance in the United States.

We have seen how the faith and practice of the Orthodox Jew have developed on the basis of the Written Law, consisting of the Bible; and the Oral Law, consisting of the Talmud. The centuries of dispersion and the many times dismemberment of Jewry have inevitably produced divergences of synagogue ritual; although they do not involve differences of doctrine. Cohen gives the following interesting description of these divergences:

There are two main systems which are grouped around the ritual of the Ashkenazim, or Jews of Germany (Heb., *Ashkenaz*), and around that of the Sephardim, or Jews of Spain (Heb., *Sephard*). The Ashkenazic liturgy, which is by far the most extensively used, has undergone minor variations in Russia and Poland as well as in

ASHKENAZIM RABBI OF JERUSALEM

England and America; whilst the Sephardic ritual, which differs in the sequence of certain prayers and the text of others and shows a preference for the compositions of writers of Spanish origin, is exclusively employed by the descendants of the exiled Jews of Spain and Portugal, who migrated mostly to Turkey and the other lands washed by the Mediterranean, as well as, in smaller groups, to England and Holland, and even to various parts of North and South America. The Sephardic ritual has also undergone certain variations, the principal being the Castilian, the Aragonian, the Catalonian, and the Provençal, whilst further variations are found among the Jews of Arabia and Morocco. The Sephardim, moreover, who probably do not number more than half a million in all, differ from the Ashkenazim in their pronunciation of Hebrew, and attach less importance to an elaborately musical service. They have their own synagogues and their own independent Rabbis, but in all the essentials of faith and observance they acknowledge the same traditional authority as the majority of Jewry.[1]

These two systems are represented in Palestine to-day. All the aspects of Judaism, in fact, are to be found among the Jews; but whatever these may be, they have their roots in the ancient faith. Zionism derives its motive force from the history of the Jewish religion. The whole of Palestine is to the Jew a symbol of the great struggle.[2]

[1] Israel Cohen, *Jewish Life in Modern Times*, pp. 275, 276.

[2] The Jewish population of Palestine at the date of the Armistice was about 55,000. (Report of the High Commissioner on the Administration of Palestine, 1920–25, p. 29.) It was found to be 84,000 at the Census of October 1922 (Report and General Abstracts of the Census of 1922. Palestine Government, 1923), and was believed by the High Commissioner to have increased to about 108,000 in March, 1925. (Report of the High Commissioner, 1920–25, p. 30.) At the end of 1925 it was estimated by the Zionist Organization at 138,000. (Report on Palestine Administration, 1925, p. 71.) On September 1, 1926, the total population, exclusive of about 110,000 nomadic Badu, was officially estimated at 777,000, including 158,000 Jews (*Jewish Telegraph Agency Bulletin*, January 22, 1927), who thus constituted about twenty per cent of the settled inhabitants, as compared with just under thirteen per cent at the Census of 1922. (*Survey of International Affairs*, 1925, vol. i. Arnold J. Toynbee, *The Islamic World Since the Peace Settlement*, p. 375.)

On August 19, 1930, the Jewish Agency's figures showed that the Jewish population of Palestine was then 172,000, or twenty per cent of the total, and that from September 1, 1929, to July 31, 1930, 5671 Jews entered Palestine, including 4663 who came in on immigration certificates. (*Jewish Daily Bulletin*, August 20, 1930.)

CHAPTER VI

THE RELIGIOUS SETTING — (2) CHRISTIANITY

IF to the Anglo-Saxon the multitude of Western religious
differences is deplorable, the Christian religion in Palestine
is the *reductio ad absurdum* of sectarianism. Ecclesiastical
quarrels among the Churches is a notorious aspect of
Christianity in the Holy Land. The friction between the
sects permeates business, education, and all kinds of social
contact. It is not merely that there are so many varieties of
religious expression, as that their differences are so accented
in every petty detail. The pilgrim in Palestine is appalled
at the wide divergence between religious bigotry with its
abnormal hatreds, and the real spirit of Christianity which
Jesus so humbly illustrated in his teaching and living. Nowhere does the Christian pilgrim more greatly deplore the
jarring of creeds than in Palestine, the birthplace of Christianity, and the land of ancient promise for the Hebrew
prophets whose wonderful story is likewise claimed as part
of the sacred history of the Church.

The Christianity of Palestine seems in some strange way
to have defied the passing of centuries, for here we find an
illustrated history of the ecclesiastical disputes of Christendom from the days of the early Church to the present time.
As the strata of the crust of the earth tell something of what
was once vigorous life, so, likewise, the various churches and
monasteries of the city of Jerusalem give quiet testimony to
the historical conflicts of creeds and races.

Perhaps the oldest stratum represented in Jerusalem is
found in the monasteries of the ancient Abyssinian Church.
The Abyssinians, together with their slightly more sophisti-
cated brethren of the ancient Egyptian Church, called Copts
from their word for Egyptian, are known as 'monophysites,'
because of their unwillingness to accept the Western theory
of Christ's 'two natures,' one human and one divine; they
insist that his nature was one, wholly divine.

These two Churches drifted away from the main stream of

historical Christianity when that comparatively new religion was adopting Greek modes of theological thinking. The Abyssinian and Coptic mind evidently was not inclined to abstractions, so, like many a boy who prematurely drops out of school in order to handle the more concrete facts of life, these African churchmen early went their own way, content to ignore the abstruse Greek theorizings. With the Abyssinians, however, the germ of growth became somewhat withered; and in consequence, their Church, as we find it to-day, is but slightly changed from the time of its primitive origin. The childlike kindliness of these black monks was interestingly illustrated in 1920, while the Nebi Musa Festival and the Passover and Easter celebrations were taking place. When the abnormally excited populace, the Jews on one side pitted against the Christians and Moslems on the other, began to pillage and massacre, the sombre African ecclesiastics energetically rang their church bells — to drive away the demons of hate.

A living picture of the asceticism of the Middle Ages is preserved in the religious orders of monasticism, especially in the freer life of the Greek Orthodox faith. More removed from the conflicts of modern life than the Franciscans and the Dominicans of the Roman Church, they live in quiet and rather easy-going seclusion. At the Monastery of Mar Saba, perched picturesquely halfway up a perpendicular cliff in the Valley of the Kedron, where neither climbing up from below nor down from above appears physically possible; at the Monastery of the Temptation, high on a forbidding mountain back of Jericho, the traditional site of the temptation of Jesus, where monks disobedient to the rules of their order have been exiled to a strange troglodyte existence; at the Monastery of el-Hajlah, in the nauseatingly humid heat of the salt wilderness near the Dead Sea, where brackish water and a bleached desert leave man naught else to think of but God — in such places as these, the long-haired, much-bearded monks of the Greek faith seek the Kingdom of Heaven.

In marked contrast to the naïveté of the Greek Orthodox are the Franciscan and Dominican monasteries. The monks of these Roman Catholic orders are largely foreign — French,

Italian, and other nationals — who bring to the country a certain amount of outside culture. Having more or less of the missionary spirit, they have earnestly endeavored to learn the language and the customs of the Palestinians whom they have come to influence. And, because of the sacred associations of the land, the various monastic orders of the Roman Catholic Church have evidently sent to Palestine only their best. The Franciscans have long had large responsibility in maintaining the Catholic organization in the country; while the Dominicans have acquired an enviable reputation for scholarship.

Of the total number of Christians in Palestine, there are adherents of more than fourteen different historic communions. The most important in local prestige, and by far the largest numerically is the Greek Orthodox. The Roman Catholic, Maronite, Coptic, and Anglican Churches; the Armenian, Gregorian, Jacobite, and Abyssinian Churches, and their Uniate counterparts; as well as the Greek Uniate and the Nestorian Uniate, or Chaldean — all share in the principal shrines. The pageantry of ecclesiasticism is unending; but the tragedy of it all lies in the ever-present and repulsive friction. The old Turkish régime felt scorn for the quarrelling infidel, and realistically dealt out the peace by keeping military guards in the important churches.

Comic-tragic stories of the disunity are part of everyday gossip: there is the carpet in the Church of the Nativity at Bethlehem from which the priestly owners cut out a section to prevent the members of an opposing sect from walking across the carpet to the Crypt, the place of Christ's Nativity.[1] There is an occasional bit of excitement over the repair of a wall or column or tiling separating the property of two opposing sects: if the Armenians, for example, employ an

---

[1] The Roman Catholics had been granted the right by the Sultan, who possessed the title deed to the Church of the Nativity, to have a procession to the Crypt, the place of Christ's Nativity. Since the Latin Church lies diagonally from the Crypt, it would be necessary to cross the carpet which the Armenians, who had been granted by the same authority the left apse of the Basilica, had put in front of their altar. The Armenians protested against this; and sallying forth one night gave the carpet its diagonal shape. Thereupon, the sovereign power marked off a passage from the Latin Church to the semi-circular stairs leading to the Crypt, which henceforth might not be covered with a carpet.

The Sultan also held the title deed to the Church of the Holy Sepulchre.

Armenian to do the repairing, then the Greeks, or whatever the opposing sect may be, will have lost their claim to it. There are the scores of gossipy arguments about ecclesiastical questions, whose only logical conclusions would result in the strangling of sincere religion. The Syrian Maronite Church, for example, claims to be the true representative of God upon earth because it alone preserves its ritual in the ancient Syriac language, once spoken by Jesus of Nazareth. And often, when ecclesiastical arguments become heated, some person conveniently appears, avowing to have had a vision which satisfactorily settles the whole problem.

The Orthodox Patriarchate originated in the sub-apostolic Bishopric of Jerusalem. For some thirteen centuries, with varying fortunes, this Patriarchate represented a Christian minority living in the midst of a ruling Moslem civilization. Waves of persecution, poverty and galling limitations of freedom by Moslem overlords had weakened the dignity of the ecclesiastical office. Moslems were offended by the sound of Christian church bells, and for that reason they were not allowed to be rung; [1] the privilege of a prominent tomb with any structure built aboveground was reserved only for the Faithful; Christians were not permitted to ride upon horses, but must content themselves with those humbler animals whose slowness and other peculiarities have vexed every traveller in the Orient; and during considerable periods within the Moslem dominance, Christians paid higher taxes than the true followers of the Prophet.

Although these discriminations no longer exist, undoubtedly they have helped to shape the spirit of the present Patriarchal Church. Such continued oppression would obviously leave its marks. Moreover, because of the cutting-off of the revenues from Russia, brought in by the coming of vast numbers of Russian pilgrims to visit the holy shrines, the activities of the Church have been greatly reduced for

[1] Concerning the ringing of Christian church bells, the following, which appeared in the *Christian Science Monitor*, dated Belgrade, May 16, 1928, is an interesting statement: 'For nearly five centuries the sound of church bells was not heard in Serbia. Now, however, ringing of church bells on every side at Easter is generally regarded as a most natural thing. After the downfall of the Servian Empire at Kossovo in 1389, the Turks, who conquered Servia, refused in their Moslem fanaticism, to allow bells to be rung.'

lack of income. The War put a stop to this Russian pilgrimage,[1] in consequence of which the great church celebrations, such as the festival of the Baptism at the Jordan River near Jericho, the famous ceremonies of Easter Week, including the foot-washing of the assembled bishops, and the giving of the Holy Fire on Easter Eve, have dwindled perceptibly from their former greatness.

In addition to these trying circumstances, a deadlock arose between the Patriarch and his Synod, one underlying cause being the disproportionate authority of foreign priests. To relieve the vexed situation, the Mandatory Government appointed a Commission to inquire into the difficulties; and its Report, published by the Oxford University Press in 1921,[2] found in favor of the Patriarchate whose jurisdiction now covers practically all of Palestine and Trans-Jordan.[3]

During the Easter season, which, because of the two calendars, lasts about a fortnight, the Church of the Holy Sepulchre is the scene of an amazing diversity of Christian ceremonial. For fifteen days, the church is almost continually crowded. There is the celebration of, the Roman Catholics, or Latins, as they are commonly called in Jerusalem, and also the Easter Week celebration of the Eastern Churches.[4]

[1] It is recorded in the Report of the Palestine Administration for 1924 that: 'The arrival of a few Russian pilgrims is noteworthy.' (Colonial No. 12. Report by His Britannic Majesty's Government on the Administration Under Mandate of Palestine and Trans-Jordan for the year 1924, p. 58.)

Besides the cessation of the flow of pilgrims, confiscation of large landed properties belonging to the Orthodox Patriarchate in Russia and Rumania have seriously crippled the Convent finances. Ten thousand pounds were annually derived from one of these.

[2] Report of the Commission, appointed by the Government of Palestine to inquire into the affairs of the Orthodox Patriarchate of Jerusalem. The Commissioners were Sir Anton Bertram, Chief Justice of Ceylon, sometime Puisne Judge of the Supreme Court of Cyprus; and Harry Charles Luke, Assistant Governor of Jerusalem. Oxford University Press. 1921.

[3] On June 17, 1921, the Orthodox Patriarchate Ordinance was enacted. This Ordinance provided for the appointment of a Commission to liquidate the debts of the Patriarchate and for the recognition of the reconstructed Synod. (Cmd. 1499.) An Interim Report on the Civil Administration of Palestine, during the period 1st July, 1920–30th June, 1921, p. 24. Presented to Parliament by Command of His Majesty, August, 1921.

Legislation of Palestine, 1918–25. Compiled by Norman Bentwich, Attorney-General of Palestine. Orders-in-Council and Ordinances, vol. 1. p. 163.

[4] As our Easter is controlled by the moon and the vernal equinox, it follows that

The most spectacular of the Eastern ceremonies is the noonday service of the Holy Fire, which comes on Holy Saturday, by the Eastern calendar. In this ceremony, when the annual miracle is witnessed of the holy fire descending from Heaven on the tomb of Christ, the 'Orthodox' or 'Greek' Christians play the leading part, though the independent Armenian, Syrian, and Coptic Churches are also represented. Every one who sees this spectacle seems inclined to write about it; and we have in consequence several excellent narrations of this stirring performance.

A remarkably vivid description of the ceremony in 1922 is given by Philip Graves, and is well worth recording:

The Eastern Churches meet on Easter Eve in a religious festival that is Christian and particularly Oriental Christian. Copts, Syrians and Armenians share the same frenzy as the Orthodox Arabs of Palestine, wait in the same tense emotion for the coming of the sacred and absolutory fire, press with the same impatient longing against the cordon of guards that keeps the way clear for the Orthodox Patriarch to enter the Holy Sepulchre. When I watched the ceremony in 1922 the only reference to a secular monarch or Government that I heard was in the couplet roared out again and again by the waiting multitude before the entry of the Patriarch:

> 'Oh, King George, may you merry be,[1]
> God to our faith gives victory'

— to translate Arabic doggerel into English doggerel. And this was a reference to the fact that for the first time since the Crusades a Christian — and not a Moslem — ruled Palestine. And when the Patriarch laid down his crown, and cast off his outer robes before the Holy Place and entered in, an Armenian bishop followed him. It was a Copt who had bought the privilege of first receiving the fire as it flashed from the narrow loophole in the northern wall of the Sepulchre. Men of all the Eastern Churches shouted, gesticulated and swirled like waves in an eddying sea around Damianos the Patriarch, as, ringed round by his struggling guards, passing on the fire to the tapers thrust towards him by imploring hands, he

the nearer this occurs to March 21, the more space there will be between the Eastern and Western observance of the festivity. On the other hand, if it occurs on a date sufficiently removed from the equinox to allow of the thirteen days' difference between the Julian and Gregorian calendars the celebrations may synchronize — one indispensable requisite of the Orthodox Church being that it should not occur at the same time as the Jewish Passover.

[1] Mr. Fosdick, who witnessed the ceremony in 1926, records the throng as singing: 'O Jew! O Jew! Yours is the feast of the Devil, but ours is the feast of the Lord.' (Harry Emerson Fosdick, *A Pilgrimage to Palestine*, p. 263.)

fought through that maddened crowd like a white boat in a sea of night and fire to the safety of the High Altar. Three processions, each formed by the chiefs of an ancient Church — Armenians in flowered robes, brown-faced Copts in purple and crimson, Jacobite Syrians in green and amaranth — followed by their bishop, his face hidden by the folds of his pointed hood, gorgeous and mysterious in his robes of deep chrome, thrice circled chanting and rejoicing around the Holy Sepulchre. I have never seen a more moving and a more terrifying spectacle. One felt that on this one day the peoples that had lived for centuries under the yoke of the robber kings who came from Inner Asia, the men of the sword and the book, the Vice-regents of the Sultan of the Sky, forgot the yoke that had galled them, and the shadow of the poised sword, and exulted with the frenzy that follows long repression. And I think I shall never see anything more moving and more terrifying, unless one day I witness the sack of Constantinople by the Orthodox armies of the Balkans of Russia, and the first thanksgiving service held by their leaders under the dome of Santa Sophia.[1]

The ceremony of receiving the 'fire from heaven' is undoubtedly derived from the ritual of the very early Church. Bernard the Wise first mentions this ceremony, in the eighth century. In comparatively early Moslem literature, we find Arabs and Turks making merciless fun of the credulity of the Christian subjects. Upon one occasion, it is related, when a Moslem entered the tomb with the Bishops to await the coming of the fire, there was no miracle! Father Barnabas Meistermann, in his 'New Guide to the Holy Land,' refers to the ceremony as a 'base fraud' (p. 136; p. 86 in the original French). The Catholic Church, it might be noted, has no share in the celebration.

The same fanaticism attends the foot-washing ceremony on Maundy Thursday, when the Greek Patriarch, divested of his robes and girded with a towel, washes the feet of twelve Greek priests, while thousands of Christian pilgrims, Moslems, and Jews look on. The rite depicts the story of the Saviour, who, having finished the Last Supper, girded himself with a towel and washed the feet of his disciples (Matthew XIII. 5–12).[2] Let us read the description of the cere-

---

[1] Philip Graves, *Palestine, the Land of Three Faiths* (London: Jonathan Cape, Limited), pp. 93–95.

[2] An Associated Press despatch (*Boston Evening Transcript*, April 13, 1928), describing the 1928 ceremony, relates that: 'The Patriarch was divested of his mitre and ornate vestments and was girdled with a towel. A priest handed him a silver

mony as given by Mr. Fosdick who saw the performance in 1926:

A great concourse of people fills the beautiful court of the church and, from every possible ledge, roof, window, and balustrade within seeing distance, watches the famous scene. The diverse crowds at the first Pentecost (Acts II. 5–11) made a homogeneous assembly compared with the throng here now. They come from the ends of the earth to gather around this upraised platform where the Greek Patriarch of Jerusalem will wash the feet of his fellow-prelates. The expectant, chattering crowd, the pealing of the bells, the procession of ecclesiastics gorgeous in embroidered robes of rich brocade, the chanting, the reading of the Scripture, then the disrobing of the Patriarch and the formal washing of the feet — all this is obviously not a sobering performance but a show for most of the spectators. No hush pervades the throng as though a spiritual and genuine act of symbolic humility were being performed, and, while one recognizes in the scene an interesting survival of dramatic teaching, I, for one, felt chiefly the contrast between that first foot-washing somewhere in Jerusalem, so spontaneous, simple, and significant, and this ethically inconsequential performance. If only the ecclesiasticism represented here were known as a fountain of unselfish service, then the formal act might symbolize reality but, as it is, one spectator at least felt little of Christ — only Christianity.[1]

A Western Christian might well exclaim with Mr. Fosdick: 'And this is Christianity in the land of Christ!' [2] As for myself, this Eastern spectacle gives a painful shock to my previous conception of the Holy Land.

The Roman Catholic Church was first officially established in Jerusalem on the capture of the city in 1099, by the Crusaders. For two hundred years the Roman Patriarchate and the Latin Kingdom of Jerusalem were closely united. On the capture of the city by Saladin in 1187, the Patriarchs were removed to Acre; and when that famous fortress fell in 1291, the Patriarchate was laid down. Not until 1847 was it revived, when Pope Pius IX was able to reëstablish the office in Jerusalem.

gilt basin and ewer, the gift of a Russian emperor. The Greek holy father then knelt and in turn washed the bared right foot of each of the twelve priests. When it came "Peter's" turn he refused the ceremony, saying: "Thou shalt never wash my feet." But the bearded Patriarch insisted, repeating the words of Jesus Christ. "If I wash thee not, thou hast no part with me." The scene was then shifted in imagination to the Garden of Gethsemane, while the Patriarch and his twelve assistants reproduced the last hours on earth of Christ.'

[1] Harry Emerson Fosdick, *A Pilgrimage to Palestine*, pp. 264–65.

[2] *Ibid.*, p. 264.

The impressiveness of the Catholic faith, as it is seen in Palestine to-day, is emphasized by its missionary zeal and by the high quality of much of its leadership. Among the members are notable linguists, historians, archeologists, and educators. Some Catholic scholars exercise a surprising amount of intellectual freedom. The Roman Catholics have been longer in the country as missionaries than the Protestants; and they have made many more converts. In several Christian villages, especially the more prosperous, such as Bethlehem, Nazareth, and Ramallah, a considerable proportion of the Greek Orthodox Palestinians have gone over to the Catholic faith; and in the cities, Catholic schools, with comparatively low tuition and organized charities of various sorts, continue to win new converts. Among the Churches not native to the country, only the Catholics and the several branches of Protestantism have gained proselytes. The non-Palestinian Oriental churches are established only for the sake of representation at the different shrines and for the convenience of pilgrims.[1]

There are many Roman Catholic religious Orders represented in Palestine. It was the Franciscan Order which cared for the holy shrines and the religious welfare of Catholic pilgrims when no Roman Patriarch could officiate in the city. The Father Custodian came to have a sort of episcopal jurisdiction; he administered confirmation and the minor orders; was privileged to the Latin Order of the Holy Sepulchre on behalf of its Grand Master, the Pope; and he had the right to maintain a merchant marine flying the flag of Terra Santa. At the present time, the Franciscan Fathers Custodians are appointed for a period of six years by the General of the Order, and are always of Italian nationality. Appointed also are a French Vicar, a Spanish Procurator, and a Council of Four composed of an Englishman, a Frenchman, an Italian, and a Spaniard.

The Order was founded by Saint Francis of Assisi, the 'little' friend to all. Saint Francis did not wish to found a monastic Order of brethren who should have all things in

---

[1] Some two hundred years ago, the Catholics, desiring to strengthen their community in Palestine, offered houses free of rent to any one who desired to come to the country. This led to a similar offer by the other communities.

common; he desired to have his followers embrace complete poverty, holding neither money nor other property, but begging their bread, and living lives of constant service for the sick and the poor.

After the great leader's death, there was a long struggle inside the Franciscan movement to maintain apostolic poverty; and one whole section, in their fanatic assertion of the fundamental Franciscan doctrine, was finally persecuted by the Church, and whole groups of them burned by order of the Inquisition. The Order, in time, acquired estates and regular income. But in spite of the change from their Master's way of life, the Franciscans have always been the willing servants of the needy; and their rope girdle perpetuates the symbol of giving up all material comfort in the service of 'Christ's poor.'

In addition to the Franciscans, many Roman Catholic religious Orders are represented in Palestine. There are the Dominicans with their admirable library and the École Biblique in the Convent of Saint Stephen at Jerusalem; the Discalced Carmelites, who take their name from the parent house on Mount Carmel; the Benedictines, Salesians, White Fathers, Lazarists, Passionists, and Assumptionists. Among the Orders for women are the Franciscans, Benedictines, Carmelites, Clarisses, Dames de Sion, Sœurs Reparatrices, Sœurs de Saint Vincent de Paul, and others.[1]

The White Fathers are the guardians of the Pool of Bethesda, where Christ healed the sick man on a Sabbath.[2] Although this is only mentioned in the fifth chapter of Saint John, one is prone to consider the place genuinely associated with Christ's ministry. It is rectangular in shape and has the five porches, as described in the Gospel; and besides this, the White Father who shows the place to visitors confidently supports the view of Père Vincent that this is Bethesda. Standing at the edge of the pool, I vividly pictured that helpless mass of humanity who sought the Master's healing; and there I felt the humility of standing in the footsteps of Jesus.

[1] *The Handbook of Palestine*, p. 43. Edited by Harry Charles Luke and Edward Keith-Roach, 1922.

[2] John v: 2–9.

A Christian pilgrimage, conducted by the Franciscan friars, takes place every Friday afternoon. The pilgrimage follows the Via Dolorosa, which the Franciscans, and many others, believe to be the route over which Jesus walked to his Crucifixion. The procession stops for prayer at nine stations of the Cross, and passes into the Basilica of the Holy Sepulchre, where four stations are made at Calvary, the last of the fourteen stations being before the Holy Sepulchre itself. The pilgrimage is attended by many Latin Orders. 'Franciscan friars in brown habits and with waists girt about with knotted cords; Dominican fathers in white; the White Fathers; Passionists wearing the sign of the heart; nuns in habits of white, black, and silver-gray, their veils and head-dresses of all descriptions, go in procession, followed by the laity.' [1]

Of the various Uniate Churches (Eastern Churches acknowledging the general supremacy of the Pope, but preserving in a greater or lesser degree their own liturgies and customs) the following are represented in Palestine: Melchites, Maronites, Armenian Uniates, Nestorian Uniates or Chaldeans, Jacobite Uniates or Syrians, and Abyssinian Uniates. These churches are represented in Palestine by very small flocks, principally resident in Jerusalem. Their presence in the Holy City is due to the famous shrines in whose veneration they share.

The most considerable of these communities as regards Palestine is that of the Melchites, who have a seminary connected with the Church of Saint Anne in Jerusalem, governed since 1878 by the White Fathers.

The Armenian Uniates possess a handsome cathedral in Jerusalem (Our Lady of the Spasm). The jurisdiction of the Armenian (Gregorian) Patriarch of Jerusalem extends over that communion in Palestine, Cyprus, and parts of Syria. From early times there has been a Bishop of that Church in Jerusalem, where the Armenians have a community of some hundreds which enjoys the ownership or part ownership of several of the Holy Places. Their Cathedral of Saint James the Less, together with a vast patriarchal property — schools, gardens, and chapels — occupies most of the southwest

[1] Major Edward Keith-Roach, 'The Pageant of Jerusalem.' *The National Geographic Magazine*, December, 1927, p. 672.

corner of the old city and forms the largest conventual enclosure in Palestine.[1]

The wealth of this property is a matter of much comment. Local gossip has it that during the War the Armenians took all their gold and silver from the cathedral in large boxes and left them in a cellar, marking them 'Bricks'; the Turks, seeking much-needed booty, scoured the cathedral in vain, naïvely supposing the crated articles to be genuine bricks. Whether or not the story is true, it gives an intimation of the feeling of the Arab regarding the comparative cleverness of the Armenian and the Turk. It is a common saying in Arabic that 'it takes two Jews to beat one Greek in trade, but it takes two Greeks to beat one Armenian.'

The Jacobites date back to the sixth century. There is a Jacobite Bishop, assisted by a Suffragan, with the residence built around the traditional house of Saint Mark in Jerusalem. The Copts, or Egyptian Christians, are in communion with the Jacobites.[2]

In the heart of Africa, the black Abyssinian Christians have preserved the Christianity to which they were converted, according to tradition, in the fourth century. We have already seen how the primitive ideas of the Abyssinian Church are reflected in the kindly deeds of these Christians, living in the midst of the warring Christian sects in Palestine. The Abyssinians are loosely bound to the Coptic communion; the 'Abuna' of Ethiopia, who is the head of the church in the Abyssinian capital at Adis Abeba, is an appointee of the Coptic Metropolitan of Alexandria. The Abyssinians are represented in Jerusalem, in common with the other Christian Episcopal Churches. They have two important convents, one of which is situated on the roof of Saint Helena's Chapel in the Church of the Holy Sepulchre.

The official representation of the Anglican Faith is the

[1] *The Handbook of Palestine*, pp. 43, 44. Edited by Harry Charles Luke and Edward Keith-Roach. 1922.

[2] Copt, Qupt in the language of the Church, in Greek was written Egypt, from which we have received our word. Cf. the popular term Gypsy, with the initial *E* again lost. The first Coptic Metropolitan was appointed in the middle of the thirteenth century. The episcopal residence adjoins the eastern end of the Church of the Holy Sepulchre, and there is a large convent at Jaffa, principally intended for the accommodation of the pilgrims coming from Egypt.

youngest of the important ecclesiastics of Jerusalem. The first Bishop was consecrated in accordance with the 'Jerusalem Bishopric Act' of 1841.[1] The aims and procedure of the founders of the original Bishopric in 1841 constitute an interesting event in Church history.

Bishop MacInnes cites the following interesting narrative:

The failure of several attempts on the part of Lutheran Germany to secure episcopal orders through Rome led King Frederick William IV of Prussia to approach England with the purpose of founding a Bishopric in Jerusalem in the hope of attaining that object, and in 1841 it was founded. Its income was provided by £600 a year, the interest of an endowment fund raised in England, and a further £600, the interest of a capital sum set aside from the privy purse of the King of Prussia. The nomination to the See thus provided for was alternately with England and Prussia; the Archbishop of Canterbury nominating for England to the Crown, and having the right of veto on the Prussian nomination.

The Bishopric, as then founded, was unpopular with many churchmen on account of its connexion with a non-episcopal communion, and from their failure to appreciate the difference between episcopal jurisdiction as exercised in the West, where it is territorial, and in the East, where several Bishops rule in the same area, each over members of their own communion. This led to the unfounded fear that there was an intrusion on the rights of the Orthodox Patriarch as Bishop of Jerusalem.

A further failure to obtain episcopal orders for the Lutherans resulted in the withdrawal of Prussia from the contract (together with the portion of income guaranteed by the King) on the death of Bishop Barclay in 1881, when the Bishopric fell into abeyance for nearly six years.

After considerable inquiry and much careful thought Archbishop Benson revived the See as an Anglican Bishopric; and Dr. Blyth,

[1] Bill, intituled An Act to amend an Act made in the Twenty-sixth Year of the Reign of His Majesty King George the Third intituled, 'An Act to empower the Archbishop of Canterbury or the Archbishop of York for the time being to consecrate to the Office of a Bishop Persons being Subjects or Citizens of Countries out of his Majesty's Dominions.' Accounts and Papers, vol. I. 1841. Bills, Public; Reports from Committees; and Reports from Commissioners. Session 19 August — 7 October 1841, pp. 73–75. Bill (as amended by the Committee) intituled, etc., pp. 77–79.

The 'Jerusalem Bishopric Act,' passed in 1841, sanctioned the consecration (in England) of Bishops for places outside the British Dominions. The Act was used not only for the first consecration of an Anglican Bishop in Jerusalem, but under its provisions all other such Bishops have since been consecrated, the King giving his mandate to the Archbishop of Canterbury in each case.

The first Anglican Bishop was Michael Solomon Alexander, a convert from Judaism.

then Archdeacon of Rangoon, was consecrated Bishop of the Church of England in Jerusalem on the 25th March, 1887, the Orthodox Patriarch of Jerusalem having said that it was 'necessary that a Bishop of the Church of England... should be placed in this Holy City.' Ever since that date the Anglican Bishopric has been growing more and more part of the religious life of the city, until it now holds a position which is unique in opportunity for promoting a good understanding among its many churches.

The aims of the Bishopric may be summed up as follows: To represent the Anglican Church as worthily as possible amongst the other Churches represented in the Holy City; to cultivate relations of friendship and sympathy with the ancient Churches of the East, always remembering the Redeemer's prayer, 'that they all may be one'; to provide churches and chaplains for Anglican communities within the diocese; and to present the Christian Faith in its fulness to non-Christians and to commend the Faith by two special means, the training and education of the young, and the healing of the sick.[1]

The British Mission, known as the 'Jerusalem and the East Mission,' is especially interested in the education of the young, both by means of its own schools, and in coöperation with other societies. It maintains the English College for young men and Saint George's School for Boys. The British High School for Girls in Jerusalem is maintained by the Jerusalem and the East Mission, by the London Jews' Society, both of which supported their independent Girls' Schools in Jerusalem before the War, and by the Church Missionary Society.

In addition to the Cathedral Church of Saint George the Martyr, there are other churches and British or Palestinian clergy and congregations in Jerusalem; so also in Gaza, Jaffa, Ramleh, Bethlehem, al Salt (Trans-Jordan), Ramallah, Nablus, Haifa and Nazareth, besides various other places in the country districts, as well as in Cyprus and Syria. Much of the work among the Arabs is carried on through the Church Missionary Society; while in Jerusalem, especially, work is done by the London Society for Promoting Christianity among the Jews.[2]

---

[1] *The Handbook of Palestine*, pp. 46, 47. Edited by Harry Charles Luke and Edward Keith-Roach. 1922.

An Outline of the Activities of the Anglican Church in Palestine, pp. 5, 6.

[2] As to the efficacy of this work, Hyamson says, in speaking of the efforts of the house of industry conducted by the society for improving the condition of unem-

The English Order of Saint John of Jerusalem is represented in Palestine by the Ophthalmic Hospital in Jerusalem, which offers service alike to Moslems, Jews, and Christians. The Order, which has fitted up the Chapel of Saint John of Jerusalem in Saint George's Cathedral, enjoys through the courtesy of the Orthodox Patriarch, the privilege of holding services in the crypt of the Orthodox Church of Saint John the Baptist in the old city.

The Anglican Church, because of its rich ritual, its kindly leniency toward Oriental environment, and its sincere concern with a real Christian brotherhood ministering to the needs of the East, presents without doubt the strongest appeal to Church unity of any force working in Palestine to-day.

A picture in Jerusalem which I shall never forget is the quiet, restful scene surrounding the Cathedral of Saint George's Close. One might for the moment imagine himself transplanted to an English cathedral town, so suggestive is this picture of British cathedrals. The scene is beautifully portrayed in a photograph taken by the American Colony Photographers, which brings out in clear detail the 'Latin campaniles, bulbous Slavic domes, solid Teutonic architecture, and Gothic towers,' 'a touch of England in a cosmopolitan capital.' [1]

In contrasting the fanatical and artificial customs of the

ployment among the Jews in the middle of the last century: 'It was doomed to inefficacy from its initiation. The conversionist movement has never had the slightest success among the Jews of the Holy Land, despite their extreme poverty. The institution aroused suspicion on account of its sponsors, and the Jews of Palestine preferred death from starvation to living by bread which to them was tainted.' (Albert M. Hyamson, *Palestine: The Rebirth of an Ancient People*, pp. 71, 72.)

On the subject of missionary activity among the Jews, Cohen says: 'Until the beginning of the nineteenth century the efforts of missionaries to convert the Jews were carried on only sporadically, but since the establishment in 1809 of the London Society for the Propagation of Christianity amongst the Jews missionary societies have sprung up in all parts of the world. There are now 112 Protestant missionary societies, employing 816 missionary workers — mostly converted Jews — at 229 stations.... Between the years 1863 and 1894 the London Society spent from £600 to £3000 upon the conversion of a single Jew; and in 1898 it spent £28,439 upon the baptism of 28 Jews.' (Israel Cohen, *Jewish Life in Modern Times*, pp. 295, 296.)

See also: *Missions to Jews*, by the late Rev. W. T. Gidney, M.A. (London, 1912.) Jewish Encyclopædia, vol. IV, p. 252. *Judentaufen im 19 Jahrhundert*, von Dr. N. Samter (Berlin, 1906), p. 64.

[1] Major Edward Keith-Roach, 'The Pageant of Jerusalem.' *The National Geographic Magazine* (December, 1927), p. 647.

Eastern Christians with the Knights of Saint John, Mr. Fosdick relates:

> The Knights of Saint John, lineal descendants of the old crusaders, made a pilgrimage to Palestine while we were there. In full panoply they worshiped in the Anglican cathedral at Jerusalem, and the bishop preached the sermon. It was a simple, Christian homily with no false glorification of a checkered past, concerned with real issues of the spirit, and in particular pleading for the Ophthalmic Hospital in Jerusalem. That was a crusade of service startlingly different from the old assault by arms in which the forefathers of these knightly pilgrims once engaged upon this very spot. From the Knights of Saint John sacking Jerusalem to the Knights of Saint John building ophthalmic hospitals in the Holy City for Moslems, Jews, and Christians alike is a great advance. Perhaps our children's children yet may see Christ genuinely honored in this city that he loved, where for centuries he has been crucified.[1]

It is comforting to see even the slightest evidence of religious harmony in the Holy Land. There are, happily, some instances of true brotherliness, among which may be cited the celebration of the Festival at the Tomb of Simon the Just. Every spring, Christians and Moslems, as well as Jews, assemble at the Tomb which is situated in the north end of Jerusalem. Simon, a Jewish scribe, was one of a line who passed on the oral law given to Moses, which was not recorded in the Pentateuch.[2] So, too, is the tolerance displayed by the Moslem guardians of the mosque [3] on the summit of the Mount of Olives, in turning over the chapel for Mass to Christian priests on certain days of the year, another illustration of religious harmony.

There are many shrines in Jerusalem sacred to more than one religion. A conspicuous example of such is the Cænaculum or Tomb of David in the southern part of Jerusalem. So fully has local Islam adopted David and his tomb that the clan of impoverished Moslem Arabs dwelling in this district has taken the name — the Dahûdi family. They claim that they are David's royal descendants; and, with a typically Oriental view of history, say that King David was a follower of Mo-

---

[1] Harry Emerson Fosdick, *A Pilgrimage to Palestine*, pp. 269–70.

[2] Major Edward Keith-Roach, 'The Pageant of Jerusalem.' *The National Geographic Magazine* (December, 1927), p. 673.

[3] Formerly the Christian Church of the Ascension.

hammed. The shrine itself has numerous legends associated with it. In the Middle Ages, it was supposed to be the house of the Virgin Mary and the place where the Last Supper was celebrated.

The Gothic church which marks the spot was built in the middle of the fourteenth century, probably by Cypriote masons. It was first in possession of the Augustinian canons and afterwards of the Franciscans, who, until they were expelled by the Turks, cared for the relics found there. Since 1547, the church has belonged to the Moslems, who allow all pilgrims to visit the 'Upper Chamber,' but to the lower room, which is alleged to contain the Tomb of David, it pleases the fanaticism of the local community to withhold admittance to all but believers in the true Faith.

Passing through the crowded markets to the northwest side of the city, we wended our way through narrow streets and alleyways to the Church of the Holy Sepulchre. This was my first visit to this unique edifice. With the exception of the southern façade, it is concealed from view by the many monasteries, chapels, and other ecclesiastical buildings built around the structure. The holy sites, still believed recognizable as late as the fourth century, are marked by small separate churches, chapels, shrines, and monasteries, all of which are embraced in one large Romanesque church, erected by the Crusaders. In 1799, a great part of the church was rebuilt, and nine years after, it was almost destroyed by fire. Another rebuilding followed in 1810; and in 1927, the dome, which was badly cracked by the earthquake of that year, was taken down. In the 1928 Report on the Administration of Palestine, it is stated that 'plans have been made for the reconstruction of the dome of the Catholicon of the Church of the Holy Sepulchre, to repair the ravages of time and the damage caused by the earthquake of 1927.' [1]

In the courtyard of the Church of the Holy Sepulchre, near the entrance, we paused at the tomb of Philip d'Aubigny, mediæval crusader, and the tutor of Henry the Third of England. This was encased by a grating, which, my guide in-

[1] Colonial No. 40. Report by His Majesty's Government in the United Kingdom of Great Britain and Northern Ireland to the Council of the League of Nations on the Administration of Palestine and Trans-Jordan for the year 1928, p. 98.

formed me, was put up to protect the tombstone from the inroads of pilgrims after six hundred and eighty-nine years of wear and tear.[1]

We succeeded in extricating ourselves from the numerous peddlers and beggars in the courtyard of the church and entered the Christian edifice. Just inside the vestibule sat a Moslem doorkeeper, who locks up the building every night and opens it in the morning. For nearly seven hundred years, no Christian has held the keys to the Church of the Holy Sepulchre. One must accustom one's self to such incongruities if he would understand the real significance of this Christian Church. So, too, must one adjust his thinking to Eastern ways, if he would save himself the jars and shocks experienced by the Westerner, in contrasting the uses to which the church is put with the Western idea of reverence for religious buildings. One learns with astonishment, for example, that at Easter time pilgrims often remain all night in this sacred building. An excellent picture, photographed by the American Colony photographer,[2] shows the Moslem guardian locking the door, which contains a round hole through which food is passed to pilgrims who spend the night in the church.

The interior of the church is divided into two principal parts, the rotunda and the Orthodox cathedral. We stopped in the rotunda, directly under the great central dome, to view the small shrine covering the Tomb of Christ — the Holy Sepulchre itself, the Fourteenth or final Station of the Cross. This is divided into two chambers. The first, called the Angel's Chapel, contains the stone, said to be the one rolled away by the angel. As we went forward through a low doorway we came to the Tomb itself, marked by a cracked marble slab used as an altar for the Mass which is said there daily; then we ascended a steep flight of stairs to Golgotha, where,

---

[1] Philip d'Aubigny's tomb was until recently covered by a masonry seat, which, being removed within living man's memory, disclosed the tombstone protruding above the pavement a couple of inches. Then, fearing that the inscription would be worn out by being constantly walked over, it was lowered and protected by the grating.

[2] The picture illustrates the text of an article by Harold J. Shepstone, entitled 'Treasures of the Holy Sepulchre.' Mr. Shepstone relates, that he has seen the doorkeeper sipping coffee and smoking cigarettes, 'which, to say the least,' he says, 'is deportment hardly in good taste within a sacred building.' (*Asia*, May, 1928, p. 398.)

as every visitor is told, the cross was erected upon which Christ was crucified.

Descending a flight of steps from the apse, we came to the Chapel of Saint Helena, named after Queen Helena, mother of Constantine, who believed that she had located the place where Christ was crucified. There was no record concerning the site of the Crucifixion before Queen Helena came to Jerusalem in the year 325.

Meistermann, who accepts the legend of the finding of the Cross, relates:

> When Saint Helena came to Jerusalem to seek for the Cross of the Redeemer, Eusebius of Cæsarea and Saint Marcarius, Bishop of Jerusalem, knowing the laws and customs of the Jews, were aware that to find it they must dig up the ground about Golgotha. The instruments of death were discovered in a neighbouring cistern filled with earth. A double miracle, the instantaneous recovery of a dying woman and the raising to life of a dead man by the mere touch of one of the three crosses made known, says Eusebius and Saint Cyril, the one on which our divine Master died.[1]

According to tradition, the search was carried on by Helena's orders; and in the Chapel of Saint Helena there is the chair in which, it is alleged, the Empress sat. Simple-minded pilgrims believe this to be genuine, although it has been renewed several times.

Going down another flight of stairs, we were in the Chapel of the Finding of the Cross, which really has the appearance of an old cavern. It was here that the three broken crosses were found. The church holds among its treasures two heavily bejewelled crosses said to contain fragments of the cross on which Christ died.

Coming back toward the entrance, we glanced at the Chapels of Melchizedek and Adam; but at Golgotha, with its many altars, we stood for several minutes, keenly conscious of the animosities of the owners of these places of veneration, and painfully impressed with the deception of the priests as they play upon the credulity of the pilgrim. We were solemnly told, as we again looked at the alleged spot where the cross stood upon which the Saviour was crucified, that his

---

[1] Meistermann, *New Guide to the Holy Land*, p. 132. (In the original French, p. 82.)

blood seeped through the earth at the foot of the cross, reached the skull of Adam who was buried there, and thus washed away the sins of the whole world.

We saw the statue of the Virgin in the Chapel of Calvary, with its vulgar decoration of jewels, said to be the most costly statue of the Virgin in the world. This, the pilgrim is told, is the traditional spot where Mary received the body of Christ; and adjoining is the Chapel of the Nailing to the Cross where Christ was disrobed and crucified — marking the Tenth and Eleventh Stations of the Cross.

Lastly, we were taken to the Stone of Unction, upon which, visitors are told, the body of Christ was anointed and prepared for burial. Four different sects own this slab, over which burn a number of lamps. Although the stone has changed ownership many times, and has been seen in different localities, the Latin priests solemnly assert that this is the authentic stone, standing on the original spot.

I had no desire to see more of this; there seemed little else but fallacy and superstition in it all, and I rejoiced with many another Christian pilgrim that perhaps after all this was not the authentic spot of Christ's Crucifixion. I felt the need of quiet reflection.

As I now look back on my visit to the Church of the Holy Sepulchre, owned and occupied in fact by six Christian sects,[1] I am inclined to regard the place with less repulsion. More than this, when I picture those centuries of Christian oppression, I almost wonder that there is not more fanaticism, and even greater friction. We must admit in truth that in this church there is a Christian faith, abused and distorted as it obviously is, but nevertheless a faith expressing in outward form the Eastern conception of Christianity. Is it, I often ask myself, too much to hope that these various creeds and liturgies, having their home under one roof, to-day clashing in strife and discord painful beyond expression to one who goes to this holiest of Christian shrines in humble devotion, may some day compose a rich synthesis? This I conceive to be the future ideal of the Eastern Churches, toward the attainment of which Western Christians have a great opportunity for service.

[1] Greek, Latin, Armenian, Copt, Jacobite, Abyssinian.

From the Church of the Holy Sepulchre, we walked along the Via Dolorosa. Although there is little evidence to substantiate the authenticity of the present route, it is an interesting experience to walk over its course as it twists in and out and follows the rise and fall of the hills on which Jerusalem is built, all the while remembering that the present way is many feet above the true 'Way of the Cross.'

Above the Via Dolorosa, near the alleged site of the Prætorium, curves the Ecce Homo Arch, so called because it is claimed to be a part of the Prætorium where Pilate uttered his memorable words. This is the middle section of a triple arch which formerly curved over the roadway leading into the city from Saint Stephen's Gate.

On the north side of the street is the church and convent of the Sisters of Zion. We were conducted through the building by one of the Sisters, who led us down to the ancient level. We walked over the pavement on which we saw designs for games of draughts and marbles, supposed to be made by the Roman soldiers of the Tower of Antonia; and we were taken to the very spot, so the Sister told us, where Jesus was condemned. We bought a picture of the chapel which the Sisters reverently show as the site of Pilate's court. Before we left, we were reassured of the authenticity of it all by a breezy, bright-faced Sister from New York, who seemed delighted to see some of her own countrymen.

Although the most authentic archeological opinion places Pilate's court in the old palace of Herod, in the small square just inside the Jaffa Gate where David Street enters, we could indeed feel only reverence for the place venerated by the Sisters, for Jesus undoubtedly walked here.

One is constrained to worship on the Mount of Olives, regardless of the churches and convents which crowd the sacred place. Jesus came here; on this Mount he spoke of suffering and death, and in the village upon its eastern slope, at Bethany, his disciples saw the same Jesus bring to Lazarus life anew. Overlooking the brow of Scopus, at Anathoth, Jeremiah was born, who for over forty years preached to Judah. It was the words of Jeremiah that Jesus quoted when he cleansed the Temple in Jerusalem.[1]

[1] Seventh chapter of Jeremiah.

The very location of the Mount of Olives inspires reverence. Situated on the eastern side of the valley of the Kedron,
2680 feet above Jerusalem, the highest point near the Holy
City in the divide between the streams which flow westward
into the Mediterranean and those which rush toward the east
into the deep valley of the Dead Sea, the Mount of Olives
gives in its panorama a rare contrast of fertility and of death.
To the west lie the gently descending hillsides which capture
the moist winds from the Mediterranean, a landscape of
springs, gardens, fruit trees, and in the distance the rich plain,
with the ancient city in the foreground. But to the east rise
the bare, brown ranges, one after another settling deeper and
deeper in the hot valley; while at the bottom is the salt desert
and the 'Sea of Lot,' the lowest spot on the face of the earth.
How much, one might well ask, has Nature influenced the
history of this region! At least we may say: How appropriately has history conformed to its background!

Somewhere on the western slope of the Mount of Olives,
overlooking the Temple area, was the place where Jesus
stopped, with his disciples, the night of his arrest. The
Garden of Gethsemane, which got its name from an oil-press,
is now divided into two areas. One contains the Russian
Church, and the other the new Franciscan Basilica. It was
somewhere in Gethsemane that Peter, James, and John fell
asleep while Jesus prayed, and Judas gave the kiss of betrayal. The twisted olive trees in the Franciscan quarter of
the Garden are said to be those under which Jesus prayed.

It was a wonderful ride down to Bethlehem, five and a half
miles south of Jerusalem. Leaving by automobile, twenty-
five hundred feet above sea level, and traversing the main
road from Jerusalem toward Hebron, we passed many sites
associated with sacred history. Our guide pointed out the
Hill of Evil Council, on the top of which is seen the queer-
shaped tree upon which Judas is said to have hanged himself.
We soon came to the plain of El Bukaa, now generally accepted as the Valley of Rephaim, the scene of much of the
fighting between David and the Philistines.

Farther on, we saw the Greek Monastery of Mar Elias, occupying a conspicuous position on a hill. The Fathers here
declare that their monastery marks the site of the refuge of the

Prophet Elijah, although it is well known that the monastery was founded by a certain Bishop Elias, the date of which, however, being uncertain. In support of their claim, the monks point out the rock on which Elijah rested when fleeing from Jezebel to Beersheba, and they actually point to a depression in the rock which they claim to have been made by the Prophet's body.

About half a mile farther down the road, we came to the Tomb of Rachel, where the road forks from the main highway, the route to the left going to Bethlehem which is but a few minutes' ride to the southeast. This tomb is accepted by many scholars as the burial-place of Rachel. In Genesis we read how 'Rachel died, and was buried in the way to Ephrath, which is Bethlehem. And Jacob set a pillar upon her grave: that is the pillar of Rachel's grave unto this day.' [1]

Just before we reached Bethlehem, we came to David's Well, enclosed with an iron gate. This is the 'well of Bethlehem, which is by the gate,' from which 'the three mighty men' who 'brake through the host of the Philistines... drew water... and took it, and brought it to David.' [2]

We drove on to the market-place of Bethlehem. The birthplace of Christ and of King David is now a town of sixty-two hundred inhabitants, mostly Christians. The steep and narrow streets, the mediæval dress of the women, and the attractive brightly colored orange turbans of the men present a picturesque sight to be found nowhere else in Palestine.

About the town of Bethlehem, 'The House of Lehem,' some deity of ancient Canaan associated with bread [3] or meat, clusters a multitude of historical anecdotes and poetic aspirations. Here lived David, and because he had lived here, the

---

[1] Genesis xxxv: 19, 20.

[2] 'And David longed, and said, Oh, that one would give me drink of the water of the well of Bethlehem, which is by the gate!' (II Samuel xxiii: 14–17.)

See the picture of the Psalmist's Well in Bethlehem. American Colony Photographers, *The National Geographic Magazine* (December, 1926), p. 748.

[3] The Hebrew meaning of Bethlehem is 'The House of Bread.' Here the bread from heaven came to earth to give life to the world. It is said that the primeval home of the wild wheat has not been found, whereas that of all the other cereals has. About forty years ago some one recorded finding wild wheat in the Lebanon; ten years later, another person found some in Galilee. Our Mr. Dinsmore was the first to find it in Judea! This land then yielded the cereal that supports all life — and the bread from heaven. (Jacob E. Spafford.)

House of David came to be thought of as the House, par excellence, of Bethlehem.[1] Sheep still graze in the fields outside the town, and the shepherd boy, like David of old, uses his flute to call his wandering flock. It was the experience which David gained here as a shepherd that led him to write the Twenty-Third Psalm: 'The Lord is my shepherd...'

Jesus of Nazareth was born in Bethlehem, and as one moves about these hills it is with thoughts of wise men, and shepherds, and angels, and glory and peace, and good-will. With the devout pilgrim, these thoughts persist, even in the midst of the sordid conflicts of the sects which elbow one another in the shrines which commemorate the angelic good-will!

Entering into the diminutive doorway of the Basilica of the Nativity, erected over the traditional birthplace of Christ, I lost all sense of architecture. I was simply imbued with the idea of standing inside the oldest Christian Church still in use. We descended the semi-circular staircase to the Grotto, marking the place where Christ was born. This is forty feet long, twelve feet wide, and ten feet high. At the bottom of the staircase, on the left, is an altar; and in the floor we saw the silver star, said to mark the exact spot of Christ's birth. Over this star fifteen lamps burn constantly. Six belong to the Greeks, five to the Armenians, and four to the Latins.

This star, which bears the inscription, 'Hic de Virgine Maria Jesus Christus natus est,' has been the cause of much trouble among the Greeks and Latins. It has disappeared at various times. The Greeks removed it in 1847 because the inscription was in Latin and not in Greek. This brought on a long diplomatic dispute, since neither of the sects nor the Powers representing them would allow a rival to replace the star, for fear that whoever should do so would claim ownership. The matter was finally settled by the then ruling Sultan of Turkey, who presented the church with a star similar to the one which had disappeared. One begins to see the real force of religion in the Holy Land![2]

[1] 'But thou, Beth-lehem Ephratah, though thou be little among the thousands of Judah, yet out of thee shall he come forth unto me that is to be ruler in Israel; whose goings forth have been from of old, from everlasting.' (Micah v: 2.)

[2] The rivalry between the Greeks and Romans dates back to 1620, when the Sultan formally granted to the King of France the protection of all Christians in Palestine and gave the Roman Catholic ecclesiastics certain rights in the Holy Places.

Opposite the altar are three steps leading down to the Chapel of the Manger. There is here a marble manger hung with lamps, to mark the spot where Mary laid her child. In the manger a wax effigy of an infant is placed after the midnight Mass on Christmas Eve.

As Easter is the great festival of the Jerusalem Christians, so Christmas brings to Bethlehem vast throngs of pilgrims. The Roman Catholics celebrate the Western date, with a great processional and a climactic ritual which begins at dusk on the twenty-fourth of the month, and reaches a dramatic climax at midnight, when a curtain covering the image of an infant is withdrawn: Jesus natus est! This image, or the beautiful wax doll that it is, remains in the Grotto twelve days. Thirteen days after the Latin celebration comes the Greek service; while thirteen days later comes the Armenian Christmas feast. Thousands of tourists and natives visit this little town of the Nativity to take part in the Christmas celebrations.

Next to Jerusalem and Bethlehem, Nazareth [1] is the most beloved of the Christian shrines. It is a beautiful town upon the Galilean hills just north of the Plain of Esdraelon. Situated just off the main road from Haifa on the coast to Tiberias, the principal town on the Sea of Galilee, and also on one of the main thoroughfares between Palestine and Damascus, Nazareth probably has always been familiar with whatever advantage Eastern commerce could give. The modern town is a little less Oriental than most of Palestine, for Western Christianity has been impelled, both by historical sentiment and by unselfish philanthropy, to aid the local Christian community.

The history of Nazareth, unlike that of Bethlehem, is not ancient; there are no Old Testament references to the place.

These rights were confirmed by a later Sultan in 1740. During the next half-century the Orthodox Greeks in Palestine, under the protection of Russia, increased in numbers and influence. They grew year by year, and staked out claims for themselves, both material and moral. France had shown little activity until the time of Napoleon III, when his Government made a formal demand for the restoration of all the rights and privileges of which the Latins had gradually been deprived. The negotiations which proceeded out of this demand culminated in the Crimean War. (Albert M. Hyamson, *Palestine: The Rebirth of an Ancient People*, p. 56.)

[1] The population of Nazareth consists of about five thousand Christians, some twenty-five hundred Moslems, and a very few Jews.

LATIN PROCESSION AT THE CHURCH OF THE NATIVITY, BETHLEHEM, ON CHRISTMAS DAY

The church shows at the left

Its associations with the life of Jesus are its chief interest, and even with reference to these, the Gospel records concerning the place are very meagre; although legend, as always, has supplied numerous anecdotes. The town, however, is fascinating even aside from its religious associations. Schools, hospitals, orphanages; institutions both Moslem and Christian, the latter representing Orthodox, Catholic, and Protestant communities — all have contributed to making a higher level of existence in Nazareth than is usual in the Palestinian villages.

It was a thrilling experience to be spending the night in Nazareth. During the day, we had been visiting the Jewish Colonies of Nahalal and Ain Harod and arrived at Nazareth about six o'clock. Emerging from Esdraelon, we motored up the steep road to Nazareth, which is very aptly portrayed as nestling in a cup sheltered by the Galilean hills. I can never describe my sensation when I entered the Galilee Hotel where our chauffeur took us for the night. 'This is Nazareth,' I said again and again to myself; but the only thing, in fact, that seemed appropriate to the place was the name of the hotel itself — Galilee. To be sure, the people who received us —a German and his wife — were cordial hosts. The sleeping-quarters were clean, though meagrely furnished; but, what seemed more out of place here than anywhere else in Palestine, were the omnipresent petroleum tins which these thrifty German innkeepers had ingeniously converted into all sorts of useful receptacles — waste-baskets, flower-pots, water-buckets, roasting-tins. Really, these transformed exotics made the only show of plenty which the inn possessed. Had it been anywhere but Nazareth, I should probably have admired this frugality and thrift; but to see Standard Oil cans in the place so intimately associated with the life of Jesus: I had to adjust my thinking all over again.

The dining-room helped out considerably. On the table were earthen water-jars of the ancient pattern, and the Arab waiters, with the long white robe, red girdle and sandals, carried out the picture.

My first night in Nazareth was hardly one of quiet repose. I was impatient for the morning when I could visit the places sacred to the memory of Him who walked these streets and here began his Christly ministry. We were out early; our first stop was Mary's Well, the one spot in Nazareth that one can positively believe was associated with Jesus. We know that He and his mother must often have come to this well, for throughout the ages Nazareth has had only this one source of water.

I had seen pictures of the well, and therefore had no illusions as to its appearance or its commonplace setting. But to the reverent visitor, this walled-up fountain, offering its copious flow to all who come to drink or wash, recalls the memory of Him who would offer a cup of cold water 'unto one of these little ones.' [1] The donkey quenching his thirst undisturbed, the women with their earthen jars, and the boys playing around the well — all might have been in the setting in Jesus' time. But the opposite picture of the boys walking on stilts, and the ragged urchins running to catch on to our automobile as we sped away, gave just that much of the modern touch to reveal the setting as it really is — dull, drab, humdrum — as we know it must have been nineteen centuries ago.

Mary's Well reminds us of another fountain of water, in Samaria, most certainly identified with Jesus.[2] It was at Jacob's Well, in 'a city of Samaria which is called Sychar,' [3] while Jesus was resting, that the woman of Samaria came to draw water.[4] There it was that Jesus told of the living water and everlasting life; [5] and there it was that the seed was sown which developed into the peculiar religion of the Samaritans, who are represented in Palestine to-day, although by a very small community of people who still cling to Nablus.[6]

---

[1] Matthew x: 42.

[2] Jacob's Well lies outside the eastern end of Nablus, below the little village of Sychar. A Byzantine church, which was erected over the well, gave place to a Crusaders' church, on whose ruins a modern Orthodox church is partially constructed.

[3] John iv: 5.   [4] *Ibid.*, 7.   [5] John iv: 1–30.

[6] In the time of Jesus, some seven centuries after the Assyrian conquest, the Samaritans were an important people; although to-day, having been depleted by wars, Turkish oppression, intermarriage, and poverty, there are not more than one hundred of them left. Their history has become known, not only because of its peculiarity, but also because, as far back as the time when the Hebrew tribes were in Canaan, they are said to have remained continuously in the land of Palestine. As long as the Judeans remained in Palestine — that is, until A.D. 135 — they continued to despise the people of Samaria and Shechem. They taunted their neighbors with being of bad blood, a foolish people, only heterodox worshippers of the Lord. When,

From Mary's Well, we went to the Church of the Annunciation, which every visitor to Nazareth plans to see. We were shown the usual sights in the church. The old monk seemed to linger at certain places, as if perhaps to estimate how much we were ready to believe. Evidently, he gave us the full program. He showed us the grotto where Mary's house stood, the workshop of Joseph, the tomb of Joseph, Mary's kitchen, and the table from which Christ ate after his resurrection. For all of these, he affected reverence. Although we knew beforehand that not one of these particular sites was authentic, they were nevertheless full of interest to us. The whole place impels reverence, for it is situated in Jesus' home town, and has been the scene of devout worship for more than twelve centuries. Pilgrims from the ends of the earth have worshipped here, and our quest, as pilgrims, was to seek those associations in Nazareth which speak of the work of Jesus and his deeds.

The Church of the Annunciation is of Christian origin. Erected hastily in the eighteenth century — as one could imagine by its appearance — in an effort to establish and maintain recognition of the Christian faith in Palestine, it is

during the rule of Pontius Pilate (A.D. 26–36), some undisciplined Samaritan youths at Passover time entered the Temple of Herod at Jerusalem and scattered human bones about, Jewish wrath reached its climax, and the Jews forbade the Samaritans ever again to enter the sacred Temple. They continued to celebrate the Passover in their own way, at their own shrine on Mount Gerizim, which they had had from of old. And there they worship to this day.

Because the Samaritans were essentially separated from their brethren the Judeans at a time when only the first of the three parts of the Old Testament Scriptures (i.e., the Law, the Prophets, and the Writings) was considered of sacred origin, their Bible includes only the first five books, which we call the Law, or Pentateuch. The Samaritans have also preserved, however, not exactly as inspired literature, but rather as the record of sacred history, the Book of Joshua. They exhibit to travellers an ancient manuscript of the Pentateuch, which claims in an interesting colophon to have been written by the grandson of Moses. As a matter of fact, scholars are aware that the age of the manuscript is by no means so ancient; it seems to come from the tenth century A.D. Nevertheless, this is probably the oldest complete text of the Pentateuch, and furnishes valuable variants of the text handed down through Orthodox Judaism.

The little community of the Samaritans has strangely changed from being in antiquity a mixed, and, it was thought, dangerously broad-minded and disloyal 'Jewish' population, to the present fossil of ancient and mediæval peculiarities. This little community cannot long survive on account of the intermarriage and poverty. The earthquake of June, 1927, was a severe tragedy to the Samaritans, who were huddled mostly in the stricken town of Shechem. (For general information on the Samaritans, see J. A. Montgomery, *The Samaritans*. Philadelphia. 1907. For their Liturgy, see A. E. Cowley, *The Samaritan Liturgy*. Oxford. 1909.)

therefore an important part of Christian history. Not only the present church, but the basilica, erected probably as early as the time of Constantine, as well as the later Church of the Crusaders, both having probably stood on this site, belong in the history of the Christian faith.

From the Church of the Annunciation, we went to the Church of the Greek Catholics which is built on the traditional site of the synagogue where the fellow townsmen of Jesus, so angered by his teaching, dragged him to a precipice where they intended to cast him down.[1] Although there is no absolute certainty that this is the authentic site, there is a very real foundation for believing it to be the right location. My guide called attention to the old walls of a small edifice, which, by exact measurement, are thirty feet long and twenty-six feet wide.

No place in Palestine stimulated my imagination more than this spot. As I stood in the church, I was overwhelmed with the thought that here, or, if not in this exact spot, somewhere in Nazareth, Jesus had proclaimed the universality of Christianity, and its message of love to the afflicted of all classes and races. Who could fail to see the picture of the mob that dragged him to the precipice? The Mount of Precipitation is still there.

And so with these memories of the Master, I followed Him in imagination from Nazareth, to which He never returned, to his new home by the Sea of Galilee — to Capernaum, twenty miles away, which Matthew called 'his own city.'[2]

We drove down over the hills to Tiberias, passing the traditional scene of the miracle of Cana.[3] The Roman Tiberias, which was founded by Herod Antipas, in honor of the Emperor Tiberius, is now a small town 681 feet below sea-level, crowded with flat-roofed houses lying on the west bank of the

[1] Luke iv: 16–29.
'And all they in the synagogue, when they heard these things, were filled with wrath, And rose up, and thrust him out of the city, and led him unto the brow of the hill whereon their city was built, that they might cast him down headlong. But he passing through the midst of them went his way, And came down to Capernaum, a city of Galilee, and taught them on the sabbath days.' (Luke iv: 28–31.)

[2] 'And he entered into a ship, and passed over, and came into his own city.' (Matthew ix: 1.)

[3] John ii.

lake. The population of Tiberias consists of five thousand Jews, two thousand Moslems, and a few Christians of different sects. Of the nine cities encircling the lake when Jesus taught here, only Tiberias remains.

The Roman city, however, which was nearly a mile south of the present town, lies completely in ruins; we saw, in our brief stay there, the remains of the theatre, the forum, and other buildings. That this is the authentic site of the ancient Tiberias is proved beyond a doubt, if any further proof is required, by the age-old hot springs which one sees from the road, the medicinal properties of which were famous throughout the Roman world. But Tiberias had only a passing interest for me, bent as I was on studying the scenes of the Christian ministry. So far as I have been able to ascertain, Jesus never entered Tiberias.[1]

We went on to Capernaum.[2] On our way up the lake, we stopped at Tabgha, ten miles away. Father Tapper received us at the hospice. As it was an hour before lunch, we sat outside with our genial host, the head of a German Catholic settlement founded in 1892. The hospice is conveniently arranged for guests, having accommodations for about twenty, with a cool refectory on the ground floor and a comfortable sitting-room above. The vaulted roofs of the rooms give a distinctly religious aspect, quite in keeping with the nature of the house. There is a chapel in the building in which, as our host told us, seventy Bedouins have assembled. Prayers are said here every morning at half-past five.

Regardless of religious affiliation, one would go a long distance to see Father Tapper. It was indeed a prominent Jew in Jerusalem who urged me to stop at the hospice. As we sat on the pleasant veranda, overlooking the palm, lemon, and other trees which sheltered us from the hot sun, our conversation covered a wide range of subjects. Father Tapper is very well informed on the problems of Palestine. I was constantly surprised at his cosmopolitan attitude toward affairs, and his keen interpretation of the Palestine situation. His

[1] Mr. Fosdick corroborates this fact, and points out that the presence of Tiberias on the lake is mentioned only once in the Gospels. (John vi: 23.) (Harry Emerson Fosdick, *A Pilgrimage to Palestine*, p. 202.)

[2] 'And leaving Nazareth, he came and dwelt in Capernaum, which is upon the sea coast,...' (Matthew iv: 13.)

sense of humor, reflected in his youthful blue eyes, stimulated questions which, because of their critical import, I had been somewhat avoiding during my stay in Palestine.

At lunch, we met two English ladies who were spending a few weeks at the hospice. A vacation on the Sea of Galilee was an alluring thought! Right here at Tabgha, just outside the hospice grounds, Father Tapper called our attention to the ruins of an old aqueduct and the tannery and pottery mills which undoubtedly stood there when Capernaum flourished as a Roman city, and when, situated on the caravan route from Damascus to the Mediterranean ports and Egypt, the Capernaum of Jesus' time was really a great cosmopolitan city having news of the whole world. Father Tapper also pointed out the spot, where, some authorities believe, Jesus fed the five thousand.[1]

Our automobile stopped at the gate in the wall which encloses the ruins of Capernaum, situated directly on the shore of the lake at Tell Hum. In 1894, the Franciscans, believing they had located the site of Capernaum, purchased the area from the Ottoman Government, and after enclosing it with a high wall, proceeded to clear away the débris which covered the ruins. The Franciscans were supported in their claim by eminent scholars; as far back as 1865, Professor Wilson, of the Palestine Exploration Fund, found at Tell Hum what he considered to be the remains of an ancient synagogue. Since that time many noted archæologists have made scientific examinations of the ruins, the latest being Dr. Pere Orfali, Rector of the Franciscan School of Archæological Research and president of the Palestine Oriental Society. The belief

---

[1] Matthew xiv: 14–21; Mark vi: 32–44; Luke ix: 12–17; John vi: 5–14.

Meistermann says: 'Few places in Palestine possess better guarantees of authenticity than this one where Jesus fed the five thousand men.' In support of this statement, Meistermann cites Saint Jerome, describing the pilgrimage which Saint Paula made about the year 380; Saint Sylvia of Aquitaine, who went to Galilee a few years later; the *Commemoratorium* about 808; and Saint Epiphanius, the Hagiopolite, who wrote from the ninth to the tenth century. (Father Barnabas Meistermann, *New Guide to the Holy Land*, pp. 441, 442.)

On the other hand, George Adam Smith believes that Bethsaida was on the east bank of the Jordan. 'The Fourth Gospel, it is true, speaks of *Bethsaida in Galilee* (John xii: 21), but this need not mean that it lay west of the Jordan, for, as we have seen, the province of Galilee ran right round the lake, and included most of the level coast-land on the east.' (George Adam Smith, *The Historical Geography of the Holy Land*, pp. 457, 458.)

that Tell Hum is the site of Capernaum is now accepted by most scholars.

Moreover, this archæological evidence is supported by Christian tradition. Saint Sylvia of Aquitaine, who visited Galilee in the fourth century and wrote a description of Capernaum, says: 'Here also can be seen the synagogue wherein he (Christ) cured the demoniac; it is reached by steps, and is built of cut stone.' Commenting on this statement, Professors Kohl and Watzinger, the archæologists enlisted by the Franciscans, say: 'There is no doubt that this pilgrim visited Capharnaum at Tell Houm; for of all the synagogues discovered in Galilee, that of Tell Houm is the only one to which one ascended by a flight of steps.' [1]

The ruins have been appropriately described as 'a jumbled mass of broken columns, bases, capitals, and entablatures,' although examination shows that practically none of the stones of which the synagogue was built are missing. In one corner of the enclosure we saw a few upright columns standing in the the midst of large blocks of stone. This is the site of the synagogue whose main walls, reaching to the height of about five feet, are still intact.

The Franciscan Fathers are rebuilding this ancient place of worship, and when the work is finished the visitor to Capernaum will be able to see the very shape and structure of the building built by the Centurion who loved the Jewish nation,[2] and in which Jesus spoke the words: 'He that believeth on me hath everlasting life.' [3]

Reluctantly we left Capernaum, where it was that Jesus showed all humanity for all time the way to live. We went back to Nazareth, and then to Haifa and Mount Carmel, on to Syria and the land to the East.

ARMAGEDDON

No more the horsemen reap the Syrian plain
With death for harvest, such as once they sought
At Armageddon; peaceful stands the grain,
And dust is in the furrows where they fought.

[1] Father Barnabas Meistermann, *Guide to the Holy Land*, pp. 546, 549. See also, Father Barnabas Meistermann, *Capharnaum et Bethsaïde* (Paris, 1921).

[2] 'For he loveth our nation, and he hath built us a synagogue.' (Luke vii: 5.)

[3] John iii: 16; vi: 40, 27, 59.

Bugles of Pharaoh or the desert kings
Sound no reveille; shouldering his gun
No British Tommy 'Tipperary' sings;
'Tis silent on the hills — as at Verdun.

Dust in the furrows where great empires passed!
Might that was tragedy! Yet short miles away
Was dreamed a shining vision that will last,
The City of Man that knoweth no decay;
No marching troops, no threat of power or death,
Peace to all men — the dream of Nazareth.

JAMES T. SHOTWELL

To Margaret Grace
May 15, 1929

CHAPTER VII

THE RELIGIOUS SETTING — (3) ISLAM

DURING the past thirteen centuries, Islam has maintained numerical and political predominance in Palestine. The Moslems include Arabs and Syro-Palestinians; a number of Circassians, North Africans (Maghribis), and Bosnians who are immigrants in the country; and a few Turkoman nomads. The purest-blooded Arabs are those of the desert, proud of their descent direct from Ishmael, independent, scornful of the settled life of peasants and tradespeople. They call themselves Bedouin.

The Syro-Palestinians are a more mixed group, difficult to classify racially. In their veins flows not only the blood of the Arabs, but also, at least in many cases, that of the Canaanites and Phœnicians, the Crusaders and Greeks, and very likely the blood of the ancient Jewish peasants. In Jerusalem today there are two or three families that claim to be of the fine Arab stock which entered the country in the seventh century at the time of the first Moslem conquest; [1] there are numerous people who claim to be directly descended from the Crusaders; there are three or four villages near Damascus where the Aramaic Language of Jesus of Nazareth and his contemporaries can still be heard, though now rarely spoken except by the women; and there are, especially in Jericho, people whose black skins and Negro features betray a large African admixture — all of these now speak Arabic, and are glad to be called Arabs. And far more than Christianity has ever done with its adherents of different hue and type, Islam has levelled down this Palestinian multitude in a common religion and culture and a truly Arabian sense of human equality.

Two of the Moslem groups, having recently been brought into the country, still maintain their striking peculiarities. These include, first, some nine hundred Circassians in the land about Amman, east of the Jordan; they are the descend-

---

[1] Such as the al Husseini and al Khaldi families. (Major E. W. Polson Newman, *The Middle East*, p. 23, note 1.)

ants of those people who, after the Russian conquest of the Caucasus in the sixties of the last century, sought refuge in Moslem Palestine, being unwilling to live under Christian rule. After the Treaty of Berlin in 1878, 'Abdu'l-Hamid established a number of colonies of these people in the midst of certain fractious Arab tribes. The ancient Oriental theory of empire was to quell rebellion against empire by creating a balance of power between contiguous minorities within the whole. Tiglath-pileser, who ruled Assyria from 745 to 727 B.C., hit upon the scheme, and destroyed his ever-reviving enemy, Damascus, by transplanting its people into northern Assyria and substituting in their place a new population; [1] so the Damascenes, once rebellious against Nineveh, found their only safety amongst foreign tribes in being loyal to their masters from whom alone they received protection. A little later, in line with the same theory, Samarians were taken into Assyrian provinces, Jews were driven to Babylonia,[2] and in our own memory Armenians have been denationalized lest in too strong a majority they should rebel against Constantinople.

The ancient custom of transplanting dangerous tribes for the purpose of creating what might be called a systematized internal balance of power was adopted by Turkey, when, for example, in Asia Minor, where Armenians had become a strong majority, their enemies, the Kurds, were vigorously encouraged. In a smaller way, in Palestine, rivalry between the Kais and the Yemen factions was not only countenanced, but evidently encouraged by the Turks down to the time of the British occupation. And it is probably because of this policy of balancing rival groups within the same territory that so prosperous a minority of Palestinians were allowed to remain Christians.[3] Through such deportation of dangerous majorities and the encouragement of local and petty competitions, the Turkish Government may have achieved its purpose; but the method was surely unjust and barbarously cruel.

[1] R. W. Rogers, *Cuneiform Parallels to the Old Testament*, pp. 317–20. II Kings XVII: 1–6.

[2] II Kings xxv: 8–20.

[3] Sir William Muir, *The Caliphate, its Rise, Decline and Fall*, pp. 134 *seq.* (Revised edition by T. H. Weir, Edinburgh, 1915.)

The second group of distinctly foreign Moslems are the Bosnians — those Islamized Serbs, who, upon the occupation of Bosnia and Herzegovina by Austria in 1878, emigrated into Turkish territory. The Turkish authorities established some of these Bosnian families within the ruined city of Cæsarea [1] on the Mediterranean coast, just south of Haifa; and to-day this peasant community numbers about three hundred people.

Much less distinct from other Palestinians, but exceedingly interesting, is the large and ancient settlement of 'Maghribis,' or North Africans, who live within the old city of Jerusalem between the Wailing Wall of the Jews and the Dung Gate, now called the Gate of the Magharbeh. There are also more of these people in Galilee, where their number is estimated at nineteen hundred. They came into Palestine in the early years of the eighteenth century. Perhaps, because distance lends enchantment, the remote origin of these families has made them famous as enchanters, magicians, and writers of charms and spells. It is commonly supposed in this part of the East that a man from North Africa has peculiar power of seeing into the future and of controlling the doings of jinn and men. They speak an Arabic which is dialectically different from that used in Palestine, and their writing of the Arabic alphabet is less beautifully flowing, more squared and scratchy in appearance, perhaps because of its queerness the more legible to the shadowy jinn who work so much mischief.

The Moslem history of Palestine began with the conquest in 639 and 640. Within the following two centuries practically the entire population became Moslem.[2] While Islam was steadily conquering, large tax exemptions were granted to believers, and social distinctions between the followers of the Prophet and all others were very great. In Palestine,

---

[1] The ancient Tower of Straton, which was fortified and greatly enlarged by Herod the Great, who also changed the name to Cæsarea (Josephus, *Antiquities*, xiv, iv, 4; xx, viii, 7, etc.), and by Archelaus and the Roman procurators as their capital.

See Philip Khûri Hitti, *The Origins of the Islamic State*, pp. 216–19, for the description of the Moslem conquest of Cæsarea.

[2] Sir William Muir, *The Caliphate, its Rise, Decline and Fall*, pp. 133 *seq.* (Revised edition. T. H. Weir, Edinburgh, 1915.)

regulations forbidding non-Moslems — in this case, of course, Christians — from riding upon horses, from prominently marking the graves of their dead, from accepting high position of any sort, furnished a constant incentive to conversion. But there were, in fact, higher motives for accepting Islam. Seventh-century Christendom in Palestine was corrupt and ruled by a political system which was torn asunder by national strifes. Islam was now vigorous, united, and in some respects morally compelling.[1]

Many stories concerning the superiority of Islam to the Christianity of the seventh century centre about the noble character of the Caliph Omar (A.D. 634–44), second successor to the Prophet. One tale, typical of the aged Caliph, relates that a certain Christian, Jabala by name, the king of the powerful tribe of Ghassan in eastern Syria, objected strenuously to paying the heavy tax which the Faithful exacted of those of other religions whom they had conquered. In order to avoid the payment, Jabala became a Moslem. Omar accordingly relieved him of the payment of tribute. After leaving the presence of the Caliph, however, Jabala was unworthily vexed at an aged man who got in the way of his horse, and he beat the man severely. The Caliph, learning of the incident, ordered that the injured man should beat the king with an equal number of blows; for, he explained to Jabala, in Islam, high and low are equal. The haughty king was so offended with this illustration of equality among the Faithful that he fled forthwith to Constantinople, there to live and die a Christian. The simple dress and manner of Omar, who indeed had by this time come to rule the greatest of the empires of the day, was often a source of embarrassment to his fellows; while to wrong-doers, the Caliph's stern sense of justice was a constant terror.[2]

Two centuries after the Moslem invasion, Palestine was taken in 969 from the Eastern Caliphate by the Fatimids of Egypt. Soon after this, the Seljuk Turks, newly converted to the faith, overran the country; and it was their new enthusiasm for Islam that caused them to persecute Christian pil-

[1] Sir William Muir, *The Caliphate, its Rise, Decline and Fall*, pp.133 *seq.* (Revised edition. T. H. Weir, Edinburgh, 1915.)

[2] *Ibid.*, p. 138.

grims to Jerusalem. This brought about the Crusades. Jerusalem was won to the Christians in 1099; but though they maintained a kingdom more or less worthy the name for two hundred years, the city itself fell to Saladin in 1187. After Saladin's death in 1293, his empire broke into quarrelling fragments. Palestine suffered a Tartar invasion in 1244. In 1291, the country fell under the power of the Mameluke (Major-Domo) dynasty of Egypt. The new, or Western Turkish Empire's expansion incorporated Palestine in 1517; and despite various invasions, especially from Egypt in the early nineteenth century, the country remained in Turkish control until the World War.

Notwithstanding the long Turkish occupation of Palestine, there are practically no Turks left in the country; neither has Turkish influence upon language and customs been very great. On the whole, the Turks ruled rather consistently, and, perhaps because of the ease with which they were bribed, rather leniently. Their unpardonable sin was that they maintained an anachronistic empire in the modern world.

The history of Islam is thus seen to be an important element in the understanding of the Mandate. So, too, we shall find the religion itself a striking factor in the life of the country. The central creed of every Moslem everywhere is expressed in the call of the Mu'ezzin from the minaret at the hour of prayer: 'There is no god but God; and Mohammed is his Prophet.' Whether or not it is true that only one God is worshipped, the fact remains that strict monotheism is an essential part of the religion; although undoubtedly the Western mind would classify many of the saints worshipped by the peasants as minor deities. To the Moslems, the so-called Trinitarianism of Christendom is a matter of ridicule. There can be only one God.

The second statement of the Mu'ezzin's call declares the divine inspiration of Mohammed. The Book (or Kur'an, 'that which is read or recited') of the words which the Prophet spoke when God inspired him is therefore considered the guide of all true religion. Since this inspiration was literal and absolute, the Kur'an is considered in every respect perfect, containing no error and omitting no needful truth. Its language, accordingly, though a philologist would note that it is in the somewhat provincial dialect of seventh-century Mekka, is the supreme example of correct Arabic style, to be studied in the schools of rhetoric and to be emulated by every Arabic writer of to-day. According to Moslem belief, the Kur'an, because of its verbal inspiration, is not to be translated; to do this would be to change the Word of God. To a Westerner, this belief of the Moslems is one of the strangest elements in their religion. Obviously, in spite of the tendency of numerous modernized Moslems to get away from the idea of literal inspiration, this still remains a strong deterrent to religious progress.

While they recognized the Kur'an as the only true Word of God, the love of the early Moslems for their Prophet led to the preservation of a great amount of legendary material regarding the intimate affairs of his life. The writing of these stories was animated by an affectionate desire to know the Prophet and to follow his example in the minutest detail. While there is a wide variation in the historical value of the different stories, this mass of tradition may be somewhat compared to our Gospel narratives; both are read for their historical and literary value, and both furnish rules of conduct. Nevertheless, there is room for individual interpretation as to which practices are essential to the religion, and also as to those which are merely incidental. In Islam, those who follow the tradition most carefully are known as Sunnite Moslems.

It is a fact, of course, that the religion is not merely a theory of monotheism which originated in the seventh century; it has, on the contrary, developed a history which has become part of itself. Islam has perhaps suffered in the peculiar limitations of its history: having had only one Prophet,[1] its origin had the breadth of but one man's mind. Furthermore, the limitation of its history to the Orient, with a close attachment to its first home in Arabia, has circumscribed its power to promulgate the underlying essentials of religion. Islam has acquired from the Oriental peoples who have professed it many notions and customs which express very low religious ideals. Perhaps we may note, however, a hope of progress for the future. A tradition relates a saying of the Prophet: 'My

---

[1] Actually there were more, but their teachings are thought to have been lost.

people shall never agree in an error.'[1] Islam as a philosophy of life realizes that it has not yet agreed; that it must continue to seek for the truth in which there may be agreement. In this respect, therefore, Islam contains the seed of progress.

But the weakness of every religion lies in the failure of its adherents to live up to its ideals. Only a very limited number earnestly desire to live out the ideals of their faith. Indeed, because of the general illiteracy of most Moslem countries, knowledge of the faith is not widespread, and it is everywhere confused with lowered moral standards and with superstitions and intolerance. The casual traveller in Palestine sees so much of Moslem ignorance and bigotry that the true merit of the religion is largely unobserved.

Most of the Moslems in Palestine are Sunnites; that is, they follow the Prophetic Tradition. Since the faith involves a political science, the people are consequently divided in their attitude toward the four great schools of law.[2] The Turks, being themselves Hanafites, administered the law according to that rule, though most of the lawyers are Shafites.

The endowments of the Moslem religious institutions in Palestine required immediate consideration by the Mandatory Government. Arising out of a series of conferences of the Moslem 'Ulema ('Doctors of Law and Theology'), together with other notables, there was established by order of the High Commissioner on December 20, 1921,[3] a Supreme Moslem Sharia Council, clothed with authority over all Moslem

[1] D. B. Macdonald, *Muslim Theology, Jurisprudence, and Constitutional Theory*, pp. 105 *seq.*
Compare T. P. Hughes, *Dictionary of Islam*, p. 197. Article on Ijmā'.

[2] D. B. Macdonald, *Muslim Theology, Jurisprudence, and Constitutional Theory*.
With the exception of small Shiah colonies, the Moslems of Palestine are Sunnis (Traditionists), divided among the four rites (*mazhab*) approximately in the following proportions:

Shafi	70 per cent
Hanbali	19
Hanafi	10
Maliki	1

(*The Handbook of Palestine*, p. 36. Edited by Harry Charles Luke and Edward Keith-Roach.)

[3] Legislation of Palestine, 1918–25. Compiled by Norman Bentwich, Attorney-General of Palestine. Constitution and Powers of Supreme Moslem Sharia Council, vol. II, p. 398.

Waqfs,[1] and Sharia Courts in Palestine. This action was consistent with Article 9 of the Mandate, which stipulates that 'the control and administration of Waqfs shall be exercised in accordance with religious law and the dispositions of the founders.'

There is a vast amount of Waqf land in the country, against the sale of which there is a strong religious sentiment; though frequently the village in which it is located would be benefited by its transfer. Popular peasant belief attaches superstitious reverence to this Waqf land, and many stories have grown up around this superstition. One hears, for example: how a thief, having taken grapes from a Waqf vineyard, died instantly; how a person who attempted to steal sheep and goats from a Waqf enclosure was blinded so that once inside the wall he could not see his prize; [2] how Waqf wheat, when stolen, turned into ants and walked back to its proper place — and many more such stories.

It has already been pointed out that Jerusalem is to Islam a Holy City. The Arabic name for the city is Quds, 'Holiness.' [3] During the early part of Mohammed's ministry, he bade his followers to pray with their faces turned toward Jerusalem; [4] and probably the custom would have continued had not some of the Jews in Medina, to which Mohammed fled in 622 from Mecca, so annoyed him that he finally ordered his fellow Moslems to turn toward Mecca instead.[5] As a Holy City, Jerusalem receives the pious pilgrimage of many Moslem saints. There are hospices near the Haram area, for the use of North African, Indian, Bokharan, Arabian, Sudanese, and other pilgrims.

This custom of pilgrimage, common to the three great religions, has had a strange influence upon the city of Jerusalem. The religious festival which attracts the pilgrim, with its magnificent and spectacular processions of ardent worshippers, proclaims the rights of the faith, and increases

[1] A Waqf is a religious endowment — property, appropriated or dedicated by a document called a Waqfiah, to charitable uses and the service of God.

[2] Cf. Genesis xix: 11.

[3] The name on the station at Jerusalem is printed in Arabic, English, and Hebrew.

[4] J. M. Rodwell, *The Koran.* (Everyman's Library, p. 353, note 3.)

[5] Sir William Muir, *The Life of Muhammad*, pp. 121 *seq.* (Revised edition. T. H. Weir, Edinburgh, 1923.)

the determination to guard it at all costs from invidious encroachments; while the display of beautiful robes and vestments gives charm and fervor to the mystical ceremony.

A casual glance at the relief map of Palestine shows the location of Jerusalem to be particularly strong for military defence, but this is its only claim to a good location. Placed as it is on four hills, and surrounded by ravines on the east, south, and west, it is hardly fitted to serve as the political capital of the country, though it has been such during most of its history — since David, about a thousand years before Christ, established there the Hebrew capital. Nor is Jerusalem a commercial centre: Nablus — the ancient Shechem — is nearer both to the products of the country and also to the ports for shipping. The essential product of Jerusalem has always been its sanctity. In the New Testament the city is nearly always referred to in connection with some pilgrimage festival. Christian pilgrims came there, fought for the privilege, mourned its possession, hated the Saracen who had occupied and defiled it. In our own time, a few Russian Christians, Jewish and Moslem pilgrims, curious travellers from all over the world, go there to satisfy some religious sentiment. It is very largely due to this religious prestige that the city's population and commercial enterprise are maintained. And the result of all this is to make Jerusalem, the goal of the most ardent religionists, one of the most fanatical cities in the world.

Accordingly, if one wishes to get an appreciable idea of the extent and intensity of Moslem religious sentiment in Palestine, one must visit the shrines. There are many Moslem shrines in the country, but those of first importance are the Dome of the Rock and the Mesjid al-Aqsa in Haram ash-Sharif in Jerusalem, and the Mosque of Abraham at Hebron.[1]

The Guide-Book, published by the Supreme Moslem Council, notifies visitors to the area of Haram ash-Sharif that: 'the whole of the Haram area, and not only its edifices, is sacred to Moslems; and that they will be expected to pay due regard to its sanctity. In particular, they must abstain

---

[1] *Mesjid* is one of the Arabic words for Mosque. In Egypt the *j* is hard, *Mesgid*, from which the French adopted the form *Mosque*, leaving off the final *d*.

from smoking anywhere in the area and from bringing dogs with them. The visiting-hours are from seven-thirty in the morning till eleven-thirty, Fridays excepted, and visitors are particularly requested to leave punctually at eleven-thirty so as not to hinder the observance of the mid-day prayer.'

The Haram is the site of the Temple of Solomon, perhaps the spot on which 'David built there an altar unto the Lord, and offered burnt offerings and peace offerings.' [1] One of the first acts of the Caliph Omar, the Arab historians relate, was to reconsecrate the site of the Haram, which had become sacred to the Moslems because of the Vision of the Night Journey,[2] and because, as well, of Islam's connection with more ancient 'sacred history.' The history of the present buildings is supposed to begin in A.D. 685–705, in the reign of the Caliph Abd al-Malik. With the coming of the Crusaders to Jerusalem, the Dome of the Rock was changed to a Christian Church, spoken of, because of the site, as a Christian Temple of the Lord. Here the Order of the Knights Templar was founded. The Mesjid al-Aqsa was likewise transformed by the Crusaders; of it they made a royal residence known as the Palace of Solomon. The Crusader historians relate with gusto how, upon the capture of the city, the Moslems took refuge in the Haram, there to be cut down in such a terrible slaughter that the whole area ran with blood to the horses' knees. We trust that this is a pious exaggeration, though it indicates the fearful cruelty of the war.

When Saladin recaptured the city in 1187, he restored the buildings of the Haram, and added many beautiful embellishments. Arab historians tell us that the Christians during their occupation used the sacred place as a dung heap, and that it had become so piled with filth that it took a vast corps of laborers to dig it away. Since the time of Saladin, the Haram has remained in Moslem hands. During the following three centuries after Saladin, extensive repairs and alterations were made, especially during the reign of Suleiman the Magnificent, the Turkish Sultan from 1520 to 1566, who added magnificent decorations.

[1] II Samuel xxiv: 25.   [2] Kur'an, sura 17: 1.

As the Moslem guard tied on my sandals before we entered the Dome of the Rock, I saw in the process something more than mere formality. The custom of guarding lest an unholy step enter the sanctuary goes far back into the primitive Semitic religion from which Islam in part has its origin. Primitive religion is always conservative; it insisted that the clothing worn by the ancients was the correct attire for religious rites. Moses at the Burning Bush was commanded to remove his sandals; [1] because his ancestors had gone bare-footed, worshippers must return to this primitive state. The Moslems in the sacred dance about the Ka'aba at the time of the pilgrimage to Mecca wear only a loin-cloth. At the Dome of the Rock worshippers ordinarily remove their shoes, going barefooted; but the courtesy is shown to Westerners of allowing them to wear a pair of sandals over their shoes. In no case must Western shoes touch the sacred carpets.

We entered by the west gate, and in the subdued light, as the splendor of the ornamentation revealed itself to us, we could see, directly beneath the Dome, the Sacred Rock on which the Crusaders had set up their altar. The columns, the tiles, the slabs of beautiful marble, the soft rich color of the windows, and the green, blue, and gold roof presented a scene of Oriental splendor similar in general effect to the Mosque of the Caliphs which we had seen in Cairo.

The great exposed rock, whose sanctity the mosque pro-tects, is associated not only with legends of hoary Hebrew antiquity, but it is also the spot, Moslems relate, from which Mohammed leaped to heaven. Much legendary lore has arisen from a little verse in the Kur'an,[2] 'Glory be to him who carried his servant by night from the sacred temple [i.e., of Mecca] to the temple that is more remote,[3] whose precinct we have blessed, that we might show him of our signs!' In a vision, or, some say, in the flesh, Mohammed was taken, or perhaps rode upon the steed Borak (Lightning), to Jeru-salem; there he was allowed to converse with some of the prophets of olden time; and from this rock he was granted a journey into the heavens. Visitors are shown the imprint

[1] Exodus III: 5.   [2] Kur'an, sura 17: 1.

[3] In Arabic, al-Aqsa, the name of one of the present mosques in the Haram area.

of his foot, or, as some say, of his fallen turban, and also the mark left by the touch of the hand of the Angel Gabriel.

Turning toward the south, in leaving the mosque, we passed the fountain of ablutions, the purpose of which is indicated by the name. The 'brass laver,' used for washing before sacrifice, was perhaps here, in the days of Solomon.[1] We descended the steps leading to the Mesjid al-Aqsa. The building dates from different periods, in general having had the same fortunes as those of the Dome of the Rock just described. The mihrab, or prayer recess, faces Mecca. The worshippers always face the mihrab during service, thus knowing that they are facing toward Mecca as is prescribed. This mihrab, which is beautifully ornamented by mosaics and supported by slender marble columns, was placed there by Saladin; while the handsome pulpit of wood, ornamented with inlaid ivory and mother-of-pearl, was brought by his order from Aleppo to Jerusalem. One of the most strikingly beautiful things about the mosque is the vast array of Oriental rugs upon the floor; it is hard to imagine all the patient skill that has gone into their workmanship.

As we left the mosque and proceeded to the staircase leading into the subterranean structures known as Solomon's Stables, we descended a flight of stairs to a small chamber, which was believed in mediæval times to have been associated with the infancy of Jesus Christ. There is here a small niche lying horizontally, which was believed to have been the cradle of Christ. The chamber is now used occasionally as a place of Moslem worship. The Moslems account Jesus a Prophet; in fact, they usually estimate him the greatest of the prophets before Mohammed; and they delight to relate stories about 'Isa ibn Marian, as they call him, connecting the stories when they can with some local Moslem shrine. The Kur'an contains very many references to him, and tells curiously garbled narratives of his life.

Tradition asserts that this entire underground structure dates from the time of the erection of Solomon's Temple, though legend is inclined to give it the most remote origins. The actual reason for the excavation is not yet surely known. Josephus probably referred to it as the place of refuge used

[1] Exodus xxx: 17–21. I Kings vii: 38.

by the Jews when Titus besieged and captured the city in
A.D. 70. The Knights Templars used the space as stables.

From the moment one steps into the Haram area, he is on
holy ground; and we may trace its history as such for more
than three thousand years. The holy site is thought by
some people to be mentioned in Genesis,[1] when Abraham was
told to bring his son to Moriah and offer him as a burnt
offering. Tradition[2] says that David selected the site on
which to build his Temple, and that although this was refused him, he gathered material for his son Solomon who
erected his Temple in the tenth century before Christ.
Solomon's famous Temple was destroyed by Nebuchadnezzar in 586 B.C., but a 'Second Temple,' as we have seen, was
built with the encouragement of Haggai and Zechariah in
522 B.C. Herod's Temple, which replaced this second building was standing in the time of Christ; and here many incidents of his life took place. During the one hundred years
in the Middle Ages, when Palestine was under Christian
rule, an iron grill was erected around the Rock; and in spite
of the change from Christian to Moslem, the grill still remains. Thus we have a Crusader relic guarding a Moslem
shrine, and that indeed upon the hilltop sanctified through
a thousand years of Jewish pious sacrifice.

Of even more intense Moslem veneration is the Haram at
Hebron, the sacred area which is supposed to enclose the
Cave of Machpelah, the burial place of Abraham and Sarah,
and later of Isaac and Rebecca, Jacob and Leah and Joseph,
whose cenotaphs occupy enclosures in the Haram. The
chapels of Abraham and Sarah, on the north side of the old
church, are particularly richly decorated. The superstition
of the Moslems is illustrated by the custom of throwing
petitions addressed to Sarah by childless women into the
cave below. The entrance to this cave is sealed, but through
a hole in the floor of the mosque a boy is let down at frequent
intervals into the outer cave to collect the petitions which
have been thrown into it. Just outside the entrance to the
mosque there is a small aperture in the great stone wall into
which Oriental Jews cast prayers to Father Abraham. Some-

[1] Genesis XXII: 1–14.
[2] II Samuel VII.

times one may thrust his arm down into the hole — though let us hope he gropes upon no scorpion — and fish out some of these curious Hebrew prayers. The Mosque of Abraham, which occupies the southern side of the Haram, was adapted by the Arabs from a Crusaders' church of the twelfth century; it stands directly over the cave.[1]

Hebron is a town of some nineteen thousand inhabitants; the majority of the population is Moslem, having the reputation of being the most fanatical group to be found anywhere in the country. Hebron, like Damascus, is one of the oldest continuously inhabited cities known.[2] The tall stone houses, narrow streets, and the picturesque, vaulted bazaars are strikingly characteristic of a typical Arab city. In the market, or *suq*, there are displayed curious trappings for Oriental equestrians; and hand-made glass, famous in this part of the world, is made here. The ovens of the glassmakers are well worth a visit.

An exceedingly interesting Moslem festival, originally organized by Saladin for the Moslems of southern Palestine, for the purpose, it is said, of strengthening Moslem senti-

---

[1] In the issue of the *Palestine Weekly*, January 20, 1928, announcement was made that the Moslem Supreme Council had decided to allow non-Moslem visitors to enter the Cave of Makhpela at Hebron. This meant, according to the announcement, that non-Moslems were to be admitted to the Cave of the Fathers: Abraham, Isaac and Jacob and Mothers: Sara, Rebecca and Leah. The following is an interesting commentary on this decision of the Moslem Supreme Council: 'More than once this arbitrary custom has been made the subject of vehement protests in the European and American Press. The Cave of Makhpela is not held by Moslems in greater veneration than the Haram-esh-Sherif in Jerusalem. Still, visitors are allowed within the innermost precincts every day of the week and every month of the year except during High Festivals. The rule of shutting out non-Moslem visitors was instituted many centuries ago when every non-Moslem visitor was a potential "usurper" and a possible conquerer of the Holy Land. No such fear need be or is entertained now. On its part, the Palestine Government, anxious to avoid interference in the internal affairs of the religious communities, did not raise this prohibition. It was left to the good, sound sense of the members of the Supreme Moslem Council to remove the barriers which centuries of tradition have helped to raise.'

In the issue of January 27, 1928, however, the following denial of the decision of the Moslem Supreme Council to open the Cave was printed: 'We are informed by the Moslem Supreme Council that the report to the effect that the Council have decided to abolish the prohibition for non-Moslems to enter the Makhpela Cave at Hebron is incorrect. No such decision has ever been taken, and the position with regard to the admission of non-Moslems remains as it was hitherto.'

[2] *Handbook of Palestine*, pp. 84, 85. Edited by Harry Charles Luke and Edward Keith-Roach, 1922.

Numbers XIII: 22.

ment and of arousing the local patriotism of the Arabs, is that of Nebi Musa, or the Feast of the Prophet Moses. This lasts seven days and comes at the same time as the Greek Christian Holy Week. On the first day of this Feast, a religious service is held in the Haram ash-Sharif in Jerusalem attended by the chief functionaries, after which the procession starts for the Tomb of Moses, which Moslem tradition places about five miles from Jericho.

Philip Graves has described this festival most vividly, as he saw it in 1922:

One of its most picturesque features is the entry into Jerusalem of the procession of the men of Hebron, guarding their sacred banners, who enter Jerusalem through the Jaffa Gate. It was led in 1922 by a noisy procession of the men of Jerusalem and Nablus, who had marched down the Bethlehem road to greet those of the city of Abraham, bearing their green and scarlet banners. Then came the Hebron village folk carrying their flags, red, green, yellow and white, embroidered with texts from the Koran, the staff of each flag hung with handkerchiefs given by the village women to be hung in Musa's shrine that they may thus obtain a blessing and bear children to their husbands. As they entered the old city the enthusiasm of the crowds reached its highest intensity. Men with the set blank stare of extreme excitement, danced round and round, bare-headed, their long locks flying wildly as they revolved. The singers strained their throats and now and again a fugleman would jump on the shoulders of a sturdy human horse who carried him up and down between the rows of dancers while he shouted, sang or directed the dance with an amazing wealth of gesticulation. Last came the green banner of Hebron, surrounded by a guard of ten wiry swordsmen. Proudly they walked with their flag, till they came to where the narrow Street of David plunges down into the labyrinth of the old city. For the last time they whirled their bright blades above their heads and disappeared into the shadow of the streets. One thought of Highland caterans visiting a Lowland town in Claverhouse's day. Next day the Hebron men and their friends marched down to the shrine of the prophet Moses, where the festival culminates in a cheerful scene of merrymaking and prayer combined after the manner of peasant peoples all the world over....

Here the rejoicings are loudest and longest. All who can follow the procession from Jerusalem: Arabs from across Jordan stalk impressively about the slopes; a 'merry-go-round,' in full swing before the entrance, delights the swarming children and their elders; boy scouts, neat, smart, and as helpful as good boy scouts can be, camp on the hill-side, enjoying themselves mightily. Inside the shrine the notables of Moslem Jerusalem entertain their guests with their wonted dignity and hospitality — though many of them are Christian or Jewish officials of the Administration. In the courts peasants from Hebron, Beduin from the valley, Transjordanians sturdy and long limbed, dance for hours, chanting improvised rhymes or traditional songs in honour of Moses. In every corner men sell their wares — handkerchiefs of rainbow colours, sweets of kaleidoscopic variety (which one hopes will not permanently injure the digestions of Young Palestine), the blue and rich green glass of Hebron. Music plays, clouds of dust blow everywhere, carriages and motor-cars struggle through the soft earth of the road. It is a religious festival, a fair, and a National Holiday all in one; and those who have not seen it must not pretend to know the Moslems of South Palestine.[1]

Related to Islam, yet very different, is the religious community of the Druses. Much as Christianity sprang from Judaism, and as Islam is the child of both Judaism and Christianity, so is the Druse religion an offshoot from Islam. It is far easier to report the outward facts of the history of this little faith than to venture an opinion as to the present beliefs. The background of the strange fanaticism from which they are sprung is in the rivalry — as we should express it — between those who were loyal to the descendants of the fourth Caliph, 'Ali, and those who supported the Umeiyads of Damascus. 'Ali died in A.D. 661. The descendants of his children by his first wife, Fāṭima, the daughter of the Prophet, are to this day the nobility of Islam. There were two sons, Al-Ḥasan, whose family now live largely in Tunis and Algeria, and Al-Ḥusein, whose descendants form part of the aristocracy of Jerusalem. Religious fanaticism quite as much as political intrigue centred about these men long after their death. Numerous sects and schisms developed, all based upon the supposed divine authority of the line of 'Ali.

In the third century of the Faith, A.D. 873–874, there appeared one such fanatic at Jerusalem, 'Abdullah ibn Meimūn al Ḳaddāḥ, who claimed that now, in the time of the seventh in succession from 'Ali, namely, ibn Isma'il, the seventh and last religion of the world was being founded. From 'Ali's descendant, the religion was known as Ismailian-

---

[1] Philip Graves, *Palestine, the Land of Three Faiths* (London: Jonathan Cape Limited), pp. 96–98.

CROWDS IN THE TEMPLE AREA DURING HOLY WEEK

ism. It was a theosophical attempt to unite all the world's religious truth. Among the enthusiasts for this sect, some went eastward, following one Ḳarmaṭ, 'the Dwarf,' there to be known as the Carmathians; their history was filled with such tragedy and heroism that none who reads can doubt the sincerity of their glorious martyrs. Others, the followers of the doctrine of 'Abdullah, went toward the west and gained greater success than the Carmathians had been able to achieve. In A.D. 909, a certain 'Obeidullah, who claimed to be descended from the Imam Isma'il and therefore from the Prophet himself, having converted a very large part of North Africa to his cause, founded the Fatimid dynasty, named from the famous daughter of the Prophet, Fāṭima. From 909 to 1171 this dynasty was, with the exception of short periods, in command of Egypt and Syria, as well as its stronghold in Tunis. When this royal family had passed away, Saladin, who took their place in government, banished from Egypt all who followed their unorthodox beliefs.

One sect, however, within this heresy, had been founded by the impious Fatimid, al-Hakim, probably about A.D. 1000, and had been encouraged to worship him as the living incarnation of the Deity. This strange sect, known as the Druses, was hateful to the others of the Fatimid heresy, however, and was driven from Egypt to settle in the Lebanon and in northern Palestine, there to remain to the present day.[1]

Nothing so excites the curiosity about the tenets of a group as the unwillingness of its members to state or explain their beliefs. The Druses have through their history in Syria persistently refused to describe themselves or to become friendly with outsiders. Numerous volumes have been written about them. Some who have associated with the Druses, speak much of their elusive dishonesty regarding religious matters; we are told that occasionally to avoid persecution some family becomes — at least outwardly — Christian or Moslem for a generation, but that Druse traditions are kept secretly alive that they may return to their faith at some more propitious season.

[1] Sir William Muir, *The Caliphate, its Rise, Decline and Fall* (Revised Edition. T. H. Weir. Edinburgh, 1915), pp. 563, 604.

The Druses are known as the most dangerous fanatics of the population of northern Galilee and Syria, having had a very large share in the uprisings against the French. They are, of course, more of a problem in Syria than in Palestine, yet by no means are they a negligible factor in the British Mandate.[1]

Another sect, whose ultimate origin is the Persian Shi'a, or sectarian Islam, is what we know as Bahaism. Shi'a doctrine dwells much upon the loyalty to the family of 'Ali, and especially upon the millennial hopes which attach to the expectation of a coming Imam from their number. The Shi'a believes that there were twelve (some say seven) rightful Imams, or leaders, from the descendants of 'Ali and Fātima. But in A.D. 940 the twelfth disappeared into a well! He still lives, they believe, and has, through certain people, spoken to his true followers. At the beginning of the nineteenth century a sect arose in Persia, following a man named Sheikh Aḥmad of Ahsa (1752–1827), known from its leader the Sheikhi religion. Sheikh Aḥmad was able to commune with the absent Imam and to reveal his will to his followers. One of his disciples, Mirza 'Ali Muḥammad, claimed yet greater honor, saying that he was himself the Bab-ullah, 'the Gate of God.' His revelation made all previous revelation superfluous. From his self-imposed title, his followers became known as the Babis. Mirza went to Mecca on Pilgrimage, and there preached his new doctrine, but upon returning to Persia he was arrested and imprisoned. The teaching of the sect centred entirely about the person of the founder, who was the Risen Imam, the Great Guide, the Gate of God. The Bab had begun to preach in 1844, and was executed in 1850, while his followers were hounded about the kingdom and many of them were slaughtered. Mirza Yahya, whom the Bab had appointed as his successor, fled to Bagh-

[1] There are about 7000 Druses in Palestine.

Another tiny sect associated with the Druses is interesting to us because of its name, though very few of its adherents have continued in Syria down to our own time. The Assassins, although originating in Persia, have the same heretical background as the Druses. Long a menace to eastern law and order, they acquired their infamous name in the history of the Crusades, on account of their treacherous use of the dagger. Their Arabic name is from the name of a drug, ḥashīsh, which they used to inflame their madness.

dad, where he was known as Subh-i-Azal, 'The Dawn of the Eternal.'

One of the teachings of the Bab had been the announcement of the coming of 'Him whom God should manifest.' Various Babis claimed to be this incarnation, and one of the claimants, who had gone to Baghdad with Subh-i-Azal, entitled himself Baha-'llah, the Glory of God. He and Azal were taken by the Turkish Government to Adrianople, where they quarrelled. The Turks intervened, and took Azal to Cyprus and Baha to Akka (Acre) in Palestine. That was in 1868. The Babis, under Azal, came to be known as Azalis; but Baha attracted most of the sect to himself, relegated the Bab to the position of forerunner of himself, and declared that previous revelation, including that of the Bab, was superseded by his own. He considered himself the founder of a new, liberal religion, the sum total of all that is good in all the established religions.

After the death of Baha in 1892, his eldest son, Abbas Effendi took the leadership of the religious community, using the title 'Abdul-Baha, 'The servant of the Baha.' The sect was no longer confined to Acre; it spread to the west, gaining enthusiastic adherents in the United States, Germany, and other countries.[1] 'Abdul-Baha died at Acre in 1921 and was buried in Haifa.[2] The present leader and head of the movement is young Shawki Effendi, a graduate of the American University of Beirut, who also took graduate work at Oxford. The present headquarters are in Haifa.

This review of Islam and its allied faiths in Palestine gives a picture of entangled traditions, creeds, and racial peculiarities which have been handed down through the centuries. Yet Islam's fundamental appreciation of worship is easily overlooked in the confusion of its outward friction. There is little of pageantry and ritual, except in connection with the pilgrimage to Mecca, and within Palestine itself, to Nebi Musa. But every day, five times during the day, there is the

[1] The Baha'i faith counts about two millions of adherents. The number of Baha'is in Palestine is somewhat less than 300.

[2] Sir 'Abbas Effendi 'Abdu'l Baha had travelled extensively in Europe and America to expound his doctrines, and on the 4th December, 1919, was created by King George V a K.B.E. for valuable services rendered to the British Government in the early days of the Occupation. (*The Handbook of Palestine*, p. 59.)

service of prayer. To be sure, a very small percentage of the people go to the mosques; but these few are by no means negligible, for they represent the most earnest of the community. The prayers include praise of God, gratitude for His beneficent mercy, request for pardon and divine guidance. There is no priest, and the Imam, or leader, may be any one of the Faithful. This prayer custom has been a great levelling force in Islam. As rich and poor, clean and unwashed, black and white and brown, repeat together this same liturgy all through the Moslem world, the equality of men in the presence of Allah has become partially realized. This democracy of Islam is strongest away from the cities, where the poverty of the desert has stimulated man to resigned puzzling over the inscrutable ways of Providence.

The Kur'an is studied with a concentration possible only to an Oriental who believes he has found the one immutable word of God. A picture of Islam, if it is to be true, will be full of inconsistencies: there is degraded poverty, unsympathetic plenty, yet withal the ideal of brotherhood. There is the unflinching doctrine of monotheism, coupled with a devotion to local saints polytheistic in all but name. There is, as in every religion, a vast majority of adherents who are completely careless and neglectful of pious obligation; and on the other hand a select few whose daily devotion is faithful and sincere. There is the little group, often fanatical, whose enthusiasm is expressed in the dervish *zikr*, a kind of worship in which the ecstatic experience is induced by the rhythmic repetition of pious phrases. But, after all is said, this inconsistent Islam has in it germs of progress, democratic, ethical, and even philosophical. We must realize, however, how painfully slow human beings progress; and until a better light appears, the Mandatory will find the problem colored with the friction, the jealousy, and the ignorance characteristic of the Islam of to-day.

CHAPTER VIII

BRITISH PERSONALITIES

'IF you want to know institutions you must know men.' [1]
Nowhere is the truth of this statement more apparent than
in Palestine; one is continually impressed with the potency
of personality in this complex and complicated Mandate.
Everybody with political experience knows the value of tact,
and this is particularly necessary, as one can readily see, in a
land of warring creeds and rival races, where almost every
problem involves the balancing of rights and the adjustment
of intricate situations. The British official, as I observed
him in Palestine, was well versed in the art of conciliation.
Moreover, every Government officer with whom I talked
seemed to be occupying his position because of special fitness.
Most of the chief men — those who have served or who are
now serving Palestine — have held positions in Egypt, the
Sudan, and other Eastern countries — an obviously profitable experience for the efficient management of their respective offices in this unique adventure in the Holy Land.

SIR RONALD STORRS

To get to the heart of the matter, then, one must seek to
know the men who have held, or who now hold, the reins of
Government. No person was better equipped to deal with the
problems of Palestine in the first years of the Mandate than
Mr. Ronald Storrs [2] (now Sir Ronald), who before his
appointment as Military Governor of Jerusalem after the
capture of the city in 1917, was Oriental Secretary to the
Residency in Cairo.

It might almost be said that Mr. Ronald Storrs came into
Jerusalem with Allenby; for, although not the first Governor
of Jerusalem, he succeeded Borton Pasha, the first incumbent of the office, who, on account of a breakdown in health,
was obliged to resign after two weeks' service. The photo-

[1] Woodrow Wilson, *Mere Literature.* 'A Literary Politician,' p. 88.

[2] Appointed Governor and Commander-in-Chief in Cyprus, August, 1926.

graph of Allenby entering Jerusalem seemed to me quite appropriately placed on the wall of Sir Ronald's room at the Governorate.[1]

Mr. Ronald Storrs came to Jerusalem with a wide knowledge of human nature, and from the very beginning showed outstanding ability to deal with people of different races and classes. With a keen sympathy for his work, he governed, as Philip Graves says, 'a particularly difficult, divided, and faction-ridden population with astonishing tact and success.' [2] One outstanding illustration of this was his amazing skill in awakening and holding the interest of these turbulent elements in the things connected with the past. He brought together 'representatives of every creed to work in harmony for the preservation of the Holy City from vulgarization and for the revival of its ancient arts and crafts.' [3]

Mr. Ronald Storrs founded the Pro-Jerusalem Society, of which he was the President and the moving spirit. There was unquestionable insight in the forming of this Society in 1918. It came into being during the Military Administration, while the Government was involved in the many intricate problems of rehabilitation and restoration occasioned by the War, and in the midst, too, of a most delicate situation caused by the arrival in Palestine of the Zionist Commission. With far-sighted vision, the Society proceeded to lay hold on the past and to prepare plans for permanent preservation.

The Charter of the Society states its objects to be: (I) The protection of and the addition to the amenities of Jerusalem and its neighborhood; (II) the provision and maintenance of parks, gardens, and open spaces in and

---

[1] See Chapter I, pp. 19, 20, note.

A recent publication discloses that the original correspondence which produced the Arab revolt against the Turks was carried on between Mr. Ronald Storrs and Hussein. (Vincent Sheean, 'British Two-Pronged Policy in Palestine.' *Asia,* August, 1930.)

[2] Philip Graves, *Palestine, the Land of Three Faiths,* p. 202.

It must not be concluded, however, that his duties were performed without difficulties. At one time, the Jews were so enraged against him that they wired to London they would on no account tolerate his presence! At a later time, the Arabs were so indignant that they made the same representation to the London authorities, who deduced therefrom that he must be partisan to neither, and therefore a fit person for the place.

[3] *Ibid.,* p. 202.

around Jerusalem; (III) the establishment of museums, libraries, art galleries, exhibitions, musical and dramatic centres or other institutions of a similar nature for the benefit of the public; (IV) the protection and preservation, with the consent of the Government, of antiquities in and around Jerusalem; (V) the encouragement of arts, handicrafts, and industries.[1]

The Council of the Society was broadly representative of the different communities in Palestine. The Honorary President was the High Commissioner; and the President, as we have seen, was the Governor of Jerusalem. The Council, which met once a month, had as Honorary Member, Lord Milner, and numbered among its other members the Mayor of Jerusalem, the Grand Mufti, the Orthodox Latin and Armenian Patriarchs, the Anglican Bishop, the Chief Rabbi, the President of the Jewish lay community, representatives of the Dominican and Franciscan Convents, of the Department of Antiquities, etc.[2]

The achievements of the Society notably reflect the keen and learned interest of the founder. One of the first pieces of work to be undertaken was the establishment of a tile and pottery factory for the purpose of making tiles like the original to cover the bare spaces on the Mosque of the Dome of the Rock. Under the direction of the Pro-Jerusalem Society, potters from Mutahia were brought to Jerusalem to make tiles in the old manner. The kilns in which the original tiles were manufactured were discovered in the Haram precincts after the British Occupation.[3]

Through the efforts of the Society, the Suq al-Qattanin (bazaar of the cotton merchants), which forms the principal entrance to the Haram area, the most important of the old

---

[1] *The Handbook of Palestine*, p. 131. Edited by Harry Charles Luke and Edward Keith-Roach. 1922.

[2] *The Handbook of Palestine*, p. 131. Edited by Harry Charles Luke and Edward Keith-Roach. 1922.

See *Jerusalem, 1918–20: Being the Records of the Pro-Jerusalem Council During the British Military Administration.* Published by John Murray, London.

Also: *Jerusalem, 1920–22: Being the Records of the Pro-Jerusalem Council During the First Two Years of the Civil Administration*, p. xv. Edited by C. R. Ashbee. London, John Murray, April, 1924.

[3] *The Handbook of Palestine*, p. 92. Edited by Harry Charles Luke and Edward Keith-Roach. 1922.

vaulted bazaars of Palestine and Syria, was preserved from imminent destruction in 1919.[1] The Society also set up the Jerusalem looms — hand-looms upon which fabrics for everyday use were woven by Palestinians for Palestinians out of Palestinian materials.[2] Among other noted achievements were the revival of the Hebron glass industry, and the freeing and completion of the Rampart Walk, which made it possible, for the first time in several hundreds of years, to 'Walk about Zion, and go round about her: tell the towers thereof.'[3]

When the British came to Jerusalem, they found the walls around the city in a state of dilapidation. In some parts the stones were crumbling and were even being carried away for building purposes. The Turks had shown little regard for these ancient ramparts, which were in places practically hidden from view by the erection of unsightly shops and booths. To save the walls seemed a matter of first importance, and, as Sir Ronald Storrs explained to me, the greater part of the seventy-five thousand dollars which he personally collected for the Pro-Jerusalem Society was used for this restoration.[4]

Much work was done by the Society in repairing the Citadel,[5] and in clearing up the débris embedded in the moat around the Citadel, which has been converted into a garden.[6] One realizes, of course — and this is clearly explained by Mr. Ashbee — that much of the most interesting

---

[1] *The Handbook of Palestine*, p. 93. Edited by Harry Charles Luke and Edward Keith-Roach. 1922.

[2] *Ibid.*, p. 131.

[3] Psalms XLVIII: 12.

[4] In the Preface to the Records of the Pro-Jerusalem Council, edited by C. R. Ashbee, Sir Ronald Storrs refers to his visit to the United States in 1923, 'with the object,' he says, 'of enlisting the interest, sympathy, and assistance of that generous nation. I have to record with gratitude the chivalrous reception accorded to my remote and unusual quest, in so much that a sojourn forcibly limited to twenty days resulted in subscriptions and donations amounting to several thousand pounds.'

[5] The massive fortress of five mighty towers, probably occupying the site of Herod's palace.

[6] The Citadel garden has made considerable progress, and it has received some valuable gifts. The Pro-Jerusalem Society established one of its nurseries in the garden.

work historically is below the ground-level or in the blocked-up passages beneath or skirting the glacis, or even under the moat. 'But the Citadel of Jerusalem,' continues Mr. Ashbee, 'is one of those buildings upon which the architect and the archæologist join issue. The latter would wish to dig it up and search its origins. To do this he has to kill the building. The former insists that as the building is still alive and serving a purpose, noble and beautiful, it must be so kept. The later periods cannot be disturbed to reveal the earlier. Architecture here is more important than archæology.'[1]

The Society held an Academy of Fine Arts in the Tower of David[2] after its restoration in 1921. This exhibition revealed, as Sir Herbert Samuel says in his Interim Report, 'the presence in Palestine of a number of artists and craftsmen of marked talent.' 'There is,' he continued, 'reason to hope that Palestine may gradually become a centre of artistic production, rivalling perhaps in time the famous emporiums of the East of past generations.'[3] In 1922, the Government used the Tower for an exhibition of Palestinian products.[4]

On March 5, 1928, under the patronage of Lord and Lady Plumer, an Arts and Crafts Exhibition was opened which

[1] *Jerusalem,* 1920–22: Being the Records of the Pro-Jerusalem Council During the First Two Years of the Civil Administration, p. 12. Edited by C. R. Ashbee. London, John Murray, 1924.

[2] The Tower of David is the principal of a group of such towers forming the Citadel, which, according to Josephus, was Herod's Palace. The historian gives a detailed description of the structures, their upper stories, baths, banquet halls, battlements, etc.; and further says that when Titus captured the city, he preserved these mighty towers so that posterity might appreciate what he had to contend against in subjugating this capital. The upper parts date from 1542, when the present walls were built. The Tower of David measures 70 feet in height by 65 × 55, with no hollow centre. It is of solid masonry. This monument certainly stood in Christ's day!

The statement is made in the Report on Palestine and Trans-Jordan for the year 1928 (p. 98) that: 'The work of conserving the Citadel of Jerusalem and the Walls of the City has continued.'

[3] (Cmd. 1499.) An Interim Report on the Civil Administration of Palestine, during the period 1st July, 1920–30th June, 1921, p. 20. Presented to Parliament by Command of His Majesty, August, 1921.

[4] *The Handbook of Palestine,* p. 132. Edited by Harry Charles Luke and Edward Keith-Roach. 1922.

lasted eight days.[1] The Exhibition was open from 8 to 12 A.M. and from 2 to 7 P.M. The admission fee was one shilling, and all parts of the country were invited to display their handiwork. The Tower of David was reserved for Jerusalem, Bethlehem, and Ramallah; while Haifa, Gaza, and Beersheba, and other places had their exhibits in other structures in the Citadel. Ladies volunteered to serve in different stalls, where objects could be sold or ordered, and tea was served each afternoon.

Various Jewish institutions had separate exhibits of their own; so also did the Moslem Orphanage, which displayed their work in the empty mosque. They had an exhibition of furniture, printing, bookbinding, and stained-glass windows set in gypsum; such as embellish the great mosque in the Temple area. Schneller's Orphanage [2] exhibited their

---

[1] The following invitation was sent out in February, 1929:

You are invited to the opening of
THE ARTS AND CRAFTS SALE-ROOM AT THE CITADEL
BY
HIS EXCELLENCY THE HIGH COMMISSIONER
on Monday February 18th, at 3.30 P.M.

This Sale-Room is an outcome of the Exhibition held last Year, and will remain open till May, from 9 A.M. till 5 P.M. daily.
(Saturday and Sunday afternoons excepted.)
It is organized for the benefit of the producer, and a minimum percentage is added to the cost-price of each article for administrative expenses.
All goods are bona-fide productions of the people of Palestine — and all districts and all sections of the population are represented.

H. C. BENTWICH
I. CORRIE } (Committee)
E. KEITH-ROACH

[2] Schneller's Orphanage has had a very interesting history, and it is interestingly told by a friend of mine, long resident in Palestine.

After the Damascus massacres in 1860, old Mr. Schneller, who was a graduate of Saint Chrischona College, near Bâle, Switzerland, started a little home in Jerusalem for a couple of these orphans, a mile and a half distant from any habitation. The number of orphans under his care increased, and it was necessary to get more room. Appeals were made in Germany and America, which met with response and led to the establishment of the largest orphanage in the country — more than four hundred children. At first the education was very elementary and much of the building and work had to be done by the boys, whose fare was necessarily rough. Later, one department after another was added and they were taught trades by which they could earn a livelihood: carpentry, blacksmithing, printing, bookbinding, tile-making, etc. In time, it came to be the best-managed institution in the country. Groups of fifty, with housefathers and housemothers, were established, which resulted in a more personal home life. At school they were altogether, then segregated into these families for meals, study, and sleep.

Dr. Theodore Schneller succeeded his old father and devoted his life to the training and welfare of these homeless waifs. Here for the first time Mohammedans came under direct Christian influence. As a young graduate qualified, he was made head of

wrought-iron work, including artistic candlesticks; while candle-making, embroidery, filigree silver-work, basketry, costumes, carpets, and mother-of-pearl work [1] formed the mainstay of the Exhibit.

The Horticultural Show was intended to encourage the planting of gardens, the keeping-up of flower beds, flower pots and ferneries, and also the raising of flowers for bouquet purposes. Prizes were awarded for the finest specimens exhibited. To encourage interest in gardens and plants, Lady Plumer left a silver cup, to be awarded at the end of the year for the best-kept garden. The contest was open to

his trade; little cottages were then built, where these superintendents could marry, live, and bring up their families. These dot the two roads converging on the mother institution.

Later, agriculture was made an intrinsic part of the life, and a large tract of land was acquired near Ramleh, where orange groves were planted and boys were given practical experience in farming. Thereupon, dairying was undertaken, as well as garden-truck raising.

A blind institute was later added, as well as a small (about thirty) girls' orphanage. These, besides being educated, attended to the laundry, sewing and mending. Tailoring and shoemaking for the children followed of necessity, and also extended beyond their needs. In the blind institute brushes and wicker-work were taught, successfully. It should here be mentioned that, though various missions had for seventy years conducted similar industrial departments, where no wages were paid to the workers, all had operated at a loss, Schneller's included, until they established the tile factory which has paid handsomely. They own their own clay fields.

On the occupation of the country by the British and the arrival of the Red Cross workers (almost entirely American), the saving of the orphans was the most crying need; therefore, this equipped institution was taken over. At first, Dr. Schneller was kept at the head; later, the direction was undertaken and held by an American until he went back to America. Naturally the language of teaching was changed from German to English. After a couple of years the Red Cross had to wind up operations, and Dr. Schneller was invited to return and resume the reins. On account of the low ebb of the German marks at the time, he could not undertake it unless support was guaranteed. This was done for over a year.

Later, came the Near-East Relief and some of the Armenian orphans were placed there. Others were put into the Convent of the Cross, Saint James's Convent and other places, and a specified rate was paid to Dr. Schneller per capita. The policy of the Near-East Relief was to make the expense as low as feasible, so that they would be able to reach as many of the war-orphaned children as possible. The Near-East Relief did not withdraw its support until rehabilitated Germany could carry the load. Thus, after this interim the Schneller Orphanage became entirely independent.

[1] It is interesting to note that the shells are exported from the Red Sea to the United States, where large pearl buttons are cut from them. Hundreds of tons of pearl-waste are in turn exported back to Palestine; and in Bethlehem this waste is turned into crosses, beads, brooches, etc., which again find their way into the United States as articles for wear, prayer rosaries, etc. (Information received by the author in Palestine.)

those who paid a nominal fee toward the expenses of the competition.

Who could have foreseen, during the period of the British Military Occupation of Palestine, that the Tower of David would have become a centre of civic activity for the whole of Palestine!

Besides vision, Sir Ronald Storrs had a practical sense of humor. In writing of the removal of the clock-tower at the Jaffa Gate,[1] which, as everybody recognized, was not in keeping with the historic significance of the ancient wall, Sir Ronald says: 'The clock-tower erected by the loyal burgesses of Jerusalem, in a style midway between that of the Eddystone Lighthouse and a jubilee memorial to commemorate the thirty-third year of the auspicious reign of the late Sultan Abdul Hamid, has been bodily removed from the north side of the Jaffa Gate, which it too long disfigured, and is being set up again in fulfilment of a promise (less aggressively and shorn of its more offensive trimmings) in the central and suitable neighbourhood of the Post Office Square.'[2]

Sir Ronald Storrs writes enthusiastically of the improvements made by the Pro-Jerusalem Society. 'The majority of the streets,' he says, 'have been named by a special committee representative of the three great religions, and the names blazoned in the three official languages in coloured and glazed Dome of the Rock tiles. For the first time in the history of the city the houses of Jerusalem are being numbered.'[3]

The naming of streets in Jerusalem was a difficult task. The interesting story of the work, completed at the end of 1922, is given by Mr. Ashbee:

[1] The tower was a conspicuous landmark. The clock had four dials, two indicating the European time with noon as the starting-point; the other two the Arabic (not Hebrew) time, starting from sunset, i.e., twelve o clock — the way time was kept in Bible times.

[2] *Jerusalem*, 1920–22: Being the Records of the Pro-Jerusalem Council During the First Two Years of the Civil Administration, p. vi. Edited by C. R. Ashbee. John Murray, London.

[3] *Jerusalem*, 1920–22: Being the Records of the Pro-Jerusalem Council During the First Two Years of the Civil Administration, pp. vi, vii. Edited by C. R. Ashbee. John Murray, London.

Sir Herbert Samuel had suggested that, instead of having the usual blue enameled names at the street corners, the faïence ones should be used.

A special sub-committee was, at the instance of His Excellency the High Commissioner, formed to undertake this most interesting and by no means easy task. The names had to be in the three official languages, and the three traditions, Christian, Moslem, and Jewish, had, so far as possible, to be preserved. Not only that, their connotations in the language in which they had no precise meaning had often to be sought out. Here was scope not only for scholarship but acute political division, and the sub-committee had on several occasions to be steered over very dangerous rocks. That was the work of the Assistant Governor, who was chairman of the sub-committee. I give here the first set of names that have been chosen and sanctioned up to the close of 1922. Forty-six in the old city and eighty in the new city were either named or numbered for naming, and the names in some cases were painted in ceramics, and set in the streets. The list is so full of history, poetry, and folklore that it is well worth careful study.[1]

Another undertaking, worthy of the high purpose of the Pro-Jerusalem Society, was the preparation of a plan for the development of the city outside the walls. Everybody who visits Palestine is impressed with the way Modern Jerusalem is spreading out over the surrounding hills. And seeing this, one realizes how very important it is that the development of Greater Jerusalem should proceed on well-planned lines. To provide Jerusalem with the advantages of a modern city, and yet to maintain the historical value of certain sites and areas in the Holy City, were the aims of the Pro-Jerusalem Society in drawing up this plan of development.

As a preliminary measure, it was decided that Jerusalem should be divided into zones — industrial, commercial, antiquities, residential, and suburban. The delimitation of these zones roughly follows the development of the city at the present time. The Palestine Town Planning Ordinance [2]

[1] *Jerusalem*, 1920–22: Being the Records of the Pro-Jerusalem Council During the First Two Years of the Civil Administration, pp. 26, 28. Edited by C. R. Ashbee. John Murray, London.

The list of the streets, as adopted during the year, 1922, is given by Mr. Ashbee: In the Old City (within the walls), the New City (outside the walls), the Town Plan, Part II, and the Town Plan, Part III. (*Jerusalem*, 1920–22: Being the Records of the Pro-Jerusalem Council During the First Two Years of the Civil Administration, pp. 26, 27. Edited by C. R. Ashbee. John Murray, London.)

[2] An Ordinance to Secure the Orderly Planning of Towns and to Control the Erection of the Buildings and the Laying-out of Streets. (This Ordinance has been amended by the Town-Planning (Amendment) Ordinance, No. 16 of 1922. Section 26 (c) of the original Ordinance has been repealed by Section 3 of the Town-Plan-

came into existence largely as a result of the work accomplished by the Pro-Jerusalem Society, many of whose ideas have been incorporated in the legislation relating to town planning. Besides the Town Planning Ordinance, the Antiquities Ordinance,[1] and other legislation necessary to the new social order were also stimulated by, or were the direct outcome of, the efforts of the Pro-Jerusalem Society.

As these Government Departments, however, became established, with functions similar to the objects of the Pro-Jerusalem Society, there inevitably developed duplication and some cross-working. When, therefore, the Governor was appointed to Cyprus, in 1926, the Pro-Jerusalem Society was dissolved.[2] Whether this Society had finished its work is a conjecture which the future alone can answer.

The real meaning of the effort is succinctly described by Mr. Ashbee:

The disaster of the Great War has forced upon all men and women the necessity of preserving all that is possible of the beauty and the purpose, in actual form, of the civilizations that have passed before. We have come to see, moreover, that this is not a mere matter of archæology or the protection of ancient buildings. In the blind mechanical order with which we are threatened everything that we associate with our sense of beauty is alike in danger. Landscape, the unities of streets and sites, the embodied vision of the men that set the great whole together, the sense of colour which in any oriental city is still a living sense — all these things have to be considered practically; they must, to put it plainly, be protected against the incursions of the grasping trader, the ignorant workman, the self-interested property owner, and the well-intentioned Government Department.

In Jerusalem, perhaps more than in any other city, these facts are brought home to us. It is a city unique, and before all things a city of idealists, a city moreover in which the idealists through succeeding generations have torn each other and their city to pieces. Over forty times has it changed hands in history. And perhaps partly because of all this and partly because of the grandeur of its

ning (Amendment) Ordinance of 1922). Legislation of Palestine, 1918–25. Compiled by Norman Bentwich, Attorney-General of Palestine. Orders-in-Council and Ordinances, vol. 1, p. 120.

[1] An Ordinance to Provide for the Control of Antiquities in Palestine. Legislation of Palestine, 1918–25. Compiled by Norman Bentwich, Attorney-General of Palestine. Orders-in-Council and Ordinances, vol. 1, p. 76.

[2] Sir Ronald Storrs presided over the last meeting — when the Society was dissolved.

site and surrounding landscape it is a city of singular romance and beauty.

These facts are emphasized by other considerations. When the British Military Administration began work there were practically no roads. The Turks only improvised roads and most of them the Great War had destroyed. Next, in the turning of every sod or scrap of stone some historic association is affected. There are then the interminable questions of prescriptive right in venerated sites, the joint ownerships by divers and conflicting religious bodies. The city maintains a large parasitic population — priests, caretakers, monks, missionaries, pious women, clerks, lawyers, the motley order that has a vested interest in maintaining the *status quo*. Here is a force that often makes for what is picturesque and conservative, but as often checks the administrator in genuine and rational improvement, because the sanction for what he wants to do rests not in the city itself, but in the great world outside somewhere, hidden away. The actual bit of stone or the rubbish-heap we want to clean up may, it is true, belong to some Greek, or Moslem, or Jew, but the Armenian, the English Protestant, the Abyssinian, the American missionary, the Italian, the Wakf in India, the Copt — the other fellow somewhere — they all have a word to say on the matter, and before we do anything we must wait to hear it.

And, last, there has been the fact that has necessarily modified alike the enterprise of the Pro-Jerusalem Society and the Administration — there has been very little money to do anything with. This, though it may cripple historical research, may also be a protection against vandalism or ill-considered enterprise, for one great power at least the Administrator of to-day possesses, the power of sitting tight and doing nothing, of stopping unintelligent or destructive action, of waiting till a better day. If he have taste, though he himself be precluded from all creation, he can at least prevent foolish or wanton things from being done. That has, in the Holy City during the last five years, been a very great help.

And one thing we whose concern is civics must always remember. In the conservation of a city, whether it be like London, Paris, Rome, or New York, well within the great stream of the world, or whether like Jerusalem set upon a hill-top and remote, what we are conserving is not only the things themselves, the streets, the houses, spires, towers, and domes, but the way of living, the idealism, the feeling for righteousness and fitness which these things connote, and with which every city with any claim to dignity and beauty is instinct.[1]

One can only hope that the impelling motive of Sir Ronald Storrs, expressed so clearly in his statement of thanks to all

[1] *Jerusalem*, 1920–22: Being the Records of the Pro-Jerusalem Council During the First Two Years of the Civil Administration, pp. 4, 5. Edited by C. R. Ashbee. John Murray, London.

those who had supported him in carrying out the objects of
the Society, will be kept alive. 'Busy men,' he speaks of
them, 'with urgent and important duties of their own, who,
nevertheless, have not spared themselves nor their time in
keeping this constructive and unifying fellowship so far as
possible abreast with the needs of the time, and in holding it
above and out of the dust and clamour of political and other
controversy.' [1]

And he continues: 'Of our benefactors many, who live in
remote continents, may never witness the results of their
generosity; of whom we can but say that, while some little of
their achievement will be presented to their vision by picture
and by plan, their true satisfaction will rest rather in the sure
and certain knowledge that, through their loving carefulness,
Jerusalem will have been preserved nearer to the city of their
faith and of their dreams.' [2]

This is the challenge to the future!

SIR HERBERT SAMUEL

The leading official in Palestine is the High Commissioner.
He is the centre of the situation: on him fall the weighty cares
and perplexing problems. Of all the Mandates, Palestine
presents the most complicated situation; in truth, it differs
from all the others, both in plan and purpose. Furthermore,
in its own class, the Mandate of Palestine is markedly different from that of Syria or of 'Iraq.[3]

These three Mandates derive their power from the Covenant of the League of Nations, which gives to all alike a definite
and binding responsibility to prepare the communities for
self-government. Witness the text which proclaimed the new
doctrine:

Certain communities formerly belonging to the Turkish Empire
have reached a stage of development where their existence as independent nations can be provisionally recognized subject to the
rendering of administrative advice and assistance by a Mandatory
until such time as they are able to stand alone.[4]

[1] *Jerusalem*, 1920–22: Being the Records of the Pro-Jerusalem Council During the
First Two Years of the Civil Administration, p. viii. Edited by C. R. Ashbee. John
Murray, London.

[2] *Ibid.*   [3] Palestine, Syria, and 'Iraq are called the 'A' Mandates.

[4] Paragraph 4 of Article 22 of the Covenant of the League of Nations.

SIR HERBERT SAMUEL ON A VISIT TO TRANS-JORDAN

Sir Herbert is in the center. The third from the right is T. E. Lawrence

The point of departure in the Palestine Mandate is the Jewish National Home, which conspicuously finds no mention in the Covenant, although this document was drawn up two years after the announcement of the Balfour Declaration. By the terms of this Mandate, which was adopted by the Council of the League of Nations in 1922, the Mandatory's chief responsibility is to facilitate the establishment of a Jewish National Home in Palestine,[1] coupled with the duty of safeguarding the civil and religious rights of the non-Jewish population, and at the same time to provide for the development of self-governing institutions.[2]

Article 1 of the Mandate clearly provides for the special régime in Palestine: 'The Mandatory shall have full powers of legislation and of administration, save as they may be limited by the terms of this mandate.'

This plan, however, as it functions in Palestine, constitutes a situation unmistakably in conflict with the Covenant; and clearly enough, in contrast to Syria and 'Iraq, it can never be in agreement with that document, except through a basal change in its structure. The whole enterprise, in fact, is a clear diversion from the original plan laid down for these three 'communities formerly belonging to the Turkish Em-

---

[1] This is indicated in paragraphs 1, 2, and 3 of the Preamble of the Mandate for Palestine:

'Whereas the Principal Allied Powers have agreed, for the purpose of giving effect to the provisions of Article 22 of the Covenant of the League of Nations, to entrust to a Mandatory selected by the said Powers the administration of the territory of Palestine, which formerly belonged to the Turkish Empire, within such boundaries as may be fixed by them; and

'Whereas the Principal Allied Powers have also agreed that the Mandatory should be responsible for putting into effect the declaration originally made on November 2nd, 1917, by the Government of His Britannic Majesty, and adopted by the said Powers, in favour of the establishment in Palestine of a national home for the Jewish people, it being clearly understood that nothing should be done which might prejudice the civil and religious rights of existing non-Jewish communities in Palestine, or the rights and political status enjoyed by Jews in any other country; and

'Whereas recognition has thereby been given to the historical connection of the Jewish people with Palestine and to the grounds for reconstituting their national home in that country;...'

[2] Article 2 of the Mandate for Palestine: 'The Mandatory shall be responsible for placing the country under such political, administrative and economic conditions as will secure the establishment of the Jewish national home, as laid down in the preamble, and the development of self-governing institutions, and also for safeguarding the civil and religious rights of all the inhabitants of Palestine, irrespective of race and religion.'

pire.' The Covenant, let us reiterate, limits the authority of the Mandatory over these territories 'to the rendering of administrative advice and assistance... until such time as they are able to stand alone.' This is the spirit and the letter as originally conceived for these Mandates.

In the circumstance, therefore, where the Mandatory relies on the terms of the Mandate, it follows that the chief duty of the High Commissioner is to further the project for the establishment of the Jewish National Home and the development of self-governing institutions; while at the same time to direct his energies toward 'safeguarding the civil and religious rights of all the inhabitants.' Naturally enough, he encounters difficulties and embarrassments. He comes face to face with two opposing policies, aggressively furthered by the Jews on the one hand, and the native inhabitants on the other. And in pursuance of his duty to govern the country according to the provisions of the Mandate, he is constantly playing the rôle of arbiter in the well-nigh irreconcilable struggle between these two factions. The man who fills this office must have wisdom, tact, and patience.

There have been three High Commissioners in Palestine, all of whom have shouldered responsibilities that might have baffled less competent administrators. Each, in turn, has wisely dealt with problems peculiar to his own régime. Yet, if we were, in a word, to single out any one period in the ten years of the Mandate, during which the office of the High Commissioner involved exceptionally difficult circumstances, we should, I think, inevitably concede that, in the setting-up of the civil government, when new policies were being formulated — policies involving the actual working-out of these strange principles, having scant precedent in international politics — the first High Commissioner faced the most intricate task of all.

In the first place, he came to a country, torn with disappointments and dissensions, rife with racial jealousy and suspicion. Emerging from military rule, the nearly six hundred thousand Arabs and the seventy to eighty thousand Jews, covertly conjecturing on the changes which civil administration might have in store for them, made up a mass little equipped in the knowledge of political theories to be applied in the adjustment of the new régime. Such was the condition of the country which Sir Herbert Samuel, a Jew and a Zionist, came to rule. He took office on July 1, 1920, at the termination of the Military Administration (Occupied Enemy Territory Administration), June 30, 1920.[1]

The appointment of a Jew to this high office is a significant incident in the history of the Palestine Mandate. It was the outstanding feature of the new Civil Government. Everybody debated the advisability of appointing a Jew to head the Administration. Although I arrived in Palestine after the departure of Sir Herbert Samuel, I encountered lively discussions on the subject. The non-Jewish sections of the population with whom I talked were almost unanimous in criticising the selection of a Jew to the office; and as one would naturally expect, the Arabs were unalterably in opposition. They regarded Sir Herbert Samuel as the political enemy of their cause; and they looked upon his appointment as the first act in the repudiation of the British pledge for an independent Arab State.

Personally, however, many of the Arabs held Sir Herbert Samuel in high esteem. No one doubted his ability. He was formerly a member of the British Cabinet and had held parliamentary and administrative positions continuously from 1905 to 1919. All parties recognized his capacity, and, as time went on, his impartiality also. All agreed that there never was a man more passionately devoted to Palestine. Yet, at the same time, even the most disinterested among the population expressed doubts — and still express doubts — as to whether the sending of a Jew to Palestine as the first High Commissioner was the wisest procedure for the situation at that time, or even, as a matter of fact, for the ultimate working-out of this unique Mandate. Then, too, the argument gained support in the observation that the highest legal officer of the Government was also — and is to-day — a Jew and a Zionist. But whatever the case, it seems beyond de-

[1] The powers of the High Commissioner are set forth in the Palestine Order-in-Council of August 10, 1922. Legislation of Palestine, 1918–25. Compiled by Norman Bentwich, Attorney-General of Palestine. Orders-in-Council and Ordinances, vol. 1, pp. 3–6.

The Royal Instructions to the High Commissioner, dated 14th August, 1922, are printed in Legislation of Palestine, 1918–25, vol. 2, pp. 529–36.

bate that these first reactions not only helped to shape Arab thought at the time, but unmistakably stimulated the building-up of an articulate Arab viewpoint, which clearly bases its structure on the early events in the British Administration. No part of the story is forgotten.

In view of all this, one gets some idea of the task which faced the first High Commissioner. Sir Herbert Samuel showed exceptional wisdom in advancing the initial measures of government. He forwarded, for example, the free expression of public opinion, and he used the Press for pronouncements of policy.[1] The proceedings of the Advisory Council, established in October, 1920, were published in the Press; and on the King's Birthday, June 3, 1921, the High Commissioner made the announcement that 'His Majesty's Government were giving the closest attention to the question of ensuring in Palestine a free and authoritative expression of popular opinion.'[2] These were striking measures for a people who had so recently been freed from the Turkish yoke.

Almost at once, Sir Herbert Samuel attacked the Arab-Jewish problem, and his efforts disclose a keen determination to allay misapprehension. In his first report on the Civil Administration, he took occasion to point out that it was the British Government's policy to satisfy 'the legitimate aspirations of the Jewish race throughout the world in relation to Palestine, combined with a full protection of the rights of the existing population'; and he significantly added, as his own personal conviction, that 'the Zionism that is practicable is the Zionism that fulfils this essential condition.'[3]

In this same report, Sir Herbert further elucidated his opinion on Zionism: 'The measures,' he said, 'to foster the well-being of the Arabs should be precisely those which we should adopt in Palestine if there were no Zionist question and if there had been no Balfour Declaration. There is in this policy

---

[1] On the discussion of the Press, see Chapter II, pp. 33–39.

[2] Cmd. 1499. An Interim Report on the Civil Administration of Palestine, during the period 1st July, 1920–30th June, 1921, p. 10. Presented to Parliament by Command of His Majesty, August, 1921.

[3] Cmd. 1499. An Interim Report on the Civil Administration of Palestine, during the period 1st July, 1920–30th June, 1921, p. 7. Presented to Parliament by Command of His Majesty, August, 1921.

nothing incompatible with reasonable Zionist aspirations. On the contrary, if the growth of Jewish influence were accompanied by Arab degradation, or even by a neglect to promote Arab advancement, it would fail in one of its essential purposes. The grievance of the Arab would be a discredit to the Jew, and in the result the moral influence of Zionism would be gravely impaired.' [1]

All this meant satisfaction for the Arabs, but such a show of impartiality aroused severe criticism among the Jews. Dr. Eder, the then acting Chairman of the Zionist Commission, denounced the Government of Palestine as an Arab administration.[2] There were also criticisms from the Orthodox Jews, who were opposed either to a political or non-religious Zionism. These Jews complained that Sir Herbert Samuel 'allowed himself to be led astray by the Zionists,' that he was 'obsessed by the idea of "union" among the Jews of Palestine'; when, in fact, it was impossible for all the Jews to be represented by one religious chief, 'since the Ashkenazim and Sephardim could not agree, except to differ.' [3]

In spite, however, of the outspoken criticism which the Jews continued to level against the High Commissioner during his five years' term of office, Sir Herbert Samuel maintained to the end his original conception of Zionism and its application to the administration of the Mandate. Even on the point of his departure, during the testimonial tendered to him and Lady Samuel by the Jews of Palestine, he again reiterated his views. This time he spoke face to face with Palestinian Jewry, heart to heart, as it were, with the earnest hope, it would seem, of coming to some agreement as to the meaning of the doctrine.

He said that much had been achieved in carrying out the policy of the Mandate, both as it relates to the Jewish National Home and the well-being of the non-Jewish population. 'I am profoundly convinced,' he asserted, 'that these two

[1] Cmd. 1499. An Interim Report on the Civil Administration of Palestine, during the period 1st July, 1920–30th June, 1921, p. 8. Presented to Parliament by Command of His Majesty, October, 1921.

[2] Cmd. 1540. Palestine, Disturbances in May, 1921. Reports of the Commission of Inquiry with Correspondence Relating Thereto, p. 57. Presented to Parliament by Command of His Majesty, October, 1921.

[3] Philip Graves, *Palestine, the Land of Three Faiths*, pp. 177–79.

purposes are intimately bound up with one another. If the creation of the National Home proved to be injurious to the Arabs of Palestine it could never be created on a firm foundation, and, on the other hand, it is only through the development of the country, which Jewish enterprise and capital are needed to promote, that the progress and well-being of the Arab population can be achieved. The policy which has been adopted involved the combination of those two elements. It is, I am sure, the only one that would be, not only just, but also practicable.'

Then, as an intimate side-light on his interesting personality, we might quote Sir Herbert's remarks made at this same testimonial, on Jewish criticism: 'The Jewish people,' he said, 'are inclined to criticism, but not, I think, in excess; and for myself I have nothing whatever to complain of in that regard.... For my own part, I have always proceeded on the belief that the most humble piece of positive work of one's own is better than the most brilliant criticism of the work of somebody else. Here and there, however, one finds elements in the Jewish community, whether in Palestine or elsewhere, which, no doubt owing to the active vitality that characterizes the race, do not realize that restraint also is necessary, and that those who ask too much often succeed in getting nothing at all. Many a political failure, and many a tragedy, in the long course of Jewish history emphasize that lesson.'

It is not the intention here to describe in any detailed fashion the achievements of Sir Herbert Samuel as High Commissioner. They appear elsewhere in the book. The author has merely aimed to portray the personality of the first High Commissioner and to indicate his method of approach to the problems of administration. Sir Herbert Samuel's farewell message, entitled 'To the People of Palestine,' dated June 30, 1925, throws much light on this thesis and incidentally gives an admirable summary of his achievements. He speaks of these five years with proud affection for Palestine and its people, and he clings to the hope that the two factions may sometime be reconciled.

Let us quote this letter — a document which merits an honored place in the annals of Zionism and in the history of the Palestine Mandate:

At the moment of vacating the Office of High Commissioner, I desire to convey to the people of Palestine, of all classes and of all creeds, my heartfelt thanks for the kindness and good will which they have shown towards me. The ceremonies of farewell during these last weeks in all the principal towns, the appreciation that has been expressed of such efforts as I have been able to make on behalf of the country, the cordial wishes for the future that have been offered for Lady Samuel and myself, have touched us deeply.

I recall the message to the people of Palestine of His Majesty King George V, which I had the privilege to deliver in my inaugural address five years ago. His Majesty then said: 'I desire to assure you of the absolute impartiality with which the duties of the Mandatory Power will be carried out, and of the determination of my Government to respect the rights of every race and every creed represented among you.' It has been my earnest endeavor to conduct the Administration with a scrupulous observance of that pledge, in the spirit and in the letter.

In leaving Palestine I rejoice to think that the country shows every sign of a growing prosperity. Agriculture, Industry and Commerce are developing. The population is rapidly increasing. There is an accumulated balance of revenue over expenditure of more than £E.600,000. It has been possible to reduce the taxation that lay heavily upon the cultivator. The railway and postal services are efficient and remunerative to the State. Nearly a thousand kilometers of new roads have been built. Public security is completely maintained. Progress has been made in the elimination of malaria and other diseases that affected the population. Nearly two hundred village schools have been opened. The antiquities of the country, of the deepest interest to the world at large, have been carefully safeguarded. The Government has taken every opportunity to promote a greater spirit of harmony between the many religious communities which are comprised within this varied population, and those efforts have had results.

Very much remains to be done. Yet the work of these five years has not been unfruitful. Laying down my charge, I pray for the future welfare of Palestine, for the union of her people, for the strengthening of her spiritual influence over the world.

(Signed)   HERBERT SAMUEL

It is difficult to say if any other person could have taken Palestine through the early and critical period of the Mandate with greater success than that achieved by Sir Herbert Samuel. A Zionist and a liberal, and conciliatory by nature, he really made an effort to pacify the Arabs. Indeed, he was so careful to avoid any suspicion of being partial for racial reasons, that on occasion he was known to favor the Arabs to the disadvantage of the Jews. Throughout his administration, he cherished high ideals for Palestine as Palestine. All parties owe him a debt of gratitude for his painstaking, cautious, and intelligent methods. Indubitably, the foundations which he laid during those critical and eventful years will color the whole future of the Palestine Mandate.

LORD PLUMER

The coming of the second High Commissioner was a landmark in the history of this Mandate. The appointment of Lord Plumer, the soldier, gave a new turn to the situation. The Arabs were relieved that he was not a Jew, and looked upon the change as perhaps indicative of more favorable consideration; while the Jews, on the other hand, were frankly disappointed. There was general fear among the Zionists that the appointment of a non-Jew might indicate a change of policy disadvantageous to them. But the disinterested of the population generally liked the appointment and looked forward to an administration without bias or personal interest. On no subject did I find such vigorous discussion as on the coming of Lord Plumer.

The Jews objected to Lord Plumer on still another ground, namely — that this appointment had been made without consulting Dr. Weizmann and the Zionist organization. Article 4 of the Mandate [1] was quoted in support of the view that the Zionist organization should have been consulted. As far back as 1921, Dr. Eder said, in his testimony before the Commission of Inquiry appointed to investigate the Jaffa disturbances in May, 1921, that he believed the Zionist Organization should be allowed either to formulate objections to the selection of the High Commissioner for Palestine or to

---

[1] Article 4. An appropriate Jewish agency shall be recognized as a public body for the purpose of advising and co-operating with the Administration of Palestine in such economic, social and other matters as may affect the establishment of the Jewish National Home and the interests of the Jewish population in Palestine, and, subject always to the control of the Administration, to assist and take part in the development of the country.

The Zionist organization, so long as its organization and constitution are in the opinion of the Mandatory appropriate, shall be recognized as such agency. It shall take steps in consultation with His Britannic Majesty's Government to secure the co-operation of all Jews who are willing to assist in the establishment of the Jewish National Home.

submit to the British Government a list of its own nominees for consideration.[1]

Jewish apprehensions seemed to be confirmed by the remarks of the Colonial Secretary who was in Palestine about that time. On receiving an Arab delegation at Government House, Mr. Amery said that: 'It ought to be clearly understood that the whole object of the policy of the Palestine Government was to promote the welfare of Palestine as a whole, and not of one section at the expense of another.' And he significantly added that there was no reason why there should not exist in Palestine an 'Arab National Home' side by side with the 'Jewish National Home.' [2]

This was a direct answer to the Arab representations to the new High Commissioner relating to the negotiations between the Mandatory Power and the Arabs concerning the establishment of an Arab Agency.[3] Although, as a matter of fact, the Arabs rejected the British plan for such an agency, the proposition caused alarm among the Jews; and it undoubtedly stimulated more vigorous action on the part of the Zionist Organization.

Lord Plumer received the usual official welcome from the Mayor of Jerusalem, Ragheb Bey Nashashibi, who, in his address, closed with the affectionate greeting: 'I wish to assure Your Excellency that the inhabitants of Jerusalem and Palestine receive you today with open hearts and smiling faces full of hopes for the future. I ask the Almighty to keep you and Lady Plumer in good health and to guide you in all your actions.'

The real attitude of the Arabs, however, was expressed in the Arab Press. The 'Yarmuk' stated:

England has not sent us an English High Commissioner for a Zionist High Commissioner in vain.

[1] Cmd. 1540. Palestine. Disturbances in May, 1921, Reports of the Commission of Inquiry with Correspondence Relating Thereto, p. 57. Presented to Parliament by Command of His Majesty, October, 1921.

[2] Major E. W. Polson Newman, *The Middle East*, p. 81.

[3] Cmd. 1989. Proposed Formation of an Arab Agency. Correspondence with the High Commissioner for Palestine, November, 1923.

Cmd. 1889. Papers relating to the Elections for the Palestine Legislative Council, June, 1923.

'Falastin' commented as follows:

The Arab inhabitants desire progress and development, will Lord Plumer, the new High Commissioner, clear the path of obstacles?

Following a long article on the new High Commissioner, the 'Carmel' concluded:

The new High Commissioner has two qualities which we hope will benefit Palestine. These two qualities are: He is the representative of the Conservative Government and he is an openminded soldier. Accordingly the deputation that must wait on him must be composed of those Arabs who possess exceptional qualities and political knowledge, and must appreciate British quality and culture.

'Maraat-al-Sherk' addressed a formal letter to H. E. Field Marshal Lord Plumer, High Commissioner for Palestine: opening with the salutation:

Allow us to offer you our warmest welcome to Palestine as High Commissioner. We venture to express this welcome on behalf of those Arabs of Palestine — and we believe them to be the majority of the population — who gratefully acknowledge the benefits to be derived under the fostering care of a British Mandate, and who earnestly desire for our Arab leaders that education and experience which can (we believe) best be acquired under the guidance of, and in hearty and open coöperation with, trained and tried British officials.

Then follows a long accusation against the previous British administration, and an appeal for participation in the legislative affairs of the country:

We would also, Your Excellency, in the name of the Arabs of Palestine — and again, we believe they are a majority of the population — who have long deplored the system which has obtained during the last two years... of Arab non-coöperation in the legislative affairs of the country. We do not propose to touch on the rights or wrongs of this past Arab policy, beyond expressing a hope that this policy is, or soon will be a thing of the past. The Palestine Arabs, despite their inexperience in organizations and united action, have yet, more than once, shown clearly that they long for an enlightened leadership which shall state their wishes, and explain the hardships under which they labor, in a fashion that would prove to His Majesty's Government that the Arabs of Palestine are not moved solely by a vain and childish obstructiveness, or by a purely negative spirit of opposition to the present policy of the Mandatory Power. The past five years have not been without their effect. We would not have the British public (of whose interest in the people of the Holy Land we are gratefully aware) — we would not have them withdraw their sympathy from us in the belief that we 'have forgotten nothing and learned nothing.' We have learnt much: we will readily forget much.

There is a plea for the solution of the 'Arab problem':

We wish the date of Your Excellency's arrival in our country, August the Twenty-fifth, 1925, to mark a landmark in the so-called 'Arab problem' of Palestine. From this day we wish our attitude towards the officials of the Mandatory Power to be openly recognized and known as one that cheerfully discards grievances and habits acquired in past years, that cleanses from our minds all bitterness aroused by real or supposed injustice or misjudgment of the past.

Methods of dealing with the problem are vaguely described:

We realize that we are in no position to bargain with His Majesty's Government on what terms to 'offer our coöperation': nor are we blind to the fact that it is inconsonant with His Majesty's dignity to enter into a bargain with (as you think) an ill-developed, ill-educated, unorganized, inexperienced and disunited and comparatively small population. But we appeal for some, at least, of the benefits intended, to accrue to a mandated area — education in self-government. Admitted that we are as yet too politically immature wholly to steer Palestine through the shoals from destitution to prosperity, we yet permit ourselves to persist in claiming a right to sit by the side of the experienced pilot, and even from time to time make our own comments and suggestions as to the course pursued and the ultimate goal proposed.

The Arab opposition to the Mandate is vigorously set forth:

We make no pretence of reconciling our Arab consciences with the whole terms and purport of the Mandate. We see in Palestine an Arab land and a centre where, by virtue of long centuries of history and in the interests of the very great majority in the country, Arab civilization has every prior claim to consideration and the right to demur most vigorously to whatever threatens to submerge that civilization. But, for good or for ill, as a brief expedient or lengthy experiment, we are forced to admit the condition of things sanctioned by powers beyond our control. Thus much being said, we leave that question for the future — when our fears have been justified or found baseless, or when the League of Nations sees fit to reëxamine the position from the Arab standpoint.

Two definite suggestions are made:

(a) that you will as a first call on your powers, use all your knowledge of men and affairs, and the advice of your officials in ascertaining the truth of our assertion that the bulk of the Arab population of all grades is anxious to coöperate with the Government, and so far as its poor ability permits, advise in the conduct of Arab affairs that,

(b) as you gradually make acquaintance with the more thoughtful and influential among the Arabs, you endeavor to recommend to His Majesty's Government such measures of modification in the 'Order in Council' which now decrees the nature of the Constitution of Palestine, as shall render possible the free and hearty measure of coöperation in the country's government and legislation to which all sections of the population admittedly are entitled.

The letter closes with a touching benediction:

·May God bless your period of office in this country, make you beloved by all our people, and grant you health and strength to pursue your difficult work and may your name be written as a blessing in the annals of this our Holy Land.

The Jewish Press was equally articulate. 'Haaretz' wrote:

Into the ears of Lord Plumer we must convey the following clear matters this day, when he first places his foot on our land and takes up the historic task of the development of our National Home during the coming years; of the details, the solitary facts, there will be yet time to speak in the ordinary meetings between the High Commissioner and the Jewish representatives. To-day it is necessary to express our general attitude, the principle of our hopes, aspirations and demands. The principle is: Return to the Balfour Declaration, to its spirit and its letter, with sincerity and without ambiguity. No sacrifices are required of the British Nation. There is only required the usual spirit of fair play, the fulfilment of obligations with a full heart, even if there are some difficulties in the side that undertakes the obligation.

From 'Doar Hayom,' we quote:

... In this spirit, in a spirit of hope and respect in advance, we receive Lord Plumer, a soldier and a diplomat of responsibility and experience, who has taken upon his shoulders the responsible burden of the administration of the country in accordance with the Mandate.

Such was the general trend of opinion which confronted Lord Plumer as he took up the reins of administration, and probably no public official was better able than he to benefit by such outspoken expressions. Though a man of eminently independent spirit and deeply impatient of superficial criticism, Lord Plumer welcomed all information, however detailed in its nature, which would in any way throw light on the problems he was called upon to solve. Moreover, he sought information; he made direct contacts with the different elements of the population; and more important than all, perhaps, he had a great personal interest in Palestine itself.

Both he and Lady Plumer showed a lively sympathy for all Palestinian affairs. One good example of this characteristic was their participation in the Annual Police Sports at Jaffa, the social event for that part of the country. My husband and I were included in the list of invited guests, and we found it a day long to be remembered. Lord Plumer was the Patron for the affair. 'His Excellency the High Commissioner, Field Marshal Lord Plumer, G.C.B., G.C.M.G., G.C.V.O., G.B.E.,' headed the printed program. Distinguished Vice-Patrons there were also: Air Commodore E. L. Gerrard, C.M.G., D.S.O., Lt.-Col. G. S. Symes, C.M.G., D.S.O., His Worship the Mayor of Jaffa and His Worship the Mayor of Tel-Aviv. In the races, were the Englishman, the Arab and the Jew — all competing in the interesting and fascinating sports.

When the program was finished, Lord Plumer, as the names of the winners were announced, passed the prizes to Lady Plumer, who, standing at his left, made the presentations, shaking hands and giving a friendly smile to each of the winners. The men came forward at the announcement of their names, some in the very garb in which they had finished the race, while others hurriedly donned a coat out of deference to Lady Plumer. Each responded to the kindly greeting, sometimes with a smile, or again with a bow, but always with some characteristic expression of genuine good feeling. There was nothing perfunctory in this ceremony for Lord and Lady Plumer; they enjoyed the sports, as did others who were there. Besides the official party and representative groups of people, the rank and file were present also. All were enjoying the same sports, and all joined in congratulating the same winners. This one day, as Lord Plumer could well under-

stand, smoothed out more grievances than a host of Ordinances or interviews could ever have done.

Lord Plumer was admirably simple. He and Lady Plumer
had just completed their visit to the Palestine Near-East
Exhibition and Fair at Tel-Aviv when we arrived. The High
Commissioner's automobile left the grounds as inconspicu-
ously as any common Palestinian might have ridden away.
In fact, we were only aware of the visit by the exuberant
spirit of the manager, who offered apology for not greeting us
immediately because he was 'just finishing showing the
exhibits to Lord and Lady Plumer.'

This was the second Exhibition of the kind, the first having
been held in the spring of 1924. The success of the first undertaking led to the organization, under the laws of Palestine, of
the Palestine Exhibitions and Fairs Corporation, Limited.
The object of the corporation is to give an exhibition 'in the
spring and fall of each year of merchandise and products, not
only from Palestine and the Near East, but from other countries of the East and West.'

The 1925 Exhibition covered a space of eight acres, and
consisted of six main buildings. The Main Hall contained the
exhibits of Home Industries. In the Machinery Hall, there
were machines, agricultural implements, and automobiles of
foreign origin, as well as tools, parts of machinery, electric
fittings, etc., manufactured in Palestine and abroad. The
Agricultural Hall contained many of the agricultural products
of Palestine — fertilizers, dairy equipment, incubators,
sprayers for the disinfection of plants and animals. The
Agricultural Department of the Zionist Executive in Palestine
exhibited a conspicuous selection of the products of Keren
Hayesod settlements on the land of the National Fund. A
varied group of articles were exhibited in the Near-East Pavilions, which housed the exhibits from Egypt, Trans-Jordan,
'Iraq, and Syria. The Health Pavilion was arranged in two
sections — the medical and the sanitary. The aim of this
exhibit was to demonstrate what had been accomplished in
sanitation and hygiene. It contained the exhibits of various
medical units. In the Palace of Literature, there were exhibitions of books and periodicals, printed in Palestine and
abroad, and also of the history of Hebrew printing and de-

velopment, placards, photo-blocks, etc. There were also private pavilions on the grounds, used by private firms, both Palestinian and foreign. Separate enclosures were constructed for the display of motor-tractors, agricultural machines, automobiles, and wagons. In all, there were three hundred exhibitors.

Besides the serious part of the project, there was the Amusement Park, conducted on the same lines as the amusement side of any other fair or exhibition. This helped to draw the crowds. On the opening day of the Exhibition, there were more than two thousand visitors, all admitted by ticket.

This Near-East Fair not only attracted attention among manufacturers, merchants, and so on, but also among public and Government circles. Sir Ronald Storrs took part in the inaugural ceremonies, and formally declared the Exhibition 'open to the public.' Lord Plumer made his visit soon after the opening, and expressed great interest in this Palestinian display.[1] And, what is most important for our thesis, Lord Plumer's presence gave great satisfaction to those who had arranged the exhibits, and assured them of the High Com-

[1] The Jewish Telegraphic Agency sent the following interesting announcement of the opening of the Palestine Exhibition in Tel-Aviv in the spring of 1929:

Tel Aviv, Apr. 9 — The Palestine and Near East Exhibition, being the fourth annual exhibition, was opened here today coincident with the observance of the twentieth anniversary of the founding of Tel Aviv, the first all-Jewish city in Palestine.

A brilliant gathering consisting of the chiefs of the government departments, foreign consuls, representatives of the Syrian government and a number of tourists and guests from all parts of the country and abroad was present to witness the inaugural ceremonies.

Sir John Chancellor, the High Commissioner, in opening the exhibition, stated that what Tel Aviv and all Palestine Jewry has achieved is a brilliant record. 'The exhibits are numerous and interesting. Now you must learn the art of selling your products. I am glad to observe that among the exhibitors are many British firms, thus trade connections with England are being fostered,' the High Commissioner declared.

'You will learn the methods of penetrating the world markets. The availability of cheap electrical power, thanks to the Rutenberg works, will assist in the industrial development of the country.' The High Commissioner concluded with an appeal to tourists present to make investments in the country.

M. Dizengoff, Mayor of Tel Aviv, in his address of welcome emphasized that the exhibition marks the end of the crisis and the beginning of a period of prosperity. 'On its twentieth birthday Tel Aviv is showing what the Jews of Palestine have achieved in the fields of industry, agriculture and education during such a short period.'

missioner's willingness to coöperate in civic projects of this nature.

During his term of office, Lord Plumer made frequent visits to different parts of Palestine. These tours of inspection not only gave the Commissioner information about conditions in the country, but proved most valuable opportunities to come into contact with the people. One might almost say that the mingling with the different classes of people is the most important aspect of the whole enterprise of Mandatory administration.

The day spent by Lord and Lady Plumer at Tel-Aviv is an outstanding illustration of Lord Plumer's method of becoming acquainted with the country and its inhabitants. The Jews looked upon the visit as a significant and important event; and the 'Palestine Bulletin' printed a full account of it.[1] Every small detail was noted, and it is safe to say that all the Jews of the country read the article with interest and satisfaction. Let us review the occasion as described by this Jewish paper:

A large crowd greeted Their Excellencies with 'uproarious applause' in front of the Municipal Offices, where a guard of honor was furnished by Boy Scouts. They were received by the Acting Mayor of Tel-Aviv, Sir Ronald Storrs, the District Commandant of Police, and the Acting Assistant Commissioner for the Jaffa district. The Boy Scouts presented Lady Plumer with a bouquet, and Lord Plumer responded that he was glad to see Scouts there. 'I was a Scout for twenty years,' said he, 'and am pleased to fill the position of Chief Scout for Palestine. I hope that I will meet you again.'

Inside the municipality building, Lord Plumer was received by the Township Council, who discussed with him questions affecting Tel-Aviv. He then proceeded to visit the interesting sights in this wholly Jewish town. He first motored to the 'Lodzia' Textile Factory, where he was met by Colonel Kisch and other prominent Jews of Tel-Aviv. His Excellency was greatly interested in the factory, and samples of the work were presented to Their Excellencies. The party next inspected the Gouralsky-Krinizi wood-working factory, and the High Commissioner especially commended the working

[1] *The Palestine Bulletin*, Jerusalem, Tuesday, October 13, 1925.

conditions. A visit was made to the Delfiner silk factory, where Lady Plumer was presented with a piece of silk as a memento of the occasion. The 'Hadassah' Hospital was visited. Here, Lord Plumer greeted the patients, and expressed hearty good wishes for their recovery. Lady Plumer was especially interested in the children's ward, and asked many questions concerning the welfare of the little patients.

Then, as the narrative proceeds: A great crowd awaited Lord Plumer's party at the Casino where they had luncheon, following which the Acting Mayor of Tel-Aviv proposed a toast to the King. The Acting Mayor gave an address, expressing the delight of the inhabitants of Tel-Aviv in welcoming their High Commissioner. He stated that the first Jewish township looked for a continuation of the just administration, and trusted that the Jewish National Home would progress under His Excellency's régime as it had done during the administration of the previous High Commissioner. He finished by expressing the hope that His Excellency would come again to visit the township. Lord Plumer replied briefly, thanking them all for their cordial greeting. The party next visited the Rutenberg Power Station, one of the main substations in the Jordan power scheme. The High Commissioner asked many questions about this plant, which the Jews regard as a shining illustration of Jewish development in Palestine.[1]

This review of the eventful day falls far short of the inter-

---

[1] One could well envisage here the possibilities of the plan for the utilization of the power resources of the Jordan. It was in Lord Plumer's administration when the Palestine Government approved the plan of supplying Palestine with cheap electricity and of irrigating the vast unproductive areas in the Jordan Valley. The construction camp and the workshops in the heart of the wilderness in the region of the Lake of Galilee, give evidence of progress in the mastery of the Jordan which discharges over five million tons of fresh water into the Dead Sea daily.

Dr. N. Feinburg presents a fair analysis of the three verdicts pronounced by the Hague Court in the Mavrommatis case, in which the Greek citizen, Mavrommatis, endeavored to have annulled the electrification concession of Pinhas Rutenberg, claiming that he himself had been awarded the concession by the Turkish Government. (*Jewish Daily Bulletin*, September 25, 1930.)

See Publications of the Permanent Court of International Justice:

Series A: No. 5. The Mavrommatis Jerusalem Concessions.

Series A: No. 11. October 10th, 1927. Case of the Readaptation of the Mavrommatis Jerusalem Concessions.

Series C: No. 13 — III. Case of the Readaptation of the Mavrommatis Jerusalem Concessions.

esting narrative from which it is taken, but it does portray
Lord Plumer in one of his characteristic rôles. Another side
of his nature, which was universally recognized, was his kindly
fellow feeling toward those in distress. This quality of his
character was most conspicuous after the earthquake of July,
1927. Lord Plumer was not in Palestine at the time, but upon
his return, he began immediately on the task of alleviating
distress. Although, because of the damage done to Government House, he and Lady Plumer were themselves without a
residence,[1] he initiated substantial plans for relief.[2]

In his 1927 Report, he says:

The earthquake shock caused loss of life and property in many
towns and villages, notably at Amman and Es-Salt in Trans-Jordan,
and Lydda, Ramleh, and Nablus in Palestine: several villages were
almost completely destroyed. Relief was afforded by Government
making available £100,000 for loans to individuals for the repair of
their houses; and by the provision of free housing or grants of small
sums of money to necessitous persons from a fund obtained by
voluntary subscriptions, which totalled £22,500 at the end of the
year, from Palestine and abroad.[3]

The annual reports of Lord Plumer record a period of pro-

[1] Immediately another residence was sought. The only space considered spacious
enough was Tantour, near Bethlehem. Tantour was built by Count Caboga, the
Austrian Consul, where a clinic was opened for the villagers of Bethlehem and the
surrounding country, ministered by an Austrian Brotherhood affiliated with the
Knights of Saint John.

Although spacious, it was decided that Tantour was too remote, and, moreover, it
would be impossible to heat in winter. Another place was sought. A building was
found diagonally across the *carrefour* from the Italian Hospital, which was built by a
German banker and afterwards acquired by the Evelina de Rothschild School.
After considerable alteration, this was made a temporary makeshift.

The earthquake made every room in Government House (Auguste Victoria Stif-
tung) uninhabitable, and one Russian woman servant was killed by falling plaster.
This was used by Jamal Pasha as headquarters during the War, and was naturally
occupied by the British on their arrival. When peace came, rent was paid for the
building. It is interesting to note that the Germans brought suit in the Palestine
courts to recover damages from the Government for the earthquake injury to their
building, inasmuch as a British contract form had been used which renders the ten-
ant liable, they claim, in spite of *force majeure*. According to Turkish law, which is in
force in Palestine, such liability is untenable.

[2] See Colonial No. 40. Report by His Majesty's Government in the United Kingdom of Great Britain and Northern Ireland to the Council of the League of Nations
on the Administration of Palestine and Trans-Jordan for the year 1928, p. 30.

[3] Colonial No. 31. Report by His Britannic Majesty's Government to the Council of the League of Nations on the Administration of Palestine and Trans-Jordan for
the year 1927, p. 3.

gressive administration. A study of his achievements shows convincingly that the appointment was made in the interest of the whole country, and not for any special community of the population, be it Arab, Jew, or Christian.

Two policies of Lord Plumer were called in question at the Seventeenth (Extraordinary) Session of the Permanent Mandates Commission, held in June, 1930, for the purpose of examining British representatives on the disturbances in Palestine in 1929. One relates to self-government and the other to the reduction of the military and police forces.

Lord Plumer felt it inadvisable to urge the Arabs to participate in the national government; his idea was to give the Arab leaders more practical experience in local and municipal government. This policy was approved both by the Permanent Mandates Commission and the Council of the League of Nations.

An instance of such approval by the Council is to be found in the presentation by M. Unden of Sweden to the session on December 9, 1925, of the report of the Mandates Commission. M. Unden said: ' ... It is obvious that the task of developing the country, with due regard to the dual principles embodied in the mandate... does not permit of rapid development in the political field....' [1]

In the Statement of British Policy, issued in October, 1930, an explanation is made on the same subject:

With the object of enabling the people of Palestine to obtain practical experience of administrative methods and the business of government and to learn discrimination in the selection of their representatives, Lord Plumer, who was High Commissioner for Palestine from 1925 to 1928, introduced a wider measure of local self-government than had previously obtained under the British régime.[2]

With regard to the reduction in military and police forces, the statement is made in the Comments by the Mandatory Power on the Seventeenth Session of the Mandates Commission, that:

The reduction was carried out on the advice of a High Commissioner to whose knowledge of the country was added the experience

[1] *Official Journal*, League of Nations, February, 1926, p. 135.

[2] Cmd. 3692. Palestine. Statement of Policy. October, 1930, p 14.

acquired during a distinguished military career; that the reduction was a step in the direction of establishing civil government on more normal lines than before; and that it had the advantage of making available for the development of the country funds which would otherwise have been expended on defence.[1]

Dr. Drummond Shiels, in referring to Lord Plumer in this connection, before the Seventeenth Session, observed that:

The Commission should not forget that Lord Plumer, who besides having been High Commissioner for Palestine, was one of the most eminent living British soldiers, had recommended a reduction.[2]

This policy of Lord Plumer was also approved by the Permanent Mandates Commission and the Council of the League. The former, in its Seventh Session, October, 1925, phrased its report to the Council to the effect that: The Mandates Commission was able to note that political agitation had diminished; that Jewish immigration was being regulated according to the country's capacity to absorb it; that a land survey was being made; that no unemployment existed; and that a smaller armed force was needed in the territory.[3]

So, likewise, in June, 1926, at its Ninth Session, the Permanent Mandates Commission, after examining the appeals from the Zionist Organization and the Waad Leumi, and also the petition from the Executive Committee of the Arab Congress, in noting 'that political unrest in the country was decreasing,' implied its approval of Lord Plumer's policy of lessening the armed forces of the country.

Lord Plumer was not wholly satisfactory to the Jews. Some of them thought he had shown only 'a lukewarm interest' in the Jewish National Home, and for that reason, in their opinion, he had failed to consider the real problem of the Mandate. Let us read what one Jewish paper said of him just before he left Palestine:

On Tuesday morning, we shook hands in farewell with Field Marshal Lord Plumer. Although still nominally High Commis-

---

[1] C. 355. M. 147. 1930. VI. Permanent Mandates Commission. Minutes of the Seventeenth (Extraordinary) Session Held at Geneva from June 3d to 21st, 1930, including the Report of the Commission to the Council and Comments by the Mandatory Power, p. 151.

[2] *Ibid.*, p. 30.　　　　　[3] Minutes of the Seventh Session, p. 62 ff.

sioner for Palestine, during the three months' period of leave, Lord Plumer has definitely bidden 'goodbye' to Palestine, and the reins of Government taken over on that day by the Chief Secretary, Mr. H. C. Luke. These three months are more an interlude in anticipation of the assumption of office by the new High Commissioner, Sir John Chancellor, than the closing term of the past three years.

On several occasions, since the appointment of Lord Plumer as High Commissioner for Palestine was made public, we have expressed our dissatisfaction with the appointment. Then, as now, we did not have the least quarrel with the appointment so far as Lord Plumer's person was concerned. It was only because the very past of the man, short of a miraculous capacity for adaptation, precluded the possibility of his continuing in the path 'blazed' by his predecessor, Sir Herbert Samuel. Lord Plumer is essentially a soldier. As such he will live forever in the annals of British arms. The relief of Mafeking in the Boer War, and the capture of Messines Ridge and the long defence by the Second Army under his command of the Ypres Salient will never be forgotten. As a contemporary of ours fitly remarks 'Probably Lord Plumer himself would regard the culminating point of his career that day when, standing on the bridge at Cologne near the statue of the Kaiser, he took the salute from the Second Army advancing to occupy the city.' The opening of the Menin Gate last year while he was home on leave is another brilliant page in the annals of the distinguished soldier.

As an administrator he has served two terms: one in Malta and one in Palestine. We plead complete ignorance of the problems which faced Lord Plumer in Malta and hence cannot express an opinion as to how far he succeeded in solving them. In Palestine the only problems which Lord Plumer tackled successfully were those which bore some relation to similar problems arising in the work of a soldier: public security, public works and emergency measures of a humanitarian nature. As a soldier, Lord Plumer 'stood no nonsense.' Public security was kept very well. Every constable felt that the chief of his department was not only the Commandant of Police, but the High Commissioner as well. Miscreants felt that they were under the baleful eye of Lord Plumer, and 'lay low' accordingly. Foremen on the roads realised that in completing a piece of work by a given date they were carrying out an express order issued by the High Commissioner in person.

The terrible earthquake of July 11, 1927, and the lamentable extent of unemployment brought forth Lord Plumer's excellent qualities of a humanitarian and a perfect gentleman. He threw himself into the work of rescue and alleviation of distress with such praiseworthy energy as perhaps his state of health did not warrant. For all of which the entire population of Palestine is deeply grateful.

But there his merits end. As a civil administrator he only followed in the trodden path made easy by countless colonial officials

throughout the world and throughout the history of British Colonisation and given concrete expression in the Colonial Rules. He did
not seek to study the inner problems of the country, the real part
which Great Britain has been called upon to fill in the history of
Palestine. He has done nothing to inspire either his subordinates or
the population at large with the historic significance of these times.
He took a very lukewarm interest in the efforts of the Jews to build
up their National Home in Palestine. The Holy Land or the Jewish
Homeland, whichever you will, are both objects of deep study calling for the highest attributes intellectual and spiritual of an official
and an administrator. In this respect Lord Plumer was only an
average resident of the country: the type of the law-abiding, God-
fearing, church-going perfect old gentleman.

We expect something more of our High Commissioners. If we
cannot expect every one of them to inspire history, we can and do
expect them to be inspired by history; ancient, modern and contemporary. If we stressed some time ago the necessity of having an
intellectual government, it was not merely because we find it more
pleasant to deal with persons of deep learning and wide outlook but
because we consider that without these qualities an administrator
cannot possibly adequately carry out his duties as a government
servant in Palestine.[1]

But note also the statement which appeared about the same
time in the New Palestine, published in the United States:

There was disappointment, when Lord Plumer was named to succeed Sir Herbert Samuel. Every possible dire consequence was pre-
dicted. How absurd this prophecy proved it is superfluous to tell,
in the light of Lord Plumer's remarkable record of administration
in Palestine. He was not only an able executive but proved himself
most sympathetic to Jewish aims in Palestine. Every Jewish problem that arose in Palestine met with his keen understanding. He
gave advice and material aid to Jewish Palestine during the two
critical years through which the country passed, in a manner that
evoked the praise and sincere gratitude of the entire Yishub. Lord
Plumer leaves behind him a grateful Jewish people, fully appreciative of everything he has done to bring us nearer our goal. It is our
sincere hope that Sir John Robert Chancellor, the new High Commissioner, will follow in the footsteps of his distinguished predecessor and that when he will have concluded his term of office, he
will carry with him the same good will and affection which Lord
Plumer takes with him on his departure from Palestine.[2]

[1] *The Palestine Weekly*, August 3, 1928.

[2] *The New Palestine*, July 13–20, 1928.
An interesting estimate of Lord Plumer's administration appeared in *The Palestine
and Near-East Economic Magazine*:
'Lord Plumer leaves Palestine with the knowledge that he has gained the warmest

The Arabs were equally critical. Their attitude toward Lord Plumer is expressed in the Arab Executive Memorandum, presented to him before his departure.[1] In presenting the demand of the Arab Congress for a Parliamentary Government in Palestine, they say they are sure that he will give his 'recommendations in a just and equitable manner as all great Soldiers have always done from times immemorial, for we believe that Your Excellency represents the highest type of Military Honor and straightforwardness.'

And yet they declare that:

The people of Palestine still remember the good words which were uttered by you when you first arrived in Palestine, in that you hoped that your work in Palestine will gain for you many friends in this country. The people had great hopes in the said statement and expected that Your Excellency will be the means to regain for them the natural rights which have been denied them. In spite of our great belief in your desire to help the people of this country to re-

affection and highest esteem of all sections of the population. He will be remembered for his almost fatherly approach, his high sense of justice and his wholehearted acceptance of duty towards the country.

'During the past few years events were not lacking which seemed at times to make the position critical. At those very moments, Lord Plumer's presence in Jerusalem was a real source of steadiness and of confidence. The country knew that its veteran High Commissioner would stand by it and see it through all troubles.

'Particularly memorable is his attitude during the unemployment crisis. Those unfamiliar with the peculiarities of former Government policies may see nothing extraordinary in the fact that during a period of unemployment the High Commissioner should have ordered the expeditious undertaking of works of public utility. But in the past Government aloofness from Jewish pioneer effort in the country's economic reconstruction seemed to be considered a virtue. The pursuit, at all costs, of a supposed ideal of equilibrium in its dealings with the two chief sections of the population — which in fact degenerated into positive bias — appeared to have been the only concern of the Government, paralysed its movement and reduced it to the position of an indifferent onlooker. Under these conditions Lord Plumer's action was a new and a bold departure, full of significance for the future.

'The period during which Lord Plumer held office may be said to have been a period of both transition and preparation: transition in the sense of change in Government attitude, from indifference to coöperation in the country's upbuilding; and preparation in the sense of spade work done for the realisation of large schemes of development which will form the basis of future prosperity. The Palestine loan was floated and preliminary work to the construction of the Haifa Harbor begun; the Dead Sea Concession was granted in principle, so that in the not distant future the commencement of actual work will be made possible; the Rutenberg Concession was given definite status and the first stage of the scheme brought near to completion; improvements were introduced in the customs tariff which freed industrial development from some of its worst handicaps.'

[1] The Arab Executive Memorandum, July 27, 1928.

gain for them the lost rights, we still find the country run in the same absolute Colonial rule which existed when Your Excellency took your High Office.

Such statements form an important part of the history of the Mandate; they are the channels through which the two opposing sections of the population make their demands on the Government. Lord Plumer was always ready to receive the statement of any genuine grievance or alleged injustice. He was a devoted servant to Palestine; and thus it was, that the second High Commissioner, as indeed the first also, sustained the British tradition of disinterested service.

Because of the ill-health of both Lord and Lady Plumer, there was little in the way of official celebrations of their departure. Only the Government officials went to the station to see them off. Lord Plumer left a simple and touching Farewell to Palestine:

On leaving Palestine, I wish to express my grateful appreciation of the loyal support which has been accorded to me during my term as High Commissioner.

My wife and I will take away with us memories of very happy three years and of the kindness shown us by many friends.

We shall always take the deepest interest in the welfare of the country and its people.

(Signed)   PLUMER, F.M.
High Commissioner

COLONEL G. S. SYMES

Next in rank to the High Commissioner is the Chief Secretary to the Administration. The incumbent of this office is a very important official. He is the High Commissioner's principal adviser on administrative matters and is the usual channel of communication between the High Commissioner and other officials. Colonel G. S. Symes, like Lord Plumer, had only recently come to the office of Chief Secretary when I arrived in Palestine. He succeeded Sir Gilbert Clayton, who in turn followed Sir Wyndham Deedes, Chief Secretary during the first two years of Sir Herbert Samuel's Administration. All three Chief Secretaries had been soldiers in the regular army.

When the Military Administration was set up in 1917,

Brigadier-General (later Sir Gilbert) Clayton,[1] Chief Political Officer to the Commander-in-Chief, was appointed by General Allenby Chief Administrator in Palestine. He held this position until Civil Administration was instituted on July 1, 1920; in 1922, he came to the office of Chief Secretary, admirably equipped, as his past experience testifies, to fulfil the duties of the office, which he held during the last three years of Sir Herbert Samuel's Administration.

It was Sir Gilbert Clayton, as Chief Secretary, who met Lord Balfour at Ludd on March 25, 1925, when the author of the famous Declaration arrived for his triumphant visit to Zionist Palestine. Sir Gilbert Clayton also accompanied Lord Balfour to Syria, where, at Damascus, the distinguished British visitor barely escaped with his life.

From 1910 to the outbreak of the War, Sir Wyndham Deedes was attached to the Turkish Gendarmerie; and during and after the War, as an Intelligence Officer, Political Officer, and Military Attaché, rendered valuable service on the Turkish front. He was known to be a strong sympathizer with Zionism,[2] but he was regarded by all sections of

---

[1] Sir Gilbert Clayton was the chief intermediary for negotiations with Ibn Saoud, the Sultan of Nejd, and successor of King Hussein, the Sherif of Mecca. On November 1, 1925, Sir Gilbert, representing the British Government, signed the Bahra Agreement with Ibn Saoud, which definitely defined the boundaries between 'Iraq and Nejd and settled certain frontier questions in the interests of peace. Later pourparlers, however, failed. On the resignation of Sir Henry Dobbs, Sir Gilbert was appointed High Commissioner to 'Iraq, taking up his duties in the spring of 1929. In the fall he died from heart failure during a polo game. His place has been taken by Sir Francis Humphreys, formerly of Kabul.

[2] The following, quoted from the *Palestine Weekly*, March 23, 1928, is interesting evidence of Sir Wyndham Deedes' sympathy with Zionism: The following letter was sent on January 31 by the Vaad Leumi (National Council of Palestine Jews) to Sir Wyndham Deedes, London, first Chief Secretary of the Government of Palestine: 'Dear Sir Wyndham, — It is with great pleasure that we inform you that the Communities Ordinance has finally been approved and signed by His Excellency the High Commissioner. Thus, our strenuous efforts which have been carried on for a period of 7 years, have at last been rewarded. We are reminded on this occasion of your cooperation with us, and remember with keen gratitude the sympathetic interest you always displayed in our activities. We are exceedingly happy to see that, although you no longer hold office here, your sympathy is still alive, and we shall be very glad indeed if you will see your way to bringing yourself into closer touch with our endeavours.'

Sir Wyndham replied as follows: 'Dear Dr. Thon, — I received with much pleasure your kind letter of a few weeks ago and rejoice at the news which you convey that the Communities Ordinance has finally been approved and signed. Any measure which tends to promote and accelerate the establishment of the National Home

the population as a man of the greatest uprightness and a friend of humanity.

Colonel Symes came to the office of Chief Secretary with a background of peculiarly valuable experience. As Governor of the Northern District of Palestine, he was particularly conversant with the Jewish agricultural settlements in the Plain of Esdraelon and the Plain of Jezreel, as well as with the growth of the industries at Haifa. These developments are among the most striking achievements of the Jews. Colonel Symes had also given much attention to the water-supply problem for Haifa, and likewise to the need of an adequate harbor for that port.[1] Indeed, as no one could fail to per-

in Palestine is of course warmly welcomed by me. I, for my part, continue as I think you know, to make my contribution to the furtherance of your aims by the only means which lie at my disposal, namely by making known to the people of this and other countries the work which the Zionist Organization is carrying out in Palestine.'

[1] The following is a very interesting history of the Haifa Harbor project:

In 1922, Mr. F. Palmer, principal of the Firm of Rendel, Palmer and Tritton, Consulting Engineers to the Crown Agents for the Colonies, was invited by the Secretary of State on behalf of the Palestine Government to report upon the question of constructing a harbour in Palestine.

Mr. Palmer recommended that a harbour should be built at Haifa at a cost of approximately £P.1,000,000 and this recommendation was accepted. In 1928, revision of the plans necessitated an increase of the cost by some 25 per cent.

In October, 1927, a Survey Party was sent out by the Consulting Engineers to survey the littoral at Haifa, to make sea borings, to ascertain the rock formation and to investigate the quarrying.

It was at first the intention of the Palestine Government to invite selected firms to tender for the construction of the proposed harbour works; and the Mandatory considered that it would not have been in conflict with its international obligations to acquiesce in this procedure.

But, in fact, no invitations to tender were issued, as it became apparent, at the end of 1928, that factors had arisen which rendered it impracticable to proceed further with the proposed works by the method of tender. There was first the difficulty in connection with the employment of local labour. Work must be provided for Jews, and owing to the different standards of life that prevail among Jews and Arabs respectively, special provision as to wages, etc., must be made if this object is to be secured, and it would have been difficult, if not impossible, to include such provision in any contract which would be made with a firm contracting for the whole work.

A further difficulty is that the quarry at Athlit, some ten miles south of Haifa, from which the stone required for the harbour is to be taken — as it is the only quarry in the vicinity capable of supplying stone of satisfactory quality in blocks of sufficient size — was found to contain exceptionally important antiquarian remains. It is necessary therefore to impose considerable restriction on quarrying, which it would have been difficult to embody in a contract without prejudice to the interests of the Palestine Government.

In the circumstances, it was decided that the system of tendering for the con-

ceive, the scope of his interest included the whole of Palestine, and thereby embraced the problem of the Mandate itself.

In response to my request for an interview, Colonel Symes invited us to tea at his home. Our discussion dwelt principally on the permanency of the Mandate and the investment of capital in Palestine. Although our stay at his house was somewhat less than an hour, the Chief Secretary gave a careful explanation of his view on the two subjects. He contrasted the situation in Palestine with the British position in 'Iraq; and it was his opinion that direct administration was undoubtedly more efficient for Palestine than the indirect course pursued in 'Iraq.

Colonel Symes fulfilled his office very satisfactorily, frequently acting as High Commissioner — without ostentation. Faithfully he stuck to his post, although, of course, he could not be *persona grata* to all. No *incident*, however, marred his term, and his departure was regretted. Good wishes, and congratulations on his promotion went with him to his new

---

struction of the harbour works under a single contract must be abandoned, that the work must be carried out departmentally by the Palestine Government, contracts being let out locally for the supply of materials or the execution of sections of the work as circumstances permit. No discrimination would be exercised in the allocation of these local contracts.

In February, 1929, therefore, the Haifa Harbour Works Department of the Palestine Government was organised, partly by new appointment, and partly by secondments from the staff of the Consulting Engineers.

From June to August preliminary works were carried out at the harbour site and the quarry, the ground was prepared and railways were laid down for the reception of the plant. By October, several locomotives, cranes and other machinery had been erected and the construction of the main breakwater begun. On the 19th October the first consignment of stone was placed in the breakwater; at the 31st January, 1930, the end of the breakwater was 202 metres from the shore and about 19,500 cubic metres of stone had been deposited.

The following plant, costing about £P.60,000 is in use: five steam and two Diesel, locomotives, five 15-ton derricks and ten 5-ton travelling cranes, two compressors, a stonebreaker, 240 steel skips, with capacity from three up to twelve tons, and 200 12-ton wagons.

Some 600 men are engaged on the works, and as the nature of the works in the first stages is almost wholly of the common unskilled class, the labour is mainly Arab. About 15 per cent., however, are Jews, employed on piecework. As further permanent works open out at the harbour, this percentage is expected to increase.

Constant personal touch with the men is established by the responsible British officers, and the development of a team spirit among all grades of workers makes for efficient administration.

(Report on the Administration of Palestine and Trans-Jordan for the year 1929, Appendix 10, pp. 220–21.)

post. Colonel Symes was knighted as Sir John and sent to Aden as High Commissioner.

SIR JOHN ROBERT CHANCELLOR

The Government of Palestine arranged a public reception on the arrival of Sir John Robert Chancellor, the third High Commissioner. The Chief Secretary and Mrs. Luke met Their Excellencies at the Jerusalem railway station at ten-fifteen, in the morning of December 6, 1928. The Chief Justice, Group Commander R.A.F. Forces, Members of the Executive Council, and the Deputy District Commissioner of Jerusalem were formally presented. A guard of honor furnished by the Palestine Police was mounted in the station yard, and the band of the Palestine Police was in attendance. His Excellency was conducted to a saluting base, where he received the salute and inspected the guard of honor.

At ten-twenty-five, Sir John and Lady Chancellor proceeded to the Jaffa Gate, escorted by an officers' mounted escort furnished by the Palestine Police. Although it was a bitterly cold day, dense crowds lined the streets and cheered them along the route. The school-children of Jerusalem, led by their teachers, marched with banners, and thus added to the picturesqueness of the occasion.

At the Jaffa Gate, on a platform erected for the purpose, the invited guests were presented to His Excellency and Lady Chancellor. These included Government officials, foreign Consuls, the heads of the religious communities, notables, and representatives of the Press. The Mayor of Jerusalem, Ragheb Bey Nashashibi, delivered the following speech of welcome:

Your Excellency, Lady Chancellor, Ladies and Gentlemen —
In the name of this Holy City and on behalf of the inhabitants of Palestine, I welcome Your Excellency and Lady Chancellor upon your arrival at the capital of the country.
I have much pleasure in conveying to Your Excellency the confident assurance of the people that during your term of office you will carry out the valuable projects and development schemes that both the historical and social importance of the country deserve and which guarantee the welfare of the inhabitants whose affairs have been entrusted to you; I wish Your Excellency every success in your labor.

Your previous services endorse our belief that the country will prosper during the term of Your Excellency's office, and we pray the Almighty to crown your efforts with success and to keep you and Lady Chancellor in good health and happiness.

This third High Commissioner made some striking statements in his reply to the Mayor. Arriving so soon after the 1928 Wailing Wall incident, speaking, therefore, in an atmosphere of hate and suspicion, Sir John Chancellor could well understand that anything he might say in these circumstances would be interpreted as of special significance. This was a trying position for the new High Commissioner.

I am a newcomer to your country [he said], and I have everything to learn of Palestine and its peoples.... It is enough for me to say that I regard it as my solemn duty to conduct the Government of Palestine in accordance with the terms of the Mandate and in the interests of every section of the population. Palestine [he continued] has during the last few years suffered from acute economic depression, which has arrested her progress and caused hardships and suffering to many of her inhabitants.... I rejoice [said he] to think that the period of economic depression is now drawing to a close, and that the prospects for the future are brighter than they have been for some years. It is therefore my ardent hope that I shall be able to concentrate my attention upon the development of the resources of the country both by Government action and by the encouragement of private enterprise. For the economic development of the country is necessary as well to enable it to sustain a larger population, as to increase the wealth of the old inhabitants, and so improve the conditions under which they live.

Then, his conclusion:

I trust that the realisation by every section of the population of the fact that the development of their country is a common interest of all of them will lead to the creation of a common patriotism, a common love for their country — confidence in the greatness of the future that awaits it, no less than reverence of the sacredness of its historic past.

Let us examine some of these statements: 'To conduct the Government of Palestine in accordance with the terms of the Mandate'; this was simply a reiteration of British policy — hateful to the Arabs, but satisfactory to the Jews. Then again: 'The economic development of the country is necessary... to enable it to sustain a larger population'; this could

only refer to the Jews, since they are the only part of the
population for which special provision is made in the Mandate for an increase in numbers.

But the most significant part of the reply was the closing
paragraph. What Sir John Chancellor meant to convey by
'a common interest,' 'the creation of a common patriotism,'
and 'a common love for their country,' is far from clear.
Nothing of the sort had ever been uttered by a high official
in Palestine. Sir Herbert Samuel had entered the plea for
religious unity, but no voice had heretofore been raised for
a united loyalty to one political unit, and this presumably
the British Mandate.

Quite in contrast to the concept of a 'common patriotism,'
or a recognition of a common interest in the country, such
as the High Commissioner advocated, was the recently
published views of the Arab Executive:

> The Arabs of Palestine from North to South and East to West
> [so runs the Arab Memorandum presented to Lord Plumer on the
> eve of his departure] are aching from the effects of such absolute
> Colonial rule and believe that Great Britain is doing a grave and
> flagrant injustice in the application of such absolute rule in this
> twentieth century, which is called the century of liberty and free-
> dom.

There was a tense interest in these ceremonies. In spite of
the biting wind, the crowds stayed to the end of the speeches
which were repeated in Arabic and Hebrew; they then went
to the Government offices, where the oath of office was given.
There they remained in the cold until His Excellency returned from Saint George's Cathedral, where he attended
divine service. The Chief Justice administered the oaths at
one o'clock, and delivered an address, which is chiefly interesting as revealing the unique and important service previously rendered by Sir John Chancellor in colonial administration.

His Excellency, in reply, expressed the hope that the
experience he had gained in other places as administrator
would help him to overcome many of the difficulties caused
by the diversity of races and legal codes; he relied, he said,
on the officials and the population at large to assist him in
his task. Addressing particularly the officials, he said he

JORDAN HYDRO-ELECTRIC POWER-HOUSE AND WORKS, TEL-OR

THE SWEARING-IN OF SIR JOHN ROBERT CHANCELLOR

would try to come into personal touch with all of them, and in this way to work for greater efficiency and better understanding.[1]

About a month after this, the Executive Committee of the Arab Congress requested an interview with the High Commissioner. On this occasion, the Arabs reiterated in vigorous language their demand for a Parliamentary Government.

We cannot conceive [so their memorandum stated] that His Majesty's Government which is represented in Palestine by Your Excellency does not realise that they are violating their pledges and depriving the Arabs of their natural rights, and we believe that it is only that famous thorn of the Balfour Declaration which is causing His Majesty's Government to hesitate in allowing the Arabs of Palestine to enjoy the principle of self-determination. In spite of our unanimous refusal to accept the said Declaration, which protest has been registered by us before every possible authority the world over, we still are of the belief that this does not prevent the people of Palestine from enjoying a Parliamentary Government in Palestine.

The Memorandum, in fact, suggested a method:

To arrive at such a conclusion [it said], we suggest a policy of direct negotiations between Your Excellency and the Executive Committee of the Palestine Arab Congress concerning the establishment of such system of Government as referred to by the unanimous decision of the Palestine Arab Congress of the 20th of June, 1928, thus entitling the Arabs to enjoy the inherent rights of every

[1] The following Proclamation was issued, after the swearing in of the High Commissioner:

'Whereas by a Commission under the Royal Sign Manual and Signet bearing date the 17th of August, 1928, His Majesty the King has been graciously pleased to appoint me, John Robert Chancellor, Knight Grand Cross of the Most Distinguished Order of Saint Michael and Saint George, Knight Grand Cross of the Royal Victorian Order, Companion of the Most Distinguished Service Order, Lieutenant-Colonel on the retired List of the Corps of Royal Engineers, to be High Commissioner for Palestine and Commander-in-Chief therein, and did further command all and singular the Public Officers and people of Palestine, and all others whom it may concern to take due notice hereof and to give their ready obedience accordingly:

'Now, therefore, I, John Robert Chancellor, do hereby proclaim that, having taken the prescribed Oaths, I have this day entered upon the duties of the Office of High Commissioner for Palestine and Commander-in-Chief therein, and I do hereby enjoin all officers of the Government, civil and military, and all the inhabitants of Palestine to take notice thereof and to give their ready obedience accordingly.

'Given at Jerusalem, this sixth day of December, one thousand nine hundred and twenty-eight.

'By His Excellency's Command,
'H. C. LUKE, *Chief Secretary*'

nation and carrying at the same time the duties and obligations laid upon the Mandatory Power by the League of Nations.

The Jews retorted to this by printing the full text of the Arab Memorandum in the 'Palestine Weekly.' [1] And they prefaced the article as follows:

In view of the importance of the interview of the Arab Executive Committee with His Excellency the High Commissioner in which they stated their demands of the British Administration in Palestine the salient points of which are contained in the following memorandum, we deemed it necessary to publish its full text.

Such was the set-up at the beginning of the administration of Sir John Robert Chancellor. From that time on, he watched with ever-growing apprehension the succession of events which finally led to the August outbreak in 1929. It remains for some future writer, after the termination of Sir John's services in Palestine, to describe his part in the subsequent efforts to smooth out the differences between the Arabs and the Jews, and to give to each group justice under the Mandate. An interesting task this will be — to analyze these circumstances as they relate to the policy and the personality of the third High Commissioner to Palestine.

[1] *The Palestine Weekly*, January 11, 1929.

CHAPTER IX

BRITISH PERSONALITIES — *continued*

NORMAN BENTWICH

DURING the two and a half years of Military Occupation — from December, 1917, to July 1, 1920 — the administration of justice was controlled by a British official, Mr. Norman Bentwich, who was known as the Senior Judicial Officer. He took the place, on the one hand, of the Ottoman Ministry of Justice, thereby exercising administrative control over the courts and land registries that had been established by the military authorities; and on the other hand, acted as legal adviser to the Chief Administrator and the different Departments of the Administration.

The administration of justice during these eventful years involved difficulties of various sorts. In the first place, the Turks, prior to the occupation of the southern part of Palestine, at the end of 1917, had carried away with them nearly all the judges of the courts, the court records, and the land registers. Though the loss of the Turkish judges, who were ill-paid and in many cases poorly qualified both in character and in knowledge of the law, was probably more of a blessing than a hindrance, the court records and the land registers, on the other hand, were indispensable to the continuance of the courts as they existed under the Ottoman régime. The loss of these implements necessitated the setting-up of a new judicial organization, and it was some months before this could be put into working operation. In fact, the courts were not fully reëstablished until June, 1918.

The court system in Palestine under the Ottoman Government consisted of a Court of First Instance, composed of three judges in each kaza (sub-district); and also a Court of Appeal, composed of five more members in each sanjaq (district). There were three Ottoman sanjaqs — Jerusalem, Acre, and Nablus; and in this area there were thirteen Courts of First Instance and three Courts of Appeal. In addition, single judges, or justices of the peace, were appointed in the principal towns, with jurisdiction as laid down in a law passed in 1913.

Such was the basis of the legal system established under the direction of Mr. Bentwich during the Military Occupation. It was formally set in operation by the Courts Proclamation of June 24, 1918.[1] This Proclamation ordered the establishment of:

1. The Civil Courts as courts of general jurisdiction, applying 'the Ottoman Law in force at the date of the Occupation, with such modifications as may be proper having regard to international Law and to the better administration of Occupied Territory.'

2. Magistrates' Courts 'in each kaza as may be required,' having 'the jurisdiction assigned to them by the Ottoman Magistrates Law of 1913 as amended.'

3. Courts of First Instance at Jerusalem and Jaffa 'and at such other places as may from time to time be prescribed.' The area of jurisdiction of the Court of First Instance at Jerusalem included the kazas of Jerusalem, Hebron, and Beersheba; while the Court of First Instance at Jaffa had jurisdiction over the kazas of Jaffa and Gaza.

4. Special courts in any kaza where there was no Court of First Instance.

5. A Court of Appeal at Jerusalem. 'The Court shall be validly constituted by the presence of three judges, and shall decide by a majority of opinions, save when trying crime punishable by death, in which case it shall consist of four judges; and if no majority is obtained the accused shall be acquitted.' The right of recourse to the Court of Cassation was abolished.

6. Moslem Religious Courts in each kaza and in such other places as might be deemed necessary. The right of recourse from Moslem Religious Courts to the Sheikh ul Islam in Constantinople was abolished, for which there was substituted 'an appeal to a Court to be established.' [2]

---

[1] Proclamation. Establishment of Courts, 24th June, 1918. (Superseded by the Palestine Order-in-Council, 1922, and by the Courts Ordinance, No. 21 of 1924.) Legislation of Palestine, 1918–25. Compiled by Norman Bentwich, Attorney-General of Palestine. Orders-in-Council and Ordinances, vol. 1, p. 605.

[2] A Moslem Religious Court of Appeal was established by the Rules relating to Moslem Religious Courts, dated October 10, 1918. (Article 1: 'A Moslem Religious

7. Courts of the Christian and Jewish communities, whose jurisdiction 'in matters of personal status of Ottoman subjects shall be as it was before the Occupation.'

Under the new system, two Courts of First Instance, composed of a British President and two Palestinian members, were established in Jerusalem and in Jaffa. In each kaza, one or more Palestinian magistrates were appointed, who exercised the jurisdiction laid down in the Law of 1913; and in the larger towns two magistrates were appointed with jurisdiction over all contraventions and misdemeanors punishable with not more than one year's imprisonment, as well as civil actions where the value of the subject-matter did not exceed fifty Egyptian pounds. They had jurisdiction:

(*a*) As a Court of First Instance in all civil actions and in misdemeanors beyond the competence of Magistrates' Courts, and

(*b*) As an Appellate Court from judgments of the Magistrates' Courts, except in action about the possession of land.

A Court of Appeal was established in Jerusalem, composed of a British President and three Palestinian members — Moslem, Christian, and Jewish. This Court had jurisdiction to hear appeals from the Courts of First Instance both in civil and criminal matters, and from the Magistrates' Courts in actions concerning land. It also, as a Court of Assize, tried in first instance criminal offences punishable with penal servitude or death. There was no appeal from its convictions, although the Senior Judicial Officer exercised the power of revision. This court took the place of the Turkish Court of Appeal and the Cour de Cassation at Constantinople.[1]

When Northern Palestine was occupied by the British in the autumn of 1918, another Proclamation was issued, being an application of the Proclamation of June 24, 1918, to Northern Palestine.[2] This provided for:

Court of Appeal is hereby established, and will sit at Jerusalem. The Court is hereinafter referred to as the Court of Appeal.') Legislation of Palestine, 1918–25. Compiled by Norman Bentwich, Attorney-General of Palestine. Regulations, Public Notices, Proclamations, Rules of Court, Agreements, and the Royal Instructions; vol. 2, p. 461.

[1] Article 7 of the Establishment of Courts Proclamation declares: 'The right of recourse to the Court of Cassation is abolished.'

[2] Proclamation. Courts, 1st November, 1918. (Superseded by the Palestine

1. Courts of First Instance: at Nablus, whose area of jurisdiction included the kazas of Nablus, Tulkarem, and Jenin; at Haifa, in whose area of jurisdiction were the kazas of Haifa, Acre, and Nazareth; and at Tiberias, which had jurisdiction over the kazas of Tiberias and Safed.

2. The Court of Appeal at Jerusalem, which should hear appeals in civil and criminal cases from all Courts of First Instance in the Occupied Enemy Territory (South); provided that an Assize Court be constituted in the Sanjaq of Acre by any British Judicial Officer and any two judges eligible to sit as members of the Court of Appeal.

3. Moslem Religious Courts, established in such kazas of the Sanjaq of Nablus and Acre as the Senior Judicial Officer might appoint. An Appeal might be taken from any final judgment already passed by a Moslem Religious Court in the Sanjaq of Nablus and Acre to the Moslem Religious Court of Appeal.

4. The jurisdiction and law of the courts of the Christian and Jewish communities in the Sanjaqs of Nablus and Acre in matters of personal status, to remain as it was before the promulgation of the said Ottoman Laws. The importance of the position of Senior Judicial Officer in the régime of Military Occupation is indicated by the provisions of Article 28 of the Courts Proclamation of June 24, 1918, which define his duties. According to the Article, he was given 'the general superintendence and control over all Civil Courts and Religious Courts in the Occupied Territory'; and with the sanction of the Chief Administrator, he might from time to time, make rules concerning certain matters, such as:

(a) the organization, jurisdiction, procedure and business of the Courts;

(b) the functions and duties of the judges and officials of the Courts;

(c) the fees payable in the courts or in connection with any proceedings of the Courts or their officials, and the costs, charges, and expenses to be allowed to parties, witnesses and others;

Order-in-Council, 1922, and by the Courts Ordinance, No. 21 of 1924.) Legislation of Palestine, 1918–25. Compiled by Norman Bentwich, Attorney-General of Palestine. Orders-in-Council and Ordinances, vol. 1, p. 612.

(d) the profession of advocates, legal practitioners and public notaries.

These rules, moreover, might annul or add to the provisions of the Proclamation or any Ottoman rules relating to the matters just mentioned.

And further, the Senior Judicial Officer might 'withdraw any action or proceeding pending in a Civil Court and refer it for disposal to any Civil Court which is competent to try it.'

The responsibilities of the Senior Judicial Officer were greatly enlarged when the jurisdiction of the Court of Appeal was extended over the whole territory; its assize ran from Gaza to Safed. This brought about two difficulties. It was found, in the first place, that one court was not sufficient to try the serious criminal cases for the whole country; and secondly, that there was general objection to the absence of any right of appeal from conviction for the most serious crimes. No court with supreme civil and criminal jurisdiction above the Court of Appeal had been established to take the place of the right of recourse to the Court of Cassation in Constantinople, which, as we have seen, had been abolished by the Establishment of Courts Proclamation in June, 1918.

It was, therefore, decided in 1920 to widen the criminal jurisdiction of the Courts of First Instance (henceforth known as District Courts) so as to cover all the more serious offences; and further, to give an appeal on a point of law from any judgment to six months' imprisonment or a more severe penalty to the Court of Appeal.

Before the Civil Government was established, in 1920, the number of District Courts was reduced to four, namely — the Court of Jerusalem, which served the Jerusalem Administrative District; the Court of Jaffa, the Districts of Jaffa and Gaza; the Court of Phœnicia, the administrative district of Phœnicia; and the Court of Samaria and Galilee.

Special arrangements were made for the District of Beersheba, which is inhabited almost entirely by Bedouin tribes. Besides a civil magistrate, a court composed of the leading Sheikhs was set up to deal with minor offences and tribal disputes; and it was arranged that a British Judicial Official from Jerusalem should try the more serious criminal cases and hear appeals from the judgments of the Sheikhs' Tribunal as well as from the civil magistrate.

The Military Administration maintained, besides the Civil Courts, a series of Military Courts composed of British officers. The procedure followed in these courts was that of military law; while in the Civil Courts, the Ottoman codes of procedure were followed. In order, however, to simplify the somewhat cumbrous and excessive formality of the Ottoman code, a number of modifications were introduced, more especially in criminal cases.

The Civil Courts exercised jurisdiction over all persons, whether Ottoman or foreign subjects. The Military Administration maintained the suspension of the Capitulations which the Ottoman Government had declared abolished in 1914, so that the former Mixed Tribunals and Consular Courts no longer existed. The Administration, recognizing, however, the practical advisability of trying foreign subjects by a court containing a British element, issued special rules of court providing that a person who established his claim to be a foreign subject should be tried for any offence more serious than a contravention, either by a British magistrate or by a court composed of a majority of British judges. The Civil Courts received jurisdiction in matters of personal status of foreign subjects, formerly dealt with by the Consuls, subject only to two conditions: first, that they apply the national law of the parties, and, second, that they exercise no jurisdiction in divorce.

This, then, was the legal system of which Mr. Bentwich was the judicial head, when the Civil Administration was established in July, 1920. The change from the military to the civil government involved no changes of great importance in the administration of justice. The Senior Judicial Officer of the Military Administration, however, became the Legal Secretary of the Civil Administration. He continued his former functions, but, in addition, was entrusted with the general supervision of the land registries, cadastral survey, and questions concerning land. This was, indeed, a plan of large proportions; and it obviously involved complicated machinery and delicate adjustment.

The successful accomplishment of such a program required

an experienced and able executive. Norman Bentwich was notably prepared for the work. He was educated at Cambridge, and was called to the Bar in 1908. He was lecturer at the Khedivial School of Law at Cairo; and is the author of several publications on international law,[1] as well as important works on Jewish subjects.[2]

In addition to this: Norman Bentwich did service in the War. He was an officer in the Camel Transport Corps in Egypt; was promoted Lieutenant in 1916; and Captain, and then Major in 1917. He entered the Administration of the Occupied Enemy Territory as Procuror-General of Palestine in May, 1918.

The only alterations in the organization of the Civil Courts, when the Civil Administration was established, were the substitution of a Chief Justice, in 1921, for the President of the Court of Appeal; and the addition of a British Vice-President and a further Moslem member. This enabled the Court to sit in two chambers each composed of three judges. Military Courts were abolished, but governors of districts and certain district officers were given magisterial powers, in virtue of which they could try minor offences under the Penal Code and contraventions of the Ordinances issued by the Administration; they could also pass sentences up to six months' imprisonment. Minor magisterial powers were also conferred on selected Palestinian district officers in order that they should be able to try petty contraventions of the villagers on the spot.

The suspension of the Capitulations was maintained; although the Government of the United States claimed that as this suspension had never been applied to American subjects, their right to try before a Consular Court an American subject accused of any offence should be maintained. The British Government acceded to their request.

The special courts for commercial cases which existed under the Ottoman régime were not maintained; such suits

[1] The books written by Mr. Bentwich on International Law are: *The Law of War and Private Property; Principle of Domicil in relation to Succession; Leading Cases and Statutes on Public International Law; The Declaration of London.* He edited the Sixth and Seventh editions of Westlake's *Private International Law.*

[2] He has written the following books on Jewish subjects, published by the American Jewish Publication Society: *Philo-Judæus, Flavius Josephus, Hellenism.*

were heard in the District Courts with the same procedure as any other civil actions. Power was given by rules of court to appoint assessors, who had, however, no voice in the decision. The Chambers of Commerce suggested that merchants should sit with the court, and on December 16, 1921, a fresh rule [1] was issued by which a President of the District Court in trying a commercial case might appoint two merchants in lieu of the two Palestinian members of the court; the merchants were to give decision on the facts, while the President was to apply the law. In other words, the merchants were to exercise the power of a jury.

The statistics of the Magistrates' Courts at the end of 1921 showed a remarkable amount of work accomplished. In the smaller towns the magistrate, in addition to the trial of cases, supervised the investigation and made the order of committal for trial in respect of the more serious crimes.

During the latter part of 1921, Municipal Benches of Honorary Magistrates were established in the three principal towns — Jerusalem, Jaffa, and Haifa — with power to deal with contraventions of Municipal By-Laws and Government Regulations, and to impose a penalty not exceeding five Egyptian pounds or imprisonment not exceeding fifteen days. These were substituted in place of the undesirable system established under the Ottoman Municipal Law, whereby a municipality could itself fine summarily persons charged with breach of the Municipal Regulations, a system which confused the functions of prosecution and judgment.

The Ottoman law system, which, with some modifications, was in force in 1921, is based on the French Criminal Procedure, which provides for a Public Prosecutor (*Procureur*) who investigates offences and exercises certain magisterial powers in regard to accused persons. Provision is also made for criminal investigation before an Examining Judge (*Juge d'instruction*). This system, as it applied to Palestine, was simplified during the year 1921 by making the Civil Magistrate act as *Juge d'instruction*, and by the delegation of the investigating functions of the Public Prosecutor to special police officers, who carried out all criminal investigations under the supervision, in more important cases, of the Public

[1] *Official Gazette*, January 1, 1922.

Prosecutor. At the head of the whole system of prosecution was the Government Advocate.

Rules of court were issued in this year regarding the execution of foreign judgments in Palestine, which provide for the issue of an exequatur by the Palestine tribunals where the foreign court has exercised jurisdiction in accordance with the generally accepted principles of international law.

When the Civil Courts were reëstablished in June, 1918, they were prohibited, by an Article in the Proclamation, from hearing actions concerning the ownership of land and also from granting execution on immovable property.[1] As we have seen, the land registers, that were the evidence of the title of land, had been for the most part removed by the Turks; and it was therefore impossible for the courts to obtain a satisfactory basis of title. It was not until May, 1921, that steps were taken to establish courts with jurisdiction to hear actions regarding ownership.[2] The necessity of constituting the Special Court of British Judges to try the cases arising out of the Jaffa disturbances in May [3] further delayed work; and it was not until July that the Land Courts were able to proceed regularly with the hearing of actions. Two courts [4] were established, one for the Districts of Jaffa and Phœnicia and one for the Districts of Samaria and Galilee.

Pending the full operation of the Land Courts, it was found

[1] Legislation of Palestine, 1918–25. Compiled by Norman Bentwich, Attorney-General of Palestine. Orders-in-Council and Ordinances, vol. 1, p. 609, Article 23.

The Proclamation dated July 20, 1918, states the definition of land to include all forms of immovable property.

[2] Land Courts Ordinance, 1921. An Ordinance to Establish Courts for the Settlement of the Title to Land, and to Define their Powers. 8th April, 1921. Legislation of Palestine, 1918–25. Compiled by Norman Bentwich, Attorney-General of Palestine. Orders-in-Council and Ordinances, vol. 1, p. 150.

The jurisdiction of the Land Courts was subsequently altered again so as to coincide with the area of jurisdiction of the District Courts. In the Districts of Nablus and Haifa the land cases are dealt with by the President of the District Court and one member; but special Land Courts, separate from the District Courts, still exist in the Districts of Jaffa and Jerusalem.

[3] Cmd. 1540. Disturbances in May, 1921, Reports of the Commission of Inquiry with Correspondence Relating Thereto.

[4] The area of jurisdiction of the Land Courts was altered at the beginning of 1922, the Southern Court dealing with cases arising in the Districts of Jaffa and Jerusalem, and the Northern with those arising in Samaria and the Northern District.

necessary to protect persons who had adverse claims against the registered owner of land; and an Ordinance was, therefore, passed in September, 1920 — Correction of Land Registers Ordinance [1] — which empowered the Court to order a caution to be placed on the land register where a person produced documentary evidence that he had some claim to the land. This power was fully exercised during the year 1921 by the District Courts. The Ordinance also empowered the courts to order the correction of the entry in the land registers where a person produced documentary evidence that the registered owner was a nominee for another person or for a corporation. The Ottoman restrictions against foreigners and corporations holding land had led to an extended system of nominal ownership which gave rise to embarrassing complications when the nominal owner died; and it was desirable, in order that the land registers should contain a true record of ownership, that the actual proprietor should appear on the register in place of the nominee.

A number of charitable and religious corporations and individuals took advantage of the law during the year, but as there was a large number of applications still in the course of preparation when the term originally fixed had nearly expired, an Ordinance was passed in September, 1921,[2] to extend the period for making application for correction till September, 1922.[3] It is a fact of interest that most of the land belonging to the Jewish settlers in Palestine was registered in the names of a few individuals who were Ottoman subjects. Steps were, therefore, taken in the Jewish villages to have the registration corrected in accordance with the

[1] Correction of Land Registers Ordinance, September 23, 1920. Amended by Correction of Land Registers (Amendment) Ordinance dated 27th September, 1921, and by 17 of 1922, Obsolete. Legislation of Palestine, 1918–25. Compiled by Norman Bentwich, Attorney-General of Palestine. Orders-in-Council and Ordinances, vol. 1, p. 647.

[2] Correction of Land Registers Amendment Ordinance, September 27, 1921. Embodied in Principal Ordinance dated 23rd September, 1920, Obsolete. Legislation of Palestine, 1918–25. Compiled by Norman Bentwich, Attorney-General of Palestine. Orders-in-Council and Ordinances, vol. 1, p. 647 (footnote).

[3] Correction of Land Registers Ordinance, September 26, 1922. Embodied in Principal Ordinance, dated 23rd September, 1920, Obsolete. Legislation of Palestine, 1918–25. Compiled by Norman Bentwich, Attorney-General of Palestine. Orders-in-Council and Ordinances, vol. 1, p. 647.

Ordinance, so that each owner might possess a title to his land.

Under the Ottoman Administration, there were Moslem Religious Courts, that had jurisdiction in all matters of personal status of Moslems and also in matters of Waqf; and in addition they had jurisdiction in certain matters of personal status of non-Moslems, such as questions of guardianship and succession on intestacy. The exact measure of their jurisdiction over these matters in the case of Christians and Jews, however, was ill-defined, because of a number of conflicting decrees and orders issued by the Ottoman Government.

In order to systematize the religious jurisdiction, a committee of judges and others were appointed to investigate the situation. They recommended that the competence of the Moslem Religious Courts should be restricted to questions of personal status of Moslems and to Moslem Waqfs. The British Administration maintained the jurisdiction exercised by the non-Moslem communities in matters of marriage, divorce, alimony, and wills, and the judgments given by the religious courts in these matters were executed through the Execution Office of the Civil Courts.

The Rabbinical authority recognized by the Ottoman Administration was the Haham Bashi, who was appointed from Constantinople on the recommendation of the Jewish community of Palestine. The Military Administration found at the time of the Occupation an acting Haham Bashi, who was sent during the War to hold elections for the office. The large majority of the Jewish community, however, did not recognize him as their spiritual head; and a number of persons styled themselves Chief Rabbis. To inquire into the organization of the Jewish Rabbinical Courts and the system of appointment of the Chief Rabbi, the High Commissioner appointed a committee, which was presided over by the Legal Secretary.

Following the recommendations of that committee, an assembly of representatives of all the Jewish communities of Palestine was held in Jerusalem in February, 1921, and elected a Rabbinical Council composed of two Chief Rabbis for the Sephardic and Ashkenazic communities respectively, six Rabbinical members and two lay councillors. This Council, which constituted a Court of Appeal from the Rabbinical Courts of the Jewish communities in the towns and villages, was recognized by the Government as the sole Rabbinical authority.[1]

The next landmark in the development of the legal system of Palestine was the promulgation of the Palestine Order-in-Council,[2] September 1, 1922.[3] Under this Order-in-Council, the Legal Secretary became Attorney-General, with the functions of legal adviser and law officer of the Government — the office which he has held continuously to the present time. The career of Mr. Bentwich has certainly been one of great distinction.

Vigorous attacks, however, have been levelled against him. Being a Jew and an ardent Zionist, the Arabs suspect his motives. They resent the appointment of a Zionist to the highest legal position in the country; they claim it is an injustice to the majority of the population. The chief grievance seems to be the power which he wields in the drafting of Ordinances by which the Administration legislates, and also in advising the other departments of the Government on points of law. As a matter of fact, I have never been able to find a *bona fide* case where he has deviated from strict legal propriety.[4]

My interview with Mr. Bentwich was interesting and delightful. We discussed the Urtas Springs and the 'E.I.' cases, and also the subject of Capitulations as it concerned

[1] The foregoing description of the legal system of Palestine, as it was functioning in 1921, is taken from the Report on Palestine Administration, July, 1920–December, 1921. (Published by His Majesty's Stationery Office.)

[2] The Palestine Order-in-Council, 1922, as amended by the Palestine (Amendment) Order-in-Council, 1923. Legislation of Palestine, 1918–25. Compiled by Norman Bentwich, Attorney-General of Palestine. Orders-in-Council and Ordinances, vol. 1, p. 1.

[3] Proclamation bringing into effect the Palestine Order-in-Council, 1922. Legislation of Palestine, 1918–25. Compiled by Norman Bentwich, Attorney-General of Palestine. Regulations, Public Notices, Proclamations, Rules of Court, Agreements, and the Royal Instructions, vol. 2, p. 404.

[4] It is of interest to observe that the Attorney-General has been criticised by the Jews themselves. The Agudath Yisrael, or the old conservative anti-Zionist Jews, for example, accused him of making Laws or Regulations which would put them under the jurisdiction of a Rabbinical body which they did not accept. (They had in fact, not been placed under the control of the Rabbinical Council.)

the current procedure in Palestine. I was particularly anxious to get the view of the Attorney-General on the subject of Capitulations. The Mandate sustained the action of the Ottoman Government in 1914, and also the British Administration in denouncing the Capitulations for Palestine. Article 8 of the Mandate declares that the privileges and immunities of foreigners, including the benefits of consular jurisdiction and protection as formerly enjoyed by Capitulation or usage in the Ottoman Empire, shall not be applicable in Palestine.[1]

The American Consul in Jerusalem refused to be bound by the Mandate; and, as he told me that very afternoon, he was still holding Consular Courts in his office. His view was that until the United States had accepted the suspension of the Capitulations, either by ratifying the Mandate or by a subsequent Convention, his duty was to assume capitulatory rights in accordance with the agreement made by the British Government in 1920. On December 3, 1924, a Convention between the United States and Great Britain regarding Palestine was signed,[2] according to which United States

---

[1] C. 529. M. 314. 1922. VI. League of Nations. Mandate for Palestine.

Cmd. 1785. League of Nations. Mandate for Palestine, together with a Note by the Secretary-General Relating to its Application to the Territory known as Trans-Jordan, under the provisions of Article 25. Presented to Parliament by Command of His Majesty, December, 1922.

[2] Convention Between the United Kingdom and the United States of America Respecting the Rights of the Two Countries and their Respective Nationals in Palestine, signed at London, December 3, 1924. Ratifications exchanged at London, December 3, 1925. (Parliamentary Papers, Treaty Series No. 54, 1925. Cmd. 2559.)

Legislation of Palestine 1918–25. Compiled by Norman Bentwich, Attorney-General of Palestine. Regulations, Public Notices, Proclamations, Rules of Court, Agreements, and the Royal Instructions, vol. 2, p. 519.

Colonial No. 20. Report by His Britannic Majesty's Government to the Council of the League of Nations on the Administration of Palestine and Trans-Jordan for the year 1925. Text of Convention between the United States of America and Great Britain regarding Palestine, p. 163.

Article 1: Subject to the provisions of the present convention the United States consents to the administration of Palestine by His Britannic Majesty, pursuant to the mandate recited above.

Article 2: The United States and its nationals shall have and enjoy all the rights and benefits secured under the terms of the mandate to members of the League of Nations and their nationals, notwithstanding the fact that the United States is not a member of the League of Nations.

Statutes of the United States of America passed at the first session of the Sixty-Ninth Congress, 1925–26, and concurrent resolutions of the two houses of Congress. Recent Treaties and Executive Proclamations, Part 2. Private Acts and Resolu-

citizens became subject to the same rules of jurisdiction as the subjects of other foreign States. The ratifications of this Convention were exchanged on December 3, 1925.[1]

The American Consul insisted on the right to hold Consular Courts until the ratifications were exchanged. The Attorney-General, on the other hand, maintained a different point of view. It was a nice point of international law, and I was very glad to hear the Attorney-General's arguments at first hand.

The following is the substance of his opinion which I gathered from the interview:

The Capitulations of the foreign Powers had been abolished by Turkey prior to the outbreak of the war between Turkey and the Allied Powers in 1914. The Allied Powers had protested; but at the time of the Occupation of Palestine by the Egyptian Expeditionary Force in 1917 and 1918, the capitulatory rights of foreigners were in fact abrogated in Palestine.

The Military Administration was entitled to maintain the system which was in force at the time of the Occupation, and was under no obligation to restore the system of Capitulations which were based on treaties between the Ottoman Government and foreign Powers. The Allied Governments recognized the right of the Military Administration, and the courts established by the Administration exercised general jurisdiction over foreigners as well as Ottoman subjects, both in criminal and civil matters. From the beginning, however, special rules with regard to the trial of foreign subjects were laid down so as to safeguard their rights.

The Government of the United States raised the question of the maintenance of their capitulatory rights after the establishment of the Civil Government in July, 1920, and the claim was conceded by the British Government pending the entry into force of the Treaty of Peace with Turkey and the Mandate for Palestine. Accordingly, an arrangement was

tions, Concurrent Resolutions, Treaties, and Proclamations. Treaties and Conventions Concluded by the United States of America with Foreign Nations. Convention Between the United States and Great Britain Regarding Palestine, December 3, 1924 (proclaimed December 5), pp. 192–200.

[1] Legislation of Palestine, 1918–25. Compiled by Norman Bentwich, Attorney-General of Palestine. Regulations, Public Notices, Proclamations, Rules of Court, Agreements, and the Royal Instructions, vol. 2, pp. 527, 528.

made between the Government of Palestine and the American Consul with regard to the jurisdiction of the Consul over citizens of the United States.

Subsequently, however, when the Palestine Order-in-Council, 1922, was published, it was held by the courts that, in virtue of the Order-in-Council, they had jurisdiction in all matters, civil and criminal, over foreign subjects, including citizens of the United States, and that the arrangement made by the Government of Palestine had no longer validity.[1]

Matters were at a deadlock until the Convention between His Majesty's Government and the United States Government was signed and ratified.

Palestine is greatly indebted to Norman Bentwich for his valuable compilation of the legislation of Palestine.[2] The work is published in two volumes and contains a complete record of the legislation of Palestine from December, 1917, through the year 1925. The need of such a compilation is very evident. Since the British Occupation, as Mr. Bentwich points out, the legislation of Palestine has appeared in various forms and has been scattered in various collections.

During the period of Military Occupation, from December, 1917, to July 1, 1920, legislation was enacted in two ways: first, in the form of Proclamations issued by the Commander-in-Chief of the Egyptian Expeditionary Force and his principal representatives in Palestine, known as the Chief Administrator of Occupied Enemy Territory (south); and second, in the form of Public Notices and Ordinances of the Chief Administrator, and of heads of Departments of the Administration. During this time, says Mr. Bentwich, there was no exactitude in the terminology of legislation, an enactment being indifferently called an Ordinance or a Public Notice, without any apparent distinction.

---

[1] Article 38 of the Palestine Order-in-Council, 1922, declares that: 'The Civil Courts hereinafter described shall, subject to the provisions of this part of the Order, exercise jurisdiction in all matters and over all persons in Palestine.' (Legislation of Palestine, 1918–25. Compiled by Norman Bentwich, Attorney-General of Palestine. Orders-in-Council and Ordinances, vol. 1, p. 11.)

[2] Legislation of Palestine, 1918–25. Compiled by Norman Bentwich, Attorney-General of Palestine. Vol. 1: Orders-in-Council and Ordinances; vol. 2: Regulations, Public Notices, Proclamations, Rules of Court, Agreements, and the Royal Instructions.

When, however, as Mr. Bentwich further explains, the Civil Administration was established, in July, 1920, there was an attempt to differentiate the forms of legislation. Three terms were included in the nomenclature: Ordinances, Public Notices, and Regulations. A measure submitted to the Advisory Council which made some substantial changes in the early Ottoman law, or introduced regulation or penalties in respect of a topic not covered by the Ottoman law, was entitled an Ordinance. On the other hand, an enactment which was designed to be an application of the Ottoman law, or concerned some departmental matter, was normally entitled a Public Notice, while a body of Rules which applied in detail an Ordinance of the Administration or an existing Ottoman law was entitled Regulations. There were, as Mr. Bentwich observes, some lapses from these principles, but in general this was the system till the issue of the Palestine Constitution by the Order-in-Council of 1922.

The plan of numbering consecutively the Ordinances of each year and of giving to each Ordinance a short title was adopted in the early part of 1923. When legislation superseded former enactments of the British Administration or the earlier Ottoman law, it was usual, though not invariable, to insert a repeal clause to that effect. In the more recent legislation, a clause has been introduced giving power to make Rules or Regulations under which the general objects of the Ordinance may be amplified. The rule-making power was originally vested in the head of a Department, who exercised it with the approval of the High Commissioner, but the power of making Regulations was later conferred upon the High Commissioner himself, as shown in the Ordinances issued in 1925.

This compilation also includes the Orders-in-Council, issued by His Majesty-in-Council, which form, as the Attorney-General says, the supreme source of the Palestine Law Book. These Orders-in-Council comprise the Constitution issued in 1922, the Citizenship Order issued in 1925, and several measures dealing with the jurisdiction of the courts. An Appendix to the publication contains the Ordinances and parts of Ordinances which have been repealed.

Mr. Bentwich points out that the compilation was designed as a preparation for a thorough restatement of the Law of Palestine, which, it is contemplated, he says, will be consolidated and arranged in chapter form at no distant date. This law-making is a continuous piece of work.[1] The Report on Palestine for 1927 states that:

The preparation of Ordinances and Regulations, required to bring the Law of Palestine into conformity with modern needs, is still the principal and most exacting part of the Law Officers' work: and as yet there is no prospect of finality.

The curve of legislation is indeed rising still: in 1925 thirty-nine Ordinances were enacted; in 1926, forty-seven; and in this year fifty-two.[2]

Much of the legislation of 1927 comprises measures concerned with the administration of justice or the amendment of the Criminal Law. By degrees, the Ottoman Criminal Codes are being replaced; the Trial upon Information Ordinance, 1924, superseded most of the Ottoman Code of Criminal Procedure; and this year rules based on English Laws were introduced in place of the Ottoman provisions about release on bail and certain matters of evidence.

The authority of the Ottoman Penal Code was largely abrogated by a series of Ordinances embodying principles of English Criminal

[1] The Attorney-General has not compiled a third volume of the Legislation of Palestine. But the legislation of each year is published by the Government in two volumes, one containing Ordinances and the other containing Regulations, Public Notices, Orders, etc.

On the subject of legislation, the statement is made of the 1929 Report that: 'For the last four months of the year the Law Officers Department dealt principally with matters arising of the disturbances. Apart from the prosecution of a great number of cases of murder and rioting, and the preparation of the case of the Government of Palestine to be laid before the Commission of Inquiry, the Law Officers were concerned with the drafting of legislation to meet the conditions caused by the disturbances. The Ordinances which were enacted on this account affect partly the substantive law and partly the procedure.... Of other Ordinances passed in 1929 some were required for the purpose of making minor amendments in the existing legislation; but others were comprehensive measures, designed either to replace unsatisfactory parts of the Ottoman Law, or to supersede earlier Ordinances of the Palestine Government which required amendment and consolidation. The work of giving Palestine a modern system of law is still incomplete, but, particularly in regard to the Commercial Law, the Criminal Law, and the Procedure of the Courts, large reforms were introduced during the year.' (Colonial No. 47. Report on the Administration of Palestine and Trans-Jordan for the year 1929, pp. 50, 52.)

[2] During the year 1928, twenty-nine Ordinances were enacted. (Colonial No. 40. Report by His Majesty's Government in the United Kingdom of Great Britain and Northern Ireland to the Council of the League of Nations on the Administration of Palestine and Trans-Jordan for the year 1928, p. 33.)

Law in regard to specific offences and to general provisions about offences.[1]

The Attorney-General, the chief law officer of Palestine, has unmistakably rendered meritorious service. Nor has this been a perfunctory performance of duty; the work was done as a labor of love for Palestine, the Promised Land. This is the governing motive of his prodigious labors. And yet the intensity of his devotion to Palestine has never caused him to deviate from the rôle of an impartial public servant. Certainly, there was never a more conscientious service.

Mr. Basil Worsfold thus speaks of this idealistic pioneer:

> I think no difficulties would have robbed him of the enjoyment of serving Palestine; for Mr. Norman Bentwich, like the High Commissioner, is a Jew, and his convinced, albeit sane, Zionism provides him with motives more intimate than the tradition of disinterested service which he shares with other 'civilian soldiers of the Empire.' [2]

SIR THOMAS HAYCRAFT

At the beginning of the Civil Administration, Sir Thomas Haycraft became the head of the Judiciary in Palestine. He was, as we have seen, appointed Chief Justice in 1921. Perhaps, however, no single instance of his career will be remembered more conspicuously by the people of the country than his service as President of the Commission of Inquiry,[3] appointed to investigate the Jaffa disturbances of 1921.[4] This body, which included representatives of the Arabs and the Jews,[5] considered in the frankest fashion, the origins, the

---

[1] Colonial No. 31. Report by His Britannic Majesty's Government to the Council of the League of Nations on the Administration of Palestine and Trans-Jordan for the year 1927, p. 21.

[2] W. Basil Worsfold, *Palestine of the Mandate*, p. 93.

[3] Legislation of Palestine, 1918–25. Compiled by Norman Bentwich, Attorney-General of Palestine. Commission of Inquiry Ordinance. An Ordinance to provide for the constitution and powers of Commissions of Inquiry. January, 1921. Orders-in-Council and Ordinances, vol. 1, p. 117.

[4] Cmd. 1540. Disturbances in May, 1921. Reports of the Commission of Inquiry with Correspondence Relating Thereto.

[5] The following constitutes the 'Terms of Reference,' signed by Sir Herbert Samuel:
'I appoint His Honour Sir Thomas Haycraft, Chief Justice of Palestine, Mr. H. C. Luke, Assistant Governor of Jerusalem, and Mr. Stubbs, of the Legal Department,

minute circumstances, and the political implications of the outbreak. During the whole procedure, Sir Thomas showed himself, first of all, a man of great good sense and practical sagacity, eminently capable of impartial reasoning. Surrounded by frenzy and hatred on the part of both the Jews and the Arabs, his unfailing regard for a straightforward search after the truth, and his wide range of experience in the application of juridical principles, brought to the case those qualities which assured a just and firm decision.

The administration of the courts system in Palestine absorbed the energies of Sir Thomas Haycraft, and must always stand out as a signal achievement in his distinguished career. Under the Palestine Order-in-Council of 1922, the administration of the courts, embracing also recommendations for the appointment of judges and magistrates, was vested in the Chief Justice, together with the power of making rules for regulating the practice and procedure of the courts — powers previously exercised by Norman Bentwich as Legal Secretary.

The first article relating to the Judiciary in the Palestine Order-in-Council [1] declares that the Civil Courts shall 'exercise jurisdiction in all matters and over all persons in Palestine.' This, as we have seen, abolished the capitulatory rights of citizens of the United States, against which the United States Consul protested.

Provision is also made in the Order-in-Council for the establishment of Magistrates' Courts [2] in each district and sub-district 'as may be prescribed from time to time by Order under the hand of the High Commissioner.' These courts will exercise the same jurisdiction as that 'assigned to them by the Ottoman Magistrates' Law of 1913, as amended by any subsequent law or Ordinance or Rules for the time being in force.' This follows in the main the provision for the

---

to be a Commission to inquire into the recent disturbances in the town and neighbourhood of Jaffa, and to report thereon.

'And I appoint Sir Thomas Haycraft to be the Chairman, and Aref Pasha Dejani El Daoudi, Elias Eff. Mushabbeck and Dr. Eliash to be assessors to the Commission.

'The Commission shall have all the powers specified in Article 2 of the Commission of Inquiries Ordinance, 1921.' (Cmd. 1540. Palestine. Disturbances in May, 1921. Reports of the Commission of Inquiry with Correspondence Relating Thereto, Presented to Parliament by Command of His Majesty, October, 1921, p. 3.)

[1] Palestine Order-in-Council, Article 38.   [2] *Ibid.*, 39.

establishment of Magistrates' Courts in the Establishment of Courts Proclamation of June 24, 1918.[1]

The action in 1920 to widen the criminal jurisdiction of the Courts of First Instance[2] (known henceforth as District Courts) was sustained in the Order-in-Council: District Courts shall exercise jurisdiction:

(1) As a Court of First Instance:
   (a) In all civil matters not within the jurisdiction of the Magistrates' Courts in and for that district.
   (b) In all criminal matters which are not within the jurisdiction of the Court of Criminal Assize.
(2) As an Appellate Court from the said Magistrates' Courts subject to the provisions of any Ordinance or Rules.[3]

The widening of the criminal jurisdiction was marked by the provision for the establishment of a Court of Criminal Assize 'which shall have exclusive jurisdiction with regard to offences punishable with death and such jurisdiction with regard to other offences as may be prescribed by Ordinances.'[4]

The High Commissioner was given power to establish Land Courts as should be required 'from time to time for the hearing of such questions concerning the title to immovable property as may be prescribed.'[5]

The most striking development in the Judiciary provided by the Order-in-Council was that embodied in the provision for the establishment of a Supreme Court, the constitution of which was to be prescribed by Ordinance. The Supreme Court sits either as a Court of Appeal or as a High Court. As a Court of Appeal, it has jurisdiction, 'subject to the provisions of any Ordinance, to hear appeals from all judgments given by a District Court in first instance or by the Court of Criminal Assize or by a Land Court.' As a High Court of Justice, it has 'jurisdiction to hear and determine such mat-

---

[1] Proclamation. Establishment of Courts, 24th June, 1918. (Superseded by the Palestine Order-in-Council, 1922, and by the Courts Ordinance, No. 21 of 1924.) Legislation of Palestine, 1918–25. Compiled by Norman Bentwich, Attorney-General of Palestine. Orders-in-Council and Ordinances, vol. 1, p. 605.

[2] *Ibid.*, see page 5.   [3] Palestine Order-in-Council, Article 40.

[4] *Ibid.*, Article 41.   [5] *Ibid.*, Article 42.

THE JERUSALEM GOVERNORATE, WHERE THE SUPREME COURT SITS

ters as are not causes or trials, but petitions or applications, not within the jurisdiction of any other court and necessary to be decided for the administration of justice.' [1]

Article 44 of the Order-in-Council provides for an appeal to the Privy Council:

In civil matters when the amount or value in dispute exceeds £E.500 an appeal shall lie from the Supreme Court to His Majesty in Council. Every appeal shall be brought within such time and in such manner as may be prescribed by any rules of procedure made by His Majesty in Council.[2]

The provision for separate courts for the District of Beersheba continued the policy of the 'special arrangements' for these Bedouin tribes, established in 1920. The complete article reads:

The High Commissioner may by order establish such separate Courts for the district of Beersheba and for such other tribal areas as he may think fit. Such courts may apply tribal custom, so far as it is not repugnant to natural justice or morality.[3]

As to the law to be applied in the Civil Courts:

The jurisdiction of the Civil Courts shall be exercised in conformity with the Ottoman Law in force in Palestine on November 1st, 1914, and such later Ottoman Laws as have been or may be declared to be in force by Public Notice, and such Orders-in-Council, Ordinances, and regulations as are in force in Palestine at the date of the commencement of this Order, or may hereafter be applied or enacted; and subject thereto and so far as the same shall not extend or apply, shall be exercised in conformity with the substance of the common law, and the doctrines of equity in force in England, and with the powers vested in and according to the procedure and practice observed by or before Courts of Justice and Justices of the Peace in England, according to their respective jurisdictions and authorities at that date, save in so far as the said powers, procedure, and practice may have been or may hereafter be modified, amended, or replaced by any other provisions. Provided always that the said common law and doctrines of equity shall be in force in Palestine so far only as the circumstances of Palestine and its inhabitants and the limits of His Majesty's jurisdiction permit and subject to such qualification as local circumstances render necessary.[4]

Under the Palestine Order-in-Council, the Moslem Re-

---

[1] Palestine Order-in-Council, Article 43.   [2] *Ibid.*, Article 44.
[3] *Ibid.*, Article 45.   [4] *Ibid.*, Article 46.

ligious Courts retain their exclusive jurisdiction in all matters of personal status of Moslems, and have besides exclusive jurisdiction in cases of the constitution or administration of a Waqf, constituted for the benefit of Moslems. The Rabbinical Courts and the courts of the several Christian communities retain their former exclusive jurisdiction in matters of marriage, divorce, alimony, and confirmation of wills of the members of their community other than foreigners, and acquire jurisdiction over any case concerning the constitution or administration of a Waqf or religious endowment constituted before their courts according to the religious law of the community. An additional power is conferred upon them, namely a concurrent jurisdiction with the Civil Courts in any other matters of personal status of members of their community other than foreigners. The Religious Courts try the case where all the parties of the action consent to their jurisdiction; the Civil, in the absence of such consent, and so take the place of the Moslem Religious Courts in dealing with questions of succession and guardianship affecting Christians and Jews, where the parties concerned eschew the religious tribunal.

Until the beginning of 1922, the Moslem Religious Courts were under the general supervision of the Legal Department and subject to the Moslem Inspector of the Department. By an Order enacted on December 20, 1921,[1] concerning the constitution and functions of the Supreme Sharia Council for Moslem religious affairs, the Moslem Religious Courts were severed from the supervision of the Legal Department and placed on an autonomous basis.

The finances of the Court, according to the Palestine Order-in-Council, remain under Government control, but the legal superintendence of the courts and all questions concerned with their law and practice are assumed by the Supreme Sharia Council to which the Sharia Inspector is responsible. The Legal Department is concerned with the decisions of the Sharia Courts to the same extent as it is with those of the other Religious Courts, namely, in its responsi-

---

[1] Legislation of Palestine, 1918–25. Compiled by Norman Bentwich, Attorney-General of Palestine. Regulations, Public Notices, Proclamations, Rules of Court, Agreements, and the Royal Instructions, vol. 2, pp. 398–402.

bility for the execution of their judgments by the process and offices of the Civil Courts.[1]

The Palestine Order-in-Council accords the Rabbinical Courts and the tribunals of the Christian Communities larger jurisdiction in matters of personal status. They are also empowered to constitute charitable endowments according to their own special system.[2]

The Palestine Order-in-Council also gives the Civil Courts jurisdiction over foreigners, provided that a foreigner may claim trial by a British magistrate in the case of a minor criminal offence, and by a court consisting of a single British judge or with a majority of British judges in the case of a graver offence; in a civil case tried by the District Court, he may claim that there shall be at least one British judge, and in a civil case heard by the Supreme Court on appeal that the court shall contain a majority of British judges.[3]

A Regulation was issued, November 15, 1922,[4] defining the non-contentious matters of personal status of foreigners, and providing for the exercise of jurisdiction by foreign Consuls in Palestine. Contentious matters of personal status affecting foreigners other than Moslems are, according to the Regulation, decided by the District Courts, applying the personal law of the parties, and constituted by the British Presidents sitting alone, subject to a right of inviting the Consul of the foreigner concerned, or his representative, to sit as assessor for the purpose of advising upon the personal law. These provisions are based upon the stipulations of the Mandate that, while the benefits of consular jurisdiction as formerly enjoyed by Capitulations shall no longer exist in Palestine, the judicial system shall assure to foreigners a complete guarantee of their rights.

The Mandate became operative September 29, 1923. Although this did not affect the jurisdiction of the courts over foreigners, the United States, as we have seen, still refused to

---

[1] Palestine Order-in-Council, Articles 51, 52, 55–57, 64–67.

[2] *Ibid.*, Articles 53, 54.

[3] *Ibid.*, Articles 58–63. These provisions reproduced the Rules made by the Military Administration.

[4] Legislation of Palestine, 1918–25. Compiled by Norman Bentwich, Attorney-General of Palestine. Regulations, Public Notices, Proclamations, Rules of Court, Agreements, and the Royal Instructions, vol. 2, pp. 66–68.

surrender its capitulatory privileges. By an amendment of the Order-in-Council, a foreigner on trial by the District Court for a criminal offence, might claim that the court should either consist of a single British Judge or contain a majority of British judges.[1]

No important changes were made in the Courts Organization until the enactment of the Ordinances, which implement the provisions of the Palestine Order-in-Council with regard to the judiciary. The delay in the enactment of these Ordinances was caused by the absence of a legislative body for ten months of 1923. The Magistrates', District, and Land Courts, and the Court of Appeal, continued to exercise their former jurisdiction.

The Courts Ordinance,[2] which was promulgated September 1, 1924, established the following tribunals:

1. The existing Magistrates', District, and Land Courts. The areas of jurisdiction of the Land Courts were reorganized: in Northern Palestine their work was undertaken by the District Courts of Haifa and Nablus, and, in Southern Palestine, courts at Jerusalem and Jaffa were constituted.

2. In place of the Court of Appeal, a Supreme Court sitting as a Court of Appeal with jurisdiction unchanged; and as the High Court with original jurisdiction in two matters hitherto regulated administratively, namely, first, applications in the nature of habeas corpus, and, second, orders in the nature of mandamus directed to public officers, etc. During the year 1924, less than twenty applications were made to the newly created High Court.

3. A Court of Criminal Assize for offences in which capital sentence may be passed; this court is constituted of the Chief Justice or the Senior British Judge of the Supreme Court sitting with the District Court of the area where the Offence was

---

[1] No. 21 of 1924. An Ordinance relating to the Constitution and Jurisdiction of certain Courts in Palestine. Cited as the 'Courts Ordinance, 1924–25.' Legislation of Palestine, 1918–25. Compiled by Norman Bentwich, Attorney-General of Palestine. Orders-in-Council and Ordinances, vol. 1, p. 407, Article 11 (b).

[2] No. 21 of 1924. An Ordinance relating to the Constitution and Jurisdiction of certain Courts in Palestine — Cited as the 'Courts Ordinance, 1924–25.' The Courts Amendment Ordinance, 1925, has been incorporated in this Ordinance. Legislation of Palestine, 1918–25. Compiled by Norman Bentwich, Attorney-General of Palestine. Orders-in-Council and Ordinances, vol 1, p. 406.

committed. The assize is held in every district, at such places as the Chief Justice shall direct.

4. A Special Tribunal, referred to in Article 55 of the Palestine Order-in-Council,[1] to deal with the conflicts of jurisdiction between a Civil and a Religious Court. This consists of two British Judges of the Supreme Court and the President of the highest Court in Palestine of any religious community which is alleged by any party to the action to have exclusive jurisdiction in the matter at issue. The Chief Justice, or in his absence, the Senior British Judge of the High Court presides over the Tribunal.

The Courts Ordinance also deals with the appointment of judges of the Supreme Court or a District Court; it provides that every judge shall hold office during the pleasure of His Majesty and gives power to make probationary appointments of fit and proper persons as members of a District Court.

Rules, governing appeal from the Supreme Court to His Majesty in Council, were promulgated by Order-in-Council, dated December 15, 1924.[2] These rules are in the common form. The appeal lies:

(a) As of right, from any final judgment of the Court, where the matter in dispute on the Appeal amounts to or is of the value of £500 sterling or upwards, or where the Appeal involves directly or indirectly, some claim or question to or respecting property or some civil right amounting to or of the said value or upwards; and

(b) At the discretion of the Court, from any other judgment of the Court, whether final or interlocutory, if, in the opinion of the Court, the question involved in the Appeal is one which, by reason of its great general or public importance or otherwise, ought to be submitted to His Majesty in Council for decision.

The Magistrates' Courts Jurisdiction Ordinance [3] extended

[1] Palestine Order-in-Council, Legislation of Palestine, 1918–25. Compiled by Norman Bentwich, Attorney-General of Palestine. Orders-in-Council and Ordinances, vol. 1, Article 55, p. 14.

[1] Order-in-Council, Legislation of Palestine, 1918–25. Compiled by Norman Bentwich, Attorney-General of Palestine. Orders-in-Council and Ordinances, vol. 1, p. 31.

[3] No. 9 of 1924. An Ordinance regulating the Jurisdiction of Magistrates' Courts.

the jurisdiction of civil magistrates to (a) offences for which the maximum penalty does not exceed imprisonment for one year and a fine of £E.100, and certain other specified offences; (b) actions for the recovery of possession of immovable property of any value; (c) actions for the partition of immovable property; (d) other civil actions in which the value involved or damages claimed do not exceed £E.100; and (e) counterclaims to the same value.

According to this Ordinance, an appeal from a magistrate lies to the District Court in criminal cases by the accused in case of fine exceeding £E.10 or imprisonment exceeding fifteen days, and by the Public Prosecutor in any case. In civil cases an appeal in a possessory action lies to a Land Court, and to the District Court in any other where the value of the claim is not less than £E.20. Leave to appeal may be granted by a President of the District Court in any case in which an appeal does not lie as of right.

The Ottoman procedure in the prosecution of an offence triable before a magistrate has been changed to provide that the police may refuse to proceed if satisfied that no public interest will be served by so doing; the complainant may then lay his complaint directly before the magistrate.

In the trial of criminal cases by the District Court and the Court of Criminal Assize, the Trial upon Information Ordinance [1] replaced the Rules in the Ottoman Code of Criminal Procedure by a system based upon the English practice, providing for a preliminary judicial enquiry by the magistrate as in proceedings for committal for trial in England. Any person alleging the commission of an offence triable before a Superior Court may make a complaint or charge directly to a magistrate. The Ottoman procedure of trials in absence for serious offences is abolished; but power remains to hold an enquiry in absence to perpetuate testimony.

The Ordinance is amended by the Magistrates' Courts Jurisdiction Amendment Ordinance No. 2 of 1926. Legislation of Palestine, 1918–25, vol. 1, p. 375.

[1] No. 22 of 1924. An Ordinance to regulate the Procedure in Criminal Cases within the jurisdiction of the Court of Criminal Assize or of the District Court. The Trial upon Information (Amendment) Ordinance No. 35 of 1925 has been embodied in this Ordinance. Legislation of Palestine, 1918–25. Compiled by Norman Bentwich, Attorney-General of Palestine. Orders-in-Council and Ordinances, vol. 1, p. 412.

Where the penalty exceeds a fine of £E.100 or six months' imprisonment, the person convicted may appeal to the Court of Appeal, and in sentences of death or penal servitude for five years or more the case must be passed to the Court of Appeal as of right. The Attorney-General has a right of appeal from an acquittal only on grounds of legal error or inadequate punishment. Special leave to appeal may be given from any final judgment which is not subject to appeal as of right. The Superior Courts are empowered to deal summarily with cases of perjury or false evidence committed before them.

In amendment of the Law of Evidence based, in the Ottoman system, on the mediæval provisions of the Mejelle (Civil Code), the Law of Evidence Ordinance [1] introduced the general principle that all persons are competent to give evidence in all cases, and that no person is incompetent by reason of being a party to a civil action or complaint, or the accused in a criminal case, or a relation of a party or of the accused. Husband and wife, parent and child, however, are declared not to be competent to give evidence against each other.

The rule in the Mejelle that the evidence of one witness is insufficient proof is modified by a provision that no judgment shall be given on the evidence of a single witness unless uncontradicted in a civil, or admitted by the accused person in a criminal case, or, whether in a civil or criminal case, corroborated by some other material evidence. Tests of the credibility of witnesses are replaced by the general provision that the value of oral evidence and the credibility of witnesses are questions for the Court to decide according to the demeanor of the witnesses and the circumstances of the case. The rule that in a civil case the party cannot be a witness is cancelled; and either party may now give evidence on his own behalf or be summoned to give evidence for the other.

A further amendment of the Law of Evidence was the Proof of Foreign Documents Ordinance [2] providing rules for the

[1] No. 13 of 1924. An Ordinance to declare and amend some points in the Law of Evidence. Legislation of Palestine, 1918–25. Orders-in-Council and Ordinances, vol. 1, p. 384.

[2] No. 28 of 1924. An Ordinance to provide rules for the Proof of Foreign Docu-

proof before the Court of documents executed in the United
Kingdom or any place in His Majesty's dominions or in
foreign countries.

The rules concerning arrest of offenders and search of
suspected persons and premises were revised and consolidated
in the Arrest of Offenders and Searches Ordinance,[1] which declares that a person arrested without a warrant shall be
brought before a magistrate within forty-eight hours of arrest
and the period of remand in custody shall not exceed fifteen
days. In certain cases a police officer may enter and search
any house or place without a warrant, otherwise a search is
permissible only upon a magistrate's warrant.

The Contempt of Court Ordinance [2] amplifies the scanty
provisions in the Ottoman Penal Code in that particular. Besides the existing penalties for insult or outrage committed in
the presence of the Court, and for failure of a witness to attend or answer questions, there are now penalties for the
publication during a trial of matter prejudicial to fair trial or
likely to bring the Court into contempt.

The Civil Trial of Members of the Forces Ordinance[3] provides for the trial by the Civil Courts of members of His
Majesty's Forces in Palestine, over whom, when charged
with a criminal offence, the Civil Courts had hitherto not
exercised jurisdiction. There is a reservation that the officer
commanding may elect to bring the accused before a court-
martial. The Civil Court to try such cases is composed solely
of a British judge or judges, applying the principles of English
Law in respect of the nature and constitution of the offence,
the admissibility of evidence and the punishment, but no
sentence more severe than that prescribed by the Palestine
law for the particular offence may be imposed.

ments in Courts of Palestine. Legislation of Palestine, 1918–25. Orders-in-Council
and Ordinances, vol. 1, p. 455.

[1] No. 4 of 1924. An Ordinance to prescribe the conditions under which offenders
may be arrested and persons and premises searched. Legislation of Palestine, 1918–
25, vol. 1, p. 367.

[2] No. 11 of 1924. An Ordinance to provide for the punishment of Contempt of
Court. Legislation of Palestine, 1918–25, vol. 1, p. 380.

[3] No. 27 of 1924. An Ordinance relating to the Jurisdiction of the Civil Courts of
Palestine in certain cases affecting members of His Britannic Majesty's Fighting
Forces in Palestine. Legislation of Palestine, 1918–25, vol. 1, p. 452.

The Palestine (Holy Places) Order-in-Council,[1] dated September 15, 1924, was issued with the object of excluding from the Civil Courts actions touching matters within the purview of the Commission on the Holy Places to be set up under Article 14 of the Mandate. It provides that such actions shall not be heard or determined by any court; but does not affect or limit the jurisdiction of the Religious Courts. The High Commissioner decides, in case of question, whether any action shall be withdrawn from the Civil Courts.

The Maronite Community, on proof of having exercised jurisdiction in matters of personal status in the Ottoman régime, has been recognized as a Community under the Palestine Order-in-Council exercising that jurisdiction over its members.

The Municipal Benches at Jerusalem, Jaffa, Haifa, and Gaza dealt with a very large number of petty offences in 1924, principally against traffic and health regulations. That they might function more easily the Municipal Courts (Amendment) Ordinance [2] was passed, reducing the minimum number of each Bench to two members; where opinion is divided the case is retried by a Bench with an odd number of members. Any person sentenced to imprisonment by a Bench has a right of appeal to the District Court and, if fined, may apply to the President of the District Court for leave to appeal.

Under the Courts Ordinance a foreigner charged with a capital offence is tried by the Court of Criminal Assize composed of the Chief Justice, or the Senior British Judge of the Supreme Court, the President of the District Court and one other judge, or by a single British judge of the Supreme Court; and for an offence triable by the District Court, by a court of a single British judge or containing a majority of British judges.

The agreement between His Majesty's Government and the United States of America, signed on December 3, 1924,[3]

[1] The Palestine (Holy Places) Order-in-Council of 1924. Legislation of Palestine, 1918–25. Orders-in-Council and Ordinances, vol. 1, p. 30.

[2] No. 32 of 1924. The Municipal Courts Amendment Ordinance. Incorporated in the Municipal Courts Ordinance, 1921; An Ordinance to provide for the institution in certain towns of a Court to try petty offences. Legislation of Palestine, 1918–25, vol. 1, p. 149.

[3] See note 2, page 259.

provided that extradition treaties between the United States and Great Britain shall apply to Palestine. The Extradition Ordinance [1] applying to Palestine the extradition treaties between His Majesty's Government and foreign Powers establishes a system similar to that of the English Acts. To demands for the extradition from Palestine of foreign fugitive offenders, the treaties in existence apply as to demands for extradition from the United Kingdom.

An application under the Ordinance for extradition of two persons charged with complicity in a bankruptcy committed in Italy was made on behalf of the Italian Government. An order for extradition was issued by the British judge and confirmed by the High Court, to which an application for a writ of habeas corpus was submitted, and an application was presented to the Privy Council for special leave to appeal from its decision. The proceedings in the Privy Council were not further pursued, however, because of the suspension of the criminal prosecution in Italy. Eighteen Ordinances on administrative and fiscal matters were enacted in 1924. The provisions of these Ordinances are described in the Report by His Britannic Majesty's Government on the Administration under Mandate of Palestine and Trans-Jordan for the year 1924.[2]

Some interesting instances of court action are noted in the 1925 Report on the Administration of Palestine.[3] Before the High Court, many applications were made in alleged cases of illegal arrest or detention of persons in prison without due authority. The validity of acts of the legislature was tested. About fifty petitions were heard, including the petition which challenged the Urtas Springs Ordinance of 1925,[4] and also the

---

[1] No. 18 of 1924. An Ordinance to provide for the detention of persons for whose extradition application has been made, and for the procedure to be observed in connection with extradition. Legislation of Palestine, 1918–25. Orders-in-Council and Ordinances, vol. 1, p. 393.

[2] Colonial No. 12. Report by His Britannic Majesty's Government on the Administration under Mandate of Palestine and Trans-Jordan for the year 1924, pp. 21–23.

[3] Colonial No. 20. Report by His Britannic Majesty's Government to the Council of the League of Nations on the Administration of Palestine and Trans-Jordan for the year 1925.

[4] Legislation of Palestine, 1918–25. Compiled by Norman Bentwich, Attorney-General of Palestine. Orders-in-Council and Ordinances, vol. 1, p. 513.

application for an injunction to prevent the Government issuing postage stamps inscribed with a translation into Hebrew of the name Palestine that did not exactly reproduce the Arabic version of the name, referred to above as the 'E.I.' case.[1]

In two instances, the powers of religious authorities were contested; one touching the competence of the Supreme Moslem Council to order a judge of a Moslem Religious Court not to grant audience to a Moslem advocate holding a license to practise before the Sharia Courts; the other touching the powers of the Government to uphold the exclusive authority of the Rabbinical Council to prevent entry to the public slaughter house of Jewish slaughterers not licensed by the Council.

The Court also heard several applications for orders to declare that elections for the secondary electors to the Supreme Moslem Council were irregularly conducted and should be annulled; and it granted the applications in some cases on the ground that the Law of Elections had not been followed.

The Special Tribunal, constituted under Article 55 of the Palestine Order-in-Council, 1922, held its first sitting to decide whether a case was one of personal status within the exclusive jurisdiction of a Religious Court. The Tribunal was formed by the Chief Justice, the Latin Bishop of Tavium, and the Senior British Judge. [2]

The German Government applied for the delivery of three persons on a charge similar to the Italian case, and the High Court confirmed the magistrate's order for extradition, holding that the pre-war Anglo-German Extradition Treaty had been reinstated and was applicable in Palestine.

The following cases were decided in the year 1928, including Appeals in all Courts of Palestine other than Religious Courts: [3]

[1] Jemal Eff. Housseini *versus* Attorney-General (Government of Palestine) *re:* letters E.I. on the stamps used in Palestine.

[2] In 1926, the Special Tribunal sat on four occasions: the Religious Courts concerned being those of the Latin, Orthodox, and Moslem communities. In 1927, the Special Tribunal sat on four occasions: the Religious Courts concerned being on three occasions Moslem, and on the fourth occasion Latin Catholic.

[3] Colonial No. 40. Report by His Majesty's Government in the United Kingdom

Courts	Civil	Criminal	Total
Supreme Court...............................	183	358	541
High Court..................................	83	—	83
Court of Criminal Assize......................	—	33	33
Special Court................................	—	—	—
District Courts..............................	2,292	2,151	4,443
Land Courts.................................	572	—	572
Magistrates' Courts..........................	60,047	27,269	87,316
Municipal Courts............................	—	9,548	9,548
Persons charged before magistrates holding special warrants	—	6,810	6,810
Total...................................	63,177	46,169	109,346

The following cases were decided in the year 1929, including Appeals in all Courts of Palestine other than Religious Courts: [1]

Courts	Civil	Criminal	Total
Supreme Court...............................	255	377	632
High Court..................................	65	—	65
Court of Criminal Assize......................	—	32	32
Special Court................................	3	—	3
District Courts..............................	2,181	2,309	4,490
Land Courts.................................	678	—	678
Magistrates' Courts..........................	61,279	23,072	84,351
Municipal Courts............................	—	10,024	10,024
Persons charged before magistrates holding special warrants.........................	—	14,012	14,012
Total...................................	64,461	49,826	114,287

This brief review gives some idea of the responsibilities devolving upon the Chief Justice; [2] but, in addition to all this, other important matters come under his jurisdiction. The discipline of the Bar, for example, is in his hands: he has the power to appoint at his discretion a Council of Discipline to investigate allegations of unprofessional conduct. Up to the present time, three Advocates have been suspended from the Bar.

The office of Chief Justice is obviously complex and difficult, but it is tremendously interesting. In many respects the duties of the Attorney-General and the Chief Justice involve more human problems than any other department in the ad-

of Great Britain and Northern Ireland to the Council of the League of Nations on the Administration of Palestine and Trans-Jordan for the year 1928, p. 42.

[1] Colonial No. 47. Report by His Majesty's Government in the United Kingdom of Great Britain and Northern Ireland to the Council of the League of Nations on the Administration of Palestine and Trans-Jordan for the year 1929, p. 62.

[2] Mr. M. F. J. McDonnell succeeded Sir Thomas Haycraft as Chief Justice.

ministration of Palestine. As we have followed the development of the legal and the judicial system, which, in fact, had no precedents except the Cour de Cassation in Constantinople, relying in turn for its Rules of Court on the Ottoman Codes of Procedure, we see how important it was to have had at the beginning such admirably equipped and devotedly disposed men for the task. The pioneer work of Norman Bentwich was skilfully carried forward by Sir Thomas Haycraft. It has well been said that, of all the legal positions outside of England open to a British lawyer, the office of Chief Justice, when Sir Thomas Haycraft took it in 1921, was probably the most intricate and arduous.

Let us quote again from W. Basil Worsfold, who makes the following interesting comment:

Is it frivolous to wonder if Sir Thomas ever thinks of Joshua, Deborah, Gideon, and the rest, as far-off predecessors? Or how Hannibal, the almost-conqueror of Rome, at Carthage bore the same Hebrew title — Shophet — as the magistrates of Phœnicia and the 'judges' of the Israelites? In a sense the East *is* unchanging. On the hills of Judea and Samaria, on the crest of Mount Carmel, and in hidden valleys on both sides of the Jordan and its lakes, the life of the indigenous population of to-day must be conditioned by much the same physical and social environment as it was three thousand years ago. Some of the causes which are tried in Palestine of the Mandate are so much *in pari materia* with the cases decided by Joshua and his successors that it would not seem impossible to find points of contact between the majestic jurisprudence of Western Europe and the primitive conceptions which found concrete expression in these endeavours to regulate human relationships by reference to a standard of righteousness external to mankind.[1]

[1] W. Basil Worsfold, *Palestine of the Mandate*, pp. 91–92.

PART II
THE PROBLEM OF ZIONISM IN PALESTINE

CHAPTER X

THE HISTORICAL BACKGROUND OF THE BALFOUR DECLARATION

THE following sentence constitutes the Balfour Declaration: [1] 'His Majesty's Government view with favour the establishment in Palestine of a National Home for the Jewish people, and will use their best endeavours to facilitate the achievement of that object, it being understood that nothing shall be done which may prejudice the civil and religious rights of existing non-Jewish communities in Palestine, or the rights and political status enjoyed by the Jews in any other country.'

This remarkable contract with Jewry was announced from the British Foreign Office on the 2d of November, 1917, while the Allied Forces under General Allenby were advancing into Palestine. Immediate publicity was given to the Declaration in England, France, and the United States, and later it received the official endorsement of the Allied and Associated Powers.

The Balfour Declaration is unique in the annals of diplomacy. There never was an agreement so fraught with conflict and distrust. And for several reasons: Two years before its announcement, England had promised the independence of the Arabs throughout the Near East; [2] and this promise, as the Arabs interpreted it, included Palestine. Then, about a year later, England made an agreement with France, bound up in the terms of the Sykes-Picot Treaty, [3] which contem-

[1] House of Commons, November 2, 1917.

[2] *A History of the Peace Conference of Paris*, vol. VI, pp. 123–27, 132–33. Edited by H. W. V. Temperley. Published under the auspices of the Institute of International Affairs.

J. de V. Loder, *The Truth About Mesopotamia, Palestine and Syria*, pp. 17–23.

[3] *A History of the Peace Conference of Paris*, vol. VI, pp. 16, 17. Edited by H. W. V. Temperley. Published under the auspices of the Institute of International Affairs.

Arnold J. Toynbee, *Survey of International Affairs*, 1925, vol. I. 'The Islamic World Since the Peace Settlement,' p. 235, note 1.

The text of the Sykes-Picot Treaty, May 16, 1916, translated from the French texts reproduced in *L'Asie Française* and in *La Syrie*, by G. Sammé, is printed in *The Truth About Mesopotamia, Palestine and Syria*, by J. de V. Loder, Appendix I, p. 161.

plated an international administration for Palestine, thereby nullifying the alleged pledges to the Arabs; while both these arrangements were obviously in conflict with the establishment of a Jewish National Home in Palestine.

But the compacts with the Arabs and the French had another characteristic which was certain to engender irritation and distrust. These British agreements were secret; and the Jews, who relied on the publicly announced Balfour Declaration in 1917, were not informed of any previous commitments. So, as the result of these circumstances, England became involved in a situation momentously embarrassing, and laden with difficulties of far-reaching consequences.

After the War, England resolved her differences with France, with respect to Palestine, by concessions to France in Syria. But she found herself tightly bound by her promises to the Arabs in 1915 and her contract with the Jews in 1917. This dual obligation became a permanent and tragic legacy of the War; both the Arabs and the Jews have tenaciously insisted on the full limit of the agreements. War measures, as they both were, both sides have based their claims, not only on the promises made during the War, but on what each contended to be a clearly substantiated historical background. From the latter angle, the Jews had the immediate advantage over the Arabs, for the principle embodied in the Balfour Declaration had received British and international recognition many years before 1914; while the project for an Arab State, as outlined in the British promises, had had support neither by Great Britain nor by international agreement until Great Britain approached the Arabs for assistance in the World War. In other words: the former was prompted not only by the stress of war, but also by a desire, slight as it may have been, to obtain justice for the Jews; while the latter was undertaken solely for promised Arab assistance in defeating the Turk. To learn the full story, we must invoke the records of history.

The Balfour Declaration has a long and dramatic background. The Jews had been dispersed for nearly two thousand years, but, as we have seen, there never was a time when Jews were not to be found in Palestine. Gradually, they returned to the cradle of their faith; and at the time of the an-

THE EARL OF BALFOUR

nouncement of the Balfour Declaration, about eighty thousand Jews were living in Palestine.

The story of this modern Return may well begin with the French Revolution, which proved an epochal event in Jewish history. The law, admitting Jews to full rights of citizenship in 1791,[1] initiated the general struggle for emancipation. Under Napoleon's influence the movement progressed; and in 1796, complete equality of the Jews was decreed in Holland. In 1811, the Jews of Westphalia, those of the Hanse towns, and also those living in Frankfurt were accorded the rights of citizenship; and in 1812, the King of Prussia granted equal rights to all Jews settled in Prussia at that time.[2] The spread of the movement for emancipation, however, was a gradual process. The Jews were emancipated in England in 1858, in Italy in 1859, in Austria in 1867, and in Germany in 1869.[3] These emancipated Jews declared their loyalty to the State and became conspicuous in trade, in the professions, and in politics. They regarded themselves as Englishmen, Frenchmen, Germans, or whatever their State of allegiance might be; and naturally, their sense of Jewish solidarity gradually diminished.

These Western Jews, however, were only a handful compared to the numbers living in the eastern part of Europe, where fully half the Jews of the world were located.[4] While Western Europe was granting emancipation, the Jews in Eastern Europe were being subjected, as Dubnow says, 'to every possible mediæval experiment.'[5] Emancipation for them was out of the question. In Russia, the absolutist ré-

[1] Loi relative aux Juifs, donné à Paris, le 13 novembre 1791 (décret du 27 septembre 1791): 'L'Assemblée Nationale, considérant que les conditions nécessaires pour être citoyen français et pour devenir citoyen actif, sont fixées par la constitution, et que tout homme réunissant lesdites conditions, prête le serment civique et s'engage à remplir tous les devoirs que la constitution impose, a droit à tous les avantages qu'elle assure; Révoque tous ajournements, réserves et exceptions insérés dans les précédens décrets relativement aux individus Juifs qui prêteront le serment civique, qui sera regardé comme une renonciation à tous privilèges et exceptions introduit précédemment en leur faveur.' (Lois et Actes du Gouvernement, Paris, 1807, vol. v, p. 229.)

[2] Graetz, *History of the Jews*, vol. v, chapter XII.

[3] Max Raisin, *History of the Jews in Modern Times*, p. 25 seq.

[4] Jessie Sampter, *Guide to Zionism*.

[5] S. M. Dubnow, *History of the Jews in Russia and Poland* (translated from the Russian by I. Friedlaender), Preface to vol. I.

gime aimed not only at the disfranchisement of the Jews, but also, as Dubnow again affirms, 'at the direct physical annihilation of the Jewish people.' [1] And further, says the same author, 'The policy of the extermination of Judaism was stamped upon the forehead of Russian reaction receiving various colors at various periods, assuming the hue now of economic, now of national and religious, now of bureaucratic oppression.' [2]

It was only a few years before the adoption of the law giving full rights of citizenship to the Jews in France that Russia instituted a Pale of Settlement by attaching the Jews to definite localities which had been wrested from Poland, and forbidding them the right to reside in other parts of Russia. This was stipulated in the Ukase of 1786.

When the second and third partitions of Poland were effected in 1793 and 1795, respectively, hundreds of thousands of Jews were admitted into Russia where, less than a generation before, not a single Jew had been allowed to enter. These Jews were confronted with the law of the Pale of Settlement, which was especially obnoxious to them, owing to the fact that ancient Poland had never had a Pale of Settlement. The Jews in Poland had merely been barred from certain so-called 'privileged towns,' such as Warsaw, the capital. The Ukase of 1794 not only circumscribed the area of the Jewish right of residence in Russia, but declared that the Jews who wished to enroll themselves in the mercantile or burgher class in the cities must pay taxes 'doubly in comparison with those imposed on the burghers and merchants of the Christian religion.'

Further restrictions were prescribed in the Ukase of 1795. Thus, toward the end of the reign of Catherine II, restrictive legislation against the Jews was firmly established. At this time there was a perceptible tendency to force the Jews out of the villages, and thus to compress the Jewish masses in the towns and cities.

It was in the reign of Alexander I that the expulsion from the villages began to take place. The project affected sixty

[1] S. M. Dubnow, *History of the Jews in Russia and Poland* (translated from the Russian by I. Friedlaender), Preface to vol. I.
[2] *Ibid.*

thousand Jewish families; it was arranged that one third of the Jews would be expelled in 1808, another third in 1809, and the last third in 1810. Dubnow describes the horrors of the expulsion as follows: 'Those who did not go willingly were made to leave by force. Many were ejected ruthlessly, under the escort of peasants and soldiers. They were driven like cattle into the townlets and cities, and left there on the public squares in the open air.' [1]

The distress of the Jewish masses became so great that the governors, in their reports to the Central Government, declared that it was impossible to carry out the expulsion decree without complete ruin to the Jews. They were only saved, however, from further expulsion by the approach of Napoleon's army toward the Russian frontier.

During the period covering the years 1815 to 1848, about two million Jews were huddled together in the western part of Russia. Dubnow explains that between 1815 and 1855, the attitude of the Russian Government toward the Jews reflected

three successive tendencies: first, in the last years of Alexander I's reign (1815–1825), a mixed tendency of 'benevolent paternalism' and severe restrictions; second, during the first half of Nicholas I's reign (1826–1840), a military tendency, that of 'correcting' the Jews by subjecting their youth, from the age of childhood, to the austere discipline of conscription and barrack training, accompanied by compulsory religious assimilation and by an unprecedented recrudescence of rightlessness and oppression; and third, during the latter part of Nicholas's reign (1840–1855), the 'enlightened' tendency of improving the Jews by establishing 'crown schools' and demolishing the autonomous structure of Jewish life, while keeping in force the former cruel disabilities (1840–1855). This endless 'correctional' and 'educational' experimenting on a whole people, aggravated by the resuscitation of ritual murder trials and wholesale expulsions in approved medieval style, makes the history of Russian Jews during that period an uninterrupted tragedy.[2]

The Polish rebellion of 1863 was in its effects detrimental to the Jews throughout the Empire. The insurrection gave a strong impetus to the policy of Russification, which was felt

[1] S. M. Dubnow, *History of the Jews in Russia and Poland* (translated from the Russian by I. Friedlaender), vol. I, p. 351.

[2] *Ibid.*, p. 391

with particular force in the western provinces. The civil rights of the Jews were not only affected, but their cultural interests as well. In such an atmosphere, as one can readily see, the emancipation of the Jews was not to be thought of; and so it came to pass that some discerning minds began to see the situation in its relation to the future of Jewry and of Judaism. They looked to Palestine as a place of escape from the Czarist yoke.

In 1862, Hirsch Kalischer, an Orthodox Rabbi, born in Prussian Poland in 1795, declared that the time had come for the Jews to redeem the soil of Palestine by their own efforts. He proposed the immediate establishment of a Jewish society for the colonization of Palestine; and in 1867, issued jointly with Rabbi Gutmacher of Graetz, an 'Appeal to our Brethren,' [1] in which the Jews of England in particular were passionately urged to support 'the colonization, cultivation, and improvement' of the 'abandoned, devastated, sacred soil.'

Interestingly enough, at about the same time, a Western Jew voiced the idea of a reunited Jewry in Palestine. Moses Hess, a German born in Bonn, whose radical views on German politics caused his exile from Prussia after the Revolution of 1848, proposed a definite plan for the relief of the Jews. In his book, 'Rome and Jerusalem,' published in 1862, he urged the Jews to labor for the 'political regeneration of the Jewish people with the same energy that other Jews in other times labored for their emancipation in the lands of exile.' [2] He saw in continued exile the ultimate dissolution of Judaism. Addressing the Jewish people, he said:

> The time has arrived for you to reclaim either by way of compensation, or by other means, your ancient fatherland from Turkey.... Was not help given to Zion in order to defend and establish the wild mountaineers there? Are not things being prepared there and roads leveled, and is not the road of civilization being built on the desert in the form of the Suez Canal works and the railroad which will connect Asia and Europe? They are not thinking at present of the restoration of our people. But you know the proverb, 'Man proposes and God disposes.'

[1] *The Hebrew National*, vol. I, No. 1, February 15, 1867, p. 6. Quoted in its entirety by N. Sokolow, in his *History of Zionism*, vol. II, pp. 262–63.

[2] Moses Hess, *Rome and Jerusalem* (translated from the German by Meyer Waxman), p. 89.

Further, he goes on to say: 'For Jewish colonization on the road to India and China, there is no lack either of Jewish laborers or of Jewish talent and capital. Let only the germ be planted under the protection of the European powers, and the tree of a new life will spring forth by itself and bear excellent fruit.' He believed in the organization of the work on a legal basis and in the founding of Jewish societies of agriculture, industry and commerce on the Mosaic, that is, social principles. He furthermore 'subscribes heartily' to a program of organization suggested by a Frenchman from whom he quotes. This program includes the following suggestions:

A Society for the colonization of Palestine which should first raise a fund sufficient to buy as many towns, fields and vineyards in the Holy Land as possible. Secondly, Jews from all parts of the world, and especially from Russia, Poland and Germany, should be settled in Palestine. Thirdly, a police system should be established to protect the colonists from the attacks of the Bedouins, and to maintain law and order. Finally, an agricultural school should be opened where Jewish youths could receive an adequate preparation for the life of a Palestinian farmer.

With these definite plans already formulated, he declares that, 'as soon as the political situation in the East takes a favourable turn, the establishment of Jewish Colonies in Palestine must at once be begun, as a first step towards the resettlement of the Jews as a nation in their historic home.' [1]

It was Kalischer's propaganda which really in fact inspired the establishment in 1870 of a Jewish agricultural school in Palestine, near Jaffa. This school, which is still in existence, was significantly called Mikweh Israel ('The Hope of Israel'). [2] It was founded by the Alliance Israélite Universelle, an association formed in Paris in 1860 for the purpose of helping oppressed and persecuted Jews in all parts of the world. The Alliance, being favorably impressed with Kalischer's proposals, took immediate steps to establish this school near Jaffa.

Thus it was the French and not the English Jews who were the first to respond to Kalischer's appeal. English Jews, how-

[1] Moses Hess, *Rome and Jerusalem* (translated from the German by Meyer Waxman), pp. 145, 149, 158, 169.

[2] In 1914, it had developed into a modern and thriving farm, having an enrollment of 150 pupils, men and boys — mostly Russian Jews. (N. Sokolow, *History of Zionism*, vol. II, p. 326.)

ever, had already become interested in Palestine. As early as 1827, Sir Moses Montefiore went there on a pilgrimage, and subsequently made repeated efforts for the settlement of Jews in Palestine. In 1834, after talking the matter over with Mehemet Ali, he elaborated a scheme of colonization on a large scale, which, however, he was unable to carry out because of changes in the political situation. In 1855, he obtained a firman from the Sultan of Turkey allowing him to purchase land in Palestine; and it was at this time that he established the agricultural Colonies at Jaffa, Safed, and Tiberias. He did much also for the improvement of Colonies already established, founding schools, hospitals, and industrial plants. In 1874 on his last visit to the Holy Land he was acclaimed in every Jewish city and received with every mark of distinction and veneration. His final suggestion was embodied in a plan for housing Jews outside the city of Jerusalem in small and modern communities, with enough land to make agriculture possible. This suggestion was energetically taken up by the Montefiore Testimonial Committee.[1] The Anglo-Jewish Association, founded in 1871, has also done much for the welfare of the Jewish population in Palestine.

In 1840, Palestine had been the object of acute political action. After nine years of warfare, Mehemet Ali, the Viceroy of Egypt, succeeded in wresting Syria from the Sultan of Turkey. France was ready to support his action, but England, backed by Prussia, Russia, and Austria desired to maintain the integrity of the Turkish Empire. On July 14, 1840, a convention was signed in London between England, Russia, Austria, and Prussia, without the concurrence of France, whereby an ultimatum was delivered to Mehemet Ali, calling on him to evacuate Palestine. This ultimatum was followed by a declaration of war. In the following year, on July 18, 1841, Mehemet Ali abandoned his claim to Syria. It was also in 1840 that the Jews resident in Damascus and Rhodes were subjected to cruel persecution, on the charge, which was proved to be false, that they used human blood in the celebration of the Passover. This cruelty aroused public opinion throughout Europe and resulted in gathering fresh impetus for the Zionist movement. As the fate of Syria

[1] Lucien Wolf, *Sir Moses Montefiore.*

still remained undecided, many declared vigorously in favor of making Palestine a home for the Jews, under the protection of the European Powers.

During this period, quite naturally, people became curious to know more about the Holy Land. Several important people visited the country, and upon their return wrote interesting books describing their travels. Kinglake gives an interesting and entertaining account of the hardships he underwent in Palestine and Syria. Travelling facilities between cities and across rivers were apparently of the most primitive kind, and he was obliged upon more than one occasion to camp in the open and often to stay at inns, in very unsanitary quarters. Conditions in the cities were deplorable, and Kinglake spares his readers none of the details. He also describes his contacts with the Arabs and Bedouins in the district east of the Jordan.[1]

In contrast to this stern realist, on the other hand, Lamartine viewed the country in a spirit of lofty idealism and interpreted it with his poetic pen. He writes of Jerusalem:

The line of her walls and her towers, the points of her numerous minarets, the arches of her shining domes, stand out in bold relief against the deep blue of an orient sky; and the town, thus exhibited on its broad and elevated platform, seems again to shine in all the antique splendor of its prophecies, or to be only waiting the word to rise in dazzling glory from its seventeen successive ruins, and to be transformed into that New Jerusalem which is to come out of the bosom of the desert, radiant with brightness.[2]

These writings, as well as others, created great interest in Palestine, and they proved to be an important factor in the progress of Zionism; for they contributed, at least indirectly, towards centring people's thoughts on the Holy Land.

After the political events of 1840, Lord Shaftesbury, in a letter written to Viscount Palmerston, then Secretary of State for Foreign Affairs, claimed that:

If the Governing Power of the Syrian provinces would promulgate equal laws and equal protection to Jew and Gentile, and confirm his decrees by accepting the four Powers as guarantees of his

---

[1] A. W. Kinglake, *Eothen, or Traces of Travel Brought Home from the East.*

[2] Alphonse de Lamartine, *Voyage en Orient*, 1832–1833, vol. I, p. 410. *A Pilgrimage to the Holy Land* (the same translated into English), vol. I, p. 268.

engagement, to be set forth and ratified in an article of the Treaty (of Peace), the way would at once be opened, confidence would be revived, and prevailing throughout these regions, would bring with it some of the wealth and enterprise of the world at large, and, by allaying their suspicions, call forth to the full the hidden wealth and industry of the Jewish people.

And he continued:

Disconnected, as they are, from all the peoples of the earth, they would appeal to no national or political sympathies for assistance in the path of wrong; and the guarantee which I propose, for insertion in the Treaty to be carried out by the personal protection of the respective Consuls and Vice-Consuls of the several nations would be sufficient to protect them in the exercise of their right.[1]

The plan suggested by Lord Shaftesbury, however, failed to appeal to the British Government at that time; but in April, 1841, Lord Palmerston forwarded a circular to the diplomatic representatives in the Levant and Syria, which stated that: 'As far as documents could avail, the law of Turkey had by that time become all that might reasonably be expected for toleration of the Jews, but that the difficulty remained as to enforcing an honest administration of that law.' The circular also pointed out that the Porte had declared its determination that the law should be righteously administered and had even promised to 'attend to any representation which might be made to it by the Embassy of any act of oppression exercised upon Jews.' The Consul was, according to the circular, to investigate diligently all cases of oppression exercised upon Jews that might come to his knowledge... and that on every suitable occasion he was to make known to the local authorities that the British Government felt an interest in the welfare of Jews in general.[2]

The British people still continued to discuss projects for the resettlement of the Jews in Palestine. Among others, the Reverend A. G. H. Hollingsworth appealed to the British Government to help the Jews regain the land of their fathers. Another well-known Englishman, Colonel George Gawler

[1] Edwin Hodder, *Life and Work of the Seventh Earl of Shaftesbury*, vol. i, p. 312. Nahum Sokolow, *History of Zionism*, vol. i, p. 126 *seq*.

[2] James Finn, *Stirring Times (or Records from Jerusalem Consular Chronicles of 1853–1856)*, vol. i, p. 106 *seq*.

(1796–1869), for a time Governor of Australia, urged the colonizing of Palestine by the Jews on political grounds. 'Divine Providence,' he said, 'has placed Syria and Egypt in the very gap between England and the most important regions of her colonial and foreign trade, India, China, the Indian Archipelago and Australia.... Hence the call upon her to exert herself energetically for the amelioration of the condition of both of these Provinces... and it is now for England to set her hand to the renovation of Syria, through the only people whose energies will be extensively and permanently in the work, — the real children of the soil, the sons of Israel.'[1]

Thomas Clarke urged the same view in his book on 'India and Palestine,' published a few years later. 'The occupation of Palestine by... the Jews, under the protection of England,' he wrote, 'must be a greater necessity than ever.... If England is relying upon its commerce as the cornerstone of its greatness; if one of the nearest and best channels of that commerce is across the axis of the three great continents; and if the Jews are essentially... a trading people, what so natural as that they should be planted along that great highway of ancient traffic.'[2]

George Eliot, whose 'Daniel Deronda' was published in 1876, puts the longing of the Jews into the mouth of the character Mordecai, a Jewish visionary of the most sincere and ardent type. His words are as follows:

Revive the organic centre: let the unity of Israel which has made the growth and form of its religion be an outward reality. Looking towards a land and a polity, our dispersed people in all the ends of the earth may share the dignity of a national life which has a voice among the peoples of the East and the West.... There is a store of wisdom among us to found a new Jewish polity, grand, simple, just, like the old — a republic where there is equality of protection.... The outraged Jew shall have a defence in the court of nations, as the outraged Englishman or American. Let the reason of Israel disclose itself in a great outward deed, and let there be another great migration, another choosing of Israel to be a nationality.[3]

[1] Address delivered by Colonel Gawler in January, 1853, on 'Syria and its Near Prospects.' Quoted in the *History of Zionism*, by Nahum Sokolow, vol. I, p. 137 *seq.*

[2] Thomas Clarke, *India and Palestine*, pp. 12–15. July, 1861. Quoted in the *History of Zionism*, by Nahum Sokolow, vol. I, p. 139.

[3] George Eliot, *Daniel Deronda* (Standard edition, E. P. Dutton and Co.), vol. II, p. 387.

Interest in the Jewish situation was also stimulated by Laurence Oliphant, who offered new proposals to the British Government. Oliphant was chiefly interested in preventing the disintegration of the Turkish Empire, and he planned to establish a model Jewish Colony on a small scale within the Turkish Empire, ruled over by a Turkish official. This, he conjectured, would strengthen Turkey's position as a place of strategic importance. The land which he selected for this purpose was the territory east of the Jordan in Syria, land that was rich and arable, but thinly populated and but nominally under the control of the central government. He proposed the organization of a Colonization Company similar in its character to the East India Company, which would buy the property from the Turkish Government and establish upon it Jewish colonists, in particular those from Turkey itself, Russia, Galicia, Roumania, and Servia. These colonists would, according to his plan, become citizens of the Ottoman Empire, but being under the auspices of a company and a charter, they would secure a certain amount of self-government. It appeared to him that through the agency of a commercial enterprise, formed under the sponsorship of the King of England, with its seat at Constantinople, sufficient capital for such an undertaking would be found abroad, provided the charter contained guarantees adequate for the protection of the interests of the shareholders. Before starting on his trip to discover what could be done, he laid his plan before the Prime Minister and Lord Salisbury. In his written account of this interview, Oliphant says: 'From both ministers I received the kindest encouragement and assurances of support, so far as it was possible to afford it without officially committing the Government....'[1] Although Oliphant was never able to carry out his scheme, the interest shown by the English Government officials is worthy of notice.

Certain events, which transpired among the Western Jews, stimulated their attention on Palestine as a place of refuge. Soon after their emancipation, these Jews were confronted with various kinds of opposition, and anti-Semitism developed as an organized force. Its effects as such were first seen in Germany. As to the cause of anti-Semitism there, Raisin explains:

[1] Laurence Oliphant, *The Land of Gideon*, p. 28. See also pp. 11–30, 405–20.

It appeared in Germany as a result of party strife between the ultramontane clericals and the liberals, or more plainly, between the reactionaries who came mostly from the Catholic Church, and the progressives to whom belonged also the Jewish members of the Reichstag. Bismarck, then at the height of his power as a result of his personal triumph in carrying the war with France to success, seized upon the occasion to enhance the feeling of hatred against the Jews to further his own political ends. Soon political Antisemitism, destined later to become 'scientific' Antisemitism, engulfed the whole of the empire and in no small measure influenced the position of the Jews of other countries as well.[1]

Although emancipated by law, the Jews in almost every part of Central and Western Europe were affected by the most determined efforts to curb their civil rights. Many Jews welcomed emancipation, but continued to struggle for civil equality; while others were violently opposed to emancipation, on the ground that it might lead to submersion. The latter group rebelled against a discrimination which compelled them, as they expressed it, to choose between ostracism and extinction. Reasoning thus, their thoughts turned to Palestine.

In Russia, assimilation became the outspoken policy of official circles; and the fight was resumed against Jewish 'Separatism.' In 1871, a commission was appointed for the purpose 'of considering ways and means to weaken as far as possible the communal cohesion among the Jews.' In fact, during the last decade of Alexander II's reign, there was a general drift toward oppression, which prepared the way for the pogroms of the following decade, under Alexander III.

The period from 1881 onward marks a distinct turning-point in Russian Jewish history. The pogroms [2] which began in the spring of 1881, upon the accession of Alexander III, were outrageously cruel. Thousands of Jews were rendered homeless, and hundreds were killed. In fact, the entire Jewish population was affected. During the trial of the terrible Kiev pogrom, the Public Prosecutor shouted, in response to

[1] Max Raisin, *A History of the Jews in Modern Times*, p. 34.

[2] For a description of the horrors of the pogroms, see S. M. Dubnow, *History of the Jews in Russia and Poland* (translated from the Russian by I. Friedlaender), vol. ii, chapters XXI and XXII.

the retort of a Jewish witness that the aggravation of the economic struggle was due to the artificial congestion of the Jews in the Pale of Settlement: 'If the Eastern frontier is closed to the Jews, the Western frontier is open to them; why don't they take advantage of it?' [1] The Jews regarded this as a summons to leave the country. They had already made up their minds to flee, for in despair they saw that there was not a ray of hope left to them — not even the hope for legal justice.

The revolting pogrom at Warsaw, instigated by the Russian Government officials, made a strong impression upon Europe and America, much stronger than the previous pogroms, for according to Dubnow, the havoc wrought in Warsaw had an immediate effect upon the European market.[2] Confronted with rumors of new measures of oppression, the Jews were greatly depressed in the year 1882. Again they heard the cry, 'The Western frontier is open for the Jews'; they were publicly told that the Government wished to get rid of them and that the only 'right' they were to be granted was the right to depart.[3]

The Jewish situation called forth protests throughout Western Europe. Practically all the English newspapers expressed sympathy with the persecuted Jews, and gave full accounts of the atrocities. An outburst of protest swept throughout England, and several mass meetings were held, at which funds for the assistance of Jewish sufferers were started. Questions were addressed in Parliament to the Secretary and Under-Secretary for Foreign Affairs. In the House of Commons, Gladstone stated that reports concerning the persecutions of the Jews in Russia had been received from the English consuls and could not but inspire sentiments of the utmost pain and horror. But, he said, that since the matter concerned the internal affairs of another country, it could not become the object of official correspondence or inquiry by England.[4] This spontaneous outcry in England soon spread to other countries. In Paris, the veteran poet Victor Hugo

[1] S. M. Dubnow, *History of the Jews in Russia and Poland* (translated from the Russian by I. Friedlaender), vol. II, p. 265.

[2] *Ibid.*, p. 283.   [3] *Ibid.*, p. 285.

[4] *Ibid.*, p. 291.

headed the appeal for justice. In Holland, the University of Utrecht rivalled that of Oxford in its protest against the treatment of the Jews.[1]

In the United States, long before the accession of Alexander III, the Government had made several representations to the Russian Government concerning the treatment of American citizens of the Jewish faith, who during their stay in Russia were subjected to the same disabilities which the Russian Government imposed upon its own Jews.[2] The United States Government, however, became interested in the general condition of Jewry in Russia, and instructed its representatives at St. Petersburg [3] to report on the matter. In 1880, acting under instructions of the Secretary of State, William M. Evarts, the United States Minister at St. Petersburg, discussed the Jewish question with leading Russian officials, and sent the report of the conversations to the Secretary of State.[4]

The indignation of many Americans, aroused by the pogroms of 1881, prompted Secretary of State Frederick T. Frelinghuysen to instruct the United States Minister at St. Petersburg to convey the idea 'that the feeling of friendship which the United States entertains for Russia prompts this Government to express the hope that the Imperial Government will find means to cause the persecution of these unfortunate beings to cease.' [5]

An emphatic protest was made by Representative Samuel S. Cox of New York, in a speech before the House of Representatives on July 31, 1882. He denounced the action of the

[1] Nahum Sokolow, *History of Zionism*, vol. I, p. 213. See also Proceedings of Meetings held February 1, 1922, at New York and London to express sympathy with the oppressed Jews in Russia.

[2] See the correspondence between the United States and Russia collected in House of Representatives, 51st Congress, 1st Session. Executive Document No. 470, dated October 1, 1890.

[3] A 'memorandum on the legal position of the Hebrews in Russia' was transmitted by the American Legation to the Secretary of State on September 29, 1872. An abstract from a Russian memorandum on the Jewish right of residence was forwarded in the same manner on March 15, 1875.

[4] An account of Foster's conversation on the problem of Russian Jewry with de Giers, the Russian Minister for Foreign Affairs, Loris-Melikov, the Minister of the Interior, and 'the Minister of Worship' is found in his dispatch of December 30, 1880.

[5] Executive Document No. 470, p. 65.

Russian Government, and offered a resolution calling on the United States Government to 'exercise its influence with the Government of Russia to stay the spirit of persecution as directed against the Jews, and protect the citizens of the United States resident in Russia....' [1] The resolution was passed by the House on February 23, 1883.

At a protest meeting held in New York in February,[2] 1882, where the first refugees from Russia had begun to arrive, one of the speakers, Judge Noah Davis, said amid the enthusiastic applause of the audience: 'Let them come! I would to Heaven it were in our power to take the whole three million Jews of Russia....'

A large number of emigration societies were formed in Russia for the purpose of transferring Russian Jews to the United States. A part of the Jewish youth, however, was extremely enthusiastic over the idea of settling in Palestine, and they conducted a vigorous propaganda for their idea. There was no unity of purpose among the Jewish leaders, but the question of organizing the emigration movement became acute. It was, therefore, decided to hold a conference in St. Petersburg to consider the problem. This was held in April, 1882, after the savage pogrom at Balta; but in spite of all the persecutions, the conference rejected the thought of organizing emigration, 'as being subversive of the dignity of the Russian body politic and of the historic rights of the Jews to their present father-land.'

In May, 1882, the 'Temporary Rules'[3] were enacted. They forbade the Jews to make new settlements outside of the towns and townlets; they suspended the completion of instruments of purchase of real property and merchandise in the name of the Jews outside of the towns and townlets; and they also forbade the Jews to carry on business on Sundays

---

[1] *Congressional Record*, vol. 13, p. 6691.

[2] The meeting was held on Wednesday, February 1, 1882, on the same day as the Mansion House Meeting in London. The chair was occupied by the Mayor, William R. Grace. See the *American Hebrew* of February 3, 1882, p. 138 *seq.*

[3] The text of the 'Temporary Rules' is given in *The Russian Jews, Extermination or Emancipation?* by Leo Errera, p. 13 *seq.* The 'Temporary Rules' remained in force until March, 1917, when the Russian Edict of Emancipation conferred equal rights on all Russian subjects irrespective of 'religion, sect, or nationality.' (The text of the Russian Edict of Emancipation is given in the *Zionist Review* of 1917, p. 50.)

and Christian holidays. The pogrom policy was abolished by the Government, but the disabilities continued in full swing. The economic misery within the Pale drove a number of Jews into the Russian interior, to be met, however, with the most drastic legal restrictions. Wholesale expulsions of Jews took place in St. Petersburg, Moscow, Kiev, Kharkov, and other forbidden centres. All this forced the Jewish population of Russia to consider again the question of emigration. A large number of immigrants were dispatched from the Galician border-town of Brody to the United States; while others were sent to the centres of Western Europe.

Parallel to this emigration, the Palestinian movement, which had attracted many enthusiasts from the Jewish youth, took on a new form. In the spring of 1882, a society of Jewish young men, consisting mostly of university students, was formed in Kharkov under the name *Bilu*, from the initial letters of their Hebrew motto, *Bet Ya'akob leku we-nelka*, 'O house of Jacob, come ye, and let us go.'[1] The aim of this society was to establish a model agricultural settlement in Palestine; and at the same time to carry on a propaganda for the colonization of their ancient homeland. Several hundred Jews in various parts of Russia joined the Bilu Society, and of these a few dozen pioneers left for Palestine between June and July, 1882.[2]

At first, the leaders of the Bilu Society endeavored to obtain from the Turkish Government a large tract of land for the establishment of Colonies, but they were unsuccessful in their efforts. Those who went to Palestine worked in the agricultural settlements near Jaffa — in Mikweh Israel, a foundation of the Alliance Israélite in Paris, and in the Colony Rishon-le-Zion, which had recently been established by private initiative.

Although small, the foundations for Palestinian colonization had thus been laid; the idea of entering upon a new life in Palestine for the national restoration of the Jewish people gave hope to the many sufferers who found life unbearable in Russia. In the autumn of the first pogrom year, M. L. Lilienblum interpreted the idea of Palestinian colonization as a

[1] Isaiah II: 5.

[2] The Manifesto of the Bilu. Nahum Sokolow, *History of Zionism*, vol. II, p. 332.

common national task for the whole of Jewry. 'We must,' he said, 'undertake the colonization of Palestine on so comprehensive a scale that in the course of one century the Jews may be able to leave inhospitable Europe almost entirely and settle in the land of our forefathers to which we are legally entitled.'

The period from 1882 onwards marks a distinct turning-point in the settlement of Jews in Palestine. Previous to that time, most of those who went there, as Sir Herbert Samuel says in his Interim Report, were 'animated by religious motives; they came to pray and die in the Holy Land, and to be buried in its soil.' [1] The Jews of the Old-World settlements were wholly unconscious of anything like a Jewish society, but the Jews who came to Palestine after the persecutions were of a new and distinctive type. They came with the avowed purpose of redeeming the soil of Palestine. Although these colonists were members of the learned professions and graduates of universities, they worked on the land as common laborers, so intense was their zeal for the achievement of their goal. In his description of these activities, Sir Herbert Samuel says: 'Large sums of money were collected in Europe and America, and spent in Palestine, for forwarding the movement. Many looked forward to a steady process of Jewish immigration, of Jewish land colonization and industrial development, until at last the Jews throughout the world would be able to see one country in which their race had a political and a spiritual home, in which, perhaps, the Jewish genius might repeat the services it had rendered to mankind from the same soil long ago.' [2]

The Russian emigration societies, formed in the beginning of 1882, contained many advocates of Palestinian colonization. The foremost of the Russo-Jewish Nationalists was Perez Smolenskin, who had founded the Hebrew review 'Ha-Shachar' ('The Dawn') in 1869. [3] He carried on an incessant propaganda until his death in 1885. Smolenskin vehemently

[1] Cmd. 1499. An Interim Report on the Civil Administration of Palestine during the period 1st July, 1920–30th June, 1921, p. 4.

[2] *Ibid.*, p. 5.

[3] According to S. M. Dubnow (*History of the Jews in Russia and Poland,* vol. II, p. 218), *The Dawn* was published in Vienna, but was read principally in Russia.

protested against the idea that the Jew should merge himself in his environment. The Jews, he declared, were not a sect, but a people, bound together by common traditions and common ideals, of which Palestine is the historic symbol.

In 1882, Leo Pinsker, a prominent communal worker in Odessa, brought forward the idea of a Jewish National Home as a solution of the Jewish problem. He describes his mental agony in perceiving the physical slavery of the Jewry of Russia, and also the spiritual slavery of the emancipated Jewry of Western Europe. The following are striking points in Pinsker's argument:

The Jews are not a living nation; they are everywhere aliens, therefore they are despised.

The civil and political emancipation of the Jews is not sufficient to raise them in the estimation of the peoples. The proper, the only remedy, would be the creation of a Jewish nationality, of a people living upon its own soil, the auto-emancipation of the Jews; their emancipation as a nation among nations, by the acquisition of a home of their own.

The international Jewish question must receive a national solution. Of course, our national regeneration must proceed slowly. *We must take the first step. Our descendants* must follow us in measured and not over-hasty time.

A way must be opened for the national regeneration of the Jews by a congress of Jewish notables.

The financial accomplishment of the undertaking can, in the present state of the case, present no insuperable difficulties.[1]

This plan differs from Smolenskin's in that it contains no mention of Palestine. In fact, Pinsker plainly avers that 'we must not attach ourselves to the place where our political life was once violently interrupted.' [2] 'We need,' he says, 'nothing but... a piece of land which shall remain our own property, from which no foreign master can expel us. Thither we shall take with us the most sacred possessions which we have saved from the shipwreck of our former fatherland, the God-idea and the Bible.' [3]

Pinsker's pamphlet, which was written in German, and printed abroad [4] for the purpose of appealing to the Jews of

[1] Leo Pinsker, *Auto-Emancipation*, pp. 22–23.

[2] *Ibid.*, p. 15.   [3] *Ibid.*, p. 18.

[4] The first edition appeared in Berlin, in 1882. It has a sub-title: 'An Appeal to his Brethren by a Russian Jew.' It was published anonymously.

Western Europe, failed, however, to produce any effect upon that assimilated section of the Jewish people. In Russia, however, it became the catechism of the 'Lovers of Zion'; and in spite of his avowal that 'we must not attach ourselves to the place where our political life was once violently interrupted,' he joined in the work of the Choveve Zion ('Lovers of Zion'), whose chief aim was to acquire land in Palestine for Jewish colonization. But always Pinsker emphasized the need of 'a secure and inviolable home for the *surplus* of those Jews who live as proletarians in the different countries and are a burden to the native citizens.'[1]

While this propaganda was going on, Jewish disabilities in Russia constantly increased. There were new restrictions in education and in the legal profession, as well as humiliating discrimination in the military service. The Jewish emigration from Russia to the United States served as a barometer· of the persecutions. In 1881 there were 8193 emigrants; in 1882, 17,497; in 1883, 6907. During the following three years, from 1884 to 1886, the movement remained practically on the same level, counting 15,000 to 17,000 emigrants annually. But in the last three years of that decade, it gained considerably in volume, amounting in 1887 to 28,944, in 1888 to 31,256, and in 1889 to 31,889.[2]

Jewish emigration from Eastern and Southeastern Europe continued throughout the next thirty years in amazing numbers, more than a million and a half having been admitted to the United States during the period from 1881 to 1910, 1,119,059 coming from Russia alone, 281,150 from Austria-Hungary, and 67,057 from Roumania.[3]

---

[1] Leo Pinsker, *Auto-Emancipation*, p. 18.

[2] S. M. Dubnow, *History of the Jews in Russia and Poland* (translated from the Russian by I. Friedlaender), vol. II, p. 373.

[3] Samuel Joseph, *Jewish Immigration to the United States*, Table VI, p. 93. Several thousand went to Argentina supported by the Jewish Colonial Association, while many settled in England, South Africa, and Canada. (S. M. Dubnow, *Die Neueste Geschichte des Juedischen Volkes*, vol. III, pp. 321–26.)

CHAPTER XI

THE HISTORICAL BACKGROUND OF THE BALFOUR DECLARATION — *continued*

WHILE the main stream of emigration during the eighties flowed to the West, the Palestinian colonization movement proceeded on a parallel line, although comparatively small. The pioneer colonists met with enormous obstacles: the Turkish Government hindered in every possible way the purchase of land and the acquisition of property; the soil was in a sadly neglected condition; and the Arabs were hostile. Besides, the colonists had limited financial means and were lacking in agricultural experience. In spite of everything, however, the Colony of Rishon-le-Zion,[1] near Jaffa, was established in 1882.

Later, Colonies similar to Rishon-le-Zion were founded at Zichron-Jacob[2] in Samaria, and at Rosh-Pinah[3] in Lower Galilee by other immigrants from Russia and Roumania. They also repurchased the derelict Colony of Petach-Tikweh,[4] profiting to some extent by the experience of the earlier colonists. Another small Colony — Yesod Hamalah — was founded in Upper Galilee by a number of Polish immigrants on the western shore of the Sea of Merom.[5]

The 'Lovers of Zion' in Russia could now point to the colonization in Palestine as a real evidence of the practicability of their doctrines. Groups of Choveré Zion, which had been formed by representatives of the intelligentsia, already existed in a number of Jewish centres; but until the Kattowitz Conference in 1884, they had made no definite plans.[6] The Conference was held in this Prussian border-town,

---

[1] The First in Zion.

[2] The Memorial of Jacob — i.e., the father of Baron Edmond de Rothschild.

[3] The Cornerstone.   [4] The Gate of Hope.

[5] Albert M. Hyamson, *Palestine: The Rebirth of an Ancient People*, p. 107 *seq.*

[6] The Choveré Zion was a federation of societies, each consisting of hundreds of members. The societies formed part of a world-wide movement, having as adherents thousands of European and American Jews. See Albert M. Hyamson, *Palestine: The Rebirth of an Ancient People*, pp. 110–15.

because of the impossibility of holding it in Russia without interference. To this Conference came the delegates of the Chovevé Zion Unions, mostly, however, from Russia.

An organized plan to promote Jewish colonization in Palestine was adopted, and some provision was made for the relief of the struggling colonists. The plan also included a scheme to encourage new settlers by assisting them with advances of capital or grants of land. The Conference hoped to obtain the recognition of Chovevé Zion Society by the Russian Government; and it was also decided to send a delegation to the Turkish Government for the purpose of removing the difficulties which stood in the way of Jewish colonization in Palestine. But these objects were not realized. In Russia, the lack of governmental sanction hampered the Chovevé Zion societies; and the funds at their disposal were hardly sufficient to maintain more than one or two Colonies in Palestine.

The really constructive activity of Chovevé Zion began in 1890, when, in consequence of the endeavors of A. Zederbaum, the Russian Government gave its approval. The first general meeting of the Odessa Committee, 'The Society for Supporting Jewish Agriculturalists in Syria and Palestine,' as it called itself, followed soon after; and Pinsker assumed the leadership of the movement. It should be remembered, however, that the formal foundation of this Committee owed its existence to the pioneer Conference at Kattowitz in 1884.[1]

Odessa was the main centre of the movement, and this Committee led in making the experiments in colonization. A new settlement in Palestine was founded at Katra, not far from Jaffa; and others continued to be made until 1913. The interest in colonization, however, was not confined to Russia. The ramifications of Chovevé Zion reached out into other parts of the world — notably into Roumania, Austria, Germany, England, and the United States. Some of its daughter societies were the Kadimah in Vienna, the Ezra Society in Berlin, and the Bnei Zion associations in English-speaking countries. Indeed, in 1890, the attempt was made to weld the societies together into an organic whole by the formation

[1] Nahum Sokolow, *History of Zionism*, vol. II, pp. 418, 419.

of a Central Committee in Paris. Since, however, no one appeared who had the qualities of leadership such as Pinsker had shown in Russia, the Odessa Committee retained a preponderating influence.[1]

Though financial aid was constantly sent to Palestine from Choveve Zion societies and from individuals in many parts of the world, had it not been for Baron Edmond de Rothschild, the great Jewish philanthropist, the new colonization could not have succeeded. In 1883, Baron Edmond de Rothschild came to the rescue of the heroic settlers in Palestine. His attention was first called to the colonists by Laurence Oliphant, who had assisted the immigrants — those who had purchased land in Zichron-Jacob — to reach their destination. The agents of the colonists who had preceded them had allowed themselves to be cheated and had lost a great deal of money. Thus, when the immigrants arrived in Palestine, they were altogether destitute; and, worse still, they had had no experience in agricultural work. Oliphant succeeded in interesting the Baron in Zichron-Jacob, and in consequence this Colony became one of the most prosperous and one of the largest in Palestine. Baron Edmond also took under his protection the settlements of Rishon-le-Zion and Rosh-Pinah; and a few years later, the two other pioneer settlements, Petach-Tikweh and Yesod Hamalah.[2] He also founded two Colonies himself — Ekron, near Jaffa, in 1884, and Metullah (Upper Galilee) in 1896. In 1914, about half the Jewish rural population in Palestine lived in the seven Colonies which formed what may be called the Rothschild group.[3] Baron Edmond provided his settlers with land and houses, advanced them working capital on very easy terms, and created at his own expense the wine industry which has ever since been a profitable enterprise. It is estimated that the sum expended by the Baron in support of the Colonies amounted to about twenty million dollars.[4]

[1] Richard J. H. Gottheil, *Zionism*, p. 72.

[2] Albert M. Hyamson, *Palestine: The Rebirth of an Ancient People*, p. 107 *seq.*

[3] In 1914 there were 12,000 Jewish inhabitants in all the Colonies of Judea and Galilee together. (S. M. Dubnow, *Neueste Geschichte des Juedischen Volkes*, vol. III, p. 550.)

[4] Max Raisin, *A History of the Jews in Modern Times*, p. 380.

The Russian Government, in the concluding years of Alexander III's reign, gave its public sanction to a Jewish exodus from the Russian Empire; and to strengthen the effect of the sanction, the Jews were subjected to persecutions and expulsions of much greater severity than those of the preceding decade. In the United States, the House of Representatives, alarmed by the effects of a sudden Russian-Jewish immigration which was bound to follow the inhuman treatment of the Jews in Russia, passed several resolutions calling on the President for action. Finally, the American Minister to Russia was instructed to point out to the Russian Government that the maltreatment of Jews in Russia was not purely an internal affair of the Russian Government, inasmuch as it affected the interests of the United States; that within ten years two hundred thousand Russian Jews had come to this country; and that continued persecutions were bound to result in a much larger immigration, which was not unattended with danger.[1]

In 1891, the Jews were expelled from Moscow.[2] This called forth a resolution from the House of Representatives, which concluded as follows: 'and the President is requested to use his good offices to notify the Government of Russia to mitigate the said laws and decrees.' [3]

Then came the astonishing news that the Russian Government was negotiating with Baron Maurice de Hirsch, the Jewish philanthropist, for the gradual removal of the three million Russian Jews to Argentina. This happened at the moment when Jews were fleeing from Russia to North and South America and in a lesser degree to Palestine. Baron Hirsch investigated the situation, and endeavored to regulate the immigration. The result was the organization of the Jewish Colonization Association, which was founded in London in 1891 as a stock company. It had a capital of fifty million francs, subscribed for the purpose of undertaking on a large scale the colonization of Argentina and other

---

[1] *Foreign Relations of the United States*, 1891, p. 740.

[2] The horrors of the expulsion are described by S. M. Dubnow in *History of the Jews in Russia and Poland* (translated from the Russian by I. Friedlaender), vol. II, chapter XXIX.

[3] *Congressional Record*, vol. 23, p. 6533.

American territories with Russian Jews. The capital was almost entirely provided by Baron Hirsch.

The Russian Government sanctioned the establishment of a Central Committee of the Jewish Colonization Association in St. Petersburg, with branches in the provinces. In May, 1892, the Constitution of the Jewish Colonization Association was ratified by the Tsar; and the Government offered to facilitate emigration by issuing to the emigrants, free of charge, permits to leave the country. The scheme, however, was doomed to failure. Instead of the million Jews as planned, during the first decade, only ten thousand Jews were distributed over six Argentinian Colonies.

The main current of Jewish emigration flowed, as before, toward the United States and Canada. At the same time, the sanctioning by the Russian Government of the constitution of the 'Society for Granting Assistance to Jewish Colonists and Artisans in Syria and Palestine,' whose first president was Dr. Leo Pinsker, improved the outlook for Palestine. The Government sanction enabled the Chovevé Zion societies to collect money openly; and in consequence the Palestinian propaganda was greatly stimulated. In the beginning of 1891, delegates of the Chovevé Zion societies appeared in Palestine *en masse*, and, with the coöperation of a Jaffa representative of the Odessa Palestine Society, began to buy up land from the Arabs. This, however, led to a real-estate speculation which raised the price of land.

The Turkish Government became alarmed at this; and announced its intention to prohibit the immigration of Russian Jews or the purchase of land by them.[1] In consequence of this action, the colonization of the Holy Land with Russian Jews proceeded slowly, as it had done heretofore. It is a fact, however, that for a time Jews were prohibited from purchasing land in Palestine. Most of the old and the

---

[1] Hyamson makes the following comment: 'The rapid increase in the number of Jewish settlers, especially from Russia — a country of which Turkey has always been suspicious — caused the authorities some uneasiness, especially when the Russian Consul at Jerusalem openly boasted that he had more " subjects" than those of all the other Consuls combined.' (Albert M. Hyamson, *Palestine: The Rebirth of an Ancient People*, p. 68.)

See a 'Petition to the Sultan,' sent through the British Foreign Office, by the Chovevé Zion, and the reply from the Foreign Office, dated 11th March, 1893. (Nahum Sokolow, *History of Zionism*, vol. II, pp. 279–80.)

new settlers were under Baron Rothschild's administration; while two or three Colonies were maintained by the Palestine Society in Odessa. In 1899, Baron Rothschild transferred his interest in the Colonies to the Jewish Colonization Association, which took control in the beginning of 1900.[1]

About ten years before this, when the Turkish Government had placed restrictions on the settlement of Jews in Palestine, General Lew Wallace, United States Minister at Constantinople, visited the Turkish Minister of Foreign Affairs on behalf of the Russian refugees. His aim was to secure for the Jews the privilege of colonizing in such districts of Syria as were available for the purpose. General Wallace was told in 1882 that the Turkish Council of Ministers had decided that Jews from whatever parts could settle on any unoccupied lands in Mesopotamia, in Syria about Aleppo, or in the region of the Orontes River, but that they could not establish themselves in Palestine. The Turks took this position, because, as the Grand Vizier explained later to the United States Minister to Constantinople, Mr. Oscar Straus, they wished to avoid conflicts between the Jews and Christians; and also because they did not want the Jews to carry out at some future time the reëstablishment in Palestine of their ancient kingdom.[2] In September, 1887, the British Ambassador sent a note to the Porte protesting against these regulations on the ground that the right of British subjects to go and come within the Ottoman dominion was secured

[1] Commenting on the philanthropic aspect of Zionism, Professor Gottheil says that: 'the history of Jewish colonization in Palestine between the years 1882 and 1899 represents a further attempt at a solution of the Jewish question upon the old philanthropic basis. It was bound to prove abortive just because it was philanthropic.' Expressing his opinion on the transfer by Baron Rothschild of his interests to the Jewish Colonization Association, he asserts that 'the change was perhaps for the worse,' that 'it rendered the bureaucracy still more bureaucratic, and the absentee landlordism more pernicious.' Continuing, Professor Gottheil says: 'But even the Jewish Colonization Association was not able to resist for long the continued demands of the colonists themselves, nor combat successfully the rising and ever-increasing dissatisfaction among the Jewish masses. In 1907, the colonies were handed over to the colonists, and the duties of self-government were laid upon the shoulders of those who by rights were called upon to bear them.' Professor Gottheil states that the Wine-Growers' Association of Rishon-le-Zion and Zichron-Jacob were able to pay off a million francs of their indebtedness to Baron Rothschild in 1911. (Richard J. H. Gottheil, *Zionism*, pp. 79, 81.)

[2] Cyrus Adler, *Jews in American Diplomatic Correspondence*, pp. 7–19; *Foreign Relations of the United States*, 1888, p. 1559.

by the Capitulations and confirmed by all subsequent treaties, and that no distinctions of race and creed could be admitted with regard to British subjects or protégés, whatever religion they might profess.

In 1888, however, regulations were made by the Porte [1] limiting the stay of all foreign Jews in Palestine to a period of three months, and prescribing that only those bearing passports, 'setting forth that they are going to Jerusalem in the performance of a pilgrimage and not for the purpose of engaging in commerce or taking up their residence there,' should be permitted to enter.[2] Protests against this regulation were registered on behalf of the French, Italian, and United States Governments; and in October of that year, the Government of the United States was informed that the measure concerning Jews entering Palestine would not be applied except to those who emigrated '*en nombre*.' [3]

The laws were only fitfully enforced; but on November 19, 1898, the United States Ambassador renewed the protest to Tewfik Pasha in the following words: 'The United States does not make any discrimination between its citizens based upon religion or race, nor will it concede to any other government the right or power to make any such discrimination in respect to American citizens.' [4]

The Jewish situation had already entered upon a new chapter. Fourteen years after Leo Pinsker had brought forward the idea of a Jewish National Home, Theodor Herzl, an Austrian Jewish publicist, who was educated for the legal profession at Vienna University, became aroused by the exciting scenes in the anti-Semitic campaign in Paris during the early period of the Dreyfus affair. He proposed a Jewish State for the solution of the Jewish problem. According to his plan, the outlet for Jewish immigration should be a territory over which the Jews would have absolute control. Herzl's 'Judenstaat,' which was written in Paris in 1895 and published in Vienna in 1896, is based primarily on

[1] George Young, *Corps de Droit Ottoman* (Oxford), vol. II, p. 155 *seq.*

[2] Cyrus Adler, *Jews in American Diplomatic Correspondence*, pp. 7–19; *Foreign Relations of the United States*, 1888, p. 1567.

[3] Cyrus Adler, *Jews in American Diplomatic Correspondence*, p. 15; *Foreign Relations of the United States*, 1888, p. 1619.

[4] See United States Senate Reports, Foreign Relations, for 1898–1899, p. 1092.

the necessity of having an outlet for the oppressed Jews. He says:

> The artificial means heretofore employed to overcome the troubles of Jews have been either too petty, such as colonization; or mistaken in principle, such as attempts to convert the Jews into peasants in their present home. Speaking of gradual colonization in Palestine and Argentina, he remarks that 'an infiltration is bound to end in disaster.... It continues till the inevitable moment when the native population feels itself threatened and forces the Government to stop the further influx of Jews.

He further declares:

> Let the sovereignty be granted us over a portion of the globe large enough to satisfy the reasonable requirements of a nation and the rest we can manage for ourselves.[1]

Herzl early formulated the idea of a charter. He believed that the Jewish question could be permanently settled only if it were reached through the medium of European diplomacy.

In May, 1896, the 'Judenstaat' was brought to the attention of the Turkish Sultan, who dispatched to Herzl, as one of the editors of the 'Neue Freie Presse,' a secret emissary, with the offer of a charter for Palestine. This was to be given in return for the cessation of the European Press campaign against the Sultan because of the Armenian massacres.[2] The Sultan thought that the Jews were powerful enough with the Continental Press to do this; but, as Professor Gottheil says: 'Not only were the Jews not so powerful in this respect as the Sultan supposed; they were not so supine as to execute such a bargain and reach their own goal over the dead bodies of another race.'[3]

In his evidence before the Royal Commission on Alien Immigration which sat at London in 1902,[4] Herzl declared that 'the solution of the Jewish difficulty is the recognition of the Jews as a people and the finding by them of a legally

[1] Theodor Herzl, *Judenstaat*, pp. 9–12.

[2] Lucien Wolf, 'Zionism,' *Encyclopædia Britannica*.

[3] Richard J. H. Gottheil, *Zionism*, p. 94.

[4] An Alien Immigration Commission had been formed to consider problems relating to immigration and in particular whether the number of Jewish immigrants to England should be limited.

DR. THEODOR HERZL

recognised home, to which Jews in those parts of the world in which they are oppressed would naturally migrate.' 'Given [sic] to Jews their rightful position as a people,' he adds, 'I am convinced they would develop a distinct Jewish cult — national characteristics and national aspirations — which would make for the progress of mankind.' [1]

Yet Herzl shows that his primary problem is anti-Semitism. In his attempt to define Jewish nationhood, he says: 'A nation is, in my mind, a historical group of men of a recognisable cohesion, held together by a common enemy. Then, if you add to that the word "Jewish," you would have what I understand to be the Jewish nation.' He conceived the common enemy to be 'The anti-Semite.' [2]

In reviewing the history of the movement which led finally to the establishment of the Jewish National Home, it is a noteworthy fact that Herzl, having had practically no contact with Jewish affairs, arrived at his conclusions quite independently of any of the motives which had inspired the Jews up to that time — such as the Messianic prophecies of traditional Judaism, the Jewish nationalism which had been gradually developing in Central and Eastern Europe since 1880, or the various attempts to rebuild the land of the forefathers. [3]

It is quite as noteworthy, also, that Herzl, whose object was the founding of a Jewish State, the location of which was of secondary consideration, should be asked to lead the forces whose central idea was Palestine. Although Herzl soon recognized Palestine an indispensable factor in the solution of the Jewish problem, and declared at the first Zionist Congress in 1897 that 'One of the first results of our Movement will be the transformation of the Jewish question into a question of Zion,' [4] yet he never wholly departed from his

[1] Evidence given before the British Royal Commission in 1902 by Theodor Herzl, p. 10.

[2] *Ibid.*, pp. 26–27.

[3] After the publication of his *Judenstaat,* Herzl openly confessed that at the time of writing he did not know of the existence of Pinsker's *Auto-Emancipation* (S. M. Dubnow, *History of the Jews in Russia and Poland* (translated from the Russian by I. Friedlaender), vol. III, p. 43.)

[4] Herzl's Address at the First Zionist Congress. See *The Congress Addresses of Theodor Herzl* (translated from the German by Nellie Strauss, New York, 1917), p. 6.

original idea that the solution of the Jewish problem lay in providing an outlet for oppressed Jews. Being a Westerner by birth and training, Herzl had arrived at the conclusion that the Jews by external pressure had been welded into a nation, and that the Jews, like other nations, should have an autonomous territory of their own.

In stipulating that the Jewish problem should be settled by international agreement, Herzl gave a broader viewpoint to Zionism. He declared in his opening address at the First Zionist Congress which met at Basle in August, 1897, that:

> Colonization in its present form is not and cannot be the solution of the Jewish question.... The only reasonable course of action which our movement can pursue is to work for publicly legalized guarantees.... The confidence of the government with which we want to negotiate regarding the settlement of Jewish masses on a large scale can be gained by frank language and upright dealing.... The advantages which an entire people is able to offer in return for benefits received are so considerable that the negotiations are vested with sufficient importance *a priori*.... But one thing must be adhered to inviolably: the agreement must be based on rights and not on toleration.... If any one thinks that the Jews can steal into the land of their fathers, he is deceiving either himself or... others. It would not be to our interest to go there prematurely.

Herzl was convinced that the conditions then existent in Palestine pointed to a successful conclusion. He also felt that the financial help which the Jews could give to Turkey was by no means inconsiderable, and that it would 'surely be of advantage to all civilized peoples if the Near-East question were to be partially solved together with the Jewish question.' He moreover believed, when once a satisfactory agreement was concluded with the various political units and a systematic migration begun, that it would last only so long in each country as that country desired to be rid of its Jews, and that in this way there would be a 'gradual decrease and final cessation of anti-Semitism.' [1]

The aims of the Zionist Movement were formulated by the First Congress in 1897. Although Herzl had stimulated the Congress, the Jewish State found no endorsement in its program; whereas Herzl had in mind Palestine or any other

[1] *The Congress Addresses of Theodor Herzl* (translated from the German by Nellie Strauss, New York, 1917), p. 7 *seq*.

country that might be suitable; the home was to be 'in Palestine.' The following expresses the declaration of the Congress:

The aim of Zionism is to create for the Jewish people a legally assured home ('rechtlich gesicherte Heimstaette') in Palestine. In order to attain this object, the Congress adopts the following means:

1. To promote the settlement in Palestine of Jewish agriculturists, handicraftsmen, industrialists, and men following professions.

2. The centralization of the entire Jewish people by means of general institutions in accordance with the laws of the land.

3. To strengthen Jewish sentiment and national self-conscience.

4. To obtain the sanction of Governments necessary to the carrying out of the objects of Zionism.[1]

The Congress at Basle was an impressive gathering:[2] for the first time, representatives of Eastern and Western Jewry united in demonstrating the national awakening of the Jewish people. The Congress was made up of delegates representing all phases of Jewish life and thought — Orthodox, Reform, indifferent in religious matters, and frankly non-religious, Chovevé Zionists, and pure nationalists.[3] A strong minority insisted on Herzl's original ideas; and this opposition, as we shall see, led eventually to the Ito or territorialist group.

In Herzl's later addresses to the Congress, he held to the political view of the question, and was therefore an opponent of the Chovevé Zionists, who in 1891, as we have seen,

---

[1] *Proceedings* of the Zionist Congress of 1897, p. 42. (P. Cowen, publisher.)

[2] Raisin says of this Congress: 'For the first time in nineteen hundred years Jews from all parts of the world came together as representatives of a Jewish nation, for the first time since the downfall of Judæa Jews loudly proclaimed their right to live their own life in the historic land of their fathers. For the nonce factionalism was forgotten, and the fact that the gathering comprised men of all shades of religious belief and political opinion, orthodox, Reformers, atheists, Socialists — was proof conclusive that Zionism had indeed touched the heart of the entire Jewish people, and that the 204 delegates in the Basel Casino in themselves constituted the Jewish nation in miniature.' (Max Raisin, *A History of the Jews in Modern Times*, pp. 408–09.)

Sokolow describes the Congress as follows: 'A strange community of Jews, a representative assembly of the great Jewish *Diaspora* — from the most modern European writers to teachers in Talmud colleges in small Lithuanian towns, quiet respectable citizens and fiery students, bankers and Hebrew writers — representing all kinds of civilization and all languages — and, nevertheless, some bond unified the whole.' (Nahum Sokolow, *History of Zionism*, vol. ii, p. 5.)

[3] Richard J. H. Gottheil, *Zionism*, p. 113.

aroused the opposition of the Turkish Government by the feverish buying-up of land from the Arabs in Palestine, while the 1888 restrictions remained in abeyance. It was Herzl's opinion that, unless political guarantees were secured upon which the tenure of land in Palestine was held, the Jewish Colonies ran the risk of sudden annihilation at any moment. This view was sustained by the renewal, on November 21, 1901, of the 1888 regulations which limited the stay of Jewish visitors in Palestine to three months.[1] The instructions of 1901, which were sent to the Vali of Beirut, caused great consternation among those who were concerned with the growth of the Palestinian Colonies.[2]

Herzl had carried on negotiations with the Sultan between the years 1898 and 1903, but they seemed to lead to no satisfactory result. He reported at the Sixth Congress that the only concession he could get was a 'colonization plan calling for scattered, unrelated communities in different parts of the Turkish Empire.'[3] This information prompted one group in the Congress to insist that, if the negotiations with the Sultan should prove a failure, the Zionist leaders should try to find another land in which the Jewish home could be established. It should be noted also that Herzl was not unfavorably disposed to the plan,[4] although a previous attempt at the Third Congress in 1899 to transfer Jewish colonization to a place other than Palestine — to the island of Cyprus, for example, had created so much] opposition that the project was not even considered by the Congress.

The next proposition for a Jewish settlement outside Palestine — that of El-Arish, situated to the south of Palestine, under Anglo-Egyptian administration, was considered by Herzl in 1902. He sponsored this plan, as he himself said, 'Because of the unsuccess of the latest negotiations in Constantinople, and also in view of the increasing distress (among the Jewish masses).'[5] Although the plan did not

---

[1] George Young, *Corps de Droit Ottoman* (Oxford, 1905), vol. II, p. 156.

[2] Richard J. H. Gottheil, *Zionism*, p. 118.

[3] *Congress Addresses of Theodor Herzl*, Sixth Congress Address, p. 34.

[4] Richard J. H. Gottheil, *Zionism*, p. 225, note 5.

[5] See *Protokoll... des Sechsten Zionisten-Kongresses* (Wien, 1903), p. 6.

succeed, Herzl considered the attitude of the Anglo-Egyptian Government, in manifesting an appreciation of Jewish needs, as a most valuable asset.

The next year, while visiting the British East-African Protectorate, Joseph Chamberlain conceived the idea that this might be a convenient place for the Jewish settlement. Negotiations were thereupon undertaken, which resulted in an official letter from the Foreign Office, dated August 14, 1903, in which Sir Clement Hill writes to Mr. L. J. Greenberg in regard 'to the form of an agreement which Doctor Herzl proposes should be entered into between His Majesty's Government and the Jewish Colonial Trust, Ltd., for the establishment of a Jewish settlement in East Africa.' The letter goes on to say that the Marquis of Lansdowne

has studied the question with the interest which His Majesty's Government must always take in any well-considered scheme for the amelioration of the position of the Jewish race.... If a site can be found which the Trust and His Majesty's commissioner consider suitable, and which commends itself to his Government, Lord Lansdowne will be prepared to entertain favorably proposals for the establishment of a Jewish colony or settlement on conditions which will enable the members to observe their national customs... the details of the scheme comprising as its main features the grant of a considerable area of land, the appointment of a Jewish official as the chief of the local administration, and permission to the colony to have a free hand in regard to municipal legislation as to the management of religious and purely domestic matters, such local autonomy being conditional upon the right of His Majesty's Government to exercise general control.[1]

Professor Gottheil says that this letter marks an epoch in Jewish history, since up to that time no Government had put itself on record as taking up the Jewish cause in such a whole-hearted manner. Certainly, the letter was a significant step which led to the announcement of the Balfour Declaration.

This offer from the British Government came on the eve of the Sixth Congress in 1903; and it called for action. As for Herzl, since his negotiations with the Sultan had been wholly

[1] Richard J. H. Gottheil, *Zionism*, pp. 123–24, and p. 225, note 8. (See the text of the whole letter in *Die Welt*, August 27, 1903, p. 1; English translation in *The Maccabæan*, v. 250.)

unsatisfactory, he conjectured that the English offer might prove an effective political weapon to be used in further dealings, perhaps, with the Sultan. But regardless of any personal plan, he presented the British offer to the Sixth Congress. Acrimonious discussion arose on the part of both partisans and opponents; but no decision was taken. The proposition, however, to send a commission to East Africa to study the territory from the point of view of Jewish colonization, was adopted by the Congress.

At the Seventh Congress, in 1905, a final decision was made on the East African offer. The Congress went on record as declaring that Zionism was solely concerned with Palestine. It thanked the British Government for their offer of territory in East Africa, and also for their desire to bring about a solution of the Jewish problem; while at the same time, it expressed the hope that the British Government would in the future extend their good offices in any matter the Zionist organization might undertake 'in accordance with the Basel program.' Vice-President Wolffsohn, in the closing address, summarized the work of the Congress as follows:

We have once again proclaimed the Program of the Basle Congress; we have erected it as the basis which may not be disregarded, of the practical work to be done in Palestine, and we have through this strengthened the organization. Everything fills us with fresh strength and confidence to work out the only possible solution of the Jewish question.[1]

The failure to accept the principle of a Jewish autonomous State, regardless of its location, as a recognized outlet for Jewish immigration, caused, however, a secession from the Jewish ranks. Under the leadership of Mr. Israel Zangwill, the Jewish Territorial Organization, popularly known as the Ito, was formed in 1906; but this effort was doomed to failure from the beginning, for it wholly lacked the idealistic appeal which the ancient homeland offered. The Ito set out to find a territory where the Jews could settle; and in rapid succession considered countries like Cyrenaica, Canada, parts of Australia, and Angola. Finding no land suitable or available

[1] *Stenographisches Protokoll der Verhandlung des VII Zionisten-Kongresses*, 1905, p. 316.

for the purpose, it finally settled down to regulating immigration to the United States by directing Jewish emigrants to land at Galveston, Texas, rather than at the large Eastern ports. In this way, it was hoped to reduce the frightful overcrowding of the large Jewish quarters of New York, Philadelphia, Baltimore, and other cities. This plan, although obviously with merits, failed to satisfy most of the immigrants. The great Jewish centres of the East proved too great an attraction for many of the Galveston arrivals, who found themselves quite out of accord with the quiet and uneventful life of the South. Therefore, with this short-lived existence, the Ito became practically dead at the outbreak of the World War; and the Galveston immigration bureau was finally closed.[1]

Herzl continued to regard political guarantees as the *sine qua non* in the colonization plan; but after his death in 1904, there appeared to be no leader with sufficient vision and skill to work toward the accomplishment of this goal. Numerically the Zionist organization went backward rather than forward. Attention was shifted from the 'great programme' to the support of the existing Jewish settlements in Palestine and to the piecemeal construction of new enterprises — more especially of educational enterprises.[2]

With the outbreak of the Turkish Revolution in 1908, the Jews looked for amelioration from the hostile attitude of the old régime, but they were quickly disillusioned by the Young Turks, who held to the policy of Abdul Hamid in limiting Jewish immigration. The law which allowed the Jews to enter Palestine for a temporary stay of three months remained in force; and the new Government apparently had not the slightest intention of giving a favorable response to the Jewish demands. Indeed, the attitude of the Young Turks became entirely unfriendly. During the Parliamentary Session of March, 1911, the Grand Vizier Hakki Pasha referred to the desire of the Jews to establish a Jewish State in Palestine by means of mass immigration as mere fancy; he explained that the law restricting Jewish immigration was a 'measure of safety taken to prevent the realization of any

[1] Max Raisin, *The History of the Jews in Modern Times*, pp. 421–22.

[2] H. M. Kallen, *Zionism and World Politics*, chapter x.

such whim.'[1] On the other hand, the Turkefying policy which the Young Turks assumed toward the Arabs was much milder treatment than that meted to the Jews. In the former case, there were friendly enough relations so long as the Arabs were willing to be submerged and live the Turkish life; while in respect of the Jews, the Turks were not willing to have them at all.

Jewish immigration formed the subject of an animated debate in the Turkish Chamber in 1912, in which Talaat Bey declared emphatically against Zionism.[2] In the same year, the Turkish authorities in Palestine were reminded by Constantinople that foreigners were prohibited by law from acquiring land in Ottoman territory and that the prohibition was to be strictly enforced. In spite of this official obstruction, it is interesting to note, Jewish colonization continued — though slowly. But all hope of obtaining a charter was abandoned.

This situation forced the Zionists to change their method. They were confronted with a new outlook. They now began to realize that Palestine had settled inhabitants, a fact which Herzl and others had seemingly overlooked. The Arabs considered themselves the rightful rulers of Syria and Palestine and therefore looked upon the Jews as interlopers. The Pan-Arab movement, which had developed before the War, was opposed to Zionism and the mass immigration of the Jews.[3] This situation brought Zionism face to face with a problem from which there has been no escape down to the present moment.

In the further progress of Zionism, two principles, the political and the cultural, have been constantly struggling for mastery. Asher Ginzberg, better known under his pen name Achad Ha'am ('One of the People'),[4] the most distinguished figure in Hebrew literature, was the leader of the latter idea. His feeling was that the mere colonization of Palestine could not in itself solve the Jewish problem. In an essay entitled 'The Wrong Way,' he wrote:

[1] S. M. Dubnow, *Neueste Geschichte des Juedischen Volkes*, vol. iii, p. 541.

[2] Leonard Stein, *Zionism*, p. 98.

[3] S. M. Dubnow, *Neueste Geschichte des Juedischen Volkes*, vol. iii, p. 541.

[4] Achad Ha'am, whose death was greatly lamented by the Zionists, died on January 2, 1927, at his home in Tel-Aviv.

Our first object ought to have been to bring about a revival — to inspire men with a deeper attachment ·to the national life and a more ardent desire for the national well-being.... We should have striven gradually to extend the empire of our ideal in Jewry, till at last it could find genuine, whole-hearted devotees, with all the qualities needed to enable them to work for its practical realization.[1]

In his discussion of the 'Jewish State and Jewish Problem,' he explains:

Chibbath Zion no less than 'Zionism' wants a Jewish State and believes in the possibility of the establishment of a Jewish State in the future. But while 'Zionism' looks to the Jewish State to provide a remedy for poverty, complete tranquility and national glory, Chibbath Zion knows that our State will not give us all these things until 'universal Righteousness is enthroned and holds sway over nations and States:' and it looks to a Jewish State to provide only a 'secure refuge' for Judaism and a cultural bond of unity for our nation.' [2]

Writing in 1912, looking back over years of progress, he says:

What has already been accomplished in Palestine entitles one to say with confidence that the country will be 'a national spiritual centre of Judaism, to which all Jews will turn with affection, and which will bind all Jews together; a centre of study and learning, of language and literature, of bodily work and spiritual purification; a true miniature of the people of Israel as it ought to be.' [3]

The political Zionists objected to the form which Zionism had taken, and they continued their objections as late as the 1913 Congress. Jean Fischer, of Antwerp, in a speech which

[1] Achad Ha'am, *Essays on Zionism and Judaism* (translated from the Hebrew by Leon Simon, London, 1922), p. 12 *seq.*

[2] *Ibid.*, p. 48.

Achad Ha'am died on January 2, 1927, at Tel-Aviv. The following appeared in the issue of the *Palestine Weekly*, January 27, 1928, in a note, under 'Tel-Aviv,' entitled, 'The Achad Haam Mourning Day': 'On Sunday the first anniversary of the death of Achad Haam, the Hebrew author and thinker, was proclaimed a mourning day. At noon the procession of the school children to Achad Haam grave began. All shops were closed. At 3 P.M. Ch. N. Bialik, the Hebrew poet-laureate, delivered an address in which the importance of Achad Haam's work for Jewish national life was explained. Then the big crowd in deep mourning surrounded the newly laid tombstone on the grave. Only one word — " Achad Haam " — is engraved on the stone. Prayers were said. In the evening the Tel-Aviv teachers held a memorial meeting at the Gymnasia Hall. Messrs. D. Levin and Dr. J. Kaufman spoke.'

[3] *Ibid.*, *Summa Summarum*, p. 155.

caused considerable uneasiness among the assembled delegates, defended the Herzlian program, which included political as well as practical Zionism. He tried to prove — what
he and others believed, though in the minority — that the
'practical work of the organization was to do what a State
ordinarily did for its people.' Appealing directly to the
delegates, he exclaimed: 'But to carry on trade, to open a
shoe store, to direct a workshop, things which are accomplished among all peoples by individuals is not and cannot
be our task. Such work is bound from the very beginning
to remain sterile.'[1] This protest, however, produced no
practical results. The feeling of the majority of the Congress
was expressed by Dr. M. Gaster of London who claimed that
the political program had only 'led to Uganda and Terri-
torialism.'[2]

Enthusiasm for Hebrew developed, and in 1911, at the
Tenth Congress, the proceedings were conducted in Hebrew.
At this Congress, a resolution was passed favoring the
support of education in Palestine from Zionist funds,[3] to
which the Mizrachi, the Orthodox element in Zionism, who
saw in the Jewish homeland a means of conserving and en-
hancing traditional Judaism, made serious objections. The
Mizrachi felt that the whole complexus of Jewish life, its
culture, social organization, educational system, etc., was
merely secondary to this sectarian interest. They wished to
keep the schools distinct from the secular organization.[4]

The particular question at issue was a grant-in-aid to the
Jaffa Hebrew Gymnasium, which was supposed to set its
teaching in a direction away from rather than toward
traditional beliefs. The position taken by the Mizrachi was,
that no official recognition should be given to the Jaffa
Gymnasium, but that if such recognition were made, a

---

[1] *Stenographisches Protokoll der Verhandlung des XI Zionisten-Kongresses*, 1913,
pp. 95–97.

[2] *Ibid.*, p. 110.

[3] *Ibid.*, 1911, p. 329. The resolution reads as follows: 'I. The Tenth Zionist Congress authorizes the Inner Actions Committee to organize and centralize the cultural
work in Palestine. II. The Tenth Zionist Congress proclaims that nothing which
conflicts with the Jewish religion may be taught in any of the Institutions of culture
organized by the Zionist Organization.'

[4] H. M. Kallen, *Zionism and World Politics*, p. 86 *seq.*

similar recognition should be given to the Mizrachi schools. Although the vote taken was unfavorable to the Mizrachi, and threatened to drive them from the Zionist organization, education in the future became an integral part of the Zionist program and Hebrew the language of the schools.

At the Vienna Congress in 1913, Dr. Weizmann suggested the opening of a Hebrew University as the crowning point of Zionist education. This was originally suggested by Professor Hermann Schapiro, of Heidelberg, who died in 1898.[1] Dr. Weizmann said there was great need for a school of higher education in Palestine which would equal in every way the European universities, where Jewish students could work with perfect freedom and do credit to the Jewish people. Furthermore, he expressed the firm belief that the language of the University should be Hebrew.[2] These ideas were approved, and the Congress instructed the Zionist Executive to work out a definite scheme for the establishment of a Hebrew University in Jerusalem.

A new impulse to the colonization movement was given at this Congress by the scheme of colonization [3] submitted by Dr. A. Ruppin, the head of the Palestine Office.[4] This embodied a complete plan for the settlement of Jews in Palestine.

By the year 1914, the Jews had created fifty-nine Colonies,[5] with a population of some twelve thousand inhabitants [6] and an annual output valued at nearly five million francs. Their holdings of land, which had nearly doubled since 1898, had risen to about one hundred thousand acres, representing from eight to fourteen per cent of the cultivated surface of Palestine.

Sir Herbert Samuel says of these colonists:

---

[1] The Hebrew University was opened in April, 1925.

[2] *Stenographisches Protokoll der Verhandlung des XI Zionisten-Kongresses*, 1913, p. 300 *seq.*

[3] *Ibid.* Listed at the end of the Minutes.

[4] Early in 1908 the Zionist Organization had founded a branch in Palestine, called 'The Palestine Office.' The object of this was to coördinate all the efforts for the Jewish colonization of the country.

[5] Nahum Sokolow (*History of Zionism*, vol. II, p. 328 *seq.*) gives a list of these Colonies.

[6] S. M. Dubnow, *Neueste Geschichte des Juedischen Volkes*, vol. III, p. 550.

[They] gave importance to the Jaffa orange trade. They culti-vated the vine, and manufactured and exported wine. They drained swamps. They planted eucalyptus trees. They practised, with modern methods, all the processes of agriculture.... The success of these agricultural Colonies attracted the eager interest of the masses of the Jewish people scattered throughout the world. In many countries they were living under the pressure of laws or customs which cramped their capacities and thwarted their energies; they saw in Palestine the prospect of a home in which they might live at ease. Profoundly discontented, as numbers of them were, with a life of petty trade in crowded cities, they listened with ready ears to the call of a healthier and finer life as producers on the land. Some among them, agriculturists already, saw in Palestine the prospect of a soil not less fertile, and an environment far more free, than those to which they were accustomed. Everywhere great numbers of Jews, whose religion causes them to live, spiritually, largely in the past, began to take an active interest in those passages of their ritual, that dwelt, with constant emphasis, upon the connection of their race with Palestine; passages which they had hitherto read day by day and week by week, with the lax attention that is given to contingency that is possible but remote. Among a great proportion, at least, of the fourteen million of Jews, who are dispersed in all the countries of the globe, the Zionist idea took hold. They found in it that larger and higher interest, outside and beyond the cares and concerns of daily life, which every man, who is not wholly material-ist, must seek somewhere.[1]

[1] Cmd. 1499. An Interim Report on the Civil Administration of Palestine, during the period 1st July, 1920–30th June, 1921, pp. 4–5.

CHAPTER XII

ZIONISM AND THE WORLD WAR

IT was a tragic moment for Palestine when Turkey entered the War as an ally of the Central Powers.[1] The Europeans, the Moslems, the Christians, and the Jews were faced with deprivation, terror, and all that war implies. Palestine as well as Syria was placed under the virtual dictatorship of the Young-Turk general, Djemal Pasha, a capricious tyrant who came to the country with the intention of Ottomanizing it. It is an interesting fact in this connection that, with the exception of soldiers and officials, there were no Turks in Palestine.[2] During the three years' command of Djemal Pasha, there were executions and deportations. Many Jewish and Arab families, both Moslem and Christian, were subjected to terrible hardships. It was in fact the cruel execution of Arab notables under the orders of Djemal Pasha in Damascus that finally forced the decision of the Sherif of Mecca to join the Allies against Turkey.[3]

The Europeans suffered chiefly on account of the abolition of the Capitulations, which left them without consular protection. The Jews and the Christians, who for the most part favored the cause of the Allies, were treated with greater severity than the Arab population, or at least that part of it which fell under the influence of German propaganda. German officers appeared, and pamphlets in Arabic were

[1] British Notification of the Existence of a State of War between Great Britain and Turkey — November 5, 1914. 'Owing to hostile acts committed by Turkish forces under German officers, a state of war exists between Great Britain and Turkey as from to-day.' (Foreign Office, November 5, 1914. British and Foreign State Papers, 1914, Part II, vol. 108, p. 163.)

Turkish Proclamation of War against Great Britain, Russia, and France, November 14, 1914. (International Law Documents, Naval War College volume, dated 1917, p. 219. Proclamation translated from *Corriere della Sera*, November 16, 1914.)

[2] Philip Graves, *Palestine, the Land of Three Faiths*, p. 38.

[3] William Linn Westermann, *What Really Happened at Paris*, chapter VIII, 'The Armenian Problem and the Disruption of Turkey,' pp. 184, 185.

distributed, declaring that Germany is the friend of Islam and that Germans are the descendants of the Prophet Mohammed.[1]

But the Jews suffered more than any other class. Cut off, as many of them were, from their usual support from abroad,[2] they fled to Egypt, fearing they would soon be without money and means of support. The emigrants went chiefly from the cities; although almost without exception, we are told, the villagers as well as the teachers stayed behind.[3] According to the Report of the Committee for the Assistance of Jewish Refugees in Alexandria, 11,277 refugees

---

[1] Alexander Aaronsohn, 'Saïfna Ahmar, ya Sultan!' *Atlantic Monthly*, July, 1916.

[2] In the fifteenth century, as the result of earthquakes, famines, and persecutions, the economic position of the Jews in Palestine became critical; and in 1601, the Jewish congregations in Venice came to their aid. They established a fund, known as 'A Fund for the Support of the Inhabitants of the Holy Land.' Later on, the Jews in Poland, Bohemia, and Germany offered similar aid. This was the origin of the Haluka, a scanty financial subsidy which, though small in amount, was distributed amongst the Jews of the Holy Land for their support. The money was sent, not so much for the purpose of mere charity as to enable the Jewish scholars and students to interpret the Scriptures and to pray in Palestine for the Jews exiled among the Gentiles. As might be imagined, the Haluka was soon abused. There was an increasing number of Jews who made a pretence of study, and in reality lived on the contributions sent from Europe. It is said that, for one Rabbi or student whom the Haluka helped, there were three who were useless impostors. In spite of the efforts of the Zionists to curtail this misplaced charity, the Haluka Jews of Safed, Tiberias, and most all of Jerusalem increased in numbers. But when the War broke out, the money ceased to come in, and thousands of these underfed Jews succumbed to disease and hunger.

[3] The interest of the Jews in education is shown by their determination to keep the schools open during the War, as described in the following statement: 'Still the people never lost their zeal for the spiritual goods of the Yishub. Neither war nor want could undermine their love of education, and their ardour for their precious Hebraism. The schools all continued in session; and this at least may be said for the Turkish authorities, they did not for a time attempt to close them. Where institutions were staffed by enemy subjects, as with the schools of the French Alliance Israélite and the Evelina de Rothschild girls' school, the enemy teachers had indeed to leave the country. But the authorities permitted substitutes to be appointed from among the Ottoman-Jewish subjects, and the only innovation in the curriculum was to substitute Turkish for the enemy language. The two directors of the Gymnasium at Jaffa, who were Russian subjects by origin, were both compelled to go, despite the Ottomanisation of the institute. But, even so, the school kept its doors open, and the directors carried on a vigorous propaganda for their Hebraic method in the countries of their exile. One of them led the movement for the foundation of a Hebrew high school in Alexandria for the elder children of the refugees, and the other went as an apostle of Hebraism to America.' (Norman Bentwich, *Palestine of the Jews*, pp. 187–88.)

left Syria and Palestine for Alexandria in 1914.[1] Five hundred of these Jewish refugees, known as the 'Zion Mule Corps,' served as a transport unit of the British army under the command of Colonel Patterson in the Gallipoli campaign.[2] Hundreds of Jews were transported free of charge to places of safety by United States cruisers. Thousands became naturalized in order to remain in Palestine; but naturalization by no means assured safety. Although, according to the Young-Turk Constitution of 1909, the Jews were liable to military service, under the law they might purchase exemption. Any man could secure this for a sum equivalent to two hundred dollars. At first the Jews were allowed to opt for military exemption, but later on they were either compelled to serve in the Turkish armies or were thrown into Turkish prisons.[3] In one instance only were the Jews, as

[1] Reports received by the Joint Distribution Committee of Funds for Jewish War Sufferers (New York, 1916), p. 141.

The Jewish Joint Distribution Committee of New York did relief work in Palestine on a very large scale during the War, and for several years after the Armistice.

[2] Lieutenant-Colonel Patterson, *With the Zionists in Gallipoli*, 1916; Max Raisin, *History of the Jews in Modern Times*, pp. 429–31.

The following is an interesting account of the Zion Mule Corps: 'Some thousands of the Jewish settlers in Palestine had preserved their foreign nationality, or at least had not assumed Ottoman citizenship, and upon the declaration of war they were given the alternative of accepting forthwith that citizenship and its obligations, or of leaving the country at short notice. Many chose the former course, especially among those who had a stake in the land. Becoming naturalised Ottomans they remained on their farms. They were promised release from military service, and were prepared to take the risk of the Turks keeping faith. Some thousands, however, of Russian, French, and English subjects, preferred a fresh exile to the tender mercies of the Ottoman Government and the prospect of famine which was already looming. They were mainly sprung from the towns, and a considerable proportion were recipients of the Chaluka; but some hundreds were labourers (Poalim) of the colonies who were willing to take their part in the war, but desired to serve in the ranks of the Allies. These were afterwards embodied in the Zion Mule Corps which went through the Gallipoli campaign from beginning to end, as a transport unit of the British army at Cape Hellas, and acquitted itself well under the command of Colonel Patterson, who published a very popular book on the achievements of his little Jewish force.' (Norman Bentwich, *Palestine of the Jews*, pp. 182–83.)

[3] When Turkey entered the War as an ally of the Central Powers, the situation of the fifty thousand Russian Jews, who constituted more than one half of the Jewish population, was precarious. As nationals of an enemy country, they became liable to any restrictions or deprivations of rights which military necessity dictated. Upon the intervention of the German and American Embassies, however, the Ottoman Government made special concessions to these Jews. Several weeks' time was allowed for those who so desired to become Turkish subjects by naturalization. Upon the expiration of this period, those who had not availed themselves of this offer were

well as the Christians, relieved of military service. In the expedition against the Suez Canal, namely, no Jew nor Christian, except a few non-Mohammedan physicians who had been forced into the army, was allowed to pass beyond Beersheba, the southern base of operations.[1]

Djemal Pasha, whose tenure was also notorious for his independence of the Turkish central authorities and of the German officers, on whom he looked with disfavor, was particularly hostile to the Zionists. He prohibited the use of Zionist insignia — the flag, the shekel, and the national fund stamps. He initiated investigations, and commanded the surrender of all firearms or weapons. The leaders in Zionist work were arrested and many innocent Jews were expelled without explanation or warning. On any pretext house-to-house searches were made; Jewish banks were closed; remittances sent to Jewish institutions were inhibited; and on two occasions great numbers of Jews were expelled from Jaffa.[2]

When War was declared, the plan was to send the Russian Jews in Palestine to the Mesopotamian town of Urfa. Although this was prevented through the representations of Ambassador Morgenthau, the Russian Jews were herded together and sent to Jaffa, where they boarded United States cruisers which were to transfer them to Egypt. But even on a friendly ship they were robbed and maltreated by the Arab boatmen.[3]

Jews accused of espionage were tortured and terrified; the case of Sara Aaronson, of Zichron-Jacob, who after torture committed suicide, illustrates the extreme cruelty of the Turkish authorities.[4]

forced to leave. About six hundred were forcibly expelled and about seven thousand others left voluntarily. (*Jews in the Eastern War Zone*, p. 95. Published by the American Jewish Committee.)

[1] Alexander Aaronsohn, 'Saïfna Ahmar, ya Sultan!' *Atlantic Monthly*, July, 1916.

[2] Philip Graves, *Palestine, the Land of Three Faiths*, p. 39.

[3] Alexander Aaronsohn, 'Saïfna Ahmar, ya Sultan!' *Atlantic Monthly*, July, 1916.

[4] The following is a vivid description of the severe measures inaugurated by Djemal Pasha: 'Djemal Pasha, the local autocrat, issued an almost savage proclamation against all Zionist enterprises, threatening with extreme penalties any who should make outward profession of adherence to the Jewish nationalist cause, or show the Jewish flag. He disarmed the Jewish police of the colonies, the Shomerim, who were the only security against robbery. And, what was even more serious, he took extreme

Not only did Palestine suffer from War cruelties, economic hardships, and serious epidemics which broke out among the underfed and distracted people; but in 1917, the country was invaded by swarms of locusts from the Soudan. The menace was so great, not only to the inhabitants, but to the army as well, that Djemal Pasha initiated a campaign against the insects; but after two months of hopeless toil, the campaign was abandoned and the locusts spread over the country, destroying everything. The damage to the Jewish agricultural Colonies alone was estimated at about five hundred thousand dollars.[1]

A vivid picture of the condition of Palestine after the War is found in the opening sentences of the first official report of the British administration of Palestine:

When General Allenby's army swept over Palestine, in a campaign as brilliant and decisive as any recorded in history, it occupied a country exhausted by war. The population had been depleted; the people of the towns were in severe distress; much cultivated land was left untilled; the stocks of cattle and horses had fallen to a low ebb; the woodlands, always scanty, had almost disappeared; orange groves had been ruined by lack of irrigation; commerce had long been at a standstill.[2]

measures against the principal Jewish financial institution, the Anglo-Palestine Bank, which had become the mainstay of the colonies. The bank was constituted as an English trading company, and therefore came within the scope of the action taken against enemy concerns. It was suddenly ordered to liquidate its business in Palestine, and to shut down all its branches. The distress of the masses, owing to want of money and of food, increased day by day. The Turkish army destined for the invasion of Egypt scoured the country-side for provisions and made pitiless requisitions. It cut down the trees and laid bare the forest colony of Chederah. Again it was American Jewry which came to the aid of its hard-pressed brethren. It had the means, and it gave them, as its way is when moved, with a large hand. Soup kitchens were organised for feeding those in greatest want, and some thousands more of the destitute were brought away to Egypt, and admitted to the refugee camp at Alexandria.' (Norman Bentwich, *Palestine of the Jews*, pp. 185–86.)

A striking statement is the following from Bentwich: 'The misery of the poor,' wrote a correspondent from Jerusalem, at the end of June, 'is unspeakable. The roads are lined with starving persons who lie about begging for a mouthful of bread. The poor Jews sell all their belongings and clothes, linen and bed covers, to the soldiers to get a few metalliks for food.' The words of the writer of Lamentations were realized: 'The young children ask bread, and no man breaketh it unto them.' (Norman Bentwich, *Palestine of the Jews*, pp. 189–90.)

[1] Philip Graves, *Palestine, the Land of Three Faiths*, pp. 38–39.
Jessie Sampter, *A Guide to Zionism*, p. 219.

[2] Cmd. 1499. An Interim Report on the Civil Administration of Palestine, during

In other parts of the world, at the outbreak of the War, Jews were found in both belligerent groups. During the War, particularly in Eastern Europe, hundreds of thousands of Jews were fighting against each other in the hostile camps of the belligerent countries. The Jews enlisted from the same sense of duty as the rest of the population. Even in Russia before the Revolution, there were many who were serving voluntarily in the Russian army.[1]

There were also, of course, large numbers of Jews living in neutral states at the outbreak of the War; and as long as these States remained neutral, the attitude of the Jews was governed by their attitude toward Russia. In the United States, Jewish public opinion was divided. Many Jews whose sympathies would have been with the Allies could not whole-heartedly identify themselves with Russia, particularly as they watched the cruel and unjust treatment meted out to their fellow Jews as the War progressed. But when the United States entered the War, Jews responded like any other citizens.

Especially irritating were the conditions in the Polish provinces which contained the bulk of the Jews in Russia. There, the Russian military leaders unjustly accused the Jews, and imposed many cruel penalties. Rigorous censorship of the Jewish Press was enforced; the Jews were forbidden to speak Yiddish; hostages were taken from among them and shut up in Russian prisons; while in March, 1915, the climax came, when the authorities began systematically to expel the Jews from the Polish provinces, including the lands not occupied by German troops.[2] This action against

the period 1st July, 1920–30th June, 1921. Presented to Parliament by Command of His Majesty, August, 1921, p. 3.

[1] Nahum Sokolow, *History of Zionism*, vol. II, p. 2.

In England, according to estimates prepared by Lord Rothschild, the Jewish population furnished more than its share of recruits in the British army, its quota of 17,000 comprising about eight and a half per cent of the total Jewish population as compared with the six per cent furnished by the non-Jewish population. (*Jews in the Eastern War Zone*, p. 14. Published by the American Jewish Committee.)

In peace-time the Jewish contingent in the Russian army numbered between 350,000 and 400,000. The Russian Jewish Relief Committee reported only 300,000 Jews in the Russian army in May, 1915. (*Jews in the Eastern War Zone*, p. 84. Published by the American Jewish Committee.)

[2] *Jews in the Eastern War Zone*, p. 41. (Published by the American Jewish Committee.)

DEVASTATION OF PALESTINE BY THE LOCUST INVASION OF 1915
Showing the vines completely stripped

the Jewish communities in Poland, said to be taken on the ground of military necessity, caused general hostility to Russia and turned many Jews to the side of the Central Powers.[1]

The activities of the Zionists, after Turkey entered the War, form a chapter of interesting history. The Zionist Organization itself, being established on the federative principle, continued its propaganda through the organizations of the different countries, and several new societies were formed. Although the central organ of the movement, 'Die Welt,' had to be suspended, a series of new Zionist publications made their appearance. Zionist conferences were held in nearly a score of countries, and the contributions to the Jewish National Fund were about doubled. The greater part of the practical work of the Zionist Organization consisted in relieving Jewish war sufferers, and also in safeguarding in every possible way the Jewish Colonies in Palestine.[2]

Events made it clear that England was to be the centre of Zionist activities; and the English Zionists so interpreted the situation. Distinguished representatives of the Zionist idea, such as the Rev. Dr. Moses Gaster and the Rev. Dr. Joseph Herman Hertz, became articulate; but the leading spirit was Dr. Chaim Weizmann, who afterward became President of the Zionist Organization. After consulting with a small circle of Zionists, Dr. Weizmann made the first attempts to confer with Government representatives about Zionism. Encouraged by these conferences, he and his colleagues inaugurated a definitely regulated propaganda to win over the Jews who were either non-Zionist or anti-Zionist.[3]

Articles on the subject appeared in the English Press; and the editor of the 'Manchester Guardian' was especially sympathetic. He, together with Dr. Weizmann, had conversations with some of the leaders in British politics; and again the results seemed favorable for Zionism.

---

[1] Philip Graves says that a knowledge of the conditions in Poland was deliberately kept from the British public by the censorship. (Philip Graves, *Palestine, the Land of Three Faiths*, p. 41.)

[2] Nahum Sokolow, *History of Zionism*, vol. ii, pp. 21–38.

[3] The account of Zionist activities during the War until the promulgation of the Balfour Declaration is mainly taken from Sokolow. There has been no official publication of the negotiations.

One of the influential personalities consulted at the time was Sir Herbert Samuel, who at the Zionist demonstration of December 2, 1914, declared, 'that he had stood for Zionism not only in the Cabinet but out of it.' Among other distinguished persons were certain members of the Rothschild family, who had previously approved the project of founding a Hebrew University in Jerusalem.

The next step, as Dr. Weizmann, Dr. Gaster, and others conceived it to be, was to establish in England a centre which would be representative of the great masses of Zionists throughout the world. Here, they thought, a practical scheme for Palestine could be worked out. At the request of the English leaders, the Zionist Organization delegated Mr. Sokolow of Warsaw and Dr. Tschlenow of Moscow to assist in the work; they arrived in London shortly before the end of the year 1914. In the early months of 1915, many conferences were held with leading personalities, with seemingly favorable results. In March, 1915, Dr. Weizmann, Mr. Sokolow, and Dr. Tschlenow went to Paris to continue the conferences which Dr. Weizmann had had previously in Paris; and shortly afterward, Dr. Tschlenow returned to Russia, where he reported to the Zionists that the political efforts in England had filled him with great hopes.

The next phase of the movement, as these leaders conceived it to be, was to strengthen Zionism from within; and so the years 1915–16 were devoted chiefly to this purpose. A large group of Zionist writers joined the leaders, conspicuous among whom was Major Norman Bentwich, now the Attorney-General of Palestine.

In October, 1916, the Zionist leaders submitted to the British Government a formal 'programme for a new administration of Palestine and for a Jewish resettlement of Palestine in accordance with the aspirations of the Zionist Movement.' The main features of this program were 'the recognition of a separate Jewish nationality or national unit in Palestine,' and 'the establishment of a Jewish chartered company for the resettlement of Palestine by Jewish settlers.' [1] There was no immediate response to these proposals, but as Stein says: 'It

[1] Leonard Stein, *Zionism*, pp. 111, 112.

was not long... before the claims of Zionism began to receive serious attention.' [1]

The 2d of February, 1917, is considered by Zionists an important date in Zionism; for it marks the beginning of consecutive official negotiations with the British Government. Shortly before this, Lieutenant-Colonel Sir Mark Sykes, Bart., M.P., joint author with M. Georges Picot in the Sykes-Picot Agreement, had communicated with Dr. Weizmann and Mr. Sokolow on the subject of Zionism. Having now been entrusted with the study of the Zionist problem, he carried on conversations with Dr. Moses Gaster, in conjunction with M. Georges Picot, who represented the French Government; and at the commencement of the year 1917, entered into closer relations with Dr. Weizmann and Mr. Sokolow. The results of the meeting which followed were considered favorable by the Zionists.[2]

Mr. Sokolow was appointed to continue conversations with Sir Mark Sykes and M. Georges Picot; and in consequence was called to Paris in March, 1917, by the French Government. On the 22d of March, he was received at the Ministry of Foreign Affairs in Paris, where he outlined the principles of the Zionist program. He received the assurance that the French Government viewed the program very favorably; and he was authorized so to inform the Zionist Organizations of the United States and Russia.

After a period of a month, Mr. Sokolow went to Rome on a similar mission. The leading Italian Jews accepted the program, but advised him to enter into negotiations with the Vatican with respect to the Holy Places. He was received by the Pope; and before he left Italy was assured that the Italian Government, in conjunction with the Allied Powers, would support the Zionist program. Similarly, as in France, he was authorized to telegraph this information to the Zionist Organizations in the United States and Russia.

On May 28, Mr. Sokolow was received by the French

---

[1] Leonard Stein, *Zionism*, p. 112.

[2] Besides Sir Mark Sykes, the following took part in this meeting: Lord Rothschild, Mr. Herbert Bentwich, Mr. Joseph Cowen, Dr. M. Gaster (at whose house the meeting took place), Mr. James de Rothschild, Mr. Harry Sacher, Right Hon. Herbert Samuel, M.P., Dr. Chaim Weizmann, and Mr. Sokolow. (Nahum Sokolow, *History of Zionism*, vol. II, p. 52.)

Prime Minister; and after later negotiations, received the following statement from the French Government:

PARIS, *June* 4, 1917

Sir,

You were good enough to present the project to which you are devoting your efforts, which has for its object the development of Jewish colonization in Palestine. You consider that, circumstances permitting, and the independence of the Holy Places being safeguarded on the other hand, it would be a deed of justice and of reparation to assist, by the protection of the Allied Powers, in the renaissance of the Jewish nationality in that Land from which the people of Israel were exiled so many centuries ago.

The French Government, which entered this present war to defend a people wrongfully attacked, and which continues the struggle to assure the victory of right over might, can but feel sympathy for your cause, the triumph of which is bound up with that of the Allies.

I am happy to give you herewith such assurance.

Please accept, Sir, the assurance of my most distinguished consideration.

(Signed)   JULES CAMBON

M. N. SOKOLOW
   Hôtel Meurice, Paris [1]

In England, the work had gone on with great zeal under the leadership of Dr. Weizmann. Two periodicals were founded, the 'Zionist Review' in London, and the weekly 'Palestine' in Manchester. A special conference of the English Zionist Federation was held on May 20, 1917, when the President, Dr. Weizmann, explained the political situation as it affected the Jewish National Movement. Extreme opposition developed against the political features of the program; a Manifesto was published in the London 'Times,' May 24, 1917, signed jointly by the President of the Board of Deputies of British Jews and the President of the Anglo-Jewish Association, declaring their opposition to the plan. Their reasons were: first, that it recognized the Jewish settlements in Palestine 'as possessing a national character in a political sense'; and second, that since the plan stipulated that the rights of Jewish settlers in Palestine were to be embodied in a charter and administered by a Jewish chartered company, there would develop a situation which would involve the Jews 'in the bit-

[1] Nahum Sokolow, *History of Zionism*, vol. II, p. 53.

terest feuds with their neighbors of other races and religions.'
This called forth an amazing storm of protest.

In July, 1917, a formula for a proposed declaration was submitted to the Government by the Zionist representatives.
This formula recognized Palestine as 'the national home of
the Jewish people' and provided for the establishment of 'a
Jewish National Colonising Corporation for the resettlement
and economic development of the country.'[1] The Government replied with an alternative draft which formed the basis
of the Balfour Declaration. From that time until November,
1917, the Zionists kept up the *pourparlers* with the British
Government, in the endeavor to obtain official acceptance of
their principles.[2] In this, they were actively assisted by a considerable number of Zionists abroad, especially by the American Zionists.[3] 'Every idea born in London was tested by the

---

[1] Leonard Stein, *Zionism*, pp. 114, 115.

[2] In describing the nature of these *pourparlers*, Philip Graves says: 'On July 18,
1917, a draft text of what was afterwards known as the Balfour Declaration was submitted by Lord Rothschild to Mr. Balfour. But both the British Government and a
number of non-Zionist British Jews raised objections to the wording of the draft. Mr.
J. M. Jeffries, in one of a series of anti-Zionist articles recently published in the *Daily
Mail* (January 9, 1923), suggests that the word "National" in the "key-phrase,"
viz., "National Home of the Jewish People," was retained in the Balfour Declaration
against the wishes of these non-Zionist Jews and in deference to the insistence of the
Zionists. On the other hand, the great Jewish writer and philosopher, Dr. Asher
Ginzberg (Achad Ha-Am), who was a member of the Zionist Political Committee,
says in an introduction, written in June, 1920, to a new edition of his Hebrew Essays:
'"This is not the text suggested to the Government by the Zionist spokesmen.
They wished it to read, 'the reconstitution of Palestine as the National Home of the
Jewish People,' but when the happy day arrived on which the Declaration was signed
and sealed by the Government, it was found to contain the first formula and not the
second. That is to say, the allusion to the fact that we are about to rebuild our national home was dropped, and at the same time the words 'constitution of Palestine
as the National Home' were replaced by 'establishment of a National Home in
Palestine.'...
'"There were some who thought that the difference was merely one of form. Hence
they sometimes attempted on subsequent occasions, when the negotiations with the
Government afforded an opportunity, to formulate the promise in their own wording, as though it had not been changed. But every time they found in the Government's reply a repetition of the actual text of the Declaration, which proves that it is
not a case where the same thing may be put equally well in either of two ways, but
that the promise is really defined in this particular form of words and goes no further."' (Philip Graves, *Palestine, the Land of Three Faiths*, pp. 44–45.)
A translation of this introduction is given in part on p. xiii *seq.* of the volume entitled, *Ten Essays on Zionism and Judaism by Achad Ha'am*, translated from the
Hebrew by Leon Simon, London, 1922.

[3] The United States entered the war on April 7, 1917.

Zionist Organization in America, and every suggestion from America received the most careful attention in London.' [1]

It is generally accepted that the successful issue of the negotiations was due in part to President Wilson. His attention was drawn to the Zionist Movement by the 'Provisional Executive Committee for General Zionist Affairs,' which was formed in New York in August, 1914, under the chairmanship of Mr. L. D. Brandeis, now Justice of the Supreme Court. When the British decision was about to be made, President Wilson allowed it to be known that he would welcome a British pronouncement in favor of Zionist aspirations. Philip Graves asserts that President Wilson's sympathy with Zionist aims 'undoubtedly influenced both the French and Italian Governments, which had hitherto shown no particular sympathy with the Zionist movement, and led them to associate themselves with the British in this question.' [2]

As to the Declaration itself, however, the Jews give full credit to Lord Balfour for the policy involved. In the Report of the Executive of the Zionist Organization to the Twelfth Zionist Congress, we find the following statement: 'The Balfour Declaration is justly so-called, not only because it fell to Sir Arthur Balfour as Foreign Secretary to write the historic letter, but also because he, more than any other single statesman, is responsible for the policy embodied in the Declaration.' [3]

On November 2, 1917, Mr. Arthur J. Balfour, Secretary of State for Foreign Affairs, formally announced the sympathy of the British Government with Zionist aspirations and its favorable attitude toward the establishment of a national home for the Jewish people in the following letter:

FOREIGN OFFICE
November 2, 1917

Dear Lord Rothschild, — I have much pleasure in conveying to you on behalf of His Majesty's Government the following declaration of sympathy with Jewish Zionist aspirations, which has been submitted to and approved by the Cabinet:
'His Majesty's Government view with favour the establishment in Palestine of a national home for the Jewish people, and will use

[1] Nahum Sokolow, *History of Zionism*, vol. II, p. 82.
[2] Philip Graves, *Palestine, the Land of Three Faiths*, pp. 45, 46.
[3] See Philip Graves, *Palestine, the Land of Three Faiths*, p. 46.

their best endeavours to facilitate the achievement of this object, it being clearly understood that nothing shall be done which may prejudice the civil and religious rights of existing non-Jewish communities in Palestine or the rights and political status enjoyed by Jews in any other country.'

I should be grateful if you would bring this declaration to the knowledge of the Zionist Federation.

Yours sincerely[1]

(Signed)   ARTHUR JAMES BALFOUR [1]

Another side to the story of the Balfour Declaration has been discussed by several writers, and should therefore find a place in a work of this sort, which is aiming to weigh and balance all considerations that may throw light on the motives underlying the Balfour Declaration. More than one writer refers to the rumor, alleged to have come to the knowledge of the British Government, that Germany contemplated making certain offers to the Zionist Jews for their support, and that Talaat Pasha, the Grand Vizier of Turkey, had made similar offers to prominent German and neutral Zionists, through the notorious communist Parvus Helphand. It is, moreover, stated that these rumors came just about the time the Zionist leaders were submitting their formal program to the British Government.[2]

The story continues: that when further proofs of these attempts to secure moral support and perhaps financial assistance from the Zionists came to the attention of the British Government, the Zionist situation became a live matter for their consideration; and that thereafter it was held of supreme importance to the Entente cause to prevent the influence of Jewry going to the side of the Central Powers.

The following citation from W. J. M. Childs seems to sum up this opinion:

Support of Zionist ambitions, indeed, promised much for the

---

[1] The above account of the steps leading to the negotiations between the Zionist leaders, on the one hand, and the British, French, and Italian Governments, on the other, which finally resulted in the Balfour Declaration, is taken from Nahum Sokolow, *History of Zionism*, vol. II, pp. 42–83.

See also Philip Graves, *Palestine, the Land of Three Faiths*, pp. 41–47.

The Balfour Declaration was pronounced when the greater part of Palestine was in Turkish hands; when, in fact, the results of the war were in no wise certain.

[2] The account of the Jewish negotiations with the Government has never been officially published.

cause of the Entente. Quite naturally Jewish sympathies were to a great extent anti-Russian, and therefore in favour of the Central Powers. No ally of Russia, in fact, could escape sharing that immediate and inevitable penalty for long and savage Russian persecution of the Jewish race. But the German General Staff desired to attach Jewish support yet more closely to the German side. With their wide outlook on possibilities, they seem to have urged, early in 1916, the advantages of promising Jewish restoration in Palestine under an arrangement to be made between Zionists and Turkey backed by a German guarantee. The practical difficulties were considerable; the subject perhaps dangerous to German relations with Turkey; and the German Government acted cautiously. But the scheme was by no means rejected or even shelved, and at any moment the Allies might have been forestalled in offering this supreme bid. In fact in September, 1917, the German Government were making the most serious efforts to capture the Zionist movement.[1]

Another reason why Great Britain might have considered it advantageous to have an organized Jewish community in Palestine under the British ægis is given by the same writer. He says that the 'obvious advantages of covering the Suez Canal by an outpost territory in which important elements of the population would not only be bound to her by every interest, but would command the support of world Jewry.' [2]

The same idea is expressed by J. de V. Loder:

Apart from the question of abstract justice and its bearing on a solution of the Jewish problem as a whole... Zionism offered certain definite advantages to Great Britain. There was the chance of an alliance with the international force of Jewry which the circumstances of the war made specially attractive and which might survive as of permanent value, and there was the chance of introducing a Jewish element into Palestine, bound by ties of gratitude to Great Britain, which would turn Palestine into an advanced bastion for the defence of the Suez Canal. The Balfour Declaration must have been influenced by such considerations, though they were certainly not its ultimate motive.[3]

Concerning the strategic importance of Palestine, Major Newman says:

[1] *A History of the Peace Conference of Paris.* Edited by H. W. V. Temperley. Published under the auspices of the Institute of International Affairs. Vol. vi, 1920, pp. 172, 173.

[2] *Ibid.,* p. 171.

[3] J. de V. Loder, *The Truth About Mesopotamia, Palestine and Syria,* pp. 149–50.

Palestine was to become one of the chief pivots of British Imperial air policy as a main aerial artery between East and West. In short, Palestine was to become the 'Suez Canal of the Air,' which was geographically side by side with the 'Suez Canal of the Sea.' [1]

In regard to the attitude of the British Cabinet toward Zionism, Mr. Childs states that:

Amongst influential English Jews, Zionism had few supporters, at all events for a Zion in Palestine. It had still fewer in France. Jewish influence both within and without the Cabinet is understood to have exerted itself strenuously and pertinaciously against the policy of the proposed Declaration.

But, as the statement explains:

Under the pressure of Allied needs the objections of the anti-Zionists were either over-ruled or the causes of objection removed, and the Balfour Declaration... was published to the world on 2nd November, 1917. That it is in purpose a definite contract with Jewry is beyond question. [2]

The same writer defines the Declaration as

a bold, imaginative, and statesmanlike effort to prevent the incalculable and universal influence of Jewry being exerted on the side of the Central Powers — as, indeed, it was, to a serious extent, then being exerted — and to transfer this highly important influence to the cause of the Entente. Nor was it a project of sudden origin, or hastily embraced. The advantages to be gained if the policy of the Declaration were adopted had long been urged; opposition to that policy had long been active. Before the British Government gave the Declaration to the world it had been closely examined in all its bearings and implications, weighed word by word, and subjected to repeated change and amendment. [3]

In March, 1917, the first Russian Revolution took place, which drove the Tsar from Petrograd and removed the restrictions affecting nationalities and creeds. [4] As to the result of this, Sokolow says, that 'far from destroying Zionism, the

[1] Major E. W. Polson Newman, *The Middle East*, p. 6.

[2] *A History of the Peace Conference of Paris.* Edited by H. W. V. Temperley. Published under the auspices of the British Institute of International Affairs. Vol. VI, p. 173.

[3] *Ibid.*, pp. 171–72.

[4] In November, 1917, Kerensky fell before Lenin and Trotsky; and in March, 1918, the Peace of Brest-Litovsk was signed with Germany, by which Russia surrendered Poland, Lithuania, the Baltic Provinces, and the Ukraine.

new liberty gave it an immense stimulus.' [1] From this time
on, Russia ceased to count as a military factor in the war; and
in April, the United States joined the Entente.

These two facts are made the basis of an interesting commentary by Philip Graves:

It was becoming painfully obvious [said he] that Russia had
ceased to count as a military factor in the war.... The New Russia
had lost interest in all but economic and social problems and longed
for peace; something must be done to bring Jewish opinion in Russia
to the side of the Allies and to influence American Jewish sentiment.
From May, 1917, the negotiations between a Zionist Political Committee and the British Government began to make more rapid
progress.[2]

After the Russian Revolution took place, the British
Foreign Office, according to Mr. Graves, appears to have laid
a memorandum before the War Cabinet imputing that British support of Zionism might have a good effect in Russia. It
is interesting in this connection to consider the following statement cited by Leonard Stein:

In its issue of January 4, 1925, the 'Rasvjet,' a Russo-
Jewish paper published in Paris, reprints from the Riga
'Narodnaja Misl' an article of which the following is a trans-
lation.

In the book, 'The Partition of Asiatic Turkey as per the Secret
Documents of the former Foreign Office,' just published by the
Soviet Commissariat for Foreign Affairs, there is a document of
considerable interest to us. It is called 'A Memorandum of the
British Embassy in Petrograd to the Minister for Foreign Affairs,
S. D. Sazonoff,' and is dated March 13, 1916. The Memorandum
reads as follows:

'A telegram has been received from Sir Edward Grey, to the
effect that the question of settling Jews in Palestine has been
brought to the notice of His Majesty's Government. Although, as
is known, many Jews are rather indifferent to the Zionist idea, a
very great and most influential part of Jewry in all countries would
greatly appreciate the proposal of an agreement relating to Palestine, which would satisfy the aspirations of the Jews.

'If the above view is correct, it is clear that by utilising the
Zionist idea, important political results could be achieved. One of
the results would be the conversion of the Jewish elements in the

[1] Nahum Sokolow, *History of Zionism*, vol. ii, p. 38.
[2] Philip Graves, *Palestine, the Land of Three Faiths*, p. 44.

East, the United States of America, and other places to the cause
of the Allies; elements whose attitude is at present rather antagonis-
tic to the Allies.'

The British Government, as is known, put the question before representative Jews of the various sections of English Jewry,
asking for their opinion on the question. The Memorandum
quotes one of the very moderate replies received from Mr. Lucien
Wolf.

'If, as a result of the War, Palestine will come into the sphere of
the interests of France and Great Britain, the French and British
Governments will not fail to take into consideration the historic
interests of Jewry in that country. Both Governments will secure
for the Jewish population equal political, civil and religious rights
with the other inhabitants, municipal rights in the colonies and
towns which may appear necessary, as well as reasonable facilities
for colonisation and immigration.'

But the British Government, it seems, found these demands too
moderate.

'The only aim of His Majesty's Government is to find some
agreement which would prove an inducement to the majority of
Jews and would facilitate the conclusion of an agreement to secure
Jewish support. Having this view in consideration, His Majesty's
Government is of opinion that a project which would grant the
Jews — when the colonists in Palestine have attained a position
which will enable them to rival the Arabs in strength — the
administration of their own internal affairs in that country (with
the exception of Jerusalem and the Holy Places) — such an agreement would be a greater inducement for the majority of Jews. His
Majesty's Government does not wish to give any preference to any
one form of the solutions of this problem. It is well aware, however,
that an international Protectorate would meet with opposition on
the part of influential Jewish sections.

'In telegraphically communicating the above, Sir Edward Grey
instructs Sir George Buchanan to request the Russian Government
to give the question their immediate serious consideration and to
ask them to communicate their point of view.' [1]

The authenticity of this document has never been proved
although it is a fact that Mr. Lucien Wolf's memorandum
is correctly quoted. Mr. Graves ventures a further commentary:

Jews were playing a prominent part in the Russian Revolution, ...
but they were greatly divided. Some were for peace at any price,
some for the maintenance of the Alliance with the Western Powers;
many were utterly uninterested in Zionism, and had found a

[1] Leonard Stein, *Zionism*, pp. 138–40.

Messiah in Karl Marx and a panacea for the world's disease in Revolutionary Communism. The War Cabinet took no immediate decision, but Zionism became an important political issue.[1]

The Russian Revolution and Zionism together had a disastrous effect on the Sykes-Picot Agreement which had already been extensively modified to meet the views of the Russian Tsarist Government in 1915 and 1916. This Agreement, as we have already noted, provided among other things for the setting-up of an international State in Palestine, with the exception of an area about Haifa, which was to be ceded to Great Britain.[2] The Zionists were strongly opposed to this internationalization of Palestine. They feared that Russian Orthodox and French and Italian Catholic interests would be strong enough to prevent any international recognition of the Jewish community in Palestine. It is a fact that the First Russian Revolution weakened the power of the Russian Orthodoxy; but, on the other hand, it left the French and the Italian Catholic opponents of Zionism in a stronger position than ever.[3]

The Balfour Declaration was an international commitment.[4] Both the French and Italian Governments, as we have learned from Jewish sources, had been kept informed of the progress of events, and the Balfour Declaration was not issued until their concurrence was assured. The French Government anticipated the pronouncement by publicly express-

---

[1] Philip Graves, *Palestine, the Land of Three Faiths*, p. 43.

[2] Articles 3 and 4 of the Sykes-Picot Agreement; text given in J. de V. Loder, *The Truth About Mesopotamia, Palestine and Syria*, Appendix, I, p. 161.

The Sykes-Picot Agreement of May, 1916, which was kept from the Zionists till the spring of 1917, and then only came to their knowledge through a French source, was revised by the end of 1918 just as the Peace Conference was opening, when France agreed to relinquish her claims to Palestine in favor of Great Britain. This was one of the secret agreements into which the Tsarist Government of Russia had entered; and it was published by the Bolsheviks as soon as they came into power. It appeared in the *Izvestia* on the 24th of November, 1917, and was reproduced in translation in the *Manchester Guardian* on the 19th of January, 1918. (*A History of the Peace Conference of Paris.* Edited by H. W. V. Temperley. Published under the auspices of the British Institute of International Affairs. Vol. vi, p. 16.)

[3] Philip Graves, *Palestine, the Land of Three Faiths*, pp. 43, 44.

[4] At this time, the greater part of Palestine was still in Turkish hands. A few weeks afterward, the British forces entered Jerusalem, and by the end of the year they had occupied nearly the whole of Judea. Six months later, the Turks were driven out of Galilee.

ing its general sympathy with Zionist aims as early as June, 1917.[1] France formally associated herself with the Declaration in February, 1918,[2] and Italy adhered in the following May.[3] Since the United States was not at war with Turkey, this Government could not formally endorse the plan, but on August 31, 1918, President Wilson allowed publicity to be given to a letter written by him to Rabbi Stephen Wise, then President of the American Zionist Federation, in which he welcomed 'the progress made by the Zionist movement in the United States and in the Allied countries since the Declaration by Mr. Balfour on behalf of the British Government of Great Britain's approval of the establishment in Palestine of a national home for the Jewish people.' [4] In December, 1918,

[1] See page 332.

[2] On February 14, 1918, M. Pichon, then Foreign Minister, sent Mr. Sokolow, as representing the Zionist Organization, a copy of an official communiqué, dated February 9, which reads as follows: 'Mr. Sokolow... was this morning received by Mons. Pichon, Minister of Foreign Affairs, who was happy to inform him that there is complete agreement between the French and British Governments, in all matters which concern the establishment of a Jewish national home in Palestine.' (Nahum Sokolow, *History of Zionism*, vol. ii, p. 128.)

[3] On May 9, 1918, the Italian Government, through its Ambassador in London, notified the Zionist Organization through Mr. Sokolow that the 'Italian Government would use its best endeavours to facilitate the establishment in Palestine of a Jewish National Centre, it being understood that this should not prejudice the civil and religious rights of existing non-Jewish communities in Palestine or the legal or political status enjoyed by Jews in any other country.' (Nahum Sokolow, *History of Zionism*, vol. ii, p. 129.)

[4] In President Wilson's address to Congress of January 8, 1918, a speech commonly regarded as a complete statement of the objects for which the Allied Powers were fighting, the twelfth of the articles in the program of the world's peace was stated thus: 'The Turkish portions of the present Ottoman Empire should be assured a secure sovereignty, but the other nationalities which are now under Turkish rule should be assured an undoubted security of life and an absolutely unmolested opportunity of autonomous development.' 'This statement,' Mr. Sokolow says, 'was regarded by Zionists as signifying the sympathetic attitude of the American Government and especially of its President to the Zionist movement.' (Nahum Sokolow, *History of Zionism*, vol. ii, p. 130.)

Four years later, both Houses of the United States Congress, when the Palestine Mandate was about to be submitted for approval to the Council of the League of Nations, unanimously adopted a resolution in favor of 'the establishment in Palestine of a national home for the Jewish people, it being clearly understood that nothing shall be done which may prejudice the civil and religious rights of the Christian and all other non-Jewish communities in Palestine, and that the Holy Places and religious buildings and sites in Palestine shall be adequately protected.' (Joint-Resolution of the Sixty-Seventh Congress, adopted by the Senate on May 3 and by the House of Representatives on June 30, 1922, and approved by President Harding on September 21, 1922.)

Japan joined with the other Principal Allied Powers in supporting the Balfour Declaration.[1]

This was immediately published throughout Europe; and it certainly rallied world Jewry to the side of the Entente. In Russia, the Central Zionist Committee requested the British Ambassador to forward to the British Government an address, on behalf of the Russian Zionists, expressing their heartfelt appreciation of the 'inspiring Declaration' and all that it stood for. Messages poured in from Italy, Switzerland, America, and even from Germany. Especially worthy of note was the telegram from Berlin stating that the German Zionist Conference had adopted the following Resolution: 'The German Zionist Association greets with satisfaction the fact that the British Government has recognized in an official declaration the right of the Jewish people to a national existence in Palestine.' [2] In America, the Declaration brought new recruits to Zionism and encouraged those who had more recently joined. It reacted immediately upon the morale of the Central Empires. According to Mr. Kallen, the Declaration accelerated the cleavage then taking place in the Central Empires between the subject nationalities and their overlords; in Germany, the attitude of the Zionists was tantamount to defiance of their rulers.[3] The Balfour Declaration has been reaffirmed by successive British Governments; [4] and to the

---

[1] The Japanese Ambassador was authorized to make the following declaration in the name of the Imperial Japanese Government: 'The Japanese Government gladly take note of the Zionist aspirations to establish in Palestine a National Home for the Jewish people, and they look forward with a sympathetic interest to the realization of such desire upon the basis proposed.' (Quoted from the *Jewish Chronicle*, January 10, 1919, by B. B. Benas in *Zionism, the Jewish National Movement*, p. 85.)

[2] *Zionist Review*, 1917–20, p. 180.

[3] Horace M. Kallen, *Zionism and World Politics*, p. 170 *seq.*

[4] Lord Curzon (Foreign Secretary) to Mr. Sokolow, November 1, 1919: 'There has been no change in the policy of the Government with regard to the establishment of a Jewish National Home in Palestine.'

The Colonial Secretary to the High Commissioner for Palestine, October 4, 1923 (Command Paper 1989 [1923]): 'The key-note of British policy in Palestine... is to be found in the Balfour Declaration... the policy of the Declaration... formed an essential part of the conditions on which Great Britain accepted the Mandate for Palestine, and thus constitutes an international obligation from which there can be no question of receding.'

Mr. J. H. Thomas (Colonial Secretary), House of Commons, February 25, 1924 (Official Report, column 63): 'His Majesty's Government have decided after careful

present day, there has been no change in British policy.

Mr. Graves makes reply to the non-Zionist claim, that the Balfour Declaration was concealed from the population of Palestine until 1920. He declares that, having himself served with the British forces in Palestine during 1917 and part of 1918, he can 'vouch for the fact that the Declaration was very well known to the inhabitants of Jerusalem and Jaffa very shortly after the capture of those towns. The German Wireless had already spread it abroad in the interval between its publication and the capture of Jerusalem on December 8, 1917.' Mr. Graves further says that he can 'remember hearing the Declaration discussed by the Military Governor of Jerusalem in January, 1918.' 'It was not made public in the form of an official proclamation,' he observes, 'since the result of the War was then in grave doubt, and obviously it was not a fitting moment to make any official proclamation of British intentions as regards hostile territory.' [1]

Mr. D. G. Hogarth says that the Balfour Declaration was communicated officially to the Arabs in January, 1918; and that when the Declaration was communicated to Hussein at this time, 'he took it philosophically, contenting himself with an expression of good-will toward a kindred Semitic race, which he understood (as his phrase made clear) was to lodge in a house owned by Arabs.' [2]

consideration of all the circumstances to adhere to the policy of giving effect to the Balfour Declaration of 1917.' (Leonard Stein, *Zionism*, p. 116.)

See vol. II, p. 273, for a statement from the Prime Minister in Parliament on April 3, 1930. See also Chapter XXII.

[1] Philip Graves, *Palestine, the Land of Three Faiths*, pp. 47–48.

[2] *A History of the Peace Conference of Paris*. Edited by H. W. V. Temperley. Published under the auspices of the British Institute of International Affairs. Vol. VI, p. 132.

CHAPTER XIII

THE JEWS AT THE PEACE CONFERENCE

ZIONISM pleaded its cause at the Peace Conference. There were present delegates from many of the Jewish organizations who had been sent to watch over the interests of the Jews. Commenting on their presence at Paris, Ray Stannard Baker says: 'The Jews maintained a powerful representation for many weeks and were shrewdly and fruitfully active.' [1]

The Zionists were not only interested in the immediate project for a Jewish Home in Palestine, but also in certain territorial settlements which were to be made by the Conference.[2] In making their demands, they relied on the Fourteen Points, enunciated by President Wilson, and accepted as one of the conditions of the Armistice. With millions of other peoples, they held the Conference responsible for putting into practice the underlying conception of the Fourteen Points: 'The principle of justice to all peoples and nationalities, and their right to live on equal terms of liberty and safety with one another, whether they be strong or weak.'

The Jews had made extensive plans for the Conference; they had kept in touch with the progress of the War and the tendencies of the settlement. They had noted, for example, the attempt, in the Peace of Bucharest, between the Central Powers and Roumania, May, 1918, to establish equal freedom in Roumania for the Jewish religion; [3] they had also learned that the Central Powers had recognized the necessity of inserting an article in the treaty extending Roumanian citizenship to Jews. These were only tendencies, to be sure; but in 1918, when the Jews were possessed of the fact, which the Allies had made plain in that year, that Poland was to become independent, they calculated that the new State would con-

---

[1] Ray Stannard Baker, *Woodrow Wilson and World Settlement*, vol. II, p. 24.

[2] Jewish insistence on minority protection was by no means confined to the Zionists. In fact, some of the Jews at Paris who advocated minority treaties, noticeably Mr. Marshall, were very anti-Zionist.

[3] This same privilege was to have been granted for the Roman Catholic, the United Greek, the Bulgarian Orthodox, the Protestant, and the Mussulman.

tain four million Jews in its population, and that therefore fourteen per cent of the inhabitants of Poland would be Jews. This, they deemed, would be a serious situation, for during recent years there had developed a strong animosity toward the Jews; and, moreover, this spirit of anti-Semitism was fostered by the rising nationalism among the Poles themselves.

The Jewish delegations at Paris followed the situation in Poland and Czecho-Slovakia — the two new States established by the Conference. They also focussed their attention on Serbia, Roumania, and Greece — States, which, in consequence of the War, were to receive important accessions of territory. The Jewish representatives claimed that it was clearly the duty of the Peace Conference to give security to the members of their race in any of these States wherever the necessity was evident.

It was a fitting moment, there at Paris, for the Jews to call attention to their lack of those safeguards enjoyed by aliens of other nationalities who could look to the protection of their own Government. But months elapsed before anything was done. It was not until the end of April that the question of protecting racial minorities in the new States was brought before the Supreme Council. The matter was first presented by President Wilson. His proposal provided for religious freedom, similar to that embodied in the Treaty of Berlin, in 1878.[1] He also included a provision for political equality.

Coincidently, at the instance of an American Jewish Committee, led by Judge Julian W. Mack and Mr. Louis Marshall, Colonel House became interested in the question of protecting the Jews; and the American delegation prepared clauses dealing with minorities in Poland for insertion in the treaty with Germany.[2] The matter, however, was so intricate, involving, as it did, so many different points of view, that the Supreme Council referred it, on May 1, to a small

[1] *British and Foreign State Papers*, LXIX, 749; *United States Foreign Relations*, 1878, 895.

[2] Manley Ottmer Hudson, Legal Adviser, American Peace Commission, 'The Protection of Minorities and Natives in Transferred Territories,' *What Really Happened at Paris*. Edited by Edward Mandell House and Charles Seymour, 1921. Chapter IX.

committee, which was later called the Committee on New States and the Protection of Minorities.[1]

The Supreme Council decided that the two new States — Poland and Czecho-Slovakia — whose independence was to be recognized by the Treaty with Germany [2] should definitely agree in the peace treaty to accept such guarantees as the Principal Powers should deem necessary for the protection of the racial minorities.

The Council of Four approved the following clause, to be inserted in the treaty with Germany (Article 93):

> Poland accepts and agrees to embody in a Treaty with the Principal Allied and Associated Powers such provisions as may be deemed necessary by the said Powers to protect the interests of the inhabitants of Poland who differ from the majority of the population in race, language or religion.

It was also decided that the same course should be adopted for the other new States. For example, the treaty with Austria obliges Jugo-Slavia, Czecho-Slovakia, and Roumania to accept similar obligations; [3] the treaty with Hungary binds Jugo-Slavia and Roumania in the same way; [4] and the treaty with Bulgaria binds Greece.[5]

There was great opposition on the part of some of the new States to the insertion of such obligations in the treaties of peace, and even more to the separate minority treaties.[6] It

---

[1] The Committee on New States and the Protection of Minorities was composed of M. Berthelot and M. Kammerrer, of France; Mr. Headlam-Morley and Mr. Carr, of Great Britain; Mr. de Martino and Colonel Castoldi, of Italy; Mr. Adatci, of Japan; and Mr. David Hunter Miller and Mr. Manley Ottmer Hudson, of the United States. In the later stages of the work, the American representative was Mr. Allen W. Dulles.

[2] The Treaty of Peace between the Allies and Associated Powers and Germany. Signed at Versailles, June 28, 1919.

[3] Cmd. 400. Treaty Series, No. 11, 1919. Treaty of Peace between the Allied and Associated Powers and Austria, together with the Protocol and Declarations annexed thereto. (Signed at Saint-Germain-en-Laye, September 10, 1919.)

[4] Cmd. 400. Treaty Series, No. 11, 1919. Treaty of Peace between the Allied and Associated Powers and Hungary, together with the Protocol and Declarations annexed thereto. (Signed at Trianon, June 4, 1920.)

[5] Cmd. 522. Treaty Series, No. 5, 1920. Treaty of Peace between the Allied and Associated Powers and Bulgaria, and Protocol. (Signed at Neuilly-sur-Seine, November 27, 1919.)

[6] Treaty of Peace between the United States of America, the British Empire, France, Italy, and Japan, and Poland. Signed at Versailles, June 28, 1919. Cmd.

was chiefly owing to the keen interest which President Wilson had in the policy that these States were not able to frustrate the attempt to give special protection to minorities.

It is pertinent to remark, however, that Czecho-Slovakia was quite in sympathy with the minority treaties. The favorable attitude of this new State is shown in the following statement:

'The Committee have received a communication from M. Benès, the representative of Czecho-Slovakia at the Peace Conference, in which he has informed them that it is the intention of the present Government to treat the Germans with the greatest liberality, and the proposals he makes go far beyond anything which the Committee would have felt justified in putting forward.[1]

While certain provisions are common to all the minority treaties, and to the minority provisions of the treaties of peace with Austria, Bulgaria, and Hungary, there are other provisions which relate only to the Jews. The general clauses [2] are designed to secure full rights of citizenship for all inhabitants, without distinction in civil rights because of any difference of race, language, or religion. They aim also to give to all inhabitants in the transferred territory the choice of acquiring the nationality of the country to which the transfer

223. Treaty Series, No. 8, 1919. (This treaty came into force January 10, 1920.)

Treaty between the Principal Allied and Associated Powers and Czecho-Slovakia. Signed at Saint-Germain-en-Laye, September 10, 1919. Cmd. 479. Treaty Series, No. 20, 1919. (This treaty came into force before end of 1920.)

Treaty between the Principal Allied and Associated Powers and the Serb-Croat-Slovene State. Signed at Saint-Germain-en-Laye, September 10, 1919. Cmd. 461. Treaty Series, No. 17, 1919. (This treaty came into force before end of 1920.)

Treaty between the Principle Allied and Associated Powers and Roumania. Signed at Paris, December 9, 1919. Cmd. 588. Treaty Series, No. 6, 1920. (This treaty came into force before end of 1920.)

[1] Committee on New States, Report No. 3.

[2] The following is a concise analysis of these general clauses: 'The general clauses described are designed to protect the Germans and white Russians and Jews and Lithuanians in Poland, the Germans and Jews and Ruthenians in Czecho-Slovakia, the Magyars and Germans and Roumanians and Albanians and Mussulmans in Jugo-Slavia, the Magyars and Serbs and Jews in Roumania, and the Mussulmans and Jews and Albanians and Vlachs in Greece. They were also included in the treaty of peace with Austria to protect the Czechs and Slavs and Jews left within the new state; in the treaty with Bulgaria to protect the Germans and Roumanians and Jews; in the treaty with Hungary to protect the Germans and Slavs and Jews; and in the treaty with Turkey to protect the Christians and Jews.' (Manley Ottmer Hudson, *What Really Happened at Paris*, chapter IX.)

is made or of retaining their old nationality by leaving the territory. All inhabitants born in the future, however, become *ipso facto* nationals of that State.

These clauses, however, although designed to protect all minorities, react, in some cases, to the special advantage of the Jews. We may cite, for example, the provision for nationality, mentioned above. This would prevent the abuses suffered by the Jews in Roumania, where the law classified as aliens people whose families had lived in Roumania for generations. And another case occurs in the Polish Minorities Treaty: [1] the provision which stipulates that there shall be an equitable share in the sums provided out of public funds, under the State, for educational, religious, or charitable purposes, particularly affects the Jews, inasmuch as in some of the towns the Jews constitute a larger proportion, sometimes a majority even, of the population.

But special protection was given to the Jews in Poland, Roumania, and Greece. The Polish Treaty contains an injunction against any legislative or administrative action which would force the Jews to violate their Sabbath, or to be placed under any disability by reason of their refusal to attend courts of law or to perform any legal business on their Sabbath. It also confers the right on the Jewish communities to appoint Educational Committees, which, subject to the general control of the State, shall provide for the distribution of the proportional share of public funds allocated to Jewish schools, and for the organization and management of these schools.

The following is an illuminating comment on the latter privilege:

This is the one point in which some concession has been made to the demand urgently pressed for the official recognition of the Jews as a community or corporation.

As is well known, there were considerable differences among the representatives of the Jews as to the objects which they desired to secure. On the whole it may be said that the English Jews tended to confine their efforts to securing to their co-religionists the widest personal liberty and full opportunities for the use of their

[1] Cmd. 223. Treaty Series, No. 8, 1919. (This treaty came into force January 10, 1920.)

own religion and the maintenance of their own customs. There was, however, a party which went farther than this and aimed at getting official recognition of what they called Jewish nationality. They seem to have hoped that the Conference would give official recognition to the Jews in Poland and in other States as an organized corporation, with definite political rights, and there are indications that if this had been secured, they might then have pressed for representation of this Jewish Nationality on the League of Nations. It need not be said that any suggestion of this kind was ruled out from the beginning. M. Clemenceau's letter specially points out that the clauses of the Treaty 'do not constitute any recognition of the Jews as a separate political community within the Polish State.'

The recognition of 'national rights' of the Jews in Poland would have been completely inconsistent with the territorial sovereignty of the State, which is the basis of our whole modern political system. It is in accordance with this that, for instance, the educational control of the schools assigned to the Jews is given not to one general Committee supervising the Jewish education for the whole of Poland, but to 'Committees' which are clearly intended to be mere local bodies. The view taken by the British Delegation throughout, and supported by the Plenipotentiaries, was that if there was to be a Jewish Nationality, it could only be by giving the Jews a local habitation and enabling them to found in Palestine a Jewish State. Any Jew, however, who was a national of a Jewish State would naturally *ipso facto* cease to be a Polish citizen.[1]

In the Minorities Treaties of Czecho-Slovakia, Jugo-Slavia, and Roumania, the special clauses regarding the Jews, which appeared in the Polish Treaty, were omitted. The Roumanian Treaty substituted for these clauses the following: 'Roumania undertakes to recognize as Rumanian nationals *ipso facto* and without the requirement of any formality, Jews inhabiting any Rumanian territory, who do not possess another nationality.'[2] It is observed in Temperley that 'the problem of the treatment of the Rumanian Jews, which has for forty years occupied their co-religionists in other countries, has, it may be hoped, been finally and definitely settled.'[3]

[1] *A History of the Peace Conference of Paris.* Edited by H. W. V. Temperley. Published under the auspices of the Institute of International Affairs. Vol. v, pp. 136, 137.

[2] *A History of the Peace Conference of Paris.* Edited by H. W. V. Temperley. Published under the auspices of the Institute of International Affairs. Vol. v, p. 149.

Besides the Jewish population of old Roumania, nearly half the population of the Bukovina, which was being assigned to Roumania, was Jewish. (*Ibid.*, vol. v, p. 128.)

[3] *Ibid.*, vol. v, p. 149.

Post-war events, on the contrary, however, have proved these Minority Treaties only measurably successful; but, as Mr. Hudson says, 'a lever has been provided by which a group in distress can advance its claim, and which the world outside can seize upon for action when a just claim would otherwise go unheeded.' [1]

An interesting post-war development in the protection of minorities is the appointment of the Committee on the Protection of Minorities by the Council of the League of Nations.[2] It is important to note that many of the countries did not object to minorities. In fact, the Turks agreed to them voluntarily.

[1] Manley Ottmer Hudson, *What Really Happened at Paris*, chapter IX, p. 229.

[2] C.C.M. 1. 1929. I. Annex 1140. Protection of Minorities. Report of the Committee Instituted by the Council Resolution of March 7, 1929:

CONTENTS

(League of Nations Official Journal. Minutes of the Fifty-Fifth Session of the Council Held at Madrid from Monday, June 10, to Saturday, June 15, 1929, pp. 1133–78.)

The long delay in shaping the Minority Treaties in Paris might well be contrasted with the speed of the Zionists in getting their cause before the Conference. Mr. Charles T. Thompson points out that the question of establishing the Zionists in Palestine was one of the earliest subjects to be discussed at Paris. In recounting what happened 'Day by Day,' he says in his notes of January 5:

Rabbi Stephen Wise, of New York, Chairman of the American Zionist Organization, has been in conference with Colonel House; he has seen Mr. Balfour at the British Foreign Office and is waiting for a conference with the President on his return from Italy.

Mr. Thompson's notes of January 5 further record:

A group of the foremost British Zionists are also in Paris conferring with the British and other delegates; following his talk with Balfour and Colonel House — and later with Tardieu, of the French delegation — Dr. Wise wrote out a statement which disclosed that a very definite plan was under way. This statement included three propositions: first, that a mandate be given to Great Britain as the trustee over Palestine; second, that a mandate be given to France as the trustee over Syria; and third, that a mandate be given to the United States as the trustee over Armenia.

The following is Dr. Wise's written statement:

Great Britain should be given, and, I believe, will be given, the Mandatory of Trusteeship over Palestine, which trusteeship Great Britain, I have reason for saying, will not accept save by the common consent of such disinterested peoples as our own. Great Britain's trusteeship over a Jewish Palestine will be because of the summons, or mandate, of the League of Nations, and for the sake of the Jewish people and the Jewish Commonwealth which they are in time to realize.

In all this, it is no secret that the President, Colonel House and Secretary Lansing have long watched with friendly interest the development of the Zionist movement. In this they have represented the judgment of the American people, including a vast majority of American Jews, and they will interpret that judgment with generosity and vision.

It is safe to forecast that France, as admirable in peace as glorious in war, will assent to the decision of the League of Nations, which will give the mandate for Palestine to Great Britain, as Great Britain and America will assent to France becoming the Mandatory over neighboring Syria.[1]

---

[1] Charles T. Thompson, *The Peace Conference Day by Day*, pp. 72, 73, 74.

Undoubtedly, as Mr. Baker observes, the Jewish propaganda at Paris prompted President Wilson to insert in his Second Draft of the Covenant an Article requiring all new States to grant equal rights to their 'racial or national minorities.' [1] One of the influential Jews who came to Paris was Justice Brandeis. Although not long in Paris, his relationships with the President were such, and the President had so much confidence in him, that he had without doubt considerable influence. Justice Brandeis was strongly in favor of the Zionist cause.

President Wilson's Third Draft of the Covenant, which was completed on January 20, 1919, included the same provision for racial minorities, and a new Article on religious equality.[2] Commenting on these articles, Mr. Baker says:

> This may well have been the President's own contribution, based upon familiar American tradition. The Jews were always insistent upon not being regarded as a religious body. The racial minority clause met their main demands. But it may have suggested the other — particularly as a means of approaching such questions in other than new States.[3]

At the Sixth Meeting of the Commission on the League of Nations, Lord Robert Cecil proposed a new text for the 'religious' Article; [4] but as several members expressed their doubts as to the advisability of including such an Article, the matter was referred to the Sub-Committee, which reported at the Seventh Meeting. The new draft [5] did not meet with

[1] Ray Stannard Baker, *Woodrow Wilson and World Settlement*, vol. i, p. 227.

See text of this: David Hunter Miller, *The Drafting of the Covenant*, vol. ii, Document 7, Article vi, of the Supplementary Agreements.

Mr. Baker makes the further assertion: 'Probably associated with this article was a new paragraph, afterward developed into the present Article xi, which Wilson has so often referred to as his "favorite article" — a set-off giving flexibility to Article x. It established the friendly right of any nation to call the attention of all to "any circumstances anywhere which threaten to disturb international peace or the good understanding between nations." This clause would enable a Lithuanian or Jugoslav state to bring before the League questions affecting the treatment of its racial kinsmen in Poland or Italy — and the United States to bring up questions of the treatment of the Jews anywhere.' (*Woodrow Wilson and World Settlement*, vol. i, pp. 227, 228.)

[2] David Hunter Miller, *The Drafting of the Covenant*, vol. ii, Document 9. Supplementary Agreements vi and viii.

[3] Ray Stannard Baker, *Woodrow Wilson and World Settlement*, vol. i, p. 230.

[4] David Hunter Miller, *The Drafting of the Covenant*, vol. ii, Document 22.

[5] *Ibid.*, vol. i, pp. 195, 196.

the approval of the Commission, and President Wilson proposed a substitute.[1]

In the draft of the Covenant delivered by the Drafting Committee, February 13, 1919, the 'religious' Article was recast;[2] but the Drafting Committee recommended its omission. The minutes of the Tenth Meeting of the Commission say that the 'religious' Article (which was then Article XXI) was dropped, although it was explained by Colonel House that the President strongly desired its inclusion.[3] Subsequently, however, President Wilson directed that the Article be omitted; and therefore the Covenant, presented at the Plenary Session on February 14, contained no mention of religious liberty.

One contributing cause to the dropping of the 'religious' Article, says David Hunter Miller, was the fact that Baron Makino proposed his 'equality' amendment [4] as an addition to the 'religious' Article. His remark, 'It would seem that matters of religion and race could well go together,' certainly worked toward the defeat of the 'religious' Article. As Thompson says, 'The entire article was withdrawn, including religious equality and the protection of the Jews.' [5]

The Zionists' plans for Palestine, which were laid before the Peace Conference, were described in a statement, dated February 3, 1919.[6] It called for an international guarantee

---

[1] David Hunter Miller, *The Drafting of the Covenant*, vol. i, p. 196.

[2] *Ibid.*, vol. i, p. 221.

[3] For the arguments on this question, see *ibid.*, vol. i, pp. 267, 268.

[4] See text: David Hunter Miller, *The Drafting of the Covenant*, vol. i, p. 183.

[5] Charles T. Thompson, *The Peace Conference Day by Day*, p. 214.

At a special Plenary Session of the Peace Conference on May 31, when representatives of some of the smaller States expressed their opposition to the Minorities Treaties, it was pointed out that a clause imposing general recognition of religious toleration, as a part of the draft of the League of Nations, on all Members of the League, had in fact been rejected, and the question could be asked why an obligation which the Great Powers refused to undertake themselves should be imposed upon others. The answer made by the Great Powers was, that through their successes they had brought about the conditions under which the transference of populations was being made, and that obviously they had a definite responsibility toward the populations. (*A History of the Peace Conference of Paris*. Edited by H. W. V. Temperley. Published under the auspices of the Institute of International Affairs. Vol. v, p. 129.)

[6] Leonard Stein, *Zionism*, pp. 122-23.

which should 'recognize the historic title of the Jewish people to Palestine and the right of the Jewish people to reconstitute in Palestine their National Home.' [1] We note here that the original desire of the Jews for the acceptance of the phrase, 'reconstitute the National Home of the Jews,' which the British Government had refused to insert in the Balfour Declaration, is again put forward.

The second demand, offered in the statement of February 3, asked that Palestine be administered by Great Britain under a Mandate of the League of Nations. It should be recalled in this connection that the Balfour Declaration contained no suggestion that Great Britain was to administer Palestine.

The third point stressed by the Zionists was that:

Palestine shall be placed under such political, administrative and economic conditions as will secure the establishment there of the Jewish National Home and ultimately render possible the creation of an autonomous Commonwealth, it being clearly understood that nothing shall be done which may prejudice the civil and religious rights of existing non-Jewish communities in Palestine or the rights and political status enjoyed by Jews in any other country.

Here we find the Zionists still asking for *the* Jewish National Home, and in close connection with it, an 'autonomous Commonwealth.' We perceive, also, the same vague expression about civil and religious rights, quoted exactly from the Balfour Declaration. Philip Graves is probably right in calling this 'purposely vague.'

The fourth point of the statement declared that: In promoting Jewish immigration and close settlement on the land, the Mandatory Power should accept the coöperation of a 'Council representing the Jews in Palestine and of the world.' This brought in an interesting complication. It was a startling thought that the Mandatory should be asked to coöperate with an organization representing Jews, not only in but beyond the borders of Palestine. The British Government had, in the Balfour Declaration, promised to 'use their best endeavours' to facilitate the establishment of a national home for the Jewish people in Palestine; but here, at the

[1] Albert M. Hyamson, 'The Zionist Movement During the War,' contained in *Awakening Palestine,* edited by Leon Simon and Leonard Stein, pp. 47–72.

Peace Conference, we find the Jews laying down the rules for the fulfilment of the promise.

Finally, the statement stipulated that: The Mandate shall guarantee 'the fullest freedom of religious worship for all creeds in Palestine' and that there shall be 'no discrimination among the inhabitants with regard to citizenship and civil rights on the grounds of religion or race.' Here, it will be observed, the Zionist proposal was simply amplifying the provisions of the Balfour Declaration.

The date of the Jewish statement, February 3, synchronized with the date of the First Meeting of the League of Nations Commission,[1] which had been preceded by a week of discussion in the Council of Ten on the subject of mandates. This discussion, although it almost brought the Council to an open rupture,[2] resulted in an agreement, on January 30, which was later incorporated in the Covenant of the League of Nations as Article XXII.[3] According to this Article, the

[1] From February 3 to February 14, the League of Nations Commission drew up the Covenant of the League of Nations.

[2] Ray Stannard Baker, *Woodrow Wilson and World Settlement,* vol. i, p. 268.

[3] 'To those colonies and territories which as a consequence of the late war have ceased to be under the sovereignty of the States which formerly governed them and which are inhabited by peoples not yet able to stand by themselves under the strenuous conditions of the modern world, there should be applied the principle that the well-being and development of such peoples form a sacred trust of civilization and that securities for the performance of this trust should be embodied in this Covenant.

'The best method of giving practical effect to this principle is that the tutelage of such peoples should be entrusted to advanced nations who by reason of their resources, their experience or their geographical position can best undertake this responsibility, and who are willing to accept it, and that this tutelage should be exercised by them as Mandatories on behalf of the League.

'The character of the mandate must differ according to the stage of the development of the people, the geographical situation of the territory, its economic conditions and other similar circumstances.

'Certain communities formerly belonging to the Turkish Empire have reached a stage of development where their existence as independent nations can be provisionally recognized subject to the rendering of administrative advice and assistance by a Mandatory until such time as they are able to stand alone. The wishes of these communities must be a principal consideration in the selection of the Mandatory.

'Other peoples, especially those of Central Africa, are at such a stage that the Mandatory must be responsible for the administration of the territory under conditions which will guarantee freedom of conscience and religion, subject only to the maintenance of public order and morals, the prohibition of abuses such as the slave trade, the arms traffic and the liquor traffic, and the prevention of the establishment of fortifications or military and naval bases and of military training of the natives for

Turkish Provinces were to be placed under mandatories acting on behalf of the League of Nations.

Mr. Thompson's notes, dated January 30, record the following:

Jan. 30. An official communiqué issued to-night makes the announcement that 'a provisional agreement has been reached on the German colonies and the occupied territory of Turkey-in-Asia.' This gives official confirmation to the acceptance by the great powers of the American proposal put forward by the President for the administration of the colonies by mandatories, appointed and supervised by the League of Nations. The provisional agreement referred to in the communiqué is the Smuts-House plan approved by the President and the British Imperial Cabinet. The reference to Turkey-in-Asia discloses for the first time that Mesopotamia, Palestine, Armenia, and Syria come within the scope of this new colonial policy, so that if England and France divide up Turkey when the break-up comes, they must do it under 'mandatories.'

Thus has suddenly come within range of practical accomplishment the most sweeping revolution in colonial management that has ever occurred. The basic idea of this change is that hereafter colonies shall be administered for the benefit of their own people, and shall not be a field of profit-making enterprises. The exchanges now going on indicate that the principle will be accepted by all the colonial powers, including Japan, Belgium, Portugal, as well as the great colonizers, England and France.[1]

Following the reading of the Covenant of the League of Nations by President Wilson at the Plenary Session of the Peace Conference on February 14, 1919, the Council of Ten, on February 27, President Wilson being in the United States,

other than police purposes and the defence of territory, and will also secure equal opportunities for the trade and commerce of other Members of the League.

'There are territories, such as South-West Africa and certain of the South Pacific Islands, which, owing to the sparseness of their population, or their small size, or their remoteness from the centres of civilization, or their geographical contiguity to the territory of the Mandatory, and other circumstances, can be best administered under the laws of the Mandatory as integral portions of its territory, subject to the safeguards above mentioned in the interests of the indigenous population.

'In every case of mandate, the Mandatory shall render to the Council an annual report in reference to the territory committed to its charge.

'The degree of authority, control, or administration to be exercised by the Mandatory shall, if not previously agreed upon by the Members of the League, be explicitly defined in each case by the Council.

'A permanent Commission shall be constituted to receive and examine the annual reports of the Mandatories and to advise the Council on all matters relating to the observance of the mandates.'

[1] Charles T. Thompson, *The Peace Conference Day by Day*, pp. 163–64.

received Dr. Weizmann and Mr. Sokolow, who represented the Zionists.[1] The Council also heard representatives of the Russian Jews, the French Jews, and the French Zionists. President Wilson sailed for the United States, the next morning after the Plenary Session on February 14, to be absent from Paris a month.

Bearing the date of March 1, 1919, Memorials on 'The Jewish Title to Palestine' and 'The Rights of Jews in Other Lands' were submitted to the President.[2] They were signed

[1] Mr. Hyamson describes the meeting with the Supreme Council as follows: 'The Zionist Representatives were heard by the Supreme Council of the Allies on the 27th of February, 1919, when they put forward the Zionist case and outlined the settlement for which they asked. Their proposals were: (1) The Powers should recognize the historic title of the Jewish people to Palestine and the right of the Jews to reconstitute their national home; (2) the sovereign possession of Palestine should be vested in the League of Nations, and the Government entrusted to Great Britain as Mandatory of the League; (3) the inclusion in the Mandate for the government of Palestine of the following special conditions: (a) Palestine shall be placed under such political, administrative and economic conditions as will secure the establishment there of a Jewish national home, and ultimately render possible the creation of an autonomous commonwealth, it being clearly understood that nothing shall be done which may prejudice the civil and religious rights of existing non-Jewish communities in Palestine and the rights and political status enjoyed by Jews in any other country. (b) To this end the Mandatory Power shall *inter alia* — (i) promote Jewish immigration and close settlement on the land, the established rights of the present non-Jewish population being equitably safeguarded; (ii) accept the co-operation in such measures of a council representative of the Jews of Palestine and of the world that may be established for the development of the Jewish national home in Palestine, and entrust the organization of Jewish education to that council; (iii) on being satisfied that the constitution of such council precludes the making of private profit, offer to the council in priority any concession for public works or for the development of natural resources which it may be found desirable to grant. (c) The Mandatory Power shall encourage the widest measure of self-government for localities practicable in the conditions of the country. (d) There shall be forever the fullest freedom of religious worship for all creeds in Palestine, and no discrimination among the inhabitants with regard to citizenship and civil rights on the grounds of religion or race.

'No suggestions were made as to the conditions that were to govern the Holy Places, a matter which, it was thought, should be left entirely to the uninfluenced decision of the Powers. Suggested boundaries were, however, laid down.

'The Council heard the Zionist representatives but more pressing matters engaged the attention of the Allies and although the Palestine question was always on the agenda of the Conference, it was never taken up again in Paris, and, in fact, was not considered until April, 1920, when the force of circumstances, namely the anti-Jewish demonstrations in Jerusalem, made further postponement impossible.' (Albert M. Hyamson, 'The Zionist Movement During the War,' contained in *Awakening Palestine*, edited by Leon Simon and Leonard Stein, pp. 47–72.)

[2] Memorials submitted to President Wilson on The Jewish Title to Palestine and The Rights of the Jews in Other Lands by Representatives of The American Jewish Congress. Second Day of March, Nineteen Hundred and Nineteen. Thirtieth Day

by the Secretary of the American Jewish Congress and also
by three representatives of the Congress — Julian W. Mack,
Louis Marshall, and Stephen S. Wise — delegates elected at
the American Jewish Congress at Philadelphia, December 18,
1918.

This Memorial presents practically the same appeal as that
contained in the statement of February 3. The historic basis
of the Jewish claims is set forth in the Memorial quite at
length:

Palestine is the historic home of the Jews. There they achieved
their greatest development. From that center, through their
agency, there emanated spiritual and moral influences of supreme
value to mankind. By violence they were driven from Palestine,
and through the ages large numbers of them never ceased to cherish
the longing and hope of return.

Palestine is not large enough to contain more than a part of the
Jews of the world. The greater portion of the fourteen millions or
more scattered through all countries must remain where they now
abide, and it will doubtless be one of the cares of the Peace Conference, as we have already urged upon you, to ensure for them
wherever they have been oppressed, as for all peoples, equal rights.
Such a Palestine would be of value to the world at large, whose
happiness is in large measure derived from the healthy diversities
of its civilization.

The land itself needs rehabilitation. Its present condition is a
standing reproach. Two things are necessary for its reconstruction:
A stable and enlightened Government and an addition to the
present population of energetic and intelligent men and women,
devoted to the country, and supported by such resources as are
indispensable to development. Such a population the Jews alone,
it is believed, could supply.

Inspired by these convictions, Jewish activities during the last
thirty years have operated in Palestine to the extent permitted by
the Turkish administrative system. Large sums have been expended in the establishment of Jewish agricultural settlements,
which have for the most part proven highly successful. With
commendable enterprise the Jews have adopted modern scientific
methods and have proven themselves to be capable agriculturists.
Hebrew has been revived as a living language. It is the medium of
instruction in the schools, and is in daily use. A Jewish university
has been founded at Jerusalem, and funds have been pledged for
its creation and support. For the further development of the

of Adar, Five Thousand Six Hundred and Seventy-Nine. Reprinted from *The
Maccabœan*, March, 1919. Zionist Organization of America, 55 Fifth Avenue, New
York.

country, large sums will be required for drainage, irrigation, the building of highways, railways, harbors, and public works of all kinds.

Great Britain is designated in the Memorial as trustee or mandatory of the League of Nations for Palestine; and the terms of the trusteeship are given as follows:

In connection with the Government to be established by the mandatory or trustee of the League of Nations until such time as the people of Palestine shall be prepared to undertake the establishment of a representative and responsible Government, the following terms are deemed important:

(1) In any instrument establishing the constitution of Palestine, the declaration of the Peace Conference shall be recited as forming an integral part of such constitution.

(2) The Jewish people shall be entitled to fair representation in the executive and legislative bodies and in the selection of public and civil servants.

(3) In encouraging the self-government of localities, the mandatory or trustee shall secure the maintenance by local communities of proper standards of administration in matters of education and communal or regional activities. In granting or enlarging autonomy, regard shall be had to the readiness and ability of the community to attain such standards. Local autonomous communities shall be empowered and encouraged to combine and cooperate for common purposes.

(4) Assistance shall be rendered from the public funds for the education of the inhabitants without distinction of race or creed. Hebrew shall be one of the official languages and shall be employed in all documents, decrees and announcements issued by the Government.

(5) The Jewish Sabbath and Holy Days shall be recognized as legal days of rest.

(6) The established rights of the present population shall be equitably safeguarded.

(7) All inhabitants of Palestine who, on a date to be specified, shall have their domicile therein, except those who, within a period to be stated, shall in writing elect to retain their citizenship in any other country, shall be citizens of Palestine, and they and all persons born in Palestine or naturalized under its laws after the day named shall be citizens thereof and entitled to the protection of the mandatory or trustee.

A list of the States which 'have officially endorsed the project to establish a Jewish Homeland' is appended to the Memorial, as follows: Serbia, December 27, 1917; France,

February 12, 1918; Italy, February 25, 1918; Greece, March 14, 1918; Holland, April 25, 1918; Siam, August 22, 1918; China, December 14, 1918; Japan, December 27, 1918.

President Wilson replied to the Memorial concerning the rights of the Jewish people in Palestine, as follows:

WHITE HOUSE, *March 2, 1919*

As for your representations touching Palestine, I have before this expressed my personal approval of the declaration of the British Government regarding the aspirations and historic claims of the Jewish people in regard to Palestine. I am, moreover, persuaded that the Allied nations, with the fullest concurrence of our own Government and people, are agreed that in Palestine shall be laid the foundations of a Jewish Commonwealth.

WOODROW WILSON [1]

President Wilson returned to Paris on March 14, 1919; but no action was taken on the establishment of the Jewish Homeland in Palestine during the remainder of the Peace Conference. It is a fact, however, that on March 20, during a secret session of the Four Heads of States — President Wilson, Lloyd George, Clemenceau, and Orlando — the question of partitioning Turkey under the old secret treaties came up for discussion.[2] The minutes disclose the President's opposition to both French and British claims.

It is indeed true that the Jews were fruitfully active while the Peace Conference was sitting. Though the Conference itself gave no definite answer to the demands for a Jewish National Home, the Allied Powers, after the meeting in Paris, proceeded to put their program into effect. We have seen, how at San Remo,[3] the Mandate for Palestine was awarded to Great Britain; and that three months later, civil government was established and a Jew appointed High Commissioner.

We have seen, also, how the Council of the League of Nations approved the first [4] and also the revised [5] draft man-

---

[1] This letter is printed in the same document containing the Memorial.

[2] Ray Stannard Baker, *Woodrow Wilson and World Settlement*, vol. II, pp. 26, 27. See vol. III, Document 1, for full minutes of this meeting.

[3] *A History of the Peace Conference of Paris.* Edited by H. W. V. Temperley. Published under the auspices of the Institute of International Affairs. Vol. VI, pp. 505–06, 519, 521–23, and Appendix V, p. 645.

[4] Cmd. 1176 (1921).   [5] Cmd. 1500 (1921).

THE BIG FOUR AT PARIS
Orlando, Lloyd George, Clemenceau, President Wilson

dates, prepared by Great Britain in consultation with Zionist representatives; and that when the Mandate was finally approved on July 24, 1922, the Preamble included the Balfour Declaration, and also the significant statement: 'recognition has thereby been given to the historical connection of the Jewish people with Palestine and to the grounds for reconstituting their national home in that country.' The word 'reconstituting,' which had been persistently discarded by the British Government, had finally found a place in the Palestine Mandate.

Thus, under a world sanction, the original desire of the Zionists was at last conceded; and the Jews, thereupon, began a new and thrilling chapter of their history — a chapter of hopes fulfilled — and of hopes deferred.

END OF VOLUME I